ALSO BY JAMES BUCHAN

DAYS OF GOD

The Revolution in Iran and Its Consequences

JAMES BUCHAN

SIMON & SCHUSTER

New York   London   Toronto   Sydney   New Delhi

Simon & Schuster
1230 Avenue of the Americas
New York, NY 10020

First Simon & Schuster hardcover edition September 2013
Originally published in Great Britain in 2012
by John Murray Publishers, an Hachette UK Company.

Illustration Credits are on page 387.

For information about special discounts for bulk purchases,
please contact Simon & Schuster Special Sales at 1-866-506-1949
or business@simonandschuster.com.

The Simon & Schuster Speakers Bureau can bring authors to your live event.
For more information or to book an event, contact the Simon & Schuster Speakers Bureau
at 1-866-248-3049 or visit our website at www.simonspeakers.com.

Manufactured in the United States of America

1   3   5   7   9   10   8   6   4   2

Library of Congress Cataloging-in-Publication Data

Buchan, James.
Days of God : the revolution in Iran and its consequences / James Buchan.
— First Simon & Schuster hardcover edition.
pages cm
"Originally published in Great Britain in 2012 by John Murray Publishers."—
Includes bibliographical references and index.
1. Iran—History—Revolution, 1979. 2. Iran—History—Revolution, 1979—Influence.
3. Iran—History—Revolution, 1979—Causes. 4. Iran—History—1979–1997. 5. Khomeini,
Ruhollah—Influence. 6. Political violence—Iran—History—20th century. I. Title.
DS318.8.B82 2013
955.05'4—dc23
2013008890

ISBN 978-1-4165-9777-3
ISBN 978-1-4165-9782-7 (ebook)

For Rose

Contents

Iran under Pahlavi Rule

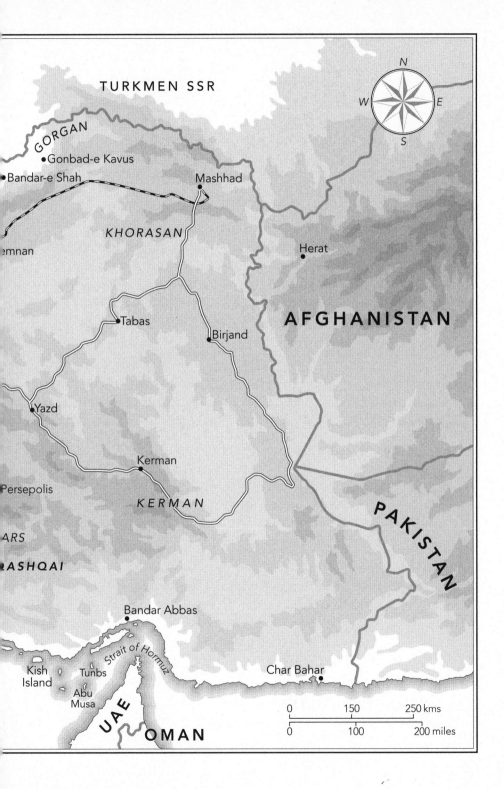

The Southern Front in the Iran–Iraq War

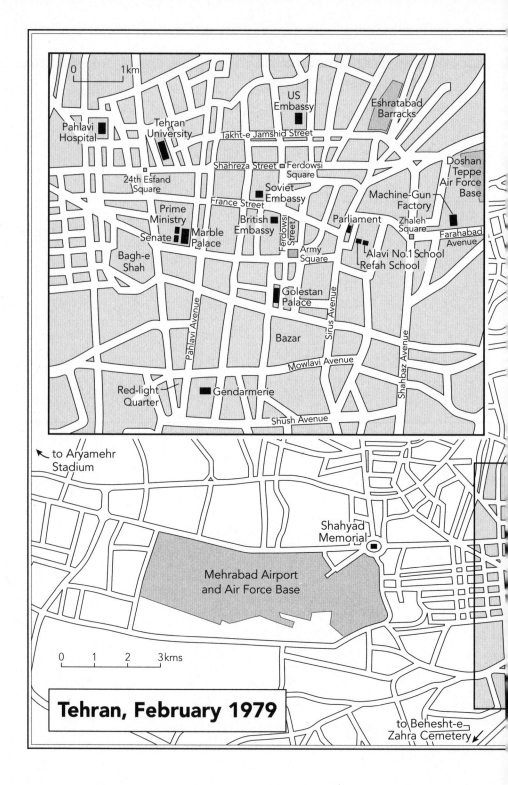

Tehran, February 1979

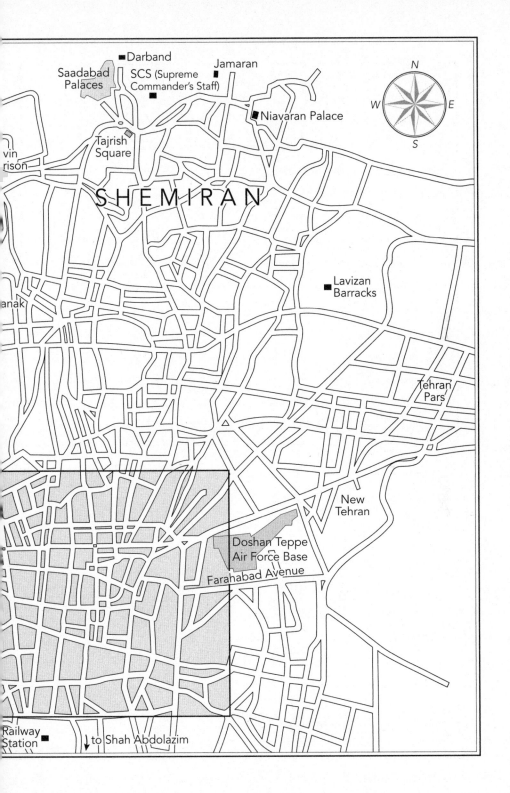

Introduction

I first came to Iran in 1974, the year the price of crude oil rose fourfold and Europe switched off its power stations. After the darkness of the autobahns, I found the city of Tabriz illuminated as if for a perpetual wedding. On my first day in Tehran, the capital, I was taken on by a school teaching the English language to cadets of the Imperial Iranian Air Force. The rows of desks receded out of sight. It was Ramazan, when Muslims fast the daylight hours, and the pupils dozed on their pen-cases or glared at the wrapped sandwiches they had brought in to eat at sundown. Among those Turkoman boys, there must have been the makings of at least one military aviator, and it was I who was going to make the start on him. I was the smallest component in one of the greatest military expansions ever undertaken. The owner of the school was a brigadier general and I used to see him, in uniform in the afternoons, striking the male secretaries. At payday, the cashier, an old man with stubble on his chin, who was the general's father, took half an hour to sign my check. An Indian colleague whispered that a tip was expected. I quit.

I moved to Isfahan, the famous old city in the heart of the country. I found a job in a morning, teaching schoolgirls. I was a bad teacher, but I was an Oxford sophomore and nineteen years old. The class doubled in size and halved in fluency. My pupils cultivated feeling to a pitch, and sighed over adjectives. They made fun of me, as if I had been a bashful seminary student.

Bred up in the medieval Persian of Oxford University, I was baffled by Iranian modernity. In this famous town, with its palaces so flimsy you could blow them over with a sigh, there were military instructors from Grumman Corp. and Bell Helicopter International, with their

Asian women and a screw loose from Vietnam, sobbing in hotel lob-
bies. I thought I had come too late to see what I had come to see, forgetting an ancient lesson: that in a year or two even this, also, would
be obliterated.

I did not know, as I know now, that nations salvage what they can
from the wreck of history, and the warriors of the national poet Ferdowsi were the tough guys or *lutis* ("buggers") of the bazaar, and the
lyrics of Hafez were the songs on the car radio: *Black-eyed, tall and
slender, Oh to win Leila!* The Isfahan women rose early, buying their
food from the grocery fresh each day, a clay bowl of yoghurt which
they smashed after use, or those bundles of green herbs that Khomeini
liked to eat, all to cook the daily lunch. For an Englishman, standing in
line to buy cigarettes, it was tempting enough to stay and settle down
with one of these angels, and pass his life in inconsequential fantasies.
The grocer wore a double-breasted suit of wide 1930s cut, a tribal cap,
and the rag-soled cotton slippers known as *giveh*. It was as if he had
thrown off a tyrannical dress code, but only at its up and down extremities. It seemed to me that the Shah had run a blunt saw across the very
grain of Iranianness.

In the cool vaults of the Isfahan bazaar, where I supplemented my
wages by dealing in bad antiques, a lane would end in a chaos of smashed
brick and a blinding highway, as if Mohammed Reza Pahlavi was trying to abolish something other than medieval masonry: an entire and
traditional way of life, with its procession from shop to mosque to bath
to shop to mosque and its interminable religious ceremonies.

Somebody, presumably the Russians, had given the Iranians a taste
for assassination and vodka. Somebody else, no doubt the Americans,
had given them Pepsi and ice cream. A third, perhaps the British, had
taught them to love opium. Laid across that beautiful town was some
personality that expressed itself in straight roads crossing at right
angles, mosques turned into mere works of art, and all the frowstiness
of an overtaken modernity. It was uneducated or even illiterate, violent,
avaricious, in a hurry to get somewhere it never arrived. I know now
that that personality was the Shah's father, Reza. Over that was another
impression, not at all forceful, but cynical, melancholy, pleasure-loving, distrustful, also in a hurry. I supposed that was Mohammed Reza.
I did not understand why those kings were in such a hurry but I knew

that haste, as the Iranians say, is the devil's work. I could see that Iran was going to hell but could not for the life of me descry what kind of hell.

James Buchan
England, 2013

DAYS
OF GOD

CHAPTER 1

The Origins
of the Pahlavi State

◆

*The foundation of injustice in the world was at first very
small.*

—Sadi[1]

On the afternoon of Sunday, April 25, 1926, at the Golestan Palace
in Tehran, a former stable lad crowned himself King of Kings. In the
vaulted and mirrored hall known as "the Museum," attended by cabinet
ministers in cashmere robes and felt hats, civil servants, military officers in European uniforms, clergymen, cadets of the military school,
and one or two European women, Reza Khan Savadkuhi of the Iranian
Cossack Brigade placed on his head the new Pahlavi crown, inset with
more than three thousand diamonds.[2]

The guests were in their places by three o'clock. The doors to the
Museum opened and Reza's six-year-old son, Mohammed Reza,
entered, dressed in miniature general's uniform of khaki, his right
hand at the salute. Next came the ministers of state in two lines, carrying on red velvet cushions the regalia of the Iranian monarchy: the
three crowns; the diamond-encrusted saber known as "World-Con-
queror," with which Nader Shah in 1739 had overrun India and
sacked Delhi; the inlaid scepter; the royal gauntlet; the colossal pink
diamond called the "Sea of Light." Behind them, field marshals carried Nader's bow, quiver, and buckler; the inlaid mace; the sword and
coat-of-mail of the Safavid Shah Ismail and the sword of Shah Abbas
the Great. For a country so desert and poor, and so ravaged by revolu-

1

tion and war for a quarter of a century, there was nonetheless always jewelry.[3]

The banners dipped, the European ladies bobbed, and attended by adjutants and courtiers, Reza strode in. "I say 'strode' advisedly," wrote an Englishwoman who was present, "because the man was so impressively tall, towering head and shoulders above the crowd."[4] Reza was in uniform, under a blue silk cape embroidered with pearls, at his waist a belt with an emerald the size of a hen's egg and in his peaked French cavalry cap Nader's aigrette or spray of emeralds.[5] He seated himself on the throne. From the parade ground to the northwest there was a twenty-one-gun salute. Reza took the Pahlavi crown from his minister of court, Abdolhosein Teymourtache, and placed it on his own head, while the minister of war, General Abdullah Khan Tahmasebi, buckled on Nader's sword. The scepter was placed in his right hand.

"Immobile," wrote the British minister to Tehran, Sir Percy Loraine, "and almost sacerdotal, his commanding profile outlined against the afternoon sun, His Imperial Majesty then read in a low and toneless voice [a] short declaration."[6] In it, Reza promised to safeguard and strengthen religion in Iran, to improve the country's defenses, to encourage education, trade, transport, and agriculture, and to reform the justice system. In an omen of what was to come, he called on the whole country for "energy and application."[7] His prime minister, Mohammed Ali Foroughi, spoke at greater length, sketching what was to become the royal ideology: that Reza and his son were heirs to two and a half millennia of Iranian monarchy as witnessed by the ancient authors and the national epic, the "Book of Kings" or *Shahnameh* of the poet Ferdowsi.[8]

The ceremony over, Reza marched out, with the Sea of Light now flashing in his cap, to an old glass coach waiting with its team of six gray horses in the palace garden. Behind him, little Mohammed Reza, his eyes closed from exhaustion and sunlight, let his hand drop from the salute. Attended by a mounted escort of police and 350 curvetting tribal horsemen, the coaches set off by way of Artillery Square and the modern district of Lalehzar to the edge of town, where Reza transferred to a Rolls-Royce motorcar for the nine-mile ride to his new palace at Saadabad in the north.

The coronation was, Sir Percy wrote to London on May 1, "economical, not unimpressive and short."[9] (As well it must have been, since Louise, Lady Loraine, her mother, and her friends directed Teymourtache on the costumes and decorations.)[10] The only untidy note came from the Muslim clergy, who "shambled" away from their allotted position, and turned on the fussing chamberlains with glowers and frowns. That, too, was an omen. For three nights, Tehran was illuminated with candles, gas, kerosene lights, and fireworks. A day or two later, there was a fly-past of eleven war-surplus British, French, and German biplanes and their *émigré* pilots that constituted the new Imperial Iranian Air Force.[11]

In the annals of Iranian monarchy, which recede into antiquity, the Pahlavis may be overlooked. Neither Reza the father, nor Mohammed Reza the son, was born to the throne, and both died in exile in Africa. Though to themselves they were the founders of an Iranian dynasty, they had more in common with Nader, who blazed like a meteor over Iran, Afghanistan, and India for a few years in the mid-eighteenth century, than the Safavids (1501–1722) and the Qajars (1796–1925), who flourished and decayed over many generations.

For all the sabers and diamonds, the Pahlavi idea of kingship was a novelty in a country where the royal power, while in theory covering the whole earth, was limited by ancient customs and privileges, dirt-poor, and a military shambles. The Pahlavis wanted a monopoly of authority, which would penetrate every village and town quarter, prescribing how Iranians should speak, dress, and conduct themselves. They wanted modernity, order, uniformity, and hard work. On his way into exile in 1941, Reza told his British escort that "he had been the first man for hundreds of years to make the Persians work."[12] In introducing the notion of a powerful state, Reza was the most influential Iranian of the last century, more influential even than Ruhollah Khomeini.

Iran is a dry country. Apart from the provinces north of the Elburz Mountains, which have rain from the Caspian Sea, Iran sees less rain in a year—ten inches—than the Pacific Northwest or the English Lake District in a month. So arid is the country that villages are not, as in western Europe, settled at walking distance apart, but scores of miles away across trackless waste. Different words might be used for the same agricultural or hydraulic process in two neighboring villages.[13] Most of the 40,000 or 50,000 villages in Qajar times were no bigger than hamlets, a cluster of flat-roofed houses of mud and poplar poles, with maybe a saint's shrine to keep off earthquakes.[14] The larger landlords lived in the towns, their agents collecting the produce from their sharecroppers in kind at harvest.

Half the country could not be cultivated, or was given over to pastoral tribes who supplied meat and wool to the cities and supplemented their living by blackmail and raiding. There were no harbors or shipping and just one navigable river, the Karun, which empties into the Shatt al-Arab at the head of the Persian Gulf. There were no carriage roads, or any wheeled traffic. All transport was by pack animal, where even a camel carried just 400 pounds, and some caravans might be one hundred days on the road. A British mission to Fath Ali Shah Qajar in 1811–14 carried seventy looking-glasses as presents to the Shah and his ladies. At the end of the 600-mile trek from Bushehr on the Gulf to Tehran, only a third of the glasses were unbroken.[15] There was no gold or silver, or indeed any mining but for a little shaley coal, transported on donkeyback, and some ancient turquoise workings in Khorasan in the northeast. There were no factories or any division of labor. Nine tenths of the population could not read nor write.

Dependent for their revenue on the product of dry farming, the Qajars were often short of ready cash. Governorships, military ranks, and aristocratic titles were peddled to the highest bidder. Crown land was parceled out to officials in lieu of cash salaries, and those fiefs or allotments often became hereditary. Even the British and Russian legations held fiefs over villages in the Shemiranat, the summer resorts or hill-stations north of Tehran. Without money to finance the collection of revenue, the Qajars "farmed" the collecting of land taxes, customs dues, and the Mint. Merchants bid for the right to collect a certain annual sum and pocketed any surplus they could extract. The comte de Gobineau, who served two missions at the French legation in Tehran in the 1850s and 1860s, concluded that the Qajar state was imaginary. There were no fortresses, no arsenals, no public storehouses, a bureaucracy of pensioners, and an army prone to accident. "In sum," he wrote, "if one says the government of Persia does not exist, it is but a very slight exaggeration."[16] The Qajars tried intermittently to reform the administration, to field a standing army, and to introduce modern industries, but those efforts failed for lack of revenue, the jealousy of the bazaar and clergy, and Anglo-Russian rivalry. In the end, such obstacles proved insuperable.

At the opening of the nineteenth century, and the wars of Napoleon in Europe, Iran was drawn into the field of European politics. Under the blandishments of Napoleon's envoys, and then British and Indian counter-envoys, and with one eye to the military reforms in the Ottoman Empire, Crown Prince Abbas Mirza began to develop a European army or "modern system"—*nezam-e jadid*—based on a type of quasi-feudal recruitment called *bonicheh*. In resisting czarist encroachment in the Caucasus, Abbas Mirza and the modern army were defeated. On February 21, 1828, at the village of Turkmanchay east of Tabriz, the czarist government imposed on Iran a Carthaginian peace, including a war indemnity of 10 crores of tomans (reduced, through British intervention, to 9 crores, or about £2.5m), capitulations or extraterritorial rights for Russian subjects, and a court etiquette favorable to Russian dignity. In return, the Russians recognized the Qajar house on the throne which, more than anything, preserved the dynasty in power until Lenin abrogated the treaty in 1918.

In a separate commercial compact, Turkmanchay provided a universal 5 percent tariff for Russian goods which, extended to the other powers on the principle of equal treatment with the most-favored nation, buried Iranian handicrafts under a heap of Russian chintzes and Manchester piece goods.[17] In time, imported tea and sugar reached remote villages, and tobacco and opium became staples. The ancient Iranian practice of seeking sanctuary or *bast* in mosques or royal palaces extended to the foreign legations.

The exposure to European power and ruthlessness was a shock from which Iran could not recover. In late 1828, the Russian playwright and diplomat Alexander Griboyedov arrived in Tehran to deliver the ratified Turkmanchay Treaty. At two audiences with Fath Ali Shah Qajar, monarch and envoy caused each other offense.[18] When the confidential treasurer of the Shah's harem and two women in a separate household sought Russian protection under the treaty, the mission's lodging in the south of town was overrun by a bazaar mob, and on February 11, 1829, Griboyedov, his Cossack escort, and all but one of his staff were cut to pieces.[19] Years later, Nassereddin Shah Qajar (1848–1896) wrote that ever since "that never-to-be-named day" when Turkmanchay was signed, Iran had been "sick."[20] *Griboedovschina*, or "doing a Griboyedov," haunted Russian diplomacy into the Soviet era.

Yet Iran was growing in prosperity. The population appears to have risen from about 5 or 6 million at the beginning of the nineteenth century to 9 or 10 million in 1900.[21] By midcentury, Tehran had broken out of its bounds, and in 1867 a new wall and ditch, pierced by twelve gates with faience decoration and irregular bastions in the modern manner (though without cannon), were laid out by a French military engineer, Alexandre Buhler. (The ditch later became the haunt of arak drinkers, prostitutes, gamblers, and pederasts.) The center of town life moved northward from the old Safavid citadel by the bazaar to the artillery ground (later Army Square), and a European suburbs grew up in the streets to the north. The British built a grand legation in the Anglo-Indian style, with fifty yards of verandah shaded by wisteria. Isfahan, once as populous as London, and Tabriz began to recover some of their Safavid prosperity.

Prices, recorded by British consular officers, rose in the second half of the century.[22] A demand for money was met by debasement (particularly of the copper coinage) and, after 1890, the introduction of bank notes. An export industry for carpets, financed and marketed from about 1875 by the Tabriz bazaar and from the next decade by such European and American houses as Ziegler, Oriental Carpet Manufacturers, Nearco Castelli, and the Persische Teppich AG (Petag), grew up on the ruins of the domestic cloth industry. In addition to silk in Gilan above the Caspian, managed by Greek traders from the Ottoman Empire, from the 1850s new cash crops were established such as cotton, tobacco, and opium.

Opium, in particular, which requires little water and only in the spring and is much easier to transport on bad roads than wheat, made fortunes for the bazaar and clergy of Isfahan and other southern cities. "Isfahan is a lodge in a garden of poppies," wrote Edward Stack, of the Bengal civil service, in May 1881. He thought the Isfahan crop might one day come to rival, or even replace, the Indian opium monopoly.[23] The British banker Joseph Rabino reported that all the free currency in the provinces poured into Isfahan at the harvest.[24] Zeinolabedin Maraghei, in a novel of social criticism published at the end of the nineteenth century, *The Travel Diary of Ebrahim Beg*, inveighed against the drug: "Worse than everything is the spread of opium smoking in this country, such that men and women, young and old, are addicted to that killer poison." [25] "His Excellency Lord Pipe" has draped its pall of melancholy over Iranian life to this day. [26]

The dilemma for the Qajars was that the new prosperity accrued not to the throne or the administration, but to the merchants of the traditional quarters of the cities and the clergy, both as landowners in their own right, objects of bazaar charity, or as administrators of pious endowments known as *auqaf* (plural of *vaqf*). Land taxes, assessed using private ciphers by a hereditary class of accountants known as *mostofis*, failed to recognize the yield from valuable cash crops such as opium. In contrast, the bazaar (pronounced "bAAzAAr") was becoming prosperous, and with prosperity came self-assertion.

The bazaar was the heart of Iranian life. Since the Middle Ages, it combined in its covered lanes both the merchant capital of the country and, among men constantly in view of one another, its social decorum and religious propriety. In a country without a police force or reliable military, the bazaar had learned to impose its will: rumors, murmurs, closed shops, and migration in a body to the mosque or other places of asylum, petitions and telegrams, menacing leaflets and flyers known as *shabnamehs* or "night letters," insurrection and, from the 1890s (and then again from the 1940s), assassination. The Qajars never succeeded in binding the bazaar to the state. The merchants paid no taxes, except a levy on the traditional guilds, and until 1925 supplied no troops to the army. They lived in unostentatious style. Their surpluses went, instead, to maintain the clerical establishment of mosques and seminaries, and by 1979 could stretch to leasing for Khomeini a Boeing 747 with fuel and crew. It is impossible to exaggerate the importance of that point. For just as the Pahlavi state grew in power, extent, and wealth in the twentieth century, so too did the Iranian clergy, till they met on the cold streets of Tehran in 1979, like *Titanic* and iceberg.

The Qajars' other headache was this. The Iranian currency, the *kran*, was a silver coin, but the expenses of the administration and the court, from capital goods to luxuries and European jaunts, arose in the lands of the international gold standard. Throughout the last part of the nineteenth century, as new lodes of silver in Nevada and elsewhere were mined, the *kran* fell on the exchanges. The Shah found himself with his income in a deteriorating currency while much of his expense was in hard gold. Joseph Rabino, the chief manager of the British bank founded in 1889, the Imperial Bank of Persia, reckoned that government revenue fell from about £1.85 million in gold sterling in 1839–40 to about £1.6 million in 1888–89.[27] Maraghei, in *Ebrahim Beg*, complained that "the revenues of the publishing house for the *Times* newspaper printed in London are more than one year's taxes of Iran."[28] The labor of Iranians, not least the women and children who knotted carpets for foreign buyers, became ever cheaper, and the hand-knotted Persian rugs from the Hamadan and Sultanabad districts and Kerman brought romance and glamour to quite modest households in Europe and the United States. (Even today, a late nineteenth-century Persian carpet sells for less than an equivalent modern European carpet colored with chemical dyestuffs and woven on a machine loom.) Foreign capital began to search out Iran as a location for other export industries, such as cereals and tobacco.

In 1872, in the midst of a severe famine, Nassereddin's chancellor or prime minister Mirza Hosein Khan, who as Iranian ambassador in Istanbul had been impressed by the reforms of the Ottoman administration, cut the Gordian knot. On July 25, an exclusive concession was signed in Tehran with a representative of Baron Julius de Reuter, founder of the Reuters news agency, to develop railways and tramways, to exploit mineral resources, petroleum, water, and forests, to "farm" the customs, and, eventually, to establish a bank. At the same time, Mirza Hosein Khan persuaded Nassereddin to make a visit to Europe—the first by a ruling Iranian monarch since Xerxes—so as to witness the progress in industry and government there.

The Reuter Concession caused a sensation in Europe. Adolphe Thiers, the French statesman, commented that the terms left nothing of Persia to the Shah except the atmosphere.[29] Nathaniel Curzon, who later became Britain's foreign secretary, called the concession "the most complete and extraordinary surrender of the entire industrial resources of a kingdom into foreign hands that has probably ever been dreamed of, much less accomplished, in history."[30] Progressive Iranians, influenced by nationalist ideas from Europe, saw the country sold out to a louche foreigner. (De Reuter later claimed that he had spent £180,000 in inducements to have the concession signed.)

In reality, for all its naïveté and haste, the concession was a sincere attempt by a country without capital or industrial expertise to break out of its backwardness. As a committee of Iranian ministers commented, de Reuter had the right only to exploit "unemployed resources which up to now have conferred no benefit on the government and, should they remain in our hands, will after this confer no benefit either."[31] On the exchanges, the *kran* rose in value in expectation that a railway line between Tehran and Rasht/Enzeli on the Caspian would lead to a demand for Iranian produce.[32]

As it turned out, the concession fell prey to a mixture of British indifference, Russian mischief, bazaar hostility, clerical xenophobia, and harem intrigue. Anis od-Dowleh, Nassereddin's senior wife, was humiliated when the unwieldy harem, with its paraphernalia of litters, curtains, and eunuchs, was sent back from Moscow. She blamed Mirza Hosein Khan. Back on his home soil in September 1873, Nassereddin was confronted by a *bast* or sit-in of ministers and officials at Anis od-Dowleh's residence. Nassereddin showed every sign of difficulties within doors. He dismissed his prime minister, reinstated him the next morning, then dismissed him the day after that.

De Reuter's contractors were still awaiting the first consignment of rails for the line between Rasht and Tehran. Since the contract stipulated that work on the line must begin within fifteen months, Nassereddin had a pretext for canceling the entire concession. De Reuter was obliged to forgo a £40,000 performance bond, deposited at the Bank of England, and was to spend the next twenty years lobbying British and continental ministers to recover it.

The cancellation of the concession shook the "credit" or ability to raise funds of Iranian projects in the City of London and the European capital markets. British officials, who were never enthusiastic about de Reuter, as a foreigner and a Jew, now championed his prior claims so as to block Russian schemes to build a railway in Iran that they feared might project Russian power toward British India. The rivalry of Britain and Russia induced a paralysis in Iran, preventing not just railroads but financial organization, a national budget, tax collection, the police, the security of the roads. Compared to the Ottoman Empire and Egypt, all embarked on railway building, foreign borrowing, and capital investment by the 1860s, Iran remained a backwater. In 1888,

Nassereddin grumbled: "Should I wish to go out for an excursion or a shooting expedition in the north, east and west of my country, I must consult the English, and should I intend to go south I must consult the Russians."[33] As the German consul in Tabriz, Wilhelm Litten, later commented: "Russia, as it pushed towards the South, and England, as it avoided any push to the North, had something in common in their policy: to have no thought for the development, reform or restoration of Persia."[34]

Nonetheless, Nassereddin capitalized and sold off for a lump sum any source of income he could find, real or imaginary. In 1873, a Russian subject was given a concession for a sturgeon fishery in the Caspian. Iranians do not eat caviar and did not miss that particular component of the Gilded Age. In the course of the next quarter century, concessions were signed with British, Russian, or Belgian capitalists for a steamer service on the Karun (which the British had to subsidize), toll carriage roads, a match factory (1890), a gasworks in Tehran (1891), a glassworks (1891), a cotton spinning works (1894), a sugar factory in Kahrizak (1895), a horse tramway that took four times as long to reach the bazaar as a man on foot stopping at two coffee-houses in a mile,[35] a wine and liquor monopoly (canceled), a lottery (also canceled), and six miles of railway from the Tehran bazaar to the shrine of Shah Abdolazim, which men rode, for convenience in case of fatal accident, in their burial shrouds.[36]

Meanwhile, a monopoly on the production, sale, and export of tobacco, on the pattern of the *régies* in France and the Ottoman Empire, was awarded to a shady City of London syndicate during Nassereddin's third visit to Europe in 1889. That was too much. Iranians had been smoking tobacco since the sixteenth century. It was a lucrative trade in the hands of the bazaar and clergy. The agitation against the tobacco monopoly revealed the power of the merchants and clergy not just to the world but to themselves.

As desert is the principal fact of Iranian geography, so is religion of Iranian history. In 1501, a fifteen-year-old boy named Ismail Safavi imposed the Shia faith on the country he and his Turkoman tribesmen had conquered. Warned the night before his coronation in Tabriz in northwestern Iran that at least two thirds of the population followed the mainstream or Sunni school of Islam, Ismail replied: "If the people utter one word of protest, so help me God Almighty, I will draw my sword and leave not one of them alive." [37] Although Sunni Muslims live and worship in Tehran and the outlying regions of Iran, as do isolated populations of Jews, Christians, and Zoroastrians, for most Iranians Iran *is* the Shia. There are Shia adherents in southern Lebanon and southern and central Iraq, Bahrain, ex-Soviet Azerbaijan, Afghanistan, Kashmir, Karachi, Burma, and the old capital of Oudh, Lucknow, yet for most Iranians and, indeed, for most people, the Shia *is* Iran.

Shia means "party" or "faction" in Arabic because it began as a political movement. With the death of the Prophet Mohammed in AD 632, differences arose among the Muslim pioneers as to who was to succeed him as leader of the prayers and the army. For many of the Muslims, the best candidate was Ali ibn Abi Taleb, who had married the Prophet's daughter Fatemeh, but he was passed over three times, only acceding to the Succession (or Caliphate) in 656.

On January 29, 661, Ali was assassinated in the mosque at Kufa in Iraq, and nineteen years later, on the tenth day of the lunar month of Moharram, his younger son, Hosein, was cut to pieces not far from the Euphrates at Karbala. Under persecution from the Caliphate, the Shia leadership passed down a succession of commanders or imams, each in direct male descent from Ali and Fatemeh. The twelfth in line, a young boy named Abulqasim Mohammed ibn Hasan, appeared at his father's funeral in the mosque in Samarra in Iraq in 874, and vanished. [38]

For a period of an earthly lifetime, the Mahdi (or "rightly guided one") communicated with the Shia through four successive lieutenants, or Gates, but at the death of the fourth Gate in 941, the Twelfth Imam passed out of communication. The light went out of the world. Yet at the outer limit of perception, in dreams or the daytime visions of certain men and women, the Lord of the Age walks the earth, incognito, and will return to usher in justice and bring the world to its end. [39] Until such time, all attempts to legislate or govern are at best provisional and, at worst, usurpations.

This story of martyrdom and redemption gave birth to immense shrines, with their pilgrimage hostels and seminaries, at Karbala in Iraq and around the tomb of Ali "Commander of the Faithful" at Najaf to the south; at Mashhad in northeastern Iran, a city which grew up round the tomb of the Eighth Imam Reza; and the old Shia town of Qom in the desert south of Tehran, where Imam Reza's sister Fatemeh, known as *Hazrat Masoumeh* or the Immaculate Lady, is buried.

From the time of the Safavids, the stories of the saints became the stock-in-trade of professional storytellers who would visit houses in the first ten days of the mourning month of Moharram, reciting behind screens in the private quarters to sobbing women and frightened children. These ceremonies culminated in the marches of the 9th and 10th of the month, known by the Arabic ordinal numbers *Tassua* and *Ashura*, where men in bloodstained shirts marched through the cities in step, beating their chests or backs with metal chains, or cutting their scalps with swords, so that they could partake of Hosein's agony or substitute for it.

All the while, there was a paradox. In the absence of the Hidden Imam, all government is a delegation, and yet the Shia has from the time of Ismail been the key to marshaling the population and seizing power in Iran. The clergy saw themselves as protectors of the poor and weak, and guarantors of religious orthodoxy, social propriety, honest commerce, and an Iranian way of life of which they felt themselves to be the embodiment. At times, they felt entitled to govern Iran either in conjunction with the sovereign, or in his place. Such clerical politics are recorded by European travelers to Iran as early as the seventeenth century.[40]

At least until the production of petroleum in Iran, the revenues of clergy were probably not much less than those of the state. With contributions from pious followers through the so-called Imams' Share, a learned man could assemble a following of students indistinguishable from a private army. In a desert land ravaged by warfare and always subject to arbitrary government, where there were no castles or manors, where even the tribal leaders had no certainty of tenure, no feudal or quasi-feudal aristocracy could establish itself for long. The senior clergy, and those who claimed blood descent from the Prophet's family or *sayyids*, took on the manners of an aristocracy.

By the nineteenth century, the Iranian clergy consisted of a hierarchy reaching up from the mendicant dervish, through the hedge-molla or *akhund* and the Moharram reciter or *rowzehkhan* to those men, known as *mojtaheds*, who had mastered the grueling seminary education to its conclusion and could pronounce on the law of the Prophet and the Imams. As such jurists proliferated, so a supercategory of scholar emerged first in Najaf and then in Qom, the "Source of Imitation" or, in Arabic, *marja al-taqlid*, whose readings or *fatwas* were law to believers as far away as India.

All the while, the Shia adjusted itself to accommodate modernity. By the nineteenth century, senior *mojtaheds* were relying on imaginative analogy, rather than just scripture or reports of the conduct of the Prophet and Imams, on matters such as the propriety of war with Russia. The clergy needed new powers because they had discovered new enemies: the mystics known as Sufis; adventists such as the Sheikhis, Babis, and Bahais; assertive Anglican and Presbyterian missionaries; and Jews and Zoroastrians who were becoming aware of the civil rights granted their co-religionists in Europe and India.

In 1844, the clerical class was torn apart by schism when a young *sayyid* from Shiraz, Ali Mohammed Shirazi (1819–1850), announced himself as the new lieutenant or Gate to the Lord of the Age and, from 1848, the Mahdi himself. Islamic law was abrogated and the Resurrection announced. Babism (from the Arabic for Gate, *Bab*) spread like wildfire. The best foreign observers, Gobineau and Edward Browne, were fascinated that, with no press or postal service or carriage road, the movement could in a matter of a few months radiate across the vast distances of Iran. They were thrilled by the courage of the Babis under persecution by the orthodox clergy and the new ideas—of tolerance and female emancipation—which had percolated from Europe, India, and the Ottoman Empire. Weary to death of Victorian Christianity, they thought to be assisting at the birth of a new monotheism.

The Bab was imprisoned in 1848, taken to Tabriz, and interrogated by the local clergy in the presence of Nassereddin, then crown prince. On July 8 or 9, 1850, the Bab was brought before a firing squad in front of the wall of the Tabriz Citadel, but the first fusillade merely cut the rope that bound him. Had the Bab, wrote Gobineau, instead of taking refuge in a guardroom, walked forward into the crowd, Tabriz and even all Iran would now be Babi.[41] On August 15, 1852, while out riding near his palace north of Tehran, Nassereddin was accosted by three Babis who fired pistols loaded with buckshot into his midriff. Nassereddin Shah survived.

There followed an orgy of persecution. In a macabre illumination to celebrate the Shah's survival, Babis were driven through the streets with lighted candles inserted into wounds in their flesh. Frightened of retaliation, the Shah's executioners or "Lords of Wrath" distributed the thirty Babi prisoners through the sketchy Qajar bureaucracy, the mosques, and the guilds. Even the cadets of the Technical College, founded by the reforming minister Mirza Taqi Khan with foreign instructors, were given a prisoner to slash at. In this holocaust, the Babi movement split with the majority group, known as Bahais after their leader, Bahaullah (1817–1892), establishing themselves at Haifa in Palestine and gaining adherents even in the United States, while the minority Azalis became one of the modernizing strands in Iran. Many Bahais were to drift into the Pahlavi camp and court, where the Bahai Abdolkarim Ayadi became Mohammed Reza's personal physician and confidant.[42]

This first display of Islamic revolution shook the Iranian clergy to the core, but was turned to use. Under the leading cleric of Isfahan, the rich and disreputable Mohammed Taqi, known as Aqa Najafi, there were thirteen anti-Babi pogroms between 1864 and 1914, leaving hundreds dead.[43] After the bloodiest of those, at New Year 1890, Mohammed Taqi was summoned to Tehran. He took two months on the way, stopping to be greeted at every village, and it was later said that Nassereddin's favorite wife, Amineh Aqdas, had asked for the basin of water in which he had washed his hands.

News of the tobacco monopoly reached Isfahan that spring along with rumors, which were well founded, that the Russians would use Turkmanchay to demand a countervailing *régie* in the opium trade.[44] In Shiraz to the south, Sayyid Ali Akbar Fal Asiri stood at the pulpit with a drawn sword and made the call to public defense, or *jihad*: "O people, you must ensure your women are not stripped [raped]. I have here a sword and a couple of drops of blood. Any foreigner who comes to Shiraz to monopolise the tobacco will have his belly ripped with this sword."[45] From the provincial towns, the agitation spread to the capital. The clergy of Tehran extracted—or, more probably, forged—a ruling from the most revered scholar of his day, "The Renewer" Hassan Shirazi, that until the tobacco monopoly was withdrawn, nobody should smoke. Under the orders of his senior wife, Anis od-Dowleh, the Shah could not even smoke in his private quarters.[46] For Edward

Browne in England, the tobacco protest was the inauguration of "a real public spirit and public opinions" in Iran.[47] In January 1892, Nassereddin, "weary of governing a nation of non-smokers,"[48] as his grandson's British tutor in Isfahan put it, canceled the concession. In the City of London, the "Persian Bubble" burst.

Dejected, Nassereddin lost his relish for reform, confining himself to hunting game or the teenaged daughters of his gardener, and enjoying the antics of his favorite, a Kurdish boy he named *Aziz os-Soltan* ("The King's Darling"). He was pestered by his harem, infiltrated by bazaar spies and agents of the legations and foreign syndicates. The British deciphered his cables and read his private correspondence. Nassereddin was at his wits' end: "When I go to my 'Anderun' [harem], five hundred women swarm around me and annoy me with their complaints. I come out, and disturbing reports are put into my hands. I go to the Amin es-Sultan [prime minister] and he heaps coals of fire on my head."[49] On May 1, 1896, just a few days short of his fifty-year jubilee by the lunar calendar, at the shrine of Shah Abdolazim south of the capital, Nassereddin was assassinated by a religious radical.

The clock could not be turned back. A £500,000 indemnity, demanded as price of the cancelation of the tobacco *régie,* inaugurated Iran's foreign debt and was used to capitalize the new British Imperial Bank of Persia, which received a monopoly on issuing bank notes. The bank survived repeated runs, organized by the rival Russian bank, the *sarrafs* or moneychangers of the bazaar, or the two in cooperation. Between them the Imperial Bank and the Russian Banque d'Escompte or Discount Bank, begun as a pawnshop and auctioneer in 1890 but taken over by an expansionary Russian state in 1899, kept the Qajars afloat and financed the transfer of power in 1896 to the new Shah, Muzaffareddin. In 1898, a group of low-ranking Belgian officials under Joseph Naus was brought in to oversee the collection of customs receipts and was so successful that Iran was able to borrow against them 32.5 million roubles (£3m) in two loans from Russia in 1900 and 1902.

Meanwhile, on May 28, 1901, all but unnoticed, William D'Arcy, an Englishman who had made a fortune in the Australian gold fields, received an exclusive concession of sixty years to prospect for petroleum over 480,000 square miles at a royalty of 16 percent of net profits (which was then standard in the southern United States). Since the concession did not cross any entrenched bazaar interests, excluded the five northern provinces that bordered Russia (Article 6), and concerned products (petroleum and natural gas) that were not used in Iran, the concession attracted little interest and is barely mentioned even in the British diplomatic correspondence.[50]

In the capital, it was different. The Constitutional Revolution had its origins in the bazaar's objection to the Belgian customs regime and the Russian loans but soon expanded to embrace the new concept of a monarchy subject to law. On September 20, 1906, the historian Ahmad Kasravi, then a sixteen-year-old seminary student in Tabriz, saw crowds gathering at the bazaar and overheard two men in the street:

"It's not cheap bread they're calling for. So what do they want?"

"They want a Constitution!"

"Constitution? What's a Constitution?"

"Go yourself and ask them."[51]

What originated as a revolt against the expansion of the state and the introduction of alien habits of business, dress, thought, and conduct became infused with ideas of freedom and equality, brought back from Europe (as Kasravi put it) like souvenirs. In the capital, the agitation was led by two prominent clergymen, the "Two Proofs of Islam," Sayyid Abdullah Behbehani and Mirza Sayyid Mohammed Tabatabai. They were supported by the principal clergy of Najaf. In Tabriz, open to influence from the Caucasus, there was a more democratic atmosphere, while in Isfahan, Aqa Najafi's brother Nurullah thought to promote a Muslim republic.

The original Constitutionalist demand was for an advisory council or House of Justice, as it was called; but in the turmoil of the summer of 1906, including a mass *bast* or asylum of the merchants and guilds in the grounds of the British legation, the demands crystallized into a bicameral Parliament of European character, elected on a limited male franchise. Muzaffareddin, desperately sick of gout and kidney stones, granted that request on August 5 and the inaugural meeting of the Tehran deputies occurred in October. With the Shah slipping away, a Constitution was drafted quickly with articles taken over from the constitutions of the kingdoms of Belgium (1831), Bulgaria (1879), and Russia (1906). It was signed by Muzaffareddin on December 30,

1906. He died ten days later. The Constitution was soon found inadequate and a Supplement of one hundred and five Articles and a Bill of Rights was presented to Muzaffareddin's son, Mohammed Ali Shah, and signed into law in October 1907. While the principles of popular sovereignty and the rule of law were established, there was ambiguity about the royal prerogative which the Pahlavi family would exploit and then explode.

The Shia clergy, bred up to think in categories of law, were attracted to constitutionalism, but many were alarmed when they became aware of what a Parliament did. Fazlollah Nuri, the most learned of the Tehran clergy and a hero later to Khomeini, attended one or two sessions of the new Parliament, which met in the public quarters and garden of a nobleman's house that had been confiscated by Nassereddin for his favorite and was known as the Baharestan ("Abode of Spring").

Nuri was horrified that the deputies, sitting on the floor in a square four rows deep, were actually making laws, and he feared that a foreign notion—*demokrasi*—was being set up to rival revealed religion. Nuri drafted Article 2 of the Supplement that declared no "laws of the National consultative assembly . . . may be at variance with the sacred principles of Islam." A committee of five jurists or *mojtaheds* was to "reject or repudiate any proposal that is at variance with the sacred laws of Islam. . . . In such matters the decision of this committee of learned men shall be followed and obeyed, and this article shall continue unchanged until the appearance of the Hidden Imam."[52] In fact, the democrat deputies ensured the clerical committee was appointed by Parliament, and it fell into abeyance until it was revived as the heart of the revolutionary Constitution of 1979.

On June 20, 1907, with about five hundred students and followers, Nuri took refuge in the shrine of Shah Abdolazim (linked by a light railway to the capital), where he issued a series of leaflets, first photographed and then lithographed, and now known as the "Journal of Sheikh Fazlollah." In those leaflets, which have been gathered up and printed since the Revolution of 1979, Nuri argued God had given the world all the law it needed. There was no call for legislation since there was clerical deduction or *ijtihad* and its practitioners, *mojtaheds*. In the slogan of the time, *mashrueh* or canonical law had juridical precedence over *mashruteh* or constitutional law.

17

If there was to be a parliament, it should confine itself to the little matters of administration or what the European eighteenth century called "police." That was essentially Khomeini's view before the triumph of the revolutionaries in 1979 introduced him to the range of powers at the state's disposal. In his scholastic logic, Nuri concluded that until the return of the Lord of the Age, absolutism was preferable to constitutionalism precisely because it made no claim to a legitimacy that might rival religion.

All the while, he fulminated against foreign influence: "These fireworks, receptions of ambassadors, these foreign manners, hurrahs, banners saying Long live! Long live! Long live equality! Long live fraternity! Why not write on one of them: Long live the holy law! Long live the Koran, Long live Islam."[53] ("If you wear a tie and collar/ He'll fuck you till you fart and holler," wrote the libertine poet Iraj Mirza.)[54]

Mohammed Ali Shah, who had been brought up by Russian tutors and was plotting to restore royal autocracy, fanned the religious flames and, on August 16, sent a carriage to bring Nuri to the palace. The parliamentarians fortified the Baharestan and the next-door Sepahsalar Mosque, while Nuri and the court marshaled their forces in the square in front. A Belgian customs officer wrote to his brother on December 17: "The roofs of the Parliament building and the mosque next door are teeming with armed men. The gardens have been turned into entrenchments. The Cossacks, artillery and the army are mobilised and waiting, armed to the teeth, in Artillery Square. There the partisans of the Shah, low stable boys and domestics of every sort are assembled in a terrific hubbub around several *sayyids* who preach war against the Parliament."[55]

After months of shifting fortunes, on June 23, 1908, the Shah's Brigade of Cossacks, under Russian officers, bombarded the Parliament building, killed many of the defenders, put the deputies to flight, and reestablished absolute rule. Constitutionalist reinforcements from Tabriz, Rasht, and Isfahan defeated the royalists the following summer and drove Mohammed Ali Shah to take refuge in the Russian legation. On July 16, 1909, he was deposed and replaced by his twelve-year-old son Ahmad, who was to be the last Qajar ruler. Nuri, who was courageous as well as learned, barricaded himself into his house in the Sangelaj district, was captured, tried for the Koranic offense of "corruption on earth" by a special tribunal under the presidency of a Constitutionalist *mojtahed*, and sentenced to death. On July 31, 1909, in Artillery Square, the turban that was the badge of clerical impunity was taken off his head and he was hanged. His last words were a couple of verses: "If we have been a burden, we are gone / If we were unkind, we are gone." Modern school textbooks in Iran portray him as the first of the clerical martyrs and a pioneer of Islamic government.

Nuri's execution, as well as the assassination of Behbehani the following summer, troubled the Iranian clergy. Whereas there were seventeen *mojtaheds* and sixty-five clergy at the inaugural Parliament (almost as great a proportion as in 1980), this number fell, and by the 1930s there was no well-known clerical member. The clergy felt betrayed by the secular reformers and that was to have consequences later in the twentieth century. Meanwhile, in the south of the country, D'Arcy's concession was about to transform the country and, in time, make parliamentary government an irrelevance.

On May 26, 1908, at four in the morning and about 110 degrees of the thermometer, at a depth of 1,180 feet below the treeless gravel near an ancient ruin called Solomon's Mosque or Masjed-e Suleiman in southern Iran, liquid petroleum was found. Lieutenant Arnold Wilson, an Indian army officer who had brought a troop of twenty Bengal Lancers to protect the drillers from the Bakhtiari tribesmen, was sleeping outside his tent and woke to the shouting of the crew and the roar of the gusher.

"It rose 50 feet or so above the top of the rig," Wilson wrote, "smothering the drillers and their devoted Persian staffs who were nearly suffocated by the accompanying gas." [56]

The breakthrough at Masjed-e Suleiman was not just into oil-bearing rock but into a new phase of Iranian history, for after some delay it was to transform Iran as no other event between the coming to power of the Safavids in 1501 and the Revolution of 1979. Iran no longer depended for its revenue on the product of subsistence farming in a dry land. On April 14, 1909, the Anglo-Persian Oil Company (APOC) was formed in London with a capital of £2 million. To bring the oil to seaboard, Anglo-Persian leased from the semi-independent Sheikh Khazal of Mohammareh a square mile of land on the alluvial island of

Abadan, some forty miles from the mouth of the Shatt al-Arab, constructed on it a bench-still refinery, and linked it to Masjed-e Suleiman by a 140-mile pipeline.

With its antiquated Indian-style management agency, Anglo-Persian at first could produce nothing of value. Its kerosene filmed the chimneys of lamps, while its motor spirit (known in the United States as gasoline, and elsewhere as benzine) was sulphurous and foul-smelling. That left a product unevaporated in the refinery process, the viscous residue known as fuel oil or bunker. To generate some revenue, Anglo-Persian was selling the fuel oil to Royal Dutch-Shell, into whose embrace the whole enterprise seemed destined to fall. By the eve of war, the company had run through its £2.5 million in capital and debentures and was surviving by bilking suppliers and borrowing from D'Arcy and its chairman, the ninety-three-year-old railway baron Lord Strathcona.[57] Rescue came in the person of Winston Churchill, First Lord of the Admiralty, who had been persuaded that the Royal Navy should convert its ships from burning coal to burning oil.

On May 20, 1914, in return for an investment of £2 million, Anglo-Persian sold a majority voting interest to the UK Treasury and promised to supply the Admiralty with fuel oil at 30 shillings a ton f.o.b. Abadan. Edward Browne, the doyen of Iranian studies in Britain, in a letter to *The Times* suggested that the agreement would force Britain to take more interest in the welfare of Iran.[58] In reality, Britain and its allies in the war with Germany were "floated to victory on a wave of oil" (said Lord Curzon)[59] while Iran, by 1917, had received a royalty of £30,537 6s 8d.[60] British government and British corporation became inextricably bound, at first to the profit of both and then, amid rising nationalism in Iran, to their fatal detriment.

In an attempt to dilute Russian and British influence, Parliament in Tehran brought in a succession of advisers from far-away lands without a history of interference in Iran. First Morgan Shuster, a brilliant but bullheaded American who ran afoul of the Russian legation, then Naus's successor, Joseph Mornard, published budgets. By the outbreak of war in 1914, there were Belgians in the customs and treasury, British in the telegraph houses, Swedes in the Gendarmerie and police, Russians in the Cossack Brigade, French jurists in the Ministries of Justice and Interior and the polytechnic, and Germans (in an irony that was not lost on them) running the government hospital and the machine-gun brigade.[61] With the entry of Turkey into the war, Iran declared its neutrality to no effect. The country became a battleground between Turkish, Russian, and British armed forces and German agents. The weak Iranian military forces were divided in their sympathies, with the Cossack Brigade under Russian control while the Government Gendarmerie, a rural police force and highway patrol set up on the eve of the war under Swedish officers and training, leaned toward Imperial Germany.

By November 1915, with Russian forces approaching Tehran, the Government Gendarmerie organized a migration of government officials, parliamentary deputies, and nationalists to the holy city of Qom, ninety miles to the southwest. A cavalry squadron under the Swede Major Gustav Edwall waited for Ahmad Shah at the Qom gate, but he was dissuaded from leaving by the ambassadors of the anti-German Entente powers. The Committee of National Defense, a sort of provisional nationalist government, was set up in Qom. The nationalist forces were gradually driven west by Russian advances to Hamadan, Kermanshah, and Qasr-e Shirin and, in the end, exile in the Ottoman territories.

With the Russian Revolution of 1917 and the defeat of Germany the following year, Britain sought a free hand in Iran. Lord Curzon, now British foreign secretary, thinking of Iran as an Indian princely state on a colossal scale, attempted to impose a British protectorate over the financial administration and the armed forces sweetened by a £2 million loan (and a subsidy to Ahmad Shah and some £140,000 in bribes to the principal Iranian officials). The Iranian armed forces were to be reconstituted on the Indian pattern, in which the Cossacks, the Gendarmerie, the provincial units, and what remained of the army would be amalgamated under British officers. It was rumored that Iranian officers would serve only as subalterns (that is, below the rank of major or even captain). Nationalist feeling ran high.

The so-called Anglo-Persian Agreement needed parliamentary approval and had no chance of achieving it. The stage was set for a national saviour.

Reza Khan was born in the autumn of 1878 in Alasht, an Alpine valley in the Savadkuh Mountains of Mazanderan northeast of Tehran, into a long-serving military family.[62] The family house, much damaged over the years and altered, still stands with its garden courtyard on a little square facing a saint's shrine. Reza's grandfather, Murad Ali Khan Soltan, had fallen at the siege of Herat in 1838 when Mohammed Shah Qajar, already hemmed in by Russian expansion in the north and the British Empire in the south, had tried without success to push into western Afghanistan.

Reza's father, Abbas Ali Khan, commander of the district levies, died six weeks after Reza's birth, and his mother, Nushafarin, a girl originally from the Caucasus, fled her husband's relations, carrying the child over the freezing mountain tracks to Tehran. There they lodged with her younger brother, Abulqasem Beg, a non-commissioned officer in the new Brigade of Cossacks, which the Russian general staff in the Caucasus had just established as a life guard for the Qajars. Nushafarin died soon after. Reza received no schooling, and even as Shah was never at ease either reading or speaking in public. (He had a habit of burning or throwing written matter to the ground.) He was enlisted first in the local regiment and then, in 1891 at the age of thirteen, as a stable boy in the Cossack Brigade.[63] Years later, a broken man in exile in Mauritius, when his daughter Shams tried to force him into evening dress for the British governor's reception, Reza said: "I am not used to these clothes. All my life I have worn only a soldier's uniform."[64]

Reza rose through the ranks. There is a 1903 photograph of a man resembling him in Cossack uniform, with its wide skirts, sewn-in cartridge pockets, and *papakha* busby, as a soldier-groom at the Dutch legation.[65] The brigade was always, in the words of a German observer, a "ceremonial and parade-ground outfit,"[66] and not one of the Russian Cossack officers fell in service. Still, in the years of uproar and brigandage that attended the death agonies of the Qajar dynasty, Reza saw some action in Kashan in the center of Iran and Kurdestan in the west. Once, as lieutenant or captain, he marched a detachment to Hamadan in Kurdestan with his boots so worn and broken that the nails pierced the soles of his feet.[67] Reza became expert in the use of the new Maxim self-powered machine gun, which had been first deployed by Russian forces in the war with Japan of 1905. He was nicknamed, in the Iranian way, *Reza Maxeem*.

In or about 1911, Reza came to the attention of a Qajar prince named Farmanfarma whom he later, as is the way of world, treated with contempt, extracting from the family land in the west of Tehran and a Rolls-Royce, and murdering one of its sons. By the end of World War I, with the brigade now at division strength and top-heavy with officers, Reza reached field rank. Reza was a handsome man, tall, with jet black hair and mustaches not yet turned white by worry and opium, and deep-set eyes shot with yellow and red that terrified his interlocutors.[68] In photographs, he stands head and shoulders over the Russian officers, as once did Saul among the Israelites.

What Reza took from his thirty-year service with the Cossacks was a soldier's way of life, an autocratic cast of mind, a contempt for civilians and clergymen, and the bullying and cussing still rife in the Russian army today. Throughout the twenty years of his dominance, Reza relied on his fellow Iranian Cossack officers, hard and uneducated men with little to lose and much to gain from Pahlavi rule, who gave the style to the Iranian armed forces right up to the 1979 Revolution. Taking their lead from their master, those officers made themselves estates of land and town property and even, like the toughest of them, General Fazlollah Zahedi, married into the old Qajar nobility. Reza may also have heard from the Russian officers something of Czar Peter the Great, who ripped the veils off ladies at his court and once took a razor to a courtier's beard with his own hand.

With the Revolution in Russia in 1917 and the collapse of czarist power in Iran, the British feared the Cossack Brigade might fall under Bolshevik control. They enlisted Reza to help eject the brigade's Russian commander. In May 1920, a Bolshevik force landed at Enzeli on the Caspian Sea north of Tehran in support of the local Communists or *Jangalis* ("woodsmen") and drove back the British and Indian troops and the Iranian Cossacks, who withdrew in disorder across the Elburz Mountains to Qazvin, two hours by unmade road west of Tehran. On October 4, there arrived at Qazvin Major General Sir Edmund Ironside, known as "Tiny" for his immense height and breadth, a maverick officer with experience in Archangel and Turkey of extracting British Empire forces from futile and perilous foreign deployments.

During a tour of the chaotic Cossack camp on November 2, 1920, Ironside was introduced to an officer who reminded him of a Rajput, a fighting caste in India. This officer was, Ironside wrote in his diary, "a man of well over six feet in height with broad shoulders and a most distinguished-looking face. His hooked nose and sparkling eyes gave him a look of animation. His name was Reza Khan." Though "shivering from a severe bout of malaria" picked up at Enzeli, Reza "never went sick." With his habitual dispatch and confidence in his own judgment, Ironside "decided to make him Commander of the Cossack Brigade at least temporarily, and at once."[69]

Looking at first for a capable Iranian officer to hold the Bolsheviks and, as he put it in a dispatch to the British War Office on December 8, "enable us to depart in peace and honour,"[70] Ironside soon refined his requirements. By January 1, 1921, on a dejected walk around Tehran, Ironside was thinking of a "strong man" who could save Iran from dismemberment.[71] He was confirmed in that belief by an interview with the boy king, Ahmad Shah Qajar, who tried to enlist his help in a currency speculation.[72] On January 14, Ironside wrote in his diary: "A military dictatorship would solve our troubles and let us out of the country without any trouble at all. I shall have to talk to the [British] Minister about it."[73] On February 14, he noted: "Better a *coup d'état* for us than anything else."

The next day, Ironside returned to Tehran and informed the British minister, Herman Norman, that he had released Reza and the Cossack Brigade from British control. "Old Norman . . . was very fearful that the Shah would be done in," Ironside wrote. "I told him I believed in Reza. . . . I had to let the Cossacks go at some time or other."[74] Ironside did extract from Reza a promise not to unseat Ahmad Shah, though his diaries show he placed no confidence in Reza's word.[75] As it turned out, in 1925 Reza sent an envoy to Staff College, Camberley, where Ironside was commandant, to request that the Englishman release him from his promise.[76]

During the night of February 20–21, 1921, Reza marched on Tehran with two regiments of Cossacks[77] and imposed himself first as commander of the country's starving military forces, then as minister of war, then prime minister, and then as Shah.

His intention that night had been to preserve the army from disintegration, and Tehran from Bolshevik attack,[78] but he found he could do neither without smashing the bankrupt Iranian state, terrorizing the nobility and the independent tribal chiefs, and dethroning the

Qajars. In the next three years, Reza removed his co-conspirator, a cleric-turned-journalist, Sayyid Zia Tabatabai, outwitted his rivals in the military and Parliament, shook down the aristocracy, won over the British and Soviet legations, and frightened Ahmad Shah Qajar into leaving for Europe. Over the winter of 1923–24, he attempted to install himself at the head of a republic on the pattern just established in Turkey on the ruins of the Ottoman Empire by another military officer, Mustafa Kemal, who later took the surname Atatürk ("Father of the Turks").[79]

Suspicious of Reza's intentions, and disgusted by his rough methods, Parliament and the leading clergy of Tehran rebuffed him. Events in Kemal Pasha's new Turkish republic, and particularly the abolition of the religious authority known as the Caliphate and the religious schools on March 3, 1924, unsettled the Iranians. On April 1, 1924, Reza recommended by decree that no more be said about a republic.[80] When on July 18 a U.S. consular officer, Robert W. Imbrie, was murdered in a religious riot, Reza imposed martial law and deployed his new British armored cars to terrorize the city. Ahmad Shah refused to return from Paris and Monte Carlo, and on October 31, 1925, an intimidated Parliament voted to abolish the Qajar dynasty. A constituent assembly, meeting under a torn awning in the drafty national theater on December 12, named Reza to the throne.

In May the following year, Parliament passed a bill abolishing titles of nobility and military sinecures and ordering all Iranians to adopt European-style surnames. Reza chose for himself and his children the name Pahlavi, which meant both "Heroic" and an ancient Persian language and script. (PEHLEVI was the cable address of the British Imperial Bank, which grumbled at having to change it.)[81] So began the Pahlavi dynasty, of short duration.

CHAPTER 2

Cossack Government

◇

*Every country has a certain type of regime. Ours is a
one-person regime.*

—Reza Pahlavi[1]

Reza Pahlavi spoke little and wrote less. Unlike his hero in Turkey,
Kemal Pasha, who once addressed a party congress for six days in succession,[2] Reza rarely said in public more than two or three sentences.
He wrote no testament and his plans for Iran must be gleaned from
proclamations, two travel diaries—about Mazanderan in the north and
Khuzestan in the south—written by ghostwriters, and the memoirs of
his ministers and his personal secretary-cum-valet, Soleiman Behbudi.

Reza believed that for Iran to hold its own against the foreign powers, it must compress their industrial and social development into a few
years. He hated the privileges enjoyed by the foreign powers in Iran,
and despised the ruling class and military that had permitted them
to become established. He had a low opinion of merchants and the
clergy, as of all civilians, and believed religion should be kept out of
the public administration. In an account of a journey to Mazanderan
in 1926, Reza (or rather his ghostwriter) said that "the mingling of religion and politics is damaging to religion and leads to the decay of the
public administration."[3] He was ashamed of the rituals of the Shia. "I
am devoted to the Lord of Martyrs [Imam Hosein]," Reza once said,
"but do we really need all this weeping and wailing?"[4]

Although Reza maintained (as his son did) a pretense of Constitutional government, he more and more ruled by decree. He would fix his
terrifying eyes on someone who had displeased him and say, "You are

lucky that I am a constitutional monarch."[5] Unlike Kemal Pasha and his People's Party of 1923 (later Republican People's Party), or Mussolini or Hitler, Reza never established a political party or any basis of support other than his ex-Cossack comrades. He once said, "Every country has a certain type of regime. Ours is a one-person regime."[6]

After the war years, when the country had thirteen prime ministers, and was overrun by foreign armies and beset by epidemics of cholera and influenza, many Iranians were looking for a man who could strengthen the military, expel the British and other foreign advisers, and put the revenue on a sound footing. Other notions current since the end of the nineteenth century—a codified law, public schools, education for women, language reform, archaeology, state investment in industry, and the disarming of the tribes—were absorbed into Reza's program but in characteristically brusque and rough execution. Even Mohammed Mossadeq, the Pahlavis' most formidable foe until Khomeini, in 1925 praised Reza for at last bringing security to the country.[7]

Reza's scheme, which had no precedent in the history of Iran, was to create a monopoly of force through a national army drawn from the entire country. The national army was both Reza's path to supreme power and the reason why he had to seize supreme power. Beset at every stage by difficulties with money, recruitment, arms and ammunition, fuel and mobility, Reza collided with both old and new institutions of the state and ended up capturing or demolishing them. Reza subordinated everything and everybody to military dictatorship: first Parliament, which after 1928 was controlled by the court minister, Teymourtache; the clergy, which lost its privileges and emoluments; the tribes, who were mistreated and disarmed; and then the public at large, who became subject to military conscription, taxation, the Uniform Dress Law of 1928, a law on headwear, and finally the unveiling decree of 1936. After the Gowharshad massacre in 1935, Reza was feared and detested, and few Iranians regretted his abdication six years later.[8]

With his Army Order No. 1 of December 6, 1921, Reza combined Cossacks, Government Gendarmerie, and the British-officered South Persia Rifles into five army divisions with a ration strength of 30,000, under the command of ex-Cossacks. He replaced the European ranks with new-minted Iranian ranks. He dismissed all but a handful of the foreign officers and banned the legations from mounting their own guard.

Reza at once attempted to take over the revenue for the army. At the end of 1922, Parliament brought in a new American financial mission, under Arthur C. Millspaugh, which established order in the budget, abolished the pensions that had bled the Qajar treasury white, and guaranteed Reza some 700,000 tomans a month for the army. Even so, the army at first had to rely on arms confiscated from the tribes, and there was talk in 1924 of financing the fledgling air force of British, German, and French biplanes by public subscription. Pay for the lower ranks was low and in arrears, and there were mutinies over pay in the summer of 1926 in Khorasan and Azerbaijan.

Attempts to interest U.S. oil concerns—Standard Oil of New Jersey and the Sinclair Oil Company—in a concession in the northern provinces and to raise a loan on Wall Street of up to $10 million came to nothing. Millspaugh did find some money for public works and by the end of the 1920s, some 6,000 miles of just about usable roads had been surfaced. Imported haulage trucks banished the twin specters of grain hoarding and famine that had haunted the last years of the Qajars.

On June 6, 1925, Parliament passed the general conscription law. Service was to be two years, at 7½ *krans* (about 3s) a month for a private, with twenty-three years in the reserves. The mutinies of the next summer delayed conscription, which proved hard to administer. The British chargé d'affaires Harold Nicolson reported that of the 2,500 young men in Tehran aged twenty-one, 1,500 went into a lottery but only 300 could actually be found.[9] Though seminary students were exempted, the broader mass of low-rank clergy was not. Soleiman Behbudi noted that Reza once stopped his car outside Hamadan, picked up a dervish loafing by the road, and packed him off to barracks.[10] Bribes allowed all but the poorest to escape conscription, and it was not enforced with the tribes.

As for the operations of the new army, they met with mixed success and were marked, particularly in Luristan in the southwest, by brutality and treachery. Reza himself led the force that broke the Bolshevik rebellion in the north. His greatest success, over Sheikh Khazal of Mohammareh, a British client who had established quasi-independent rule in the oil fields and southwest, was achieved without much of a fight. On the evening of April 19, 1925, the ex-Cossack Fazlollah Zahedi kidnapped Khazal off his yacht, *Ivy*, in the Shatt al-Arab and had him carried to Tehran, where he passed the rest of his life under house arrest and died in 1936 in murky circumstances. The incorporation of Khazal's sheikhdom restored Reza's prestige and the morale of the army that had been troubled by his flirtation with republicanism the previous year. It helped that Lord Curzon was now dead and the British minister in Tehran, Sir Percy Loraine, was able to express his enthusiasm for Reza. In a commentary on December 16, 1925, *Izvestiya* in Moscow wrote that although Reza's was "not yet a fully bourgeois monarchy, it is no longer the Anglo-Feudalism of the Qajars."[11]

There was unrest in Tabriz and the south in 1927 and 1928, and an uprising among the Qashqai and other tribes in the south in 1929, but by the 1930s the power of the state had passed into even remote corners of Iran. Between 1930 and 1937, the army doubled in size, and by 1941 it could muster 127,000 men in sixteen divisions of varying strength. Just as important, the army was the principal means by which Reza imposed his passion for uniformity, with the officer corps first adopting the Pahlavi cap or French-style *képi* and, from 1936, appearing with their wives and daughters unveiled in public.

The military was resented not just for such novelties but for its swagger and for requisitioning labor, transport, and pack animals without payment. Senior officers were permitted to follow the example of the Shah and enrich themselves. Even Sir Percy Loraine, Reza's great supporter, in his farewell audience with the Shah on June 27, 1926, raised the matter of the "oppression and corruption" of the military, saying it was "time to put the army back firmly on the leash."[12] Millspaugh also confronted the Shah with reports of the illegal taking of men, horses, grain, and money from the villages, "looting in some places so thorough as to leave nothing for the payment of taxes. He fingered his beads rapidly, a familiar sign of anger; and in spite of the respect that I took pains to show him and in spite of the facts, his anger was directed at me and not at his Army. It was well known that Reza helped himself liberally to army funds and used the proceeds for personal purposes."[13] Millspaugh's contract was not renewed.

The Iranian clergy soon found that Reza was no pleasure-loving Qajar. Sayyid Hassan Modarres, a leading parliamentarian, was dragged out of his house in 1928 by the chief of police, imprisoned in a town by the Afghan border, and, on December 1, 1937, done to death. A new code of civil law, drawn up by a parliamentary committee that included clergy under Ali Akbar Davar, Reza's minister of justice, was presented to Parliament in early 1928. Based in large part on the French civil code, it greatly reduced the role and purview of informal religious courts, which eventually lost even their notarial function, which was the chief source of income for the ordinary mollas. (In time, the Iranian clergy became so unaccustomed to the practice of the law that, in 1979, when they assumed the right to sit in judgment on the officers of the Pahlavi regime, they made elementary errors of process and evidence. Those were generally fatal to the prisoner.) The new code permitted Davar and Reza to suspend the consular courts and other legal privileges, sometimes known as Capitulations, that foreigners had enjoyed since Turkmanchay.

On the eve of New Year's Day, that is March 20, 1928, by the equinoctial calendar, there was an incident in the shrine of the Immaculate Lady in Qom which, though barely recorded at the time, has inflated into a tale of clerical resistance and martyrdom. Queen Taj ol-Moluk, her young daughters Shams and Ashraf, and other royal ladies wished to see in the New Year at the shrine. While taking their places in the ladies' gallery, the queen displayed too much of her face for the taste of one of the clergymen, Mohammed Taqi Bafqi, who made unseemly comments. One of her bodyguards threatened to shoot him. The queen calmed the man down, left the shrine with her party, and telephoned Reza. The next morning, the Shah, accompanied by an armored car and officials in several motor vehicles, arrived at the shrine, sent in the head of the security police to find Bafqi, and when that officer came out empty-handed, beat him with his cane. Reza then entered the shrine himself, without ceremony, cleared out two men who had taken *bast* or asylum from the law or military service in the shrine, and arrested several men, including Bafqi.[14] Bafqi was imprisoned, then exiled to the shrine of Shah Abdolazim, just south of Tehran, where Khomeini used to visit him till his death in 1946.[15] The British, who had turned against Reza since Sir Percy's departure in 1926, reported the incident as just one more instance of Reza's "barrack-yard behaviour."[16]

With Modarres safely in jail, the Uniform Dress Law passed into law on December 27, 1928. It prescribed among other things a new hat, similar to the *képi* that officers had been wearing since the early 1920s (later made famous by General de Gaulle). The law again exempted the higher clergy, but lower ranks and students were required to sit an examination to enjoy exemption. It was, wrote Mehdi Qoli Hedayat, Reza's long-serving conservative prime minister, "aimed evidently at abolishing the dress of the learned class which many of the common people were wearing."[17] (Hedayat continued to wear his skirted robe until one day in cabinet Reza seized his collar and hissed: "Shall I have a [frock] coat and trousers cut for you?")[18]

Uniform dress was a passion of the early twentieth century from China to Latin America. Several impulses combined. The first was a belief, evident in Japan since the 1870s, that the sober, plain, and clean masculine dress devised in England in the early nineteenth century was in some way the cause of Western success (rather than, as we would suppose, its consequence). The second, which was particularly marked in Asia, was the hope that uniform dress might overcome the distinctions and animosities of tribe, region, caste, and condition in otherwise unorganized societies. Reza himself said: "When Shirazis, Tabrizis and all others no longer wear different costumes there will be no reason for differences among them."[19] Here, Reza followed the lead set by his neighbors Kemal Pasha in Turkey and King Amanullah in Afghanistan and, further afield, Sun Yat-sen in China. The third was the appeal of the quasi-military uniforms of the nationalist parties in Germany, Italy, Spain, England, and among the Maronite Christians of Lebanon, which seemed to promise vigor and authority in countries shaken to the core by World War I.

In 1934, during his visit to Kemal Pasha in Turkey—and no doubt preparing for a return visit—Reza ordered a change in headwear to the brimmed or "international hat." Muslims, when they pray, press their foreheads to the ground, which is not easy to do in a brimmed hat. Amid growing unease, the leading *mojtahed* Hosein Qomi and his son asked for an interview with Reza on the subject, and took asylum at Shah Abdolazim. They were invited to leave the country. On July 7, 1935, the newspaper *Ettelaat* printed a circular from the Ministry of Interior that stipulated, among other things: that a sun helmet should not be worn in winter or after sundown; a straw hat, likewise; and that both should be removed indoors or in the company of a superior or an older gentleman.[20]

On the night of July 10–11, a roving Muharram reciter named Mohammed Taqi Bohlul, well known for his high spirits, prodigious memory, and habit of preaching only in his shirt, attempted to organize a mass *bast* or sit-in against the dress reforms in the Gowharshad shrine at Mashhad. In attempting to clear the shrine, the army lost its discipline and fired on the worshippers, killing at least eighteen of them. The army commander in Mashhad, the ex-Cossack Iraj Matbui, withdrew his men from the shrine but established no picket lines. In the next three days, crowds armed with sticks, sickles, shovels, and daggers converged from the town and villages shouting, "Hosein protect us from this Shah," and dragging with them sometimes reluctant clergymen. The British consul reported that government officials walked the streets with the new hat concealed in their coat pockets, only to put it on when they saw one another.

The conscripts were confined to barracks, and at 2 a.m. on the 14th, the Marg or "Death" Regiment cleared the shrine with machine guns, killing at least 128 people and wounding 200–300. Those included a party of Afghan pilgrims who, arriving on the night of the 14th and finding nowhere to stay, were camping at the shrine and lost fifteen of their number, among them women and children. Those arrested were beaten in batches of thirty every day for a week.[21] Bohlul the reciter escaped to Kabul in Afghanistan, where he was implicated in a murder, and then Cairo. He lived to make his peace with the Pahlavis, return to Iran, and see the Revolution of 1979. Matbui, by now a senator, was shot by the revolutionaries in Evin Prison on September 24, 1979.[22]

The British minister reported: "The Shah has suffered an almost mortal blow for the sacrilege at Meshed. . . . It may well be a nail in the coffin of his dynasty."[23] He was correct in his prediction, but premature. The Gowharshad massacre broke public resistance. Attempts to organize protests in other towns came to nothing. The British consul in Kermanshah reported on August 2, 1935: "Owing to fear and lack of leadership, it would not seem likely that any upheaval need be anticipated, unless a lead be given from some other part of [the] country."[24] Iranian men, outside the tribes, the clergy, and the military, stopped wearing hats. Khomeini's favorite pupil, Hosein Ali Montazeri, then a seminary student in Isfahan, remembers that the police raided the college, rummaged through clothes and bedding and, when they found a turban, took it away or ripped it to shreds. The Isfahan students nick-named their chief police tormentor "Prince Crankhandle," no doubt because he armed himself with that item.[25]

Meanwhile, the long-planned or threatened move on women's dress, or "women's renovation," was put into action. Women, long secluded by jealousy and religious custom, had begun to emerge from their houses in the 1920s. The classical singer Qamar had broken a taboo when she appeared unveiled on stage at the Grand Hotel on Lalehzar Street, Tehran, in 1924. By the late 1920s, official government functions proceeded in tandem: mixed parties in which Teymourtache might appear with his mistress, and the all-male affairs of the conservative prime minister, Hedayat. In June 1928, King Amanullah and Queen Soraya of Afghanistan returned from Europe through Tehran, she in a cloche hat with a skimpy veil and a short flapper skirt. Amanullah's defeat in a tribal revolt the next year was presented by conservatives in Iran as a warning against change.

In the autumn of 1935, on his return from his estates in Mazan-deran, Reza was told that perhaps if His Imperial Majesty took the lead, the people would follow. "Very well," he is reported to have said. "I am an old man. I'm ready to volunteer and set an example."[26] On Jan-uary 8, 1936, at ceremonies to award diplomas at a women's teacher training college, Queen Taj ol-Moluk and the two princesses, Shams and Ashraf, appeared unveiled. The young women stride out in their Girl Scout uniforms, but the queen's face is invisible behind a wide-brimmed Florentine hat and a fox stole.[27] (She never appeared again to the general public, not even at her son's coronation.)

In his short speech, Reza said: "The women of our country, because of their exclusion from society, have been unable to display their talent and ability. I might say they have been unable to do their duty towards their beloved country and people." On February 1, the Interior Ministry announced restrictions on the all-over female wrapper known as the *chador* or "tent." Those were sometimes enforced, sometimes ignored. The British consul in Tabriz reported that the police had cleared veiled women from the main boulevard of the town by February 9.[28] Mon-tazeri remembered police officers stationed outside the ladies' bath-house in Najafabad, near Isfahan, and tearing off their head scarves.[29]

Government officials were ordered to stage tea parties and receptions and bring their wives with them. Many, from the prime minister downwards, pleaded diplomatic illnesses, or even in some cases contracted temporary marriages with women willing to appear unveiled. (Known as *sigheh* or *muta,* temporary marriage is a peculiar Iranian form of regulated concubinage that used to shock and fascinate European visitors.)[30]

Many, perhaps most women stayed home. Clergymen sent their families to the villages, or retired to their houses and closed the street door. A few Iranians saw the comedy in it all, and put it about that pious women now could not go to the bathhouse and, therefore, by long Iranian custom, could not sleep with their husbands. The poor men were Reza's cuckolds. A government spy reported from the south: "On the outside, they support the government, but inside they cling to their old superstitions. At receptions, some plead illness, others wrap up their wives in black so their faces can't be seen. They look like immense storage jars on the move. This all has no effect on the public, who scamper back and forth across the roofs to meet one another or attend the bathhouse."[31] Mohammed Reza Mahdavi-Kani, who later became the revolutionary interior minister, remembers as a child seeing a door being cut in the party wall of his house so that women could pass unseen to the bathhouse at the top of the village.[32]

A man such as Teymourtache could look like a matinée idol, whether in a Kashmir robe or a Pahlavi cap, but that was not the case for Iranian men at large. Foreign visitors grumbled that Reza had turned some of the most elegant men in the world into the shabbiest. As for women, used to concealing their clothes under a dark chador, there was nothing in the bazaar for them to wear and the state textile import monopoly had to order clothing in bulk from Germany and England. In the photographs of the period, Iranian women are bundled up in hats, stockings, and pumps like Tatar *Hausfrauen,* while a traditional woman such as the poet Parvin Etesami seems to swoon with shyness at her presentation to Mohammed Reza. After Reza's abdication in 1941, and the lifting of the oppressive atmosphere, the chador returned to the streets. (All my pupils in 1974 wore chadors of printed Isfahan chintz in the street, and about one quarter in class.) The Revolution in 1979 merely enforced Reza's decree of 1936. There was no attempt to impose on Iranian women the beehive chador and visor of Qajar days. Even in divine revolutions, discretion is sometimes the better part of valor.

• • •

One by one, the British lost their privileges. The British consulates, established in the course of the nineteenth century in all the large towns of Iran and some of the small, lost their extraterritorial jurisdiction in 1928 and were, as one consul put it, "sent to Coventry" (boycotted).[33] The British Imperial Bank of Persia was stripped of its functions as a state bank, the Indo-European Telegraph was nationalized, and the Royal Navy lost two bunkering stations on Iranian islands in the Gulf. What Reza hated above all things was the British oil concession in the southwest of the country, but he recognized that it was indispensable to his revenue, and in trying to renegotiate the contract in 1933, he was outwitted by the company and the British government.

For the British, Anglo-Persian was an experiment in benign commercial imperialism. In the course of the 1920s, the reservoir was mapped, and a second field brought on at Haft Kel. Production rose from 897,400 tons (18,000 barrels a day) in 1917–18 to 5,357,800 tons (108,000 b/d) in 1928.[34] Anglo-Persian expanded the Abadan refinery to a throughput of 4.5 million tons, dredged the Shatt al-Arab, installed pipelines, storage, telephones, and jetties. It raised some £30 million in finance in London, which was far beyond the primitive Iranian capital market. It fueled the fivefold expansion in private motoring in Britain and Continental Europe in the course of the 1920s. The company was proud that, as the sole concessionaire, it was managing the reservoir not, as in Mexico and the United States, in a cutthroat scamper but as a precious resource for the long term.[35] As Sir John Cadman, who became chairman in 1927, told the American Petroleum Institute, oil was "a store of energy to be conserved, released and applied as part of a concerted operation owing its inception to more than one nation, and therefore yielding its tribute to more than one treasury."[36] What Cadman wanted, from at least 1926, was an extension of the sixty-year concession, already almost halfway expired.

In contrast, Iranians by the late 1920s saw that Anglo-Persian had built at their expense an oil-fired British navy and merchant marine, two refineries in the United Kingdom and a network of roadside service stations there and in Belgium, France, Germany, and Ireland, as well as a fleet of eighty-one oil tankers, bunkering stations, and a succession of dry exploratory wells from Argentina to Albania. They saw that only 3.5 square miles of the concession was actually being worked, were suspicious of APOC's activities in other countries, especially Iraq, and were disgusted by the treatment of the Iranian workers at Abadan. Reza, on his first visit to the oil fields in November 1925, was struck by the large number of British and foreign (chiefly Indian) employees, amounting to half of the workforce of 29,000, and their preferential treatment and accommodation. He saw no signs of prosperity outside the company towns.[37] The journalist Ali Dashti later claimed that Anglo-Persian treated the local population as badly as "the East India Company was said to have treated the Indians two hundred years ago."[38] Cadman's talk of conservation was to the Iranians merely a screen for a worldwide cartel to manage oil production in the interests not of the producers but of the companies.

Iranians were skeptical of Anglo-Persian's accounting policies and believed that "net profits" (on which their 16 percent was struck) were depressed by charges that had nothing to do with Iran but arose in its distribution or "downstream" business worldwide. Despite the increase in the tonnage produced and refined, Iran had received under £10 million in royalties by the end of the 1920s.[39] In some years, such as 1920–21 and again in 1931, Anglo-Persian paid more in income taxes to the UK Treasury than in royalties to Iran. Above all, the company hated the involvement of the British government and feared its interference. As Reza told T. L. Jacks, the company's resident director in Tehran on May 29, 1928, his one objection to Anglo-Persian was that "the majority of its shares are held by the British Government, otherwise its work has been very good."[40]

Reza was in need of hard currency to buy arms and equipment abroad for his army and air force and for an ambitious railroad project. He was determined to achieve more favorable terms and dispatched Teymourtache to negotiate with the company in London, Paris, and Geneva. The court minister made little progress. He demanded from Anglo-Persian a minimum annual payment of £2.75 million and, *sotto voce*, something for himself (eventually, £50,000).[41] Reza became impatient.

On a tour of the south in pouring rain in November 1928, Reza stood on the roof of the railway administration in Ahvaz and seeing the gas flares from Abadan on the southern horizon, said: "Curse the Anglo-Persian Oil Company!"[42] On May Day, 1929, Iranian employees of the company went on strike and tried to break into the refinery. While the local governor crushed the strike, Teymourtache insisted to the British that the cause of the unrest was "low wages and the lack of specific regulations for their work." The Wall Street crash that October was followed by a worldwide depression in trade. The oil market collapsed, the Iranian royalties slumped to just £300,000 for 1931, and 10,000 Iranian laborers at the oil company were dismissed. The *kran*, in slow decline along with the value of silver for half a century, fell precipitately on the exchanges.

On November 26, 1932, Reza strode into a meeting of his ministers, abused Teymourtache for failing to reach an agreement, and dictated a letter canceling the concession. He then opened the stove and threw the file of the negotiations into it.[43] To celebrate the end of "this shameful remnant of the past," Tehran was illuminated for two nights. The British submitted the case to the League of Nations. On December 23, Teymourtache was dismissed as minister of court. When two newspapers praised the Shah for dismissing him, Reza ordered their editors, for their sycophancy, to be given brooms and made to sweep Army Square (as the artillery ground was now known).[44]

Of Teymourtache it was once said, "women, society, property, children, power, earth, heaven, work and reputation: all for him were a gamble."[45] He was rumored to be losing at cards up to 10,000 tomans (£1,500) a night at the Iran Club, and his affair with a colleague's wife, nicknamed "Bulbul" or Nightingale, was a scandal in a city where even the royal women did not appear in public.[46] At some point, Reza came to fear that Teymourtache was threatening his very rule. Tehran had been shaken by the revelations of G. S. Agapekov, the former OGPU Resident in Tehran, detailing the Soviet penetration of the country and a wide network of agents. Teymourtache, who had studied at the St. Petersburg military academy, fell under suspicion.

British diplomatic archives show that London was planning to put pressure on Teymourtache, threatening to produce a letter of March 25, 1932, whose effect might be "volcanic and land Teymourtache in prison for speculating in government funds." (The letter itself is not in the public British archives and I do not know if it was ever shown in Tehran.)[47] On January 9, 1933, *The Times* of London published a long article under the heading "The Shah and His Advisers," which referred to "Prince" Teymourtache. It said that Reza was now "sixty and in poor health. What chance would his 13-year-old son have, should the Regency fall to a man [Teymourtache] still young, ambitious and extremely unscrupulous? The safety of the dynasty can be ensured only by removing all men of outstanding ability." [48] The article, if it did not originate at the Foreign Office or Anglo-Persian, certainly derived from their briefing. Teymourtache himself had no doubt that the British were behind his fall. [49]

After some weeks of confinement to his house, Teymourtache was sent on February 16, 1933, to the new model prison, the Qasr, built on the site of an old Qajar hunting lodge. His tears and self-pity disgusted other prisoners. He was haunted by the crying of an owl, a bird of ill omen in Iran. [50] Teymourtache was tried in camera on charges of accepting bribes in a case unrelated to Anglo-Persian and condemned on March 17 to three years solitary confinement and the restitution of some £20,000 in bribes. He showed signs of mistreatment and at one point broke down and wept. [51] At a second trial, on June 24, he was sentenced to five years solitary confinement for accepting a bribe over the grant in 1930 of the opium concession. [52] Reza visited him in prison and ordered the guards to take away his furniture and toilet articles. [53] On October 3, 1933, Teymourtache died, officially of angina. The British legation in Tehran, in its dispatch, wept crocodile tears: "Thus the man whose brilliant talents had placed him on a pinnacle of power far above all the Shah's subjects was left by his ungrateful master without even a bed to die upon." [54]

By then, a new concession had been signed. As Sir John Cadman set off for Tehran in March 1933, his predecessor as chairman, Lord Greenway, wrote: "You will be in a strong position—much stronger than when you were dealing with T.T. [Teymourtache]." After three weeks of jousting in a "dreadful atmosphere" where the "Persian ministers . . . are almost terrified . . . to speak to or be seen with me," [55] Cadman saw Reza on April 24, 1933, and again on April 26, and gained the Shah's consent to what he most wanted. Reza agreed to an extension of the concession over 100,000 square miles (to be selected by the company) until the end of 1993. In return, Anglo-Persian agreed to a new royalty based not on "net profits" but of 4 shillings a ton delivered and, anyway, not less than £750,000 a year (which was lower than the royalty paid in the mid-

1920s). To sweeten the transaction, Anglo-Persian recalculated the royalties for 1931 and 1932 on the new basis (giving £1.3m and £1.5m) and provided a lump sum of £1 million in settlement of all past claims (allocated to the War Ministry). Before leaving Tehran, Cadman said: "The Shah, and only the Shah, made the agreement possible." [56]

The concession agreement, which was ratified by Parliament without debate on May 28, 1933, was a catastrophe for both parties. It did nothing to dispel Iranian resentment of the company. Meanwhile, for the sake of cash for industry and the armed forces, Reza had played his best card, which was the diminishing value of the lease. The original D'Arcy concession had been due to run out in 1961, at which date all of the assets of the company "for the exploitation of its industry" would have passed to Iran. With each year, the British position was becoming weaker. Sayyid Hassan Taqizadeh, who as finance minister signed the new concession agreement, later told Parliament: "The master himself made a mistake and then could not go back on it. He himself did not want the concession to be extended, and to begin with reacted against it in the most abusive terms. 'Such a thing is quite out of the question! Do you expect us, who for thirty years have been cursing our forebears because of this business, to allow ourselves to be cursed for another fifty?' But in the end he allowed himself to be persuaded." [57]

Iran's oil income from Anglo-Iranian (as it was renamed at Reza's order) rose through the 1930s, passing above £2 million in 1934 and £3 million in 1937.[58] Such revenue could certainly have paid the interest on a foreign loan of over £30 million, but the experience of the Qajars had inoculated Iran, and most particularly Reza, against foreign borrowing. Except for some ordinary trade finance, barter, or "clearing" arrangements with soft-currency countries such as Germany and Soviet Russia, and advances from the oil company and the British Imperial Bank of Persia, Reza never borrowed abroad.

The oil revenues were deposited at the Bank of England to pay for arms and industrial equipment. Reza's most ambitious project, the Trans-Iranian Railway (2.5 billion rials or $150m), the costliest in the world up to that time and the most challenging ever, might have been financed by a loan at 6 percent secured on the oil revenue of £2 million. It was paid for by a tax on his people's principal (and, in the villages, their only) luxuries, tea and sugar.

Nearly 900 miles in length, the Trans-Iranian Railway began at a silty harbor at Bandar Shahpur on the Persian Gulf, crossed the Karun River over a 1,000-yard bridge at Ahvaz, climbed through the canyons of Luristan to a peak of 7,000 feet, and crossed the Iranian plateau by way of Sultanabad and Qom to a station at Tehran that Millspaugh compared favorably with the depot at Kansas City. From Tehran, the northern section ran east, then climbed north through the Elburz to another 7,000-foot watershed at Firuzkuh and descended on a 2.8 percent gradient down the Talar Valley to the shallow harbor named Bandar Shah on the Caspian. Described by one of its legion of foreign critics as running from "nowhere to nowhere," since it bypassed such important towns as Isfahan, Hamadan, and Shiraz, and connected with no international network, the railway right-of-way reveals Reza's mental geography.[59] It linked his capital city with his estates in Mazanderan in the north and the oil fields in the south, while keeping well away from the railheads of Russia and British India. Only after the trunk line was completed did Reza contract to link Tehran to the main provincial cities. Designed to be of no strategic use to Iran's old enemies, in conditions of world war the Trans-Iranian Railway turned out to be quite useful to them, after all.

Approved by Parliament in February 1926, the project languished to Reza's growing fury until April 1933, when he appointed as project manager a firm of engineers from Denmark, a country without a history of meddling in Iran. Kampmann, Kierulff & Saxild (known as Kampsax), which had worked successfully in Kemal's Turkey, broke the line into small lots and let them out to foreign contractors, desperate for work in the depressed world market, from Britain, France, Belgium, Italy, and Germany. Employing at its peak 45,000 workers, principally Iranian laborers on a penny a day but including skilled masons from Italy, Turkey, and the Balkans, the railroad swallowed over a fifth of all investment spending. Both the northern line, where Italian engineers battled malaria, methane leaks, adverse geology, and mud slides to cross the Elburz, driving tunnels that spiraled through the mountain and laying what was then the highest bridge in the world at Veresk; and the "canyon" section in the Zagros, where fully a quarter of the track runs through tunnels, were seen by Fascist writers as a triumph of Will (and reinforced concrete) over brute nature.[60] At the completion ceremony at Sefid Cheshmeh on August 26, 1938, Reza drove in the last rail with a golden spike, then walked alone across the track and wept.[61] At a gala dinner at the Tehran station, telegrams of congratulation were read from, among others, Adolf Hitler.

The railway was a burden on a backward economy. To stabilize the currency—renamed in 1932 the rial—Reza introduced exchange controls and, responding to the trade protectionism sweeping the world, a monopoly of foreign trade. The purpose was not just to conserve hard currency for the cement, steel reinforcing bars, rails, and 4,000 tons of dynamite for the railroad and weapons for the armed forces, but to protect domestic industry from foreign competition. Foreign trade became dominated by the Third Reich and the Soviet Union, which took Iran's rice, cotton, dried fruits, and hides in return for industrial goods, including in 1936 a Krupp blast furnace at Karaj, northwest of Tehran. Industry became a series of protected monopolies, not just of oil and opium, but cotton, silk, carpets, tires, and cement.

By the mid-1930s, foreign visitors found Iran sunk in misery. The British minister, writing in August 1935, told the Foreign Office: "Poverty is more widespread and severe than at any time in living memory, with the exception of the famine year of the [Great] war." He described, from a conversation with a Hamadan landowner, peasants' houses without even a rug or an oil lamp, and women barely clothed.[62] *Time* magazine, in a cover story dedicated to Reza in April 1938, described conditions of "starvation" in the south.[63] The carpet trade, which under Reza's patronage in the 1920s had made pieces as fine as any since the Safavid era, lost its North American market and fell on hard times.[64] Most of the foreign rug companies sold out to Reza's state monopoly and withdrew from Iran. To make ends meet, weavers took to knotting on not two but four warp-strings at a time so they could make two rugs out of the wool advanced them by the bazaar for just one. These pieces, known as *jufti* or "double," became notorious even in London and further injured the export trade.[65]

Only the royal estates were prospering, where by 1934 Reza was supplying 80 percent of the army's grain, rice, boots, and clothing,[66] and Tehran, which was sucking in money and people, and was approaching a population of half a million. An Italian Fascist railway journalist, who visited Tehran in the mid-1930s, detected in Reza's capital a Futurist fantasy of speed and asphalt: "This old town, sunk in lethargy, silence and immobility, where in the centre traffic moved in single file and at the pace of half-starved hacks trotting in harness before decrepit carriages, the men of Reza Shah Pahlavi have turned into a super-modern city, handsome, new from top to bottom, fresh and clean, vibrating with life and pulsating with movement, the streets even and well-lit and coursing with automobiles, among buildings adapted to the requirements of modernity, hygiene and good taste."[67] A more conventional response came from Robert Byron, the British art historian, who breathed a sigh of relief in Isfahan in February 1934 "to have escaped from that vile stinking hideous intrigue-ridden pretentious vulgar parody of a capital, Teheran."[68] With its bitter winters and dusty summers, its streets crowded but without fashion or gaiety, spreading over the desert as if overnight, one could search for hours for a monument of the recent past. The novelist Emineh Pakravan (mother of the intelligence officer who in 1964 interceded for Khomeini) described Tehran as a "town without memory," *une ville sans mémoire*.[69] The smaller cities, with their boulevards smashed through the bazaar at right angles (the first called Shah and the second Pahlavi), or radiating out from traffic circles topped by a plaster-of-Paris statue of Reza (Ahvaz, Kermanshah, Hamadan), survive with only the streets renamed to this day.[70]

Reza Shah Pahlavi slept on the floor and washed in a basin from water poured by his soldier servant, Hosein the Beluchi, whom he called "Black Hosein."[71] He ate simple food in sparing quantities and always at the same times.[72] He worked generally in the open air, either seated on a bench in the garden of the Golestan, Marble, or Saadabad palaces, or pacing up and down (a habit his son inherited). According to Soleiman Behbudi, his secretary, Reza lived his life by the "manual," taking his tea, cigarette, or drink of water at regulated times.[73] Compared to Kemal Pasha and Churchill, who were rarely, if ever, entirely sober, Reza drank little wine.[74] He was neat and clean, and expected the same of others. He would kick cigarette ends under the carpets to check on his servants.[75] He did not tolerate unpunctuality, and ministers used to telephone to synchronize watches with his private office.[76] His son inherited his punctuality.

Reza spoke no foreign language, except some barrack-square Russian, and until his exile traveled abroad only twice, first to the Shia holy places in British-administered Iraq in 1924 and then to his hero's Turkey ten years later. Once he became Shah, he had nothing to do with the foreign envoys, did not attend his own birthday party, and discouraged any contact between his subjects and foreigners. His son's childhood friend, Hosein Fardoust, remembered: "Reza Khan never once attended an official reception. Sometimes he used to take Mohammed Reza and myself to the Golestan Palace, where receptions in his honour were held, and in the darkness spy on the guests through the trees. He used to whisper to me: 'Look at these foreign women, how they tart themselves up!' He'd point them out one by one and make fun of them." [77]

Reza treated his intimates with a savage levity. Once, according to Behbudi, when a tire punctured on the Enzeli road, Reza struck his driver so hard on the back of the neck that he broke the diamond ring he was wearing. [78] He humiliated even senior officers in public. He arrested one of his ministers on the steps of the national theater, a second at cards, a third at the races on the Turkoman steppe. As early as 1929, Teymourtache told the British minister that Reza was suspicious of "everybody and everyone. There was really nobody in the whole country whom His Majesty trusted and this was very much resented by those who had always stood faithfully by him." [79] Many of his original intimates would perish later in the new prison in northern Tehran, the Qasr, through mistreatment, murder, or suicide.

Every afternoon at two, Reza spent an hour on his private commercial interests. By the time of his abdication in 1941, he had acquired about 2,000 villages or parts of villages in some 40,000 separate transactions. Amounting to 1.5 million hectares or more, Reza's estates comprised all of the rich province of Mazanderan on the north or rainy slope of the Elburz Mountains, as well as a new port on the Caspian, the Chalus road, most of Astarabad, Fariman near Mashhad, the best land about Kermanshah, and a large estate in the hills overlooking Tehran. He built and managed hotels, rice mills, and silk and cotton factories. The British diplomatic cables tell of landowners unpaid or thrown into prison until they accepted nugatory prices. [80] Having given Black Hosein in the 1920s a tiny plot near the palace on which to build a house, with the rise in property values Reza tried to take it back. Secretary Behbudi screwed up his courage and suggested that Reza already had an estate "the size of the Kingdom of Belgium, perhaps larger."[81]

[The Shah's] face blazed with anger and he showed the whites of his eyes. From behind his writing-desk, he stood up, strode into the middle of the room, and was so altered I felt faint. I wanted to run out, but it was as if my legs had lost their power and I stood there speechless and immobile. He paced up and down the room, sighing deeply, then turned on me a face as white as a sheet. He said: "I thought you at least, who are as close to me as my shirt, would understand and explain to others, but I see, alas, that is not the case. Everything I possess is of this kingdom and for the dignity of the kingdom and remains in this kingdom. Today, I am the king but I am also a landlord and farmer, hotel keeper, factory owner and bathhouse attendant. You say a king should not engage in those activities. But I have observed that an Iranian who lays out one hundred tomans today, demands a return of one hundred tomans tomorrow, while foreigners are content to work for years, and that is why I have had to undertake these things. When I am gone in a little while, everything I have done will remain for the country." I stood in tears. We worked for an hour, and then, still furious and upset, he dismissed me.[82]

In his private life, Reza was by the standards of Iranian princes restrained. Not for Reza the harem of the Qajars, symbol of power and privilege, and comprising at one time over a thousand women including servants.[83] A perpetual drain on the revenue, the harem accompanied Nassereddin Qajar on his summer jaunts round the provinces, a train of covered litters and led horses that condemned whole villages to famine.[84] Viewing Nassereddin's night palace for the first time on November 12, 1889, the French military doctor Jean-Baptiste Feuvrier fell into a swoon: "What sweet dreams could one not dream in this quiet and secret palace, guarded by a thousand women!"[85] Reza tore the building down, and replaced it with a Ministry of Finance. The pleasure palaces outside Tehran he turned into military barracks or prisons.

Reza married at least four times. He first took to wife a girl called Maryam, an orphan living in the house of his uncle, Abulqasem Beg. She died after giving birth to a daughter, who was brought up by an aunt. In 1916, having advanced in the Cossack service, he married Nimtaj Ayromlu, the daughter of a brother officer, who as queen mother took the title of Taj ol-Moluk, or "Crown of Kings." Fair-haired and slight, she barely reached to his medals. She gave birth first to a daughter, Shams, in 1917, and then, on October 26, 1919, in a rented house near the Qazvin Gate in the west end of Tehran,[86] to Mohammed Reza and his devoted twin sister, Ashraf, who came, as she always said, "unwanted" into the world.[87] A second son, Alireza, followed in 1922.

As Reza gained in prosperity in the 1920s, tiring of Nimtaj's prudery, he took wives from the Qajar nobility: first Turan Amir Soleimani, whom he divorced soon after the birth of a third son, Gholamreza, in 1923, and then Esmat Dowlatshahi, who gave him five more children to fight for the scraps of royal precedence. According to Hosein Fardoust, who was Mohammed Reza's principal companion in childhood, Taj ol-Moluk was jealous of Esmat and once set her servants, armed with sticks, to break up her rival's house in the royal compound at Saadabad, forcing her to hide in a cellar. Reza was delighted.[88] Esmat claimed late in life that Taj ol-Moluk cast spells on her and put poison in her bath.[89] It was Esmat who accompanied the Shah into exile in Mauritius but, after eight months, returned to Iran.

Reza had no friends, but many men he hated, and no amusement, except the races once a year on the Turkoman plain, forgotten Russian card games, backgammon, and money. After the death of Teymourtache, he had nobody to rely on, and he exhausted himself in the smallest details, from the type of sleeper or tie to be laid on the railway to the serving of sheep's head-and-trotters in the Shemiran resorts.[90] His delight was the Marble Palace, built on the Farmanfarma land with marquetrywork on which 150 Isfahan craftsmen had labored for a year; his armed forces; the railway; and his eldest son, above all his son.

In Mohammed Reza, the Shah saw all that he himself lacked: manners honed in the best schools of Switzerland, beautiful French and fluent English, a mastery of difficult and complex subjects. Reza told a flatterer in the 1930s: "Yes, I have done this kingdom great service, but my greatest service has been in the choice of Crown Prince. For the moment, you do not see it, but when the Crown Prince gets down to work, then you will see what sort of Crown Prince he is. Then you will see it."[91]

At the age of six or seven, Mohammed Reza was placed in a miniature military school, with about twenty other students of different social degrees, including Hosein Fardoust, the son of a Gendarmerie officer, a silent and withdrawn lad who nevertheless became his "special friend."[92] Under a former ballerina married to an Iranian, Madame Arfa, he learned the French which was always to be his favorite language. Reza lunched with him every day and called him "Sir." Taj ol-Moluk called him "Your Highness" and stood when he came into the room.

At eleven, Mohammed Reza was sent to Switzerland. Along with his full brother Alireza and two companions, Fardoust and Teymourtache's third son, he went first to a boarding school in Lausanne and then to Le Rosey, a private school on the north shore of Lake Geneva where he stayed until 1936. On the day of his departure for Switzerland from Enzeli (now renamed Bandar Pahlavi) in September 1931, General Hassan Arfa, a soldier who served both Qajars and Pahlavis, found the Shah pacing as usual up and down, much affected, his suite in a circle about him. "It is very hard for me to part with my beloved son," Reza said, "but one must think of the country. Iran needs educated and enlightened rulers, we, the old and ignorant must go."[93]

At the Château du Rosey, Mohammed Reza excelled at sport, especially football, and became an expert tennis player and horseman and an elegant skier at the winter campus at Gstaad.[94] His third wife later saw in those years away from Iran the origins of his heaviness and melancholy.[95] The Shah used to send messengers to the Central Post Office on Army Square to pick up his son's weekly letter in Persian.[96] Mohammed Reza returned in 1936 and was followed by a young man named Ernest Perron, the son of the school janitor who had been crippled in a childhood accident and was to fascinate and repel the court until his disgrace in 1954. (The diplomatic reports are full of codewords for homosexual.)[97]

Reza took against the young Swiss and he was sent as head gardener to the new palace at Ramsar on the Caspian,[98] and later roomed with a Swiss landlady outside the Marble Palace. Mohammed Reza was enrolled in a special class at the Officers' Cadet College in Tehran, which Reza had founded on the model of the French military school at Saint-Cyr, along with Fardoust and the husbands of the princesses, Ali

Qavam and Fereydoun Djam. Where the Shah terrified his interlocutors, Mohammed Reza charmed them with his European manners.[99] In the spring of 1938, Mohammed Reza graduated as a second lieutenant and was appointed as an army inspector, responsible for observing the training and readiness of the troops on the drill ground and on maneuvers.[100] He used to say that though he was commander in chief, he was only a second lieutenant.

Reza dreamed of a dynastic match for the crown prince, and at the suggestion, it is said, of Kemal Pasha of Turkey, chose an Egyptian princess, Fauzia, sister to King Farouk.[101] The Egyptian monarchy was only three years older than the Pahlavi, but the family had been *de facto* rulers of the country for over a century, and the match was an endorsement for the Pahlavis in both dynastic politics and the world of international fashion. *Life* magazine called Fauzia "probably the prettiest royalty in the world today."[102]

To celebrate the betrothal, the junction of the north and south sections of the new Trans-Iranian Railway was renamed "Fauzia," and on March 15, 1939, the crown prince and his seventeen-year-old bride were married at the Abdin Palace in Cairo. Reza did not attend. Anxious that his court in Iran would appear dowdy to the fashionable and worldly Egyptians, Reza had the Ministry of Finance place a bulk order with Messrs Ziegler in Manchester for silk and rayon dress material, ladies' underclothing and shoes, gloves, shirts, collars, ties, ornaments and clasps, and twenty model dresses for copying. Ziegler's assembled sixty packing cases in ten days, and shipped them by the Orient and Taurus expresses to the railhead and then onward to Tehran by road.[103]

To no avail. The arrival of Princess Fauzia and Queen Nazli at Mohammareh was chaotic. The train broke down. Though Fauzia produced a daughter, Shahnaz (born on October 27, 1940), she found Tehran dull and frightening, and was oppressed by the intriguing of Princesses Shams and Ashraf, and the bullying of Taj ol-Moluk. She was ordered to dismiss her Egyptian servants. According to a later Iranian complaint to the Egyptian court, Fauzia had "not performed her duties as Queen. Instead of taking an interest in improving Iranian society and the condition of the people by visiting hospitals and kindergartens, and working in charitable affairs, she prefers to sleep until noon. Afterwards she either stays in her room or goes out alone.

She not only shows no interest in anything Iranian, she has also been remiss in carrying out her marital duties." [104]

At the outbreak of war, Reza confirmed Iran's neutrality, as if that had been effective in the war of 1914–18. An old man now, without experience of the world, and cut off for years from diplomatic intercourse, Reza was not prepared for the ruthlessness of the Allied powers fighting for their lives. He pestered the British to supply him with aircraft and munitions, to guarantee his oil payments, and to replace from the British Empire the imports of rails and other industrial goods that had come, under barter arrangements, from the Third Reich. Uncertain of the outcome of the war, but sympathetic, like all but a few Iranians, to the enemies of Britain and Russia, Reza tolerated a colony in Iran of about a thousand Germans and Austrians, many or most of them National Socialist. His military preparations against Soviet attack were sketchy.

For all Reza's expenditure, amounting to about one third of government revenue in the 1930s, the Iranian armed forces remained inexperienced, incapable of full mobilization, weak in signals, transport, commissariat, audit, and military medicine, and short of training with live ammunition. After the campaign against the Qashqai in 1929, there had been little action. For fear of losing valuable aircraft and incurring Reza's anger, the air force restricted its operations to daylight and fair weather. Unlike in Turkey, the military was not admired as a pillar of state. Above all, Reza had never demonstrated, as Kemal Pasha had at Gallipoli in 1915 and then again in the Turkish War of Independence between 1918 and 1923, that he had officers and, particularly, fighting men prepared to give the European powers a bloody nose. In the summer of 1937, Iran signed a non-aggression treaty with all of its neighbors except the Soviet Union, known as the Saadabad Pact. Reza does not seem to have imagined that the great powers would be the aggressors.

The German invasion of Russia on June 22, 1941, sealed his fate. With the Germans racing toward the Caucasus, Russia would no longer tolerate a pro-German neutral in its rear nor Britain the threat to its oil supplies from Abadan. The possibility of a "Persian Corridor" to supply a Soviet stand had taken shape by July. [105] Reza continued to drag his feet over the German colony, and that provided the Allies with a threadbare casus belli. Just after 4 a.m. on August 25, 1941, the Soviet and British ministers called separately on Ali Mansur, the prime minister, and handed him identical notes warning of military action (which, in fact, had just begun). They called on the Shah at 10 a.m. According to Reader Bullard, the British minister, Reza said that "if the cause of the attack was that Germany had seized the whole of Europe and Great Britain and the Soviet Union wished to seize Persia, then Persia was too weak to oppose this." [106] At lunch as usual with the royal family, none dared speak, not even Mohammed Reza. At length, Reza said: "This will be the end for me—the English will see to it." [107]

Faced in the south and west by tough and well-drilled Indian and Nepalese troops under British officers, and in the north by overwhelming Soviet infantry and armor, the Iranian army was outmaneuvered and scattered. General Hassan Arfa, appointed chief of staff of the still intact 1st and 2nd Divisions in the capital, pressed to withdraw the Tehran garrison to a redoubt in the mountains west of Sultanabad/Arak, destroying bridges as they went. The Shah rejected the plan, and Arfa concluded bitterly that "from the beginning the Shah did not intend to put up a real defence, and wanted only to show . . . that in the event of a German victory Iran could not be held responsible and treated as an enemy." [108]

On August 27, Reza agreed to a cease-fire and the withdrawal of his forces to the capital which, in the north, turned into a rout. When, on August 30, the general staff ordered conscripts to return home, Reza lost his self-control and took his cane to the war minister and chief of staff. [109]

The Iranians had lost several hundred men. The British and Indians had suffered twenty officers and sepoys killed, and the Russians about forty of all ranks. The British military attaché wrote: "The resistance put up by the Persian army to British and Russian troops was even less than anticipated by its severest critics." He ascribed the army's failure, first, to "its own lack of morale." The rank and file were "underpaid and underfed," senior officers were corrupt, and all lacked training in the field or "with the very good weapons they possessed." Second, there was "an almost entire lack of serious preparation for resistance." Third, there was no civilian air-raid protection and the first hint of aerial bombardment caused panic which spread to the headquarters and disrupted troop movements. Above all, he told London, "it appeared that there never had been any serious intention of resisting. It is believed that up to the last moment the Shah was confident that GB and Russia would not go to extreme lengths, and this optimism reflected itself in the faulty dispositions of the army."[110]

Moscow and London soon decided they could do nothing with the old man, and on September 12, the new BBC Persian Service started broadcasting scurrilous attacks on Reza devised by the British press attaché in Tehran, Ann Lambton. Iranians with wireless sets heard how Reza had removed the crown jewels from Tehran (which was untrue), forced men to work in his textile mills, used regressive and unfair taxation to finance his railway, and diverted the capital's water supply to water his market gardens.[111]

The Soviets moved toward the capital. On September 16, at the Marble Palace, Mohammed Ali Foroughi, who was once again prime minister, wrote a letter of abdication which Reza signed:

Having expended all my powers these last years on the nation's business and having no more strength, I feel the time has now come for younger energies to take over the affairs of state, which require continuous attention if we are to achieve the happiness and salvation of the country. For that reason I am entrusting the throne to my Crown Prince and successor and stepping aside. From this day, the 25 Shahrivar 1320, the whole nation and the armed forces must recognise the Crown Prince as my legal successor and do for him all that they, in the interests of the country, did for me.

Reza Pahlavi
Marble Palace, Tehran
25 Shahrivar, 1320

Mohammed Reza burst out: "If you go, the Russians will enter Tehran and there will be a revolution!" Reza cackled and said: "On the contrary, Sir. All that's just for show. It's me they're after. Once I am gone, that will be that, and you will rule in perfect ease and there will be no revolution."[112]

Reza set off in a single car to Isfahan and then to the small port of Bandar Abbas on the Arabian Sea. He had hoped to travel to the

Americas—he mentioned at different times Chile, Argentina, and Canada—but the British had other plans. Anxious there might be demonstrations of sympathy from Indian Muslims, the British authorities in India refused to let Reza's party of eleven (along with eight servants) land at Bombay.[113] Reza had wired £35,000 to Bombay. After sending ashore to buy supplies (including a British roadster for his sons), the party was transshipped to the SS *Burma* and taken as prisoners in all but name to Mauritius. Here, broken, listless, unable to sleep, frantic about Mohammed Reza, he remained until he was allowed to move to the more suitable climate of South Africa, where a country house was lent him on the outskirts of Johannesburg.

Reza was disgusted by reports of famine in Iran. According to his wife Esmat, he feared a resurgence of the clergy or what he called *akhundbazi* ("molla games" or priestcraft).[114] He died of a heart attack at the house in Johannesburg on what is now Young Avenue, Houghton, on July 26, 1944, but not before he was able to hear a message from his eldest son on a phonograph record brought to him by Ernest Perron. In his reply, also recorded on disc, the old man said: "These invisible waves, penetrating my heart, re-formed into your darling voice, sweet light of my eyes."[115]

CHAPTER 3

The Boy

◇

There is no more lonely and unhappy life for a man than when he decides to rule instead of to reign.

—Mohammed Reza[1]

These were wilderness years for Mohammed Reza Pahlavi. He had no goodwill, and, when he opened the new Parliament on November 13, 1941, crowds menaced his car, shouting: "Long Live Hitler!" and "Down with the Russians and the British!"[2] The British legation reported that "if unsuitable, [he] can be got rid of later."[3] Sir Reader Bullard, the British minister at Tehran, the son of a London docker or longshoreman who had risen to the heights of the British Foreign Service, treated the twenty-two-year-old Shah (and all Iranians) with such disdain that even Winston Churchill, not a man who had much time for foreigners, was disgusted.[4] In London, there was some thought of restoring the Qajars until it was found that the pretender from that house had changed his name to Drummond and was serving in the British merchant marine.[5]

With the coast clear, the men of the old regime returned from their estates, calling Mohammed Reza "the boy" (*pesareh*) and the Pahlavis "those people" (*anha*). The veil reappeared in the modern quarters of town, along with the Ashura mourning marches, and the clergy began to jockey for power and influence. To finance their occupation, the British forced Parliament to inflate the Iranian currency, but then lost control of the food supply, and there were bread shortages in Tehran and famine in the provinces. From the north of the country, the Soviets carted off grain and livestock and munitions to the Volga. Some 20,000

Polish and other refugees from the German advance added to the pressure on food supply. There were outbreaks of typhus.

In the south, the Qashqai tribe, assisted by a small commando of German agents, rose in revolt. The British informed the young Shah that when Stalingrad fell and the Germans reached the Volga delta, Tehran would come under air attack. Parliament asked the Allies to withdraw their forces from Tehran and declare the capital an "open city" (that is, undefended), but they refused. Mohammed Reza's marriage to Fauzia was under strain and Cecil Beaton photographed them for *Life* magazine in sepulchral shadow, or imprisoned behind lattices, she with a bandage on her arm, he a "Shah on probation."[6]

Mohammed Reza had few resources but his youth and his good looks, and the equivalent of about £5 million in cash that he received "for and in consideration of a lump of sugar" in a deed signed by his father on September 19, 1941, at Isfahan.[7] It was not an immense sum, but sufficient to buy influence in a poor country, to distribute alms and famine and earthquake relief, to make gifts to the Shia shrines, and to start a newspaper supportive of the court. His father's farmlands, villages, hotels, and factories he handed over to the state, but he was able later to recover them.

What aided Mohammed Reza in his solitude were several factors beyond his control but in his power to exploit. The first was the failure of the German armies in the autumn of 1942 to break through at Stalingrad, and their surrender the following February 1943. The receding German threat caused the British to treat Mohammed Reza (and his father) with greater consideration.

The second was the weakness of the 1906–07 Constitution so that Parliament paralyzed the executive and in the twelve years from Reza's abdication to 1953 there were twenty governments. The Reza period could not simply be wished away and a gulf had opened up between those allies of 1906, the clergy and democratic reformers. Under Soviet patronage, a popular front party known as the Tudeh or "Mass" was formed in the month after the invasion. It gained adherents in the oil fields and Tehran and set up clandestine cells in the army. As the Tudeh grew in response to the Soviet victories and the prestige of the Red Army, the traditional clergy saw a Communist threat to Islamic beliefs and the sanctity of private property. Mohammed Reza was prepared to woo and flatter the clergy.

The third factor was the breakdown in Allied wartime coalition, and the growing hostility of the United States to the Soviet Union and its exasperation with the colonizing habits of the United Kingdom. When the Soviets in 1946 refused to withdraw their occupying army, and set up local governments in the northwestern provinces, Iran was drawn into cold war politics at which Mohammed Reza became adept. Seeing that neutrality had not helped his father, Mohammed Reza allied himself with the British, and then the United States, while flirting with the Soviet Union when it suited him. Neutrality, he later wrote, had "dismally failed [and] co-operation with the Allies was not merely inevitable but also highly desirable."[8]

The fourth was the loyalty of the Iranian armed forces. Unpopular and humiliated, burdened by what a U.S. officer termed a "modern tradition of defeat,"[9] the senior officers knew they had little hope of advancement from the short-lived civilian governments. In contrast, Mohammed Reza concluded from the invasion not that the Iranian army was a waste of money in a poor country, but that it must be strengthened at any cost. When Eve Curie, daughter of the physicists, called on the new Shah for the *New York Times* at the close of 1941, he was dressed in pale green officer's uniform. His first remark was, "What does the world think of our non-resistance?"[10]

Mohammed Reza pressed to be admitted into the Allied coalition and declare war on the German Reich. At his first face-to-face meeting with Reader Bullard, in early October 1941, he talked about "helping us [the Allies] with an army of three or four hundred thousand men."[11] Bullard found that fantastical. Instead, under a Tripartite Treaty of Alliance of January 29, 1942, Britain and the Soviet Union committed themselves to defend Iran from attack, "to safeguard the economic existence of the Iranian people," and to withdraw their forces not later than six months after the end of hostilities with Germany. In September 1943, Iran declared war on Germany and joined the United Nations. The Shah was permitted to establish a small life guard or household regiment, on the British and French pattern, known as the Imperial Guard.

Mohammed Reza's first steps in politics were halting. He attempted to set up, behind the backs of government, a secret channel to the British, which Bullard rejected.[12] He intrigued against his prime ministers.

During a riot over bread shortages on December 8, 1942, a crowd set fire to the house of Ahmad Qavam, then prime minister. Bullard saw the hand of the young Shah in the disturbances. In a meeting with parliamentary deputies that day, Mohammed Reza let slip both a hint to his state of mind and a premonition of the future. As it was reported to Bullard, the Shah said that "unless something drastic was done there would be a revolution from below and suggested that a revolution from above would be better." [13] His twin sister, Ashraf, unhappy in her marriage as in her childhood, became notorious for meddling. She saw herself as the mirror image of her twin, [14] and never made peace with the limits Iranian custom placed on a woman's activity and scope. She was, in addition, a stranger to fear.

Time weighed on Mohammed Reza's hands. Bullard gave him Thucydides to read. [15] He convened a literary society once a week, sending cars to bring the members to the Marble Palace or, in summer, to Saadabad. The doyen of the club was the greatest Iranian literary scholar of the twentieth century, Mirza Mohammed Qazvini, the editor of the medieval lyric poet Hafez and a man of such sensitivity that once in Paris, when a visitor recited an indifferent couplet of verse, Mirza Mohammed threw up. At those meetings, Mohammed Reza was generally silent except to pose Mirza Mohammed an opening question. [16]

At the conference of the three principal Allied leaders in Tehran between November 28 and December 1, 1943, where delegates moved between the British legation and the Soviet Embassy across the street behind canvas screens, neither President Franklin D. Roosevelt nor Prime Minister Churchill called on the young Shah but, in a breach of protocol, received him on Soviet property. Joseph Stalin did call on him, and offered an armored regiment, a Trojan Horse Mohammed Reza found hard to refuse. [17] Only General de Gaulle, commander of the Free French forces, who passed through Tehran in November 1944, treated him with kindness. Mohammed Reza never forgot him. [18]

The Japanese attack on Pearl Harbor in December 1941, and the entry of the United States into the war, changed the fortunes of both Mohammed Reza and the Iranian military. To protect the road and railroad lines of supply to the Soviet Union, the United States agreed to send two advisory missions to Iran. Colonel H. Norman Schwarzkopf, Sr., founder of the New Jersey State Police and celebrated for leading the investigation into the Lindbergh baby kidnapping case in the 1930s, arrived in August 1942 at the head of a mission to improve the Gendarmerie or rural police force. Against some opposition from Mohammed Reza, a permanent U.S. mission, known as GENMISH, was established to train and arm a force of some 20,000.

The first U.S. adviser to the Iranian army, General John Greely, arrived in Iran that summer. He delighted Mohammed Reza by proposing that the Iranian army be built up and brought into the war. "This is a fine country with a virile people and more could be done with it than [General Douglas] MacArthur did with the Philippines [as military adviser after 1935]," he wrote.[19] Secretary of War Henry Stimson disagreed, saying the Iranian army was too disorganized to be effective as a combat force even after resupply, reorganization, and long training.[20] Instead, Major General Clarence S. Ridley, an engineer, was sent to Iran in late October to examine the ground for a U.S. mission to the army. Mohammed Reza at once suggested he take over the reorganization of the entire Iranian military, and offered him the rank of lieutenant general in the Iranian service.

General Ridley found the Iranian army "practically immobile."[21] Budgets were inadequate to wartime prices, and supply and auxiliary departments barely functioned. In a report for Mohammed Reza at the end of 1942, he recommended an army of 88,000, a purge of dead-wood officers, reasonable rates of pay, and, most important, adequate motor transport. That provided Mohammed Reza with support in confronting Arthur Millspaugh, who had been asked by Parliament in late 1942 to return to Iran to take over Iranian state finances and, like finance ministers always everywhere, wanted no military at all.[22] Millspaugh told the Shah that if the army budget were increased, there would be "little if anything for agriculture, education, or public health." Mohammed Reza replied: "Very well, then; we'll have to postpone those things."[23]

Meanwhile, that summer of 1942, the first U.S. military technicians of the Persian Gulf Service Command arrived at Ahvaz in the south to operate the railroad and deliver Lend-Lease supplies to the Soviet Union through what became known as the Persian Corridor. The war revealed to a hungry Iran the U.S. genius for industrial organization on a colossal scale and to their bakeries, laundries, ice cream plants, refrigerated warehouses, and dental surgeries.[24] The U.S. engineers and servicemen replaced the light rails which had buckled under the wartime tonnages, graded Reza's washboard roads, and built a highway to Andimeshk and a new port at Khorramshahr (formerly Mohammareh), which handled at its peak in mid-1944 nearly as much traffic (7,500 tons per day) as in the oil boom after 1973. In the end, the United States left behind assets of $100 million, which was probably as much as all of Reza's industrial investment at book value.

The U.S. Army historian describes the immense trains of railcars, leaving Ahvaz at night to escape the scalding daytime heat, carrying northward sheet steel, pipe, rails, oleomargarine, canned meat, galvanized wire, sugar, beans, battle tanks, alkylate, gasoline, and aviation spirit. Miles-long motor convoys rolled through small towns with their lights extinguished, past intersections patrolled by foreign MPs, while round the depots could be heard the muffled detonation of antipersonnel mines set off by starving prowlers.[25] In the mountains of Luristan, men jumped from overhanging banks onto the slow-moving trucks to throw down tires, ammunition, sugar, flour, beans, and cloth to their companions.

The U.S. Military Mission, due to leave on March 1, 1945, was extended. "Iran," wrote Secretary of State Edward Stettinius, "is perhaps the most prominent area of the world where inter-Allied friction might arise. Such friction would grow out of the chaos and disorder in Iran which would result from a weak Iranian army. It is in our interests to prevent this from happening."[26] When, at the close of the war, Stalin at first refused to withdraw the Soviet forces and encouraged the setting up of autonomous republics in the northwest, that cast of mind became entrenched. In October 1947, Mohammed Reza reached a first milestone in his quest for power with the creation of a permanent U.S. Mission to the Iranian Army, ARMISH, which was to survive until the Revolution. In 1950, it was expanded to supervise the growing volume of U.S. weaponry and training into the Military Assistance Advisory Group, usually known as ARMISH-MAAG.

By then, Fauzia had left. On June 21, 1945, six weeks after VE (Victory in Europe) Day and just as soon as it was safe to travel, she returned to Alexandria, ostensibly to recover from a bout of malaria. On August

13, King Farouk summoned the Iranian ambassador and told him that "Queen Fauzia did not intend to return to Iran ever." Despite telegrams, flowers, a valuable Tabriz carpet, heartrending messages from her daughter Shahnaz (who kept a scrapbook of her mother's press cuttings), and even a promise to send the queen mother away, Fauzia refused to come back, and even threatened Ghassem Ghani, the new Iranian envoy, that unless granted a divorce she would "act"—in other words, reveal to the world Mohammed Reza's womanizing.[27] Mohammed Reza gave in, and divorced her on October 16, 1948. Fauzia used to say she was frightened of revolution in Iran, but revolution came to Egypt first when her brother Farouk was forced by military officers to leave the country in 1952. (Fauzia lives today in retirement in Switzerland. Shahnaz, after a difficult childhood and an adolescence of conflict with her father, lived for a while in the Islamic Republic before herself moving to Switzerland.)

In his enforced idleness, Mohammed Reza drove fast cars and, like Edward of England and Hussein of Jordan, learned to pilot small aircraft. He took instruction first from a pilot of Trans World Airlines (TWA) and then from Mohammed Khatami and Hassan Toufanian, who were to reach high command in the air force. He received his pilot's license in early 1946. In a campaign to liquidate the autonomous republics set up by the Soviets in the northwest at the end of 1946, Mohammed Reza flew several reconnaissance missions in old aircraft, "always without radio."[28] The Soviet withdrawal and the collapse in short order of the Communist regimes in Azerbaijan and Kurdestan, though hardly attributable to Mohammed Reza, gave him a measure of popularity. On his return from Tabriz, the capital turned out to welcome him. Among the cheering crowds on the roof of a filling station was an eight-year-old girl, Farah Diba.[29] Still, at a meeting in March 1947 that Ernest Perron arranged with the French scholar Henry Corbin, Mohammed Reza burst out that at least Corbin had his philosophical work and "his life was not empty."[30]

In April 1947, to seal a contract to service the aircraft of Iranian Airways, TWA gave Mohammed Reza a Boeing B-17 Flying Fortress which it had converted for civilian use but for which it had found no market. (The machine carried the flattering call sign EP-HIM, as for His Imperial Majesty.)[31] It seems that in the air, at the controls of ever more complex aircraft including in 1972 the Anglo-French supersonic Concorde, Mohammed Reza found relief from the strain of his existence and a reinforcement of his self-confidence. In 1948, he had the first of several air accidents when his two-seater de Havilland Tiger Moth, the biplane trainer used by the Royal Air Force, lost power in its single engine and crashed in a ravine near Isfahan.[32]

Mohammed Reza chased girls. About the time that Fauzia left for Egypt, while driving behind dark glasses and a scarf in Zhaleh Street, he followed a young girl with a striking head of blond hair. She was Parvin or Pari Ghaffari, the daughter of an official in the research department of the Parliament. She was sixteen years old and unhappily married. His old friend Fardoust arranged for her divorce (that is, bought off her husband), and Mohammed Reza set her and her mother up in a house in Kakh Street, opposite the Marble Palace, and gave her the minimum legal status of a *sigheh* or legal concubine. The affair lasted until February 1949, when the court was shaken by an attempt on Mohammed Reza's life.[33]

On the afternoon of February 4, as Mohammed Reza stepped out of his car to visit the Faculty of Law at Tehran University, a man named Nasser Fakhrarai emerged from among the press photographers, pulled a Belgian revolver from his camera case, and fired at the Shah. The first three bullets passed through Mohammed Reza's military cap. The fourth smashed through his right cheekbone, broke his upper teeth, and came out through his upper lip. From six feet away, Fakhrarai aimed at the Shah's heart but put the fifth bullet in his shoulder. The sixth jammed in the barrel. He threw the revolver at Mohammed Reza and tried to make his escape but was surrounded and shot dead by the Shah's entourage. Fakhrarai's identity card showed that he was on assignment for a religious newspaper associated with Ayatollah Abol Qasim Kashani, but he was known to have had links with the Communist Party of Iran, the Tudeh or Mass. (He was also, as Mohammed Reza liked to point out, the lover of the daughter of a British Embassy gardener.)[34]

The attempt at assassination, and Mohammed Reza's unlikely survival, had consequences. It confirmed the Shah in his belief that he had a special destiny and was under the protection of God and His Saints.[35] There was some sympathy for the wounded Shah and admiration for his *sang-froid* and Mohammed Reza was able, three weeks later, to gain a valuable accession to his powers. On February 27, Parliament voted to set in train an alteration to the 1906–07 Constitution which would allow the Shah more easily to dissolve Parliament. It also banned the Tudeh and drove it underground.

Mohammed Reza was invited to Washington on a state visit that November. In the words of Secretary of State Dean Acheson, "the visit turned out to be a disappointment to all."[36] The Truman administration found the young Shah's military and development ambitions quite fanciful. The Iranian party was inexperienced and half of it—Fardoust, and the medical doctors Adl and Ayadi—could not speak English. The envoy Ghassem Ghani, who was a physician and a literary scholar, mistook Fardoust in Washington for "a kind of domestic servant."[37] The visit was not a complete failure: Mohammed Reza had a brief love affair with Grace Kelly, later Princess Grace of Monaco, and twenty years afterward he was still bragging about it.[38] Yet the assassination attempt reminded the Pahlavis that Mohammed Reza was still without a male heir of the body, and for that he needed not diversion with a beautiful actress but a wife.

The queen mother had heard of a sixteen-year-old girl at finishing school in Switzerland, the daughter of a chief of the Bakhtiari tribe and a German mother, named Soraya Esfandiary. A photograph was procured and shown to Mohammed Reza, who was intrigued. Princess Shams interviewed Soraya in London, where she was by now studying English and dreaming of becoming a screen actress. At her wedding to Mohammed Reza in the snow on February 12, 1951, which took place first at the Marble Palace, then amid the dirt and gloom of the Golestan Palace, the guests trampling one another on the cramped stairways, Soraya was ill with typhoid fever. She became so faint in the crush that, halfway through the reception, she took refuge in an antechamber and a lady-in-waiting took shears to her ten-yard train of white tulle and paste diamonds.[39]

In memoirs published in 1991, Soraya describes the regime at the Private Palace, a concrete box run up in the suburban German style in the 1930s in the corner of the grounds of the Marble Palace, with its worn-out sofas, greasy armchairs, and faded and washed-out silk hangings.[40] She asked her husband to engage Maison Jansen, a celebrated decorator of the Belle Epoque in the rue Royale in Paris, but there was no money. Soraya hated the valetudinarian regime, the quack doctors Adl and Ayadi, the dinners prompt at seven-thirty with their boiled vegetables and sickroom food, the dishonest cooks and tubercular milk cows, the interminable canasta, billiards, and parlor games, the Pahlavi in-talk, the insipid film shows.[41] She hated Ernest Perron, limping through her cramped apartments, closeted with the Shah, quizzing her about sex, and poisoning her relations with the sisters.[42] Just eighteen years old at her marriage, she hated the tirades of Taj ol-Moluk and the intrigues by Shams and Ashraf to control her and, through her, their adored brother.[43] She was too shy or lazy to appear in public. She was a bad stepmother to motherless Shahnaz.[44] What Soraya had, what all the Bakhtiaris in this story had, was backbone, and it would be needed.

At this time, Mohammed Reza began selling off his lands, which provided rents of about £400,000 a year and were worth £5–£10 million, on easy terms to his farming tenants. The sales, which were of property in trust and thus legally inalienable, infuriated the other large landowners but were popular.[45]

Ever since the turning of the tide in the war, both Western oil companies and the Soviets had been pressing hard for oil concessions in Iran. To persuade Stalin to withdraw from Azerbaijan, Prime Minister Ahmad Qavam agreed in principle to a Soviet oil concession in the five northern provinces to balance the long-standing British concession in the south.

It is hard at this distance to tell if Qavam was sincere or merely adroit, but Parliament balked and in October 1947, in part to mollify the Soviets, voted that the British concession, dating back to 1901 but renegotiated in 1933, should also be revised "with a view to securing Iran's national rights." The British government had been treating Anglo-Iranian as a fountain of money. In 1942, the company paid more in income taxes to the British government (£6.6m) than in taxes and royalties to Iran (£4m), and by the end of the war the difference was almost threefold (£16m: £6m). Britain made no attempt to restore the balance in the postwar years, and in 1950 the yield to the British Treasury (not including its dividends) was £36 million against £16 million to Iran.[46] In other words, the population of one of the world's poorest countries was contributing not only to Britain's war effort but also its postwar Welfare State.

The law of October 22, 1947, called on the government to enter talks with Anglo-Iranian "with a view to securing Iran's national rights." Those talks ended in 1949 in an unloved agreement, known as the Supplemental Oil Agreement or, after its principal negotiators on each side, Gass-Golshaian. Amid the thicket of provisions, the main component was an increase in royalty to 6 shillings a ton. It was rejected by the Iranian Parliament. By the new year, both Saudi Arabia and Kuwait (following Venezuela) had negotiated with the companies a fifty-fifty profit share, but by the time Anglo-Iranian came to offer that, it was too late. On March 15, 1951, Parliament voted unanimously to nationalize the oil industry, and Mohammed Reza signed the bill into law on the 20th. A month later, Mohammed Mossadeq was appointed prime minister.

With his bald head and long nose, his floods of tears, fainting fits, swoons, imaginary illnesses, and habit of receiving visitors in his pajamas on an iron bedstead, Mossadeq was a relic of old Iran. He was born in Tehran in 1882 to a princely family. His mother was a cousin to Nassereddin Shah Qajar. As a child, he received the title of nobility, *mossadeq al-saltaneh*, "certifier of the monarchy," which in Europe he shortened to Mossadeq or Mossadegh. A democrat, he was elected to the first Iranian Parliament in 1907 but barred on grounds of youth. When the next year the new Parliament was bombarded by the reactionary Mohammed Ali Shah, he set off to join the defense but was frightened by the sound of cannon.

In 1909, he traveled to Europe, first Paris and then Neuchâtel in Switzerland, and took a doctorate in law. On his return to Iran, he filled various governorships and cabinet posts including, for a while, deputy finance minister. In 1925, when Reza moved to install himself as Shah, Mossadeq was one of four men to speak in Parliament against the bill to abolish the Qajar dynasty. Characteristically, he absented himself for the vote. As Reza tightened his grip on Parliament, Mossadeq retired in 1928 to his estate at Ahmadabad, west of Tehran. In 1940, the Shah threw him into jail in the remote desert town of Birjand, where he fully expected to die had not Perron and Mohammed Reza interceded for him. With Reza's exile, he returned from his estates, was elected to Parliament in 1943, and became the heart of a movement to wrest control of the southern oil fields from the British. The following year, he was offered the premiership but (in a premonition of the future) set conditions that Parliament found intolerable. In 1949, he formed a political alliance under his leadership known as the National Front.

One of his first acts as prime minister in April 1951 was to demand that Mohammed Reza order Princess Ashraf to leave the country. On June 10, the Iranian flag was raised over the oil company's headquarters and a "provisional board of directors" appointed, including a pious and respected engineer named Mehdi Bazargan. Years later, Bazargan was to take over a greatly expanded oil industry in Ruhollah Khomeini's name and serve as the first prime minister of the provisional Islamic Republic.

Britain was not anxious to give up what was now, after Indian Independence, its most valuable foreign property.[47] It sought redress at the United Nations, at the International Court in The Hague, and through the mediation of the World Bank. It sent warships to the Gulf and the Shatt al-Arab, and used all its influence in Iran to try to have Mossadeq replaced as prime minister. The large companies that controlled the international trade in petroleum refused to buy Iranian oil, the industry in Khuzestan closed down, revenue and foreign exchange dried up, and the first essay in Soviet-style development planning, designed by the Idaho engineering consultants Morrison-Knudsen to invest $650 million over seven years, disintegrated with under a sixth of its money spent. Iraq, Kuwait, and Saudi Arabia opened the spigots to make up for the loss of Iranian oil, and Iran did not regain its place as chief producer in the Middle East until 1969.

Mossadeq was adamant. For Mossadeq, as for Iranians in general, as a British Persianist wrote, "No material benefits could compensate for personal degradation and loss of dignity."[48] On a wave of popular support, Mossadeq demanded dictatorial powers from Parliament and from Mohammed Reza command of the armed forces. When both demurred, Mossadeq resigned. Parliament reelected Qavam. There followed five days of riot and mayhem, and Mohammed Reza was forced to recall Mossadeq, who was granted emergency powers to rule by decree. The Shah's prestige sank. He was vilified in the press. He slept with a Smith & Wesson revolver under his pillow and brought it to table.[49] "Every morning I woke thinking it would be my last, and then had to plough through obscene insults in the newspapers," he later said.[50] Mossadeq purged royalist officers from the armed forces, and cut the military budget. On October 22, 1952, he broke off diplomatic relations with Britain.

Oil nationalization was popular in every corner of Iran, from the court down to remote desert towns.[51] The challenge for Mossadeq, which he never mastered, was to harness the popular elation and control the political free-for-all unleashed by the humiliation of the British. The Truman administration, which sought at first to find common ground between Iran and Britain, became exasperated. As Dean Acheson, President Truman's secretary of state, later wrote, "Mossadeq's self-defeating quality was that he never paused to see that the passions he excited to support him restricted his freedom of choice and left only extreme solutions possible."[52]

The clergy, flattered by the court, wanted above all to reverse Reza Shah's social reforms and to extirpate the Bahais, but was itself under pressure from religious radicals in uproar over the creation in 1948, on land for centuries under Muslim settlement, of the state of Israel. Principal among the radicals were the terrorists known as the "Devotees of Islam" (*fedayan-e Islam*), established in the war years by a young *sayyid* and former oil field agitator named Mojtaba Mirlohi (c. 1923–1955), who claimed descent from the Safavid dynasty and awarded himself the name of Navvab Safavi, or "Safavid Lord."

An Islamic romantic, Navvab Safavi dreamed of establishing a model Shia state purged of foreigners, alcohol, European dress and music.[53] Under the slogan "Religion and Vengeance," the Fedayan recruited from the neighborhood roughs, known as "thicknecks," "brigands," and "stiletto men," in Tehran, Qom, and Mashhad.[54] (As in Russia and southern Italy, the Iranian criminal class is devoted to religion.) Their first victim, on March 11, 1946, was the anticlerical historian and philosopher Ahmad Kasravi. Navvab Safavi and his supporters staged marches against the creation, in the war of 1948, of the Jewish state in Palestine and infiltrated the seminary in Qom. The dean of the seminary, Ayatollah Hosein Borujerdi, cleared them out in 1950, but the Fedayan merely transferred to Tehran, where they enjoyed the protection of another clergyman, Ayatollah Abol Qasim Kashani, who had built a political career of passionate opposition to the British, first in Iraq and then in Iran. In the permissive atmosphere, the Fedayan staged a series of public assassinations in the capital, including on March 7, 1951, Prime Minister Ali Razmara, who had attempted to push through Parliament the Supplemental Agreement with Anglo-Iranian. The Tudeh reorganized. To some Iranians, the fabric of state seemed to be disintegrating.

By the summer of 1952, both the Fedayan and Ayatollah Kashani had concluded that the Europeanized Mossadeq was not the man to install Islamic government in Iran. Wooed by Hosein Ala, minister of court, Kashani transferred his allegiance to General Fazlollah Zahedi, a brave and unscrupulous ex-Cossack now intriguing behind the scenes as chairman of the Retired Officers' Association. Mossadeq was caught in a vicious circle. The more his rivals hemmed him in, the more he sought to rule by decree, and the more he alienated his former allies. In January 1953, he insisted on an extension of his emergency powers. Meanwhile, the British convinced the incoming Eisenhower administration that Iran was about to fall into the Soviet sphere of influence.

In November and December 1952, the British Secret Intelligence Service (SIS) presented to the Central Intelligence Agency in Washington a plan for a *coup* to overthow Mossadeq. The CIA was taken aback, and no progress was made until after the new Republican president, Dwight Eisenhower, was inaugurated on January 20, 1953. On April 4, CIA director Allen Dulles approved a budget of $1 million for use by the Tehran CIA station and Ambassador Loy Henderson "in any way that would bring about the fall of Mossadeq."[55] On May 13, Donald Wilber, for the CIA, and the SIS resident in Tehran, Norman Darbyshire, met in Nicosia, Cyprus, a halfway station between London and Tehran. At the meeting, the two men agreed on a plan for a coup to be led by General Zahedi. In the altered conditions of the cold war, they chose to forget that the British had arrested and exiled Zahedi in 1942 for fear he would become the nucleus of a pro-Axis uprising.

The two agents agreed that "Zahedi alone of potential candidates had the vigor and courage to make him worthy of support," and, with less enthusiasm, that "the Shah must be brought into the operation; that the Shah would act only with great reluctance but that he could be forced to do so." Both men had a low opinion of Mohammed Reza, but he was needed to provide a "legal or quasi-legal" aspect to proceedings and because, "if the issue was clear-cut, the armed forces would follow the Shah rather than Mossadeq."[56]

As Foreign Secretary Anthony Eden had said of Mohammed Reza on February 27, "poor creature that he is, the Shah does represent an element of stability."[57] None foresaw that it was not Britain nor the United States, nor Zahedi nor Kashani nor the Fedayan, but Mohammed Reza who would most profit from the coup. The plan, code-named TPAJAX by the CIA and "Operation Boot" by SIS, was refined at two further meetings in Beirut (June 10–13) and London (June 14–17), and approved by Churchill and Eisenhower in early July. The "Art Department" of the CIA under Wilber began creating and distributing black propaganda.

Already in February 1953 Mohammed Reza's nerves were so frayed that, in his own words, he could not remain in Tehran. When Mossadeq, who feared the Shah was becoming the focus of opposition, suggested on February 24 that he leave the country for a while, Mohammed Reza "jumped at chance [to] get out," according to Ambassador Henderson.[58] He was prevented by a demonstration arranged by Kashani on February 28 outside the palace gates. Mossadeq was shown out by Soraya through a wicket gate, only to find crowds gathering in front of his own house nearby. In the end, he was forced to escape in his pajamas over the garden wall. Henderson believed that Mossadeq was enraged that even "inherently anti-foreign" politicians such as Kashani had turned against him and toward the court.[59] Mossadeq banned Mohammed Reza from conveying land to his tenants and took the properties back under government control.

Mohammed Reza feared Mossadeq, and believed the country was being bankrupted for the sake of a principle. He distrusted the British and had shown, during the fiasco of Qavam's five days in power, that he was reluctant to see blood shed in his name. For that reason, the plotters attempted to stiffen his resolve with secret emissaries. First his twin sister, Ashraf, returned from exile in Paris incognito on June 25. She was at once ordered to leave by both Mossadeq and her brother but defied them long enough to pass Soraya a message for Mohammed Reza.[60] She was followed, on August 1, by General Norman Schwarzkopf, who had spent the latter part of World War II in Iran reorganizing the Iranian Gendarmerie; the chief SIS agent in Iran, Asadollah Rashidian; Kermit Roosevelt, head of the Near Eastern Affairs section of the CIA and commander of the operation; and General Zahedi on August 10. According to the "London Draft" of the plan, Schwarzkopf had orders to say that the oil issue would be settled in a manner acceptable to Iran. The coup would proceed with or without Mohammed Reza's assistance, but if it failed, his dynasty would end and he would be held responsible.[61] The visit of Schwarzkopf set Tehran abuzz with rumors that what Iranians call a *koodeta* was in preparation.

The role assigned to Mohammed Reza had shrunk to signing two decrees or *firmans:* one dismissing Mossadeq as prime minister and the other appointing Zahedi (who was now in hiding). Even so, Mohammed Reza fretted whether he had the powers under the Constitution to dismiss a premier without parliamentary approval. According to Colonel Nematollah Nassiri, commander of the Imperial Guard, the British-style household division formed at the beginning of Mohammed Reza's reign, it was Soraya who finally persuaded the Shah to sign the two decrees.[62] Meanwhile, Mossadeq called a referendum on August 3 to dissolve Parliament and rule by decree. The plebiscite alarmed the influential Tehran clergyman Mohammed Behbehani, son of the Constitutionalist hero, who threatened to mobilize his supporters against it. Behbehani had many followers among the merchants of the Tehran bazaar.

On Tuesday, August 11, Mohammed Reza and Soraya and a few companions set off in a small aircraft trainer, ostensibly for the sake of the queen's health, to Kelardasht, a resort in the Elburz above Ramsar that then consisted of a few village houses among orchards and a dirt air strip.[63] There they waited, shut up in a small chalet, playing desultory cards and drinking cup after cup of coffee, over the Iranian weekend (which falls on Thursday and Friday). On the 13th, either at Kelardasht or in Ramsar, Mohammed Reza signed the two *firmans.* They remained in contact by radio-telephone with Colonel Nassiri.

The coup, delayed until August 15, was a fiasco. Early the next morning, August 16, Radio Tehran came on the air with the announcement: "Dear fellow-citizens, pay attention, please! At 7 a.m., the government will make a general announcement!" The announcement, when it came, said that the government had foiled a *coup d'état* by the Imperial

Guard. It said that at 1 a.m., Colonel Nassiri had arrived at the prime minister's house with an armored car, two jeeps, and four trucks of soldiers, but been beaten back by the prime minister's guard and arrested. The broadcast made no mention of the *firmans*.[64] Soraya says she was woken at the chalet by Mohammed Reza at 4 a.m. on the 16th, saying they were leaving for Ramsar and had not a moment to lose.[65]

Without money or luggage, they took to the air: Mohammed Reza, Soraya, the pilot Major Mohammed Khatami, and the Shah's aide-de-camp, Kambiz Atabai. In the chaos, Soraya left behind her Skye terrier. At Ramsar, they found Mohammed Reza's twin-engined Beechcraft already fueled, and they took off for Baghdad, five hundred miles away by air and just within range. Called from the Baghdad control tower to identify themselves, Mohammed Reza said they were tourists in need of fuel and were given permission to land.

The young Iraqi king, Faisal II, himself was expected by air from Amman, and the Iranians were directed to a corner of the field. They changed their clothes in the aircraft and Mohammed Reza wrote a few words on a scrap of paper and asked for it to be taken to the king. They waited by the customs building, in 110-degree heat, while Faisal inspected a guard of honor. Soraya was brought a soda. Kambiz Atabai, who was to serve the Pahlavi family until the Revolution and beyond, was pained to see the queen, "so tender and so well attended until yesterday, and now she must drink Coca-Cola from the bottle in the desert."[66]

In the end, they were taken to a government guesthouse and in the afternoon called on King Faisal. The Iranian ambassador ignored them. That evening, Mohammed Reza received the U.S. ambassador and gave his account of events. He had been approached, Mohammed Reza said, "some time ago about the desirability of a *coup*," and "he had at first agreed but had later come to the conclusion that as a constitutional monarch he should simply dismiss Mussadiq and appoint General Zahedi as Prime Minister, using sufficient forces only to ensure a smooth change-over. He had made arrangements to that end and the attempt had been made after a little delay but had failed owing, he thought, either to a leakage or to the interception of his telecommunications with General Zahedi. He had then decided that he could not resort to force since that would result in bloodshed and chaos, and that he must leave for Baghdad." He said he intended to look for work, as he had a large family and "very small means outside of Iran." The next day, at the shrine of the Shia martyrs in Karbala, Mohammed Reza disbursed 100 of the 280 Iraqi dinars he had with him, and then, over attempts by both the British and American ambassadors to make him stay, and discouraged by "scurrilous broadcasts" from Tehran, left for Rome with BOAC (forerunner of British Airways) at seven thirty the next morning, Tuesday, August 18.[67]

They arrived in Rome at 3 p.m. Once again, the Iranian Embassy cold-shouldered them, and they were taken by representatives of the Italian Foreign Ministry to the Hotel Excelsior and lodged on the fourth floor. Besieged by *paparazzi,* glued to Radio Cairo, smoking cigarette after cigarette, Mohammed Reza told Soraya they could afford to buy a little land in the United States, but not to support the remainder of the royal family. Soraya, in contrast, was for the first time in her marriage happy.[68] She had only ever wanted to be looked at. In her red strapless polka-dot dress, bought that evening on the Via Veneto, she seemed to be acting a part in a parallel, and more agreeable, history. On August 19, they were lunching all four in the dining room of the Excelsior when a correspondent of the Associated Press came to their table, and proffered a scrap of paper torn from off the news wire. Mossadeq had fallen. The army was in control of Tehran. Zahedi was prime minister. What had happened?

Back on Sunday, August 16, CIA headquarters outside Washington heard of the failure of the coup at 1:30 a.m. Though London and Washington both wanted to call off the operation, and pull out their own and Iranian agents, Zahedi, in hiding in Shemiran, and Kermit Roosevelt at the U.S. Embassy did not.[69] Zahedi's son, Ardeshir, photographed and printed the *firmans* at an Armenian shop on Naderi Street and showed them to the *New York Times* correspondents at 11 a.m.[70] Meanwhile, the National Front and the Tudeh went on the rampage, tearing down Reza's statues outside the Parliament and in Army Square. Cars with loudspeakers roamed midtown calling for a mass demonstration in Baharestan Square, where a public address system had been strung into the corners. In heat that penetrated the soles of shoes, the foreign minister and government spokesman, Hosein Fatemi, called for the abolition of the monarchy and the trial of the Pahlavis. "The crimes of the Pahlavi court make the crimes of King Farouk like driven snow," he said. There was still no word of the *firmans*.[71] Ominously for the prime minister, the Tehran bazaar shut down.

On the evening of the 18th, as CIA headquarters was signaling that, in the absence of strong recommendations from Henderson and Roosevelt, "operations against Mossadeq should be discontinued,"[72] demonstrators and police drove the nationalists and Tudeh off the streets in midtown. The next morning, a crowd armed with sticks and stones and including the athletes of the ancient weightlifting fraternities came up from the south, filled Army Square, where they were held for a while by troops firing into the air, and fanned out into the main shopping streets.

For reasons of professional prestige, both the CIA and Kermit Roosevelt have portrayed the march from the south of town as a hired mob bought with CIA money. The Islamic Republic, anxious to conceal the support of the clergy and bazaar for the Pahlavis, concurs. In fact, the *Clandestine History,* the account nearest in time to events, was baffled. Of the attacks on the nationalists and Tudeh on the evening of the 18th, the author (Donald Wilber) writes: "Just what was the major motivating force is impossible to say."[73] What is certain is that the bazaar, with its corporate links, its craft guilds and religious and athletic fraternities, its thicknecks and hoodlums, turned out on the 19th against Mossadeq and for Mohammed Reza. "The Shah is victorious," they shouted.

They sacked and set fire to Tudeh newspaper offices and, in Lalehzar, burned the Sadi Theater, long associated with the Tudeh playwright Nushin. Around noon, five tanks and about twenty truckloads of soldiers joined the crowd, and that helped decide the outcome of the day. The Central Post and Telegraph Office in Army Square was in royalist hands by 1 p.m. After a short fight, in which at least three men were killed, Radio Tehran on the Shemiran road fell just after 2 p.m. The headquarters of the chief of staff surrendered at the end of the afternoon. Some time before 7 p.m., a crowd supported by half a dozen Sherman tanks overran stiff resistance at Mossadeq's house near the Marble Palace in Kakh Street, and then sacked it. As many as thirty-five people died in the fight.[74] Mossadeq had already left over a back wall, but was arrested at 5 p.m. the next evening and taken to the Officers' Club, where General Zahedi treated him with consideration. By then, all the main provincial towns were in royalist hands. The Tudeh Military Organization, in formation under Moscow guidance since 1941 and numbering some six hundred officers and men, hesitated and then did nothing. They were ordered to collect on August 20, and then stood down on the following day.[75] A romantic plan to organize armed resistance in the woods of Gilan and in Mazanderan was not carried out.

On August 22, Mohammed Reza flew with twenty journalists in a chartered Constellation to Baghdad, said his prayers at Karbala, and then flew the Beechcraft to Tehran. At Mehrabad Airport, he was all but knocked over by men pressing to kiss his boots and knees. It was the Muslim Feast of Sacrifice and the road from the airport was stained red with the blood of camels, sheep, and chickens slaughtered in celebration. By then, Behbehani had reopened the bazaar.

The events of August 1953 altered Mohammed Reza. As the U.S. Embassy later cabled: "Mosadeq era effected major conversion. Shah today is no longer ward of foreigners as in 1941–45, nor vacillating youth of late forties."[76] Talking to an American academic in 1955, Mohammed Reza said: "There is no more lonely and unhappy life for a man than when he decides to rule instead of to reign. I am going to rule!"[77] Though marginal to events or a hindrance, he told his wife that day at the Excelsior in Rome: "Today I have just been truly elected by my people."[78] What was true was that the army remained loyal to him rather than to the prime minister, the clergy were supportive or neutral, the middle class terrified, and the bazaar keen to be back in business. Soraya is more plausible: "Neither CIA money nor Zahedi's dash nor the fervour of Molla Behbehani could have brought about the fall of Mossadegh and his policies had the Shah been unpopular."[79]

Officers who were loyal in the crisis, such as Khatami and Nassiri, received preferment. Ardeshir Zahedi was permitted to marry Princess Shahnaz. General Zahedi was passed $5 million from CIA funds.[80] Behbehani was wooed by the court. Mossadeq was tried before a military court on charges of treason, and sentenced to three years in prison. After serving his sentence, he was confined to his farm at Ahmad Abad where he died, a patriot and a gentleman, on March 5, 1967. Fatemi and the journalist who most offended Mohammed Reza, Amir Mokhtar Karimpurshirazi, were done to death.[81] Mohammed Reza fired the Iranian ambassador in Baghdad and the chargé in Rome who had refused to give him the keys to the car he kept at the Rome Embassy.

In August 1954, the military government of Tehran under a young cousin of Soraya, Teymour Bakhtiar, rolled up the Tudeh network in the army and air force, numbering according to Mohammed Reza some six hundred officers, including the commander of the best battalion of the Imperial Guard, and uncovered its clandestine printing works in the Tehran districts of Dovudieh and Narnak. Mohammed Reza said they had planned to use Mossadeq to overthrow the Pahlavi dynasty, and then kill him.[82] Twenty-seven officers were executed and 144 condemned to life imprisonment. The Tudeh leadership fled into exile and passed out of Iranian politics for a generation.

Mohammed Reza now had at last what no Shah of Iran had ever known except Nader after the sack of Delhi. Mohammed Reza had money. Under a new oil agreement, which was signed in September 1954, Anglo-Iranian (now renamed British Petroleum or BP) lost its monopoly but became a shareholder, with the major U.S. oil companies, in a consortium lifting Iranian oil under a fifty-fifty profit share. Iran still had no control over production volumes or sale prices, but the deal was incomparably better than the penury of the past three years or the see-no-evil parsimony of Anglo-Iranian. The state's revenue from oil increased from nothing in 1953 to $100 million in 1955, and thrice that in 1958, and it was swelled by development loans from the World Bank and U.S. civilian and military assistance. Soraya, who had had her clothes made by a French *émigrée* dressmaker at the Maison Ninon in Tehran, now could afford to go to Paris. In December 1954, the couple set off on a lazy three-month tour of the United States and Britain and then Germany, where the public enthusiasm for Soraya caused Mohammed Reza to sulk.

The clergy now submitted its invoice. Mohammed Reza was under criticism for his style of life and the conduct of the royal party during their two-month jaunt in the United States.[83] On a visit to Qom to see in the New Year on March 21, 1955, the Shah was snubbed by Ayatollah Borujerdi, who chose to be out of town. Interior Minister Asadollah Alam told his friend, the British diplomat Denis Wright, that Borujerdi was threatening to publish in Iran a shot of Soraya in Florida, wearing the new-fangled bikini, and to print scandal about Mohammed Reza's infidelities.[84] Borujerdi's particular concern was the Bahais, who under Bahaullah's grandson Shoghi Effendi had become more assertive and bought a large tract of land in the north of the capital to build an imposing shrine or House of Worship. Borujerdi wanted, at the very least, that Bahais be banned from government service.

On April 22, two days before the start of the fasting month of Ramazan, Mohammed Reza received a call from a popular Tehran preacher, Mohammaed Taqi Falsafi, and appears to have given him free rein to go after the Bahais. Mohammed Reza hoped, according to Interior Minister Alam, "that religious feelings stirred up over the Bahais might be channelled against Communism, and [because the Shah] wanted to keep in with the mullas."[85] This was, according to Roger Stevens, the British ambassador, "a bad miscalculation."[86]

In sermons that were broadcast over state radio, Falsafi attacked Bahais as heretics and agents of foreign powers. On May 7, their domed temple in Tehran was occupied while in Shiraz, birthplace of the Bab, a preacher named Sayyid Nureddin led a rampage against Bahai property and martial law was declared. There was uproar in the British press and in the United States, where Bahais were established in the Chicago area. Eventually, the government restored calm, Sayyid Nureddin was summoned to Tehran, and Falsafi encouraged to perform the pilgrimage to Mecca. Alam told Parliament that it was state policy that only Muslims might be employed in government service. In practice, the Bahais were invited to conceal their beliefs.

At a farewell audience with Mohammed Reza at Saadabad on the evening of September 17, 1955, Denis Wright, on instructions from London, tried to persuade the Shah to be "tougher" on the clergy. They were in deck chairs under a marquee, the Shah's dog at his knee and Alam, Bakhtiar, and Nassiri in attendance. Wright argued that the clergy were no bulwark against communism: Look at the power of the Communists in Catholic Italy![87] Wright said: "We would like to see what your father did and get much tougher with the mullahs and the ulammas [ulama, 'learned men'] and so on." The Shah said: "I'm not strong enough."[88]

But he was. The Fedayan returned to their old ways. When a Fedai tried to assassinate Prime Minister Hosein Ala as he entered the Royal Mosque in Tehran on November 17, 1955, Navvab Safavi was arrested. After a summary trial in the same military court that had condemned the Tudeh army officers, Navvab and four associates were shot on January 18, 1956. As he prepared for death, Navvab said: "Tonight my grandmother Fatemeh is waiting for me."[89] The affable Kashani, cold-shouldered by the nationalists for making possible the return of the Shah and the Consortium Agreement, and by the traditionalists for his political activism, passed out of sight and died in 1962. Defeated over the Bahais, the clergy was helpless to prevent Mohammed Reza from moving closer to the United States; from making a tactical alliance with Israel against the Arab nationalists such as Gamal Abdel Nasser of Egypt; and from creating the Savak security apparatus, which clamped down on religious demonstrations in 1958 and 1959. The clergy felt, with some justice, that Mohammed Reza had double-crossed them.

Soon Mohammed Reza was intriguing to be rid of Zahedi, and he dispatched Ernest Perron and Bahram Shahrokh (who had broadcast from Berlin during the war) to set up a backchannel to the British behind Zahedi's back. The British counselor, Denis Wright, who was eating his Christmas lunch, immediately informed the foreign minister.[90] Perron was dismissed and tried to take his own life. He went to live with Princess Shams and died in Switzerland, forgotten in Iran, in 1961.

Zahedi resigned in April 1955 and retired with his millions to Montreux. After fourteen years of frustration, Mohammed Reza had control of the armed forces. He brought Iran alongside Turkey, Iraq, Pakistan, and the United Kingdom into the anti-Soviet Baghdad Pact and used that to justify demands for modern equipment from both the United States and Britain. Though the United States was not a signatory to the pact, the Eisenhower Doctrine, under which the United States committed itself to resist Communist subversion in the Middle East, made the United States (in President Eisenhower's words of March 1957) "an effective member."

By joining the pact, Mohammed Reza exposed Iran to Soviet hostility, but gained access to U.S. weaponry under the U.S. Military Assistance Program, which amounted by 1960 to $90 million a year in new and surplus equipment, including the F-86 Sabre fighter, which had been deployed in the Korean War. With the assistance of a CIA mission of five officers, Bakhtiar's operation was expanded and renamed in 1958 the "Organization for Intelligence and Homeland Security" or, from its Persian acronym, Savak.* Before it gained its evil reputation at the end of the 1960s, Savak for a while offered a respectable career and (like the CIA and the West European external intelligence services) attracted some able men. In 1959, Dr. Eberhard Tauber, an expert in anti-Bolshevik dirty tricks under the Third Reich who had found Chancellor Adenauer's West Germany too hot for him, was taken on to combat Soviet propaganda. (Dr. Tauber was sent away after a propaganda truce and thaw in relations with the Soviets four years later.)[91] In 1958, the Iraqi monarchy was overthrown and Baghdad withdrew from the pact, which was renamed the Central Treaty Organization (CENTO). Iran began to loom larger in Western strategic thinking, and in March 1959 the United States signed with Iran a bilateral defense agreement.

In those years, Mohammed Reza consolidated his fortune and, with it, his influence. The Omran Bank, capitalized in 1952 with the proceeds from the sale of the crown farm lands, expanded into real estate development (first in Tehran and then on Kish Island in the Persian Gulf) and ultimately had a balance sheet of over $1 billion.[92] It was the chief asset of the Pahlavi Foundation, founded as a *vaqf* or charitable trust in 1958, and endowed in 1961 with the remaining farms and hotels, cement and fertilizer plants, merchant shipping and insurance company. It built gambling casinos (which are obnoxious to pious Muslims) on the Caspian shore and Kish. A source of investment capital and royal patronage, which paid for Iranians to study at college abroad, to repair mosques and so on, the Pahlavi Foundation was later swelled by commission payments or sweeteners from foreign companies seeking commercial and defense contracts. The foundation allowed Mohammed Reza to direct the country's economic development and buy influence without acting, as his father had, "as hotel keeper, factory owner and bathhouse attendant."

Mohammed Reza's private life remained the subject of gossip. As he approached his fortieth birthday without a male heir, his relations with Soraya began to break down. His only full brother, Alireza, had died in an air accident in 1954. When his daughter Shahnaz became pregnant, he faced the prospect of a male heir fathered by the bumptious

---

* Sazman-e Attalaat Va Amniat-e Keshvar—Organization for Intelligence and Homeland Security.

Ardeshir Zahedi.[93] Refusing to allow her husband to take a second wife, Soraya left the country on February 13, 1958, first to St. Moritz and then to join her mother in Cologne. On March 14, Ala, now minister of court, announced the termination of the marriage. It was, said the British ambassador, Sir Roger Stevens, who had become fond of Soraya, "a tragedy."[94] A song called *"Je veux pleurer comme Soraya"* ("I want to weep like Soraya") was a hit that summer in France. Mohammed Reza later said that "for a certain period, it was one of the greatest sorrows of my life."[95] (Soraya made two films in 1965 but was not a success as an actress. She died at her flat on the Avenue Montaigne in Paris in 2001.)

The court cast about for another bride and settled on Maria Gabriella of Savoy, the middle daughter of the exiled king of Italy. She was then eighteen years old.[96] She was also a Roman Catholic and, on February 23, 1959, the Vatican newspaper *l'Osservatore Romano* warned of a "grave danger" in the marriage of a Catholic princess to a Muslim king.[97] Maria Gabriella was discouraged, too, by stories about the backbiting at the Pahlavi court. (Mohammed Reza blamed his sister-in-law, Pari Sima, for gossiping and banned her from court for more than ten years.)[98] There was an approach to the British about Princess Alexandra, the twenty-two-year-old cousin of Queen Elizabeth II who was in the party that welcomed Mohammed Reza at Victoria Station on his state visit to England in May, and accompanied him to the Covent Garden ballet, but that came to nothing.

During the summer of 1959, Ardeshir Zahedi, who was responsible for the welfare of Iranian students abroad, interviewed a young girl named Farah Diba. The niece of Reza's treasurer, who had been done to death in the 1930s, she had also lost her father and grown up in Shemiran in the house of her maternal uncle. A brilliant schoolgirl athlete, who swept the board at the first girls' athletics championship in Tehran in 1954, Farah was studying at the École speciale d'architecture in Paris, where she lived a sociable and spotless existence.[99] She was now home for her summer vacation.

By way of his wife Princess Shahnaz, Zahedi introduced her to Mohammed Reza. The Shah took both women flying in his new Morane-Saulnier jet trainer, and proposed to Farah on her twenty-first birthday, October 14, 1959. Despite her mother's misgivings about the evil reputation of the court,[100] they were married on December 21. Farah wore a five-pound tiara made from Nader's emeralds by the New York jeweler Harry Winston[101] and a dress designed by Yves Saint Laurent of Dior.

Admired for her lovely face, hair, and hands, Farah was not melancholy like Fauzia, or hoydenish like Soraya, but tactful and economical, then considered the great virtues in an Iranian wife. In the shortest time decent, she produced a male heir, Reza, who was born on October 31, 1960, at a busy public hospital in South Tehran. Mohammed Reza, generally so ponderous, aloof, and reserved, was overjoyed. His first volume of memoirs, published that year in English as *Mission for My Country*, brims with confidence and a sense of divine right. He describes how, at the point of death from typhoid fever as a seven-year-old, he dreamed that Ali, Commander of the Faithful, extended to him a bowl to drink which cured him. On another occasion, one of Imam Hosein's companions saved him from a fall. On a third, he saw the Lord of the Age in a dream.[102] Mohammed Reza was ready for the fight of his life.

CHAPTER 4

Ruhollah

◇

To become a molla is difficult. To become a human being is impossible.

—Abdol Karim Haeri-Yazdi[1]

Like so much that appears of great antiquity in Iran, the seminary at Qom is of recent foundation. Although the shrine of the Immaculate Lady was a center of religious knowledge in the early Middle Ages, under the Safavids and then under Fath Ali Shah Qajar, who was buried there, the torch of learning had by the Constitutional Revolution long passed to the shrines of Iraq. The modern prestige of Qom arose from the turmoil that followed the British occupation of Iraq in World War I and the arrival from the weaving town of Sultanabad of Abdol Karim Haeri-Yazdi, who came to the shrine to see in the New Year of 1922 and was persuaded to stay.[2] Among his entourage was a nineteen-year-old student of great promise, Ruhollah Khomeini.

Sayyid Ruhollah Khomeini was born on September 24, 1902, in Khomein, a small farming town about forty miles south of Sultanabad. His family claimed descent from the Prophet through the line of the Seventh Imam, Musa al-Kazem. With the fall of the Safavid state to Afghan raiders in 1722, and the dispersal of the Isfahan seminary, the family had emigrated to India—some say Lucknow, some say Kashmir—but in the 1830s Ruhollah's grandfather, Sayyid Ahmad, on making a pilgrimage to the shrines in Iraq, was persuaded to settle in Khomein.

There he built a large brick and timber house and garden, which survives, and acquired orchards and wheat land in the surrounding villages. Ruhollah's father, Sayyid Mostafa, received his clerical training in Iraq, where he advanced to the level of *mojtahed*, then returned to Khomein, where he lived the pleasant life of a clerical landed gentleman, with rents of some 100–200 tomans a year (or the equivalent of a colonel in the military), and five surviving children. One day in March 1903, five months after Ruhollah was born, Sayyid Mostafa was murdered on the Sultanabad road. In the ensuing years, what remained of highway security collapsed, and Ruhollah grew up in tense and difficult circumstances, in a house fortified with two towers, looked after by his mother, his wet nurse Naneh Khavar, and his aunt, Sahebeh. He attended the Koran school in the town, and by his mid-teens had memorized hundreds or even thousands of verses by the classical poets, and was himself a competent versifier. According to his elder brother Pasandideh, he excelled at the ancient Iranian sport of wrestling.

In the chaos at the close of World War I, with the country crisscrossed by foreign armies and ravaged by cholera and influenza (which claimed both his mother and his aunt), Khomeini traveled for his clerical studies not to Iraq, or even Isfahan, but to join Haeri-Yazdi in nearby Sultanabad. There he studied a curriculum that had not changed for centuries and donned the black turban of the *sayyid*. (The turban, once worn by all adult male Muslims, was by now the badge of the seminary-trained cleric.) When surnames were introduced in 1925, he went by the name of Sayyid Ruhollah Musavi Mostafavi, and that was the name on his passport.[3]

In the battles between Reza and the clergy over conscription and uniform dress, Khomeini took no active role or concealed his opinions behind a wall of prudence, a practice known among the Shia as *ketman* or *taqiyeh*. Having mastered Arabic, the sources of religious law, and its philosophical grounding or jurisprudence, by the mid-1930s he was accepted as a *mojtahed*, a scholar who through his knowledge of the holy law could pronounce on every aspect of human life. He himself lived a spotless life without recourse to the widows and divorcees that swarm round the seminary towns in Iran and Iraq, marrying students for as little as an hour and a bride price of a couple of tomans. Always well off, in 1929 he married Qodsi, the only woman in his adult life, the daughter of a rich Tehran divine named Mirza Mohammed Saqqafi. At first reluctant to marry, as became a fifteen-year-old girl in Iran, Qodsi changed her mind after seeing the Prophet's daughter Fatemeh in a dream.[4] Ruhollah was neat in his dress, and restrained in his manners. He lived off bread, cheese, and the Iranian herbs called *sabzi*. He did not care to handle money and could not be parted from it.[5] As an adult, he never once put his hand to physical labor.[6]

What marked Khomeini out from his peers was an expertise in certain remote and demanding disciplines of higher religious knowledge, which were to occupy both his early maturity and his extreme old age. Those were grouped under the heading of "philosophy" or *falsafa* (from the Greek *philosophia*), but Khomeini was not a philosopher as Socrates understood that word. He reasoned in old-fashioned syllogisms, which are often quite vacuous, used violent and vulgar language, and was careless in matters of fact. As a mystic, some Iranians say, he was beyond compare.

All religions display two faces. The outward or manifest prescribes for its adherents forms of worship, ritual, costume, conduct, and law. In Shia Islam, those prescriptions are precise and punctual. The inward or hidden seeks to penetrate the chaos and muddle of appearances to understand the permanent reality of God. Islam, which stresses at every point the absolute oneness or unity of God, always had an affinity for this cast of inquiry, which is known in the West as monism (from the Greek *monos*, meaning "single"). Iranians, in particular, had a bent for mysticism that by the high Middle Ages had come to saturate Persian lyric poetry, which became, in a fashion not unlike the English poets of the sixteenth and seventeenth centuries, at the same time both carnal and metaphysical.

In the seminaries, the school of *falsafa* and the overlapping sciences of *erfan* and *hikmat* (from the Arabic root words for "know" and "judge") deployed intuition rather than deductive reasoning to explore the nature of God and reality. God could not only be known, through spiritual exercises and the most profound study of the Koran and the Immaculate Imams, but had (according to one theory) created the world so that He could be known. Under the Safavids, Molla Sadra, a writer all but impenetrable to the foreigner without an Iranian guide (and, in the case of this author, even with one), presented a parable of four journeys, on the last of which the adept not only subsists within God but actually may return from God to guide humanity. (Later, Khomeini's followers claimed that his political inaction until 1962 came about, in part, because he had not completed these grueling spiritual displacements.)[7]

From the mid-1930s, Khomeini taught classes in public and at his house on the works of Molla Sadra and his principal interpreter, Molla Sabzevari (who died in 1872). His students included Morteza Motahhari, one of his closest allies in the struggle against the Pahlavis, and Hosein Ali Montazeri, who was for a time in the 1980s designated his successor. Those courses of study, though tolerated by both Haeri-Yazdi and his successor after 1944, Hosein Borujerdi, exuded the whiff of brimstone, and although Khomeini wrote many theosophical treatises at this time, starting in 1928 with a meditation on one of the Ramazan prayers, none was published until after the Revolution. He stood outside the mainstream at Qom. He once said that a group of men ordered that a cup be washed from which his elder son, Mostafa, had drunk, "because his father teaches philosophy." The insult, which implied that Khomeini was an infidel and thus ritually unclean, was known all over Qom.[8]

Progress at Qom was slow. Haeri-Yazdi complained to a visitor from Lebanon in 1934: "We raise and educate the students, but when the education comes to fruition the student takes off his turban and wears the attire of the temporal power and joins one of the government departments."[9] Haeri-Yazdi dreamed of expanding the seminary into a university, with faculties of traditional medicine and mathematics, but it remained confined to Arabic and the religious sciences. When he proposed to send students abroad to study the European languages, the merchants who held his purse strings refused. The condition of some of the students was beyond desperate. The thirteen-year-old Montazeri, the son of a sharecropper in Najafabad, lived on a farthing a day and used to stand outside the confectioners' shops, breathing in the aroma of almond brittle that he could not afford to buy.[10] By his mid-twenties, the young student had ruined his eyesight by study. With his pebble spectacles, untidy dress, and coarse, even ribald, speech, Montazeri gave a rustic, even clownish, impression.

In Isfahan and other towns, the seminaries, vacated by all but a few poor students and with their endowments lost, were taken over as historical landmarks and opened to the few Western tourists. Even in

Qom, on the eve of Reza's abdication, Montazeri said there were just eight hundred students, nowhere near adequate to staff the thousands of mosques in Iran.[11] With the death of Haeri-Yazdi in 1937, the seminary began to drift and was in no state to raise popular feeling against the Anglo-Soviet invasion.

As so often with human beings, the loss of influence was compensated by an augmentation of title. The honorific Ayatollah—"sign of God"—came into widespread use first with Haeri-Yazdi, then his successor as leader of the seminary, Hosein Borujerdi, and then the nationalist politician Abol Qasim Kashani, who was not a man of learning. In time, the title became so devalued that a new category, Grand Ayatollah, was invented to honor the senior *mojtaheds* such as Montazeri. Under influence from Lebanon, Khomeini was accorded an entirely new title, Imam.

In the more open and permissive atmosphere after Reza's exile, Khomeini broke off his teaching of Molla Sadra to compose in 1944 or 1945[12] a polemic directed at a readership outside the seminary, and to take his first step in politics: or, as he put it in the language of mysticism, "to pass from the world of unity under the writ of multiplicity."[13]

This work, *The Unveiling of the Secrets*, was written not in Arabic but in Persian, and appeared without date or author's name. Composed amid signs of haste, it took on a modernizing trend in the civil service and teaching profession that sought to purify the Shia of its popular rituals and cult of saints. The occasion for the book and its title had been a work, published in 1943, called *The Secrets of the Millennium*, but Khomeini also took aim at the historian Ahmad Kasravi ("that imbecile"), whose history of the Constitutional Revolution has been quoted.

Khomeini attacked those self-styled reformers as no better than agents of the puritanical Saudis, who had overrun the sacred cities of Mecca and Medina in 1924–25, leveled the tombs of the Shia Imams, and established the kingdom of Saudi Arabia. Khomeini's hatred for "the savages of Nejd and camel-grazers of Riyadh" was lifelong and is evident in his last will and testament. Khomeini also attacked Reza Pahlavi, now safely over the water: "Reza Khan was quite unsuited to the throne. The Shah must take it on himself to protect the lives, property, chastity and honour of the masses, not exploit the throne to indulge his appetites and rapacity." As for the Pahlavi modernizers, "In your European hat, you strolled the boulevards, ogling the naked girls, and thought yourselves fine fellows, unaware that foreigners were carting off the country's patrimony and resources."[14] He fulminates against dance halls, unveiling, wineshops, mixed schools, and the decay of traditional or "Greek" medicine. He makes no explicit mention of the Allied occupation.

The book is ill-printed and unpunctuated, and but for Khomeini's later fame, might have vanished from the earth. Yet dispersed through it are hints of a political philosophy that draws on Fazlollah Nuri and the anti-Constitutional clergy and was to result in the modern Islamic Republic and its armed forces.

None but God may rule on earth,[15] and the world has in the Koran and the Traditions or sayings of the Prophet all the laws it needs. There is no place for legislation, assemblies, or elections. Sultans there must be and they must have some military competence. To forestall another Reza, the Sultan should be appointed by that class of men who have penetrated the mysteries of the Koran and are best in control of their appetites: the doctors of the religious law. "When we say that the government or the regency resides in this time with the jurists, we do not mean that the jurist must be Shah, minister, military man and road-sweeper all in one, but that a constituent assembly be formed of the senior doctors of the law . . . to elect a just man as King who will not oppose God's law."[16] As for the army, it should not be a Pahlavi-style standing force conscripted by press-gang but a militia or "mobilization" (*basij*) whose principal task will be religious propagation.

Through the tumult of the 1950s, Khomeini kept his own counsel. While sympathetic to the aims of Navvab Safavi and the Fedayan, he had profound reservations about their tactical alliances and violent methods.[17] Nonetheless, Borujerdi came to distrust Khomeini and his pupils, and a coldness or distance grew between them that lasted until Borujerdi's death in 1961.[18]

Mohammed Reza pressed ahead with his reforms. The Land Reform of the 1960s, though it developed under the pressure of events into a royal *coup d'état*, began as agricultural improvement. The chapter on agriculture in *Mission for My Country* shows Mohammed Reza had thought hard about the farmers, but came to a conclusion that suited his political purposes. He wrote that "much of the worst-managed land" was in the hands of large absentee landlords, including those with forty or more villages, and the lay stewards or farm managers of the clergy.[19] The solution was to distribute land to smallholders on the pattern of the crown lands, and provide cooperative finance to replace the old dependence on the landlord.

Bundled up with other reforms such as votes for women, renamed the White Revolution, and then the Shah-People Revolution, Land Reform had less in the end to do with tillage and husbandry than with a "revolution from above,"[20] as Mohammed Reza first conceived it in the dark 1940s: an end run past the entrenched estates of landowners and clergy to the peasantry and the laborers in industry. It was the means to complete his father's unfinished business and establish the only government he understood, which was an autocracy, paternal, enlightened, and repressive. Mohammed Reza had chosen his ground well. The rump of the Mossadeqists could not ally with clergy that opposed women's suffrage and agrarian reform.[21] The Kennedy administration, which had pressed representative democracy on Mohammed Reza, found itself bound to support him. There was a thaw in relations with the Soviet Union, which praised "the blow to the hopes of the Western colonialists who supported the Iranian feudalists."[22]

The first Land Reform Act, which was passed by the lower house of Parliament on March 16, 1960, and the Senate on May 17, was a failure. Since it ran across fundamental Islamic principles of private property and contract, it was opposed by Borujerdi. His death, much mourned, from a heart attack on March 30, 1961, left the seminary with no figure of comparable religious authority. The same day, Mohammed Reza sent the customary telegram of condolence not to the leading clergy of Qom, but to Ayatollah Mohsen al-Hakim in Iraq. Ever alert to such signals, the Qom clergy concluded that Mohammed Reza wanted them cut down to size.[23]

Khomeini was not at that time known outside the seminary. Kept at arm's length by Borujerdi, he was outranked by three senior doctors of the religious law or *mojtaheds,* the Ayatollahs Golpayegani, Shariatmadari, and Marashi-Najafi. He had few students and, unlike Shariatmadari of Tabriz, no financial backing from a merchant city. He had published nothing except a wartime polemic, unread at the time except by his students (who had to pay full price for it). At the mourning ceremonies for Borujerdi, Montazeri came away from the crowds at Golpayegani's house in the Qom bazaar to find his teacher at home, alone and unattended.[24] Khomeini refused, out of diffidence and thrift, to take over the stipends of any of the late Borujerdi's students.[25] He was haunted by the fate of Kashani.[26]

In the next three years, Khomeini revealed to Iran his implacable will, his fearlessness, and his talent for oratory. By 1964, he was the undisputed champion not just of the seminary but of the clergy in general, of Iranian customs and the Constitution, and the scourge of the monarchy, Israel, and the United States. In part to save his life, and in part as recognition of his popular support in Tehran and Qom, the Iranian clergy (though not those resident in Iraq) acquiesced in Khomeini's promotion to the status of a *marja* or "Source of Imitation" beyond the reach of the civil law. As one clergyman put it in 1963, "In the thirteen-hundred-year history of Islam, this is the first time that a clerical person has achieved the status of 'Source of Imitation' for the Shiites by way of direct action. This person is Ayatollah Khomeini to whom the other *marjas* expressed their written allegiance."[27] Like Kashani and Navvab Safavi, but unlike Fazlollah Nuri, Khomeini came to prominence not in the library but in the streets.

To remedy their master's obscurity and to bolster his claim to supreme authority or *marjiyat*, Khomeini's students began gathering up his rulings on knotty points of ritual and law, similar to the *responsa* ("Answers") of Roman jurisprudence and the Roman Catholic Church. They were published in Persian in 1962 and entitled (after a pattern set by Borujerdi) *Clarification of Problems*. What distinguished this 135-page booklet was, amid the rulings on defecation, menstruation, and the rights of temporary wives, a section dealing with the defense of Muslim life, wealth, and honor against foreigners, and the agents of foreigners.[28] Over Khomeini's objections and economies, a telephone was installed in his house (though he never paid the bill).[29] With the help of bazaar merchants in Tehran, he began paying stipends to his students.[30] These stipends were paid even when he was in jail and in exile.

In the autumn of 1962 Mohammed Reza, elated by his new marriage, a successful visit to Washington, and the thaw in relations with the Soviet Union, went on the offensive. He was encouraged by his prime minister, Asadollah Alam, scion of an ancient noble family in eastern Iran who had tied his fate with the house of Pahlavi. On October 7, Alam introduced a bill for elections to local councils in which, for the first time, women might vote and stand and where candidates would be permitted to take the oath of service not just on the Koran but on any "Heavenly Book," which might be the Torah, the Zoroastrian Avesta, or the Bible. The bundling of the two measures split the opposition, for the Mossadeqists, now congregating in a reformed National Front, had proposed the women's franchise back in 1950 only to be overruled by Borujerdi and Qom.

By now an old man in a country where life expectancy at birth was under fifty years, Khomeini saw the bill as the first step in a project "to extirpate Islam in this country." [31] No doubt, he had in mind Reza's policies of the late 1920s, which had begun with surnames and military conscription and culminated in the Gowharshad massacre.

The next evening, he managed to convene a meeting of the leading clergy in Qom, including Shariatmadari and Golpayegani, on the neutral ground of the house of the late founder of the modern seminary, Haeri-Yazdi. They could not agree on a joint telegram to Mohammed Reza, so Khomeini wrote himself, addressing the Shah as "His Serene Majesty," and requesting that "the order be given that a matter that is contrary to the sacred faith of the kingdom and its official creed be kept from government and party policy." [32] The other clergy followed suit, the Tehran bazaar mobilized, and on November 29, Mohammed Reza, "against his better judgment," allowed the bill to be dropped. [33]

Both men now had the bit between the teeth. Khomeini pressed for Prime Minister Alam's resignation and, in a speech to students on December 2, justified both his long quiescence and his entry into political action by the example of Ali, Commander of the Faithful, who had given his allegiance to the first three Sunni caliphs but had risen against the tyrannical Umayyads. [34] To consolidate his new support in the Tehran bazaar and the South Tehran underworld, he encouraged the formation of a militant front known as the "Coalition of Islamic Societies," which channeled contributions to his movement and, after his exile, attempted to revive Navvab Safavi's policy of assassination. The front consisted of leading merchants such as Asadollah Lajevardi, a bazaar draper who, as warden of Evin Prison between 1979 and 1984, would preside over the first prison massacres and was assassinated, to universal relief, in 1998. In Qom, Montazeri and such younger men as Ali Khamenei and Ali Akbar Hashemi Rafsanjani formed a secret society to agitate in the seminary.

Mohammed Reza was not to be deterred and decided to appeal over the heads of Parliament and clergy to the people. Taking a leaf out of Mossadeq's book, he proposed to put his "White Revolution" to a plebiscite. On January 9, 1963, he spoke at a congress of farmers in Tehran and announced a six-point referendum consisting of land distribution; the nationalization of forests and other natural resources; the sale of shares in government factories to landowners as compensation; profit sharing for workers; the women's franchise; and a literacy corps. Once again, Mohammed Reza's policy and tactics split the opposition and obscured the battle for foreign observers. For who among the modern classes could oppose an assault on the absentee landlords and the plutocratic clergy, or stand out against rural literacy and women's suffrage? Khomeini grasped that more quickly than his colleagues, and told his supporters to concentrate their fire not on the individual points in the White Revolution, but on the referendum itself as an assault on the 1906 Constitution.[35]

As January 26, polling day, approached, feelings ran high and then spilled over. On January 23, the Tehran bazaar closed and police broke up an attempt to stage a *bast* at the Sayyid Azizullah Mosque. The next day, Mohammed Reza traveled to Qom, in part as an act of conciliation and in part to distribute title deeds to farmers specially brought into the shrine of the Immaculate Lady for the occasion. Never a good extempore speaker in Persian, Mohammed Reza lost his self-control, and attacked the clergy in language that was to come back to haunt him, calling them "ignorant and desiccated individuals whose minds have not stirred for centuries and cannot be stirred."[36] Meanwhile, farmers and plainclothes officers jeered at the seminary students, shouting: "Your days of eating rice are over!"[37] As is the way of such things in the Near East, the referendum returned a resounding "Yes" to the six-point program.

At the equinoctial New Year (March 21), Qom was as usual thronged with pilgrims, but Montazeri noted as he hurried to the house of his old teacher that many of them, while dressed as farmers, carried marks of their military or police caps still livid on their temples.[38] By dawn of the next day, which was the anniversary of the death at the hands of the Caliphate of the Sixth Imam, the courtyard of Khomeini's house in the district of Qom, which was known as the "Judge's Icehouse," was teeming with people. A preacher who spoke of the Sixth Imam's sufferings was constantly interrupted and even drowned out by scuffles and sarcastic hosannas in all the wrong places. On Khomeini's orders, his pupil Sadeq Khalkhali snatched the microphone and warned that if there were further interruptions, his master would take himself to the shrine of the Immaculate Lady and "make his reckoning with the ruling power once and for all."[39] A similar scene played out amid Shariatmadari's congregation, but at the main event of the day, in the courtyard of the Faizieh Seminary, where Golpayegani was holding court, a pitched battle broke out between the students and the royalist "peasants" and paramilitaries.

Like many religious schools of the Safavid and Qajar eras, the Faizieh consists of a spacious court with monumental porches at each point of the compass joined by a two-story arcade where the students have their cells or rooms. In the melee, the seminarians retreated up the stairs to the upper-story arcade, where a stack of mud bricks for repairs furnished ammunition which they hurled down, killing two men. The royalist forces, reinforced by uniformed police coming across the roof of the neighboring Infirmary School, stormed the upper floor and pitched students down fifteen feet to the pavement, where one was to die from his injuries. They then rampaged through the cells, throwing turbans, cloaks, possessions, and books (even, it is said, the Koran) down into the court, where they heaped them up and set fire to them. Not until seven in the evening was order restored. Khomeini, who was about to set out to investigate the scene at the Faizieh, was prevented by his students. In a short speech, he said with his characteristic hyperbole: "With this outrage, the ruling power has revealed itself as the successor to Genghis Khan and made inevitable its own defeat and destruction."[40]

After this fight, neither side was willing to give ground. Alam maintained the pressure, conscripting seminarians (including Ali Akbar Hashemi Rafsanjani, later president of the Islamic Republic) into the army. Khomeini merely said, "A man should know how to shoot,"[41] and fell to talking of his youthful exploits with the gun, protecting his father's orchards in Khomein. The court attempted to smear Khomeini as an agent of Mohammed Reza's bugbear, Abdel Nasser of Egypt. From Iraq, Ayatollah Hakim wrote to propose a mass migration of the Iranian clergy to the Holy Thresholds of Karbala and Najaf, which would have suited Mohammed Reza. For that reason, and because they knew it would be easier to depart than to return, Khomeini and the other *mojtaheds* declined. When the governor of Qom and the chief of police came to call on him, Khomeini would not admit them. Later, he said he wished he had so he "could have punched them in the mouth."

On the fortieth day after the Faizieh fight, May 2, the clergy staged mourning ceremonies. After issuing a declaration in which he came closer than ever to blaming "His Majesty" for what had happened, Khomeini walked to the Faizieh, where he seated himself before one of the student rooms on the east side of the court, and wept without cease.[42] Looming ahead was the start on May 24 of the mourning month of Moharram, in which the enactment of Imam Hosein's passion and death was bound to inflame sentiment. Military units were sent to reinforce the Qom police, while there were rumors that the metal bazaar in Tehran was fashioning makeshift weapons. Mohammed Reza sent Farah and the two small children off early to Saadabad.[43]

All over Iran, outspoken clerics used the first nights of Moharram to attack the regime, and even the Shah in person. On the afternoon of the 10th of the month, or Ashura (June 3), Khomeini brushed aside threats from both a Savak officer and the Qom police commissioner and set off for the Faizieh, hemmed in by students, entered the college, and climbed the pulpit behind a thicket of microphones. He began with the tragedy of Karbala, blamed Israel for the attack on the Faizieh, and wondered out loud if perhaps Mohammed Reza himself was a Jew and a Bahai, and should be condemned to death. He then addressed the Shah in terms not heard in public since 1953: "Mr. Shah, Your Excellency Mr. Shah, let me give you a piece of advice. . . . When the Soviet Union, Britain and America invaded Iran and occupied our country [in 1941],* the people's property and honour was imperilled, but

---

* The United States did not invade Iran.

God knows the people were happy that Pahlavi had gone. I don't want the same to happen to you. Listen to my advice, listen to the clergy of Islam, do not listen to Israel. You worthless wretch, forty-five [i.e., forty-three] years of your life have passed, isn't it time for you to think and reflect a little, to consider where this is leading you, to learn from your father's fate."[44] No attempt was made to disrupt the sermon.

Such insults to the head of state, which might have brought prosecution even in democracies such as France and West Germany, were too much for the court. At about three in the morning of June 5, Khomeini was arrested at his house, bundled into a black Volkswagen Beetle, and then transferred to a red station wagon and driven the ninety miles to Tehran, where he was lodged first, like Mossadeq, at the Officers' Club and then in the Qasr barracks. He was among some sixty clergy arrested that day, including the leading preachers of Mashhad and Shiraz, as well as such younger men as Motahhari and Khalkhali.

As Khomeini was being taken away, his elder son Mostafa struggled up a narrow stair to the roof of a neighboring house, shouting, "People of Qom! They have taken away the Master!"[45] All over the quarter, people appeared on their roofs and then in the lanes below, and by first light the main streets and the shrine were teeming with men and women armed with makeshift weapons. As at the Gowharshad thirty years before, the officer commanding troops lost control, and panicky soldiers, isolated from their comrades, opened fire. Eleven students were killed, and as many as twice that number of townspeople, and the army took casualties. In one legendary story, a lady asked the assistance of a soldier in crossing an exposed street and, when he gave her his arm, knifed him in the stomach. It was not until midafternoon, with the arrival of an experienced officer from Tehran, that the army regrouped and cleared the streets. Four fighter aircraft flew low over the city, breaking the sound barrier.

In Tehran by 9 a.m. crowds were mobilizing in the thousands all over the bazaar. Crying "Khomeini or Death!," they attacked a police precinct in the bazaar, then attempted to overrun the radio station in Arg Square, just south of the Golestan Palace. They were repeatedly driven back with casualties. All across midtown, government buildings were attacked, and cinemas and a bus depot were set on fire. At some point that morning, Mohammed Reza, under pressure from Hosein

Ala and other elder statesmen to sack Alam and halt the bloodshed, called the prime minister and said: "Now you have your revolution, what are you going to do about it?" Alam replied: "It is I who has the firepower." According to Alam, the Shah "laughed from the depths of his heart and said: 'I agree and I am behind you.'"[46] General Nematol-lah Nassiri, the loyal colonel of 1953, was appointed military governor, the city was put under curfew, tanks and armor rumbled into midtown, and soldiers in battle gear deployed with orders to shoot to kill. By the following evening, June 6, they had control of the city and had made hundreds of arrests.

There was also violence in Kashan, Khomein, Shiraz, and Mashhad, and by June 7 the uprising had spread to the villages. That morning, Savak learned from two travelers arrived at the Saveh bus depot that some 2,000 people from the Varamin district, a farming area thirty miles southeast of Tehran, armed with makeshift weapons, were on the march to "join the troublemakers" in the capital.[47] Savak in Varamin conveyed an unconfirmed report that the marchers were wearing their shrouds, and raised the number to 4,000.[48] They were mourners who had gathered at a shrine in the hill village of Pishva to hold the Ashura mourning ceremonies and been incensed by news, relayed over the shrine loudspeaker, of the arrest of Khomeini and the other clergy. They overran the village police post, and reinforced from Varamin, were on the march to Tehran, when they came upon lines of Gendar-merie at about 11 a.m. where the road crossed the Tehran-Mashhad railway at Baqerabad. They pressed forward, falling on the Gendarmes, who opened fire, killing an unknown number.[49]

Khomeini always said that some 15,000 had lost their lives in the uprising of 1963.[50] That implies that five times as many people were killed in three days as in the four hundred days of the Revolution of 1978–79. Prime Minister Alam put the number of dead at 94 and Mohammed Reza, in exile in Nassau in 1979, at 110.[51] The new Brit-ish ambassador, Sir Denis Wright, who had served through the vio-lent uprising against Haile Selassie's government in Addis Ababa in December 1960, thought casualties were not high.[52] The U.S. Embassy reported that the uprising was suppressed with ease. After eleven days of strike, the Tehran bazaar reopened. Those old advisers who had met at Hosein Ala's house on June 5 and advised caution on the Shah, such as Ala himself, ex-Prime Minister Jafar Sharif-Emami, and Abdullah Entezam, head of the oil company, were disgraced.

Defeated on the streets, the clergy migrated in a body to Tehran to sue for the release of their colleagues. In the shrine of Shah Abdolazim, Shariatmadari sat weeping under a mulberry tree. At a meeting of clergy in the northern suburbs, at Golhak, Montazeri presented a telegram he had drafted to Khomeini, styling his teacher "Grand Ayatollah and Great Source of Imitation." When somebody objected that Khomeini was nothing of the sort, and anyway who were his imitators, Montazeri shot back: "I am."[53] Fearing that unless he were granted that title and placed beyond the law, Khomeini might be held indefinitely or sent into exile, a number of leading clergymen (including Shariatmadari) submitted to his elevation.

Khomeini was not mistreated. After three weeks, he was moved to Eshratabad, one of Nassereddin Shah Qajar's pleasure palaces that had been turned into a barracks, where he was given a small house with a courtyard and pond. Without compromising his stand, Khomeini modified his language. In early July 1963, Hassan Pakravan, who had replaced the disgraced Teymour Bakhtiar as head of Savak, persuaded Mohammed Reza to release him:[54] first to a Savak house, then, when that was overwhelmed by visitors, to a house owned by a pious Isfahan merchant who had good relations with both Pakravan and the clergy. When a pair of clergymen sympathetic to the court called on him, with a greeting from Mohammed Reza, Khomeini replied: "I hate the Shah. I hate the Shah. I hate the Shah."[55] The courteous Pakravan visited and said: "Sir, you are a gentleman, a Source of Imitation, a notable, a clergyman. Why not leave politics to us? Politics is villainy, lies and hypocrisy. Don't let yourself be sullied by it." Khomeini replied: "Of course, if politics is as you say, it is your affair and I have no part in it. But if it is a matter of the public administration and the people's business, then of course Islam has something to say."[56] Pakravan came away from their weekly lunches baffled by Khomeini's secrecy and shaken by his ambition. "You know, it made my hair stand on my head."[57] (As well it might, for it was his sentence of death.)

On March 7, 1964, Mohammed Reza appointed a new prime minister, Hassan Ali Mansur. Having had no part in the events of June 1963, Mansur felt confident enough to mollify the clergy. On April 7, 1964, ten months after his arrest and at a safe interval from the month of Moharram, Khomeini returned in state to Qom. A tank battalion was deployed on the outskirts of the city as a precautionary measure.[58] Beholden to the conservative clergy for his release, Khomeini made a show of deference to Ayatollahs Shariatmadari and Golpayegani, while searching for a new cause to which he could rally both his own battered forces and the modern classes such as the secular nationalists, headless since Mossadeq was sent into internal exile, and the left. The issue was not hard to find.

Back in March 1962, the U.S. government had proposed that the growing number of U.S. soldiers and civilians in Iran and their dependents should have the diplomatic privileges and immunities specified for "members of the administrative and technical staff" in the Vienna Convention on Diplomatic Relations of 1961.[59] Mohammed Reza, exhilarated by the early success of Land Reform and anxious to win American support for his military projects, including a $200 million loan, agreed. While to the United States this was a routine "Status of Forces" arrangement, such as was already in force in the NATO countries, Japan, and South Korea, it summoned up in Iran the ghosts of Turkmanchay and the so-called Capitulations or judicial immunities for foreigners that Reza Pahlavi had abolished in 1928, it was supposed, for all time.

The "Status" bill, introduced in the summer of 1964, passed the lower house on October 13 with a majority of only thirteen. Mansur's New Iran Party mutinied, with many deputies absenting themselves or voting against the bill. It did not help that on the day before, a U.S. serviceman had badly injured a taxi driver in a motor accident. In riotous scenes in the chamber, one speaker claimed (as the U.S. Embassy cabled Washington) that "an American noncom could henceforth slap the face of an Iranian general with impunity." The embassy reported that "not only Mansur but to some extent also the Shah's regime has paid an unexpectedly high price in getting this done."[60]

On the morning of October 27, which coincided with the birthday of the Prophet's daughter Fatemeh, a large crowd gathered at Khomeini's house to hear his sermon. Stepping outside, Khomeini turned what was traditionally a celebration into an act of mourning. He began: "Our dignity has been trampled underfoot. The dignity of the Iranian army has been trampled underfoot. . . . If some American's servant, some

American's cook, assassinates your *marja* in the middle of the bazaar, or crushes him underfoot, the Iranian police may not arrest him . . . [61] If someone runs over a dog belonging to an American, he will be prosecuted. Even if the Shah himself were to run over a dog belonging to an American, he would be prosecuted. But if an American's cook runs over the Shah, the head of state, no one will have the right to interfere with him." [62]

What could protect Iran from humiliation, when Parliament and the "wretch" Mansur were so heedless of the country's honor? "If there were five *mojtaheds* in the Parliament, or even one single clergyman, he would punch the deputies in the mouth. He would not allow this bill to be enacted. He would smash Parliament up."

Khomeini at last had the enemy he needed, and it was not Mohammed Reza (whom he did not name), nor Parliament, nor Prime Minister Mansur, nor Britain, nor the Jews, nor Bahais, but the United States. "Let the American President know that in the eyes of the Iranian people, he is the most repellent member of the human race." When, on November 4, Khomeini was arrested, driven to Tehran, and placed on one of the new Iranian air force C-130 Hercules transport aircraft to Ankara in Turkey, the U.S. Embassy in Tehran fretted that Iranians would think that it was not for treason but for opposition to the Status bill and the $200 million loan that Khomeini had been exiled.[63] As it turned out, Khomeini's expulsion passed without incident.

Khomeini was lodged in a hotel in Ankara, and then moved to Bursa, an old-fashioned silk-weaving town which had opposed Atatürk, to stay with Colonel Ali Cetiner, an officer in Turkish Military Intelligence. On his first evening, he refused to sit down with the lady of the house and hissed in bad Turkish at her daughter and made her cry. Madame Cetiner, though offended and hurt, concluded that it was all for show, and indeed, once the escort officers had left, Khomeini softened his manners and invited the ladies to come back and sit down at their own table.[64] In Melahat Cetiner Khomeini saw, at close quarters, probably for the first time, a Muslim woman who was both unveiled and chaste, and that may have altered his thinking on the rights and duties of women. Banned under Turkish law from wearing his clerical dress, he was at first reluctant to go out, or to be photographed in his civilian clothes.

Khomeini made adjustments. He became fond of the Cetiners, and they of him. He attended to his table manners. He paddled in the Sea of Marmara, wearing a towel.[65] His work from exile shows expanded horizons. In his ample leisure, he picked up his old wartime notes on another work of casuistry, written by a venerable Najaf clergyman who had been expelled by the British in 1923, Abol Hassan Isfahani (he died in 1946), and expanded them into a long commentary in Arabic comprising 4,397 answers. In this work, *Edition of the "Way,"* Khomeini gives opinions on such innovations as insurance, banking, lotteries, artificial insemination, anatomical dissection, sex-change operations, space travel, and marriage with extraterrestrials.[66] He remained busy with visitors from Iran and inundated with donations. Whether sincerely or as tactical dissimulation, he told a visitor he had become tired of the "rough and tumble" of his life, and tried to have his son Mostafa admitted back to Iran on parole.[67]

Turkey was not inclined to accommodate Mohammed Reza forever. Khomeini himself, though he seems to have kept his feelings about Kemal Pasha private, regarded Atatürk's Turkey as a land of infidels and would not permit his wife to join him. In the end, it suited all three parties that Khomeini should move to the shrines in Iraq, and on October 5, 1965, he flew with Mostafa to Baghdad. There was nobody to meet them at Baghdad Airport and so, after waiting some time in the terminal, they took a taxi to the Shia shrine of Kazemain, in the western suburbs of the city. Khomeini haggled over the fare. They roomed in a pilgrims' boardinghouse.[68]

By the next day, word of his arrival had spread, and students and clergy came out to greet him as he traveled to the holy places of Samarra and Karbala. He arrived in state in Najaf on October 14, 1965. For the next five years, Khomeini was occupied with settling into the seminary, which was as riddled with clerical politics as Qom, and under as much pressure from the government, which though secular in profession drew its chief support from the Sunni or orthodox minority in Iraq. At a long and delicate meeting on October 18, he was quite unable to win over the most senior scholar, Ayatollah Mohsen al-Hakim, to militancy or convince him that Mohammed Reza was a heretic who had to be fought.[69] He himself had to fend off the approaches of the Iraqi Baath government, which came to power in 1968 and thought to make use of

him in a long-standing border quarrel with Iran. Savak placed inform-
ers in his household.[70] His success in this period was to forge relations
with dissident Iranian students in Europe and North America, including a group of four who were to help establish the Islamic Republic in
1978–79: Abol Hassan Bani-Sadr, a perpetual student in Paris who was
the son of a millionaire clergyman of Hamadan; Ebrahim Yazdi, a surgeon in the United States; Sadeq Qotbzadeh; and Mostafa Chamran.
The first three were later to manage his exile in France, while Chamran
established contact with armed groups in Lebanon. Khomeini's failure
was to acquire any influence with the Iraqi public, even its Shia majority, and that was to prove near fatal to his revolution in the 1980s.

From a modern vantage, Khomeini's uprising of 1963–64 appears
doomed as premature. At the time, it was felt to be belated and that Iranian society had run away from a clergy still rooted in the nineteenth
century and Constitutional era. From 1964, the Iranian economy again
began to expand, this time at annual rates of about 8–9 percent. Such
rapid growth, familiar from China and India in the first years of the
twenty-first century, was at that time matched only in Japan and the
Far East. Every other sort of vital statistic beloved of economists—birth
rates, death rates, the eating of butchers' meat (which doubled between
1960 and 1975),[71] automobile production and ownership, cement, steel,
power generation, house building, hospital beds, schools and universities—showed an improvement in the material conditions of Iranian
life. The population rose from 19 million at the first national census in
1956 to 30 million by 1970. Long before the quadrupling of crude oil
prices in 1973–74, Iran was seen as a paragon of successful development under authoritarian government.

On January 21, 1965, the revived Fedayan assassinated Prime Minister Mansur at the entrance to Parliament. One of the Luger Para-
bellum revolvers used was traced to Hashemi Rafsanjani, and he and
other of Khomeini's disciples saw the inside of Mohammed Reza's jails
or were banished to uncomfortable desert towns. By the time I arrived
in Iran in the early 1970s, Khomeini was described to me as a sincere
old man, who had taken on the ruling power when it was not so strong,
and suffered defeat.

CHAPTER 5

Ruritania

◆

Kingship lasts but a moment, so enjoy it.
—Eskandar Beg Munshi[1]

On the morning of April 10, 1965, just after 9 a.m., as Mohammed Reza was mounting the steps of the Marble Palace to enter his office, a member of the Imperial Guard, Reza Shamsabadi, opened fire with his submachine gun. The Shah, showing the same presence of mind as in 1949, took refuge in a pantry. Shamsabadi, who had been groomed by the *fedayan-e Islam* ("Devotees of Islam"), was killed by two other Imperial Guardsmen, at the cost of their lives. As a result of the attempt, and on the advice of SIS among others, Mohammed Reza moved from the cramped Private Palace (which had just two bedrooms) and the midtown traffic to the safer and quieter north of the city.

The new palace, which had been built for state guests, stood at about 6,000 feet of altitude at a place called Niavaran, where the Qajars had built a multitude of garden pavilions and summer retreats. A tall white cube behind a portico of tubular columns designed by Abdolaziz Farmanfarmaian but not especially well built, it boasted an entrance hall to the roof as an echo of the *talar* of ancient Iranian palace architecture. Its glory was (and is) a park of old pine and Oriental plane trees, but they could not ventilate the summer heat coming up from the town below, and the royal family continued to use the compound at Saadabad, which the queen disliked.

With the help of the Parisian decorators Mercier Frères and the American Charles Sevigny, the queen did up the main public rooms at Niavaran in the grand French style, while the private apartments, such as her library and a cinema for Mohammed Reza's favorite film shows, gave rein to her thrift and modernism. In the park, a pavilion built by Ahmad Shah Qajar, decorated with mosaic mirrorwork and known as the Jahan Nama ("Mirror of the World"), was converted by Maison Jansen into an office for Mohammed Reza, grander than the Kennedys' rooms at the White House in Washington but more businesslike. It was from there, twelve years later, that Mohammed Reza saw his capital city burn.[2]

The consequences of the move north cannot be exaggerated. Never at ease among his subjects, Mohammed Reza was now isolated from them. Soon he was traveling even to Saadabad by helicopter (and Alam, now minister of court, vetted every house beneath the flight path). He attended military reviews in a bulletproof vest. Yet he continued to believe he was popular. "The Iranian people love me," he told Alam, "and will stay by me."[3]

His family life prospered. Farah produced three more children, whose sad lives all began well: Farahnaz, born March 12, 1963; Ali-Reza (April 28, 1966); and Leila (March 27, 1970). She also brought peace and even a little elegance to the drab and rackety Pahlavi court. She won over the queen mother, whom she called *Maman*. Princess Shams and Princess Ashraf were now rich in their own right from the rise in value of the lands left them by Reza.[4] Shams, who had remarried and secretly converted to Roman Catholicism, moved out of town, to a palace built in 1966 by the Frank Lloyd Wright Foundation near Karaj (now in a ruinous state). Ashraf pursued her ambitions abroad, seeking at one stage to be elected secretary-general of the United Nations. In private, Mohammed Reza made fun of his twin's pretensions but he indulged, sometimes with bad grace, her extravagance, questionable company, and the avarice she had inherited from her father.

Court life was a round of stiff family dinners and bridge games in the compound at Saadabad, twice a week at the queen mother's, twice a week at Ashraf's. To vary the monotony, Mohammed Reza continued to conduct love affairs or what he called *gardeshha* (diversions or strolls). After 1968, when the court moved in winter to ski at St. Moritz in Switzerland, he took care to pursue some of those affairs abroad. Many of his women were procured by Amir Houshang Daval-lou, a Qajar prince with a weakness for opium who went by the court nickname "Prince Pimp."[5] Davallou used a network in Paris managed by Fernande Grudet, who traded under the name "Madame Claude." There was competition both to remove and to supplant Davallou,[6] and a rival once tipped off the police at Zurich Airport that he was carrying a small supply of opium.[7] Minou Reeves, a secretary in the Iranian Embassy in Berne, describes seeing in the bar of the Hôtel Suvretta House at St. Moritz a swarm of Iranian men buzzing round a pretty woman at a window table. They were the Iranian ambassador to Switzerland; Asadollah Alam; Ardeshir Zahedi, now foreign minister; and old Dr. Ayadi. The woman was the actress Brigitte Bardot.[8]

Mohammed Reza's womanizing put the court at sixes and sevens, and elevated Alam and Princess Ashraf, who connived in his affairs, over Amir Abbas Hoveyda, his prime minister, who was known to be cold in matters of the heart. The Shah's infidelities made for tension with Farah, the most levelheaded of his circle, while her relations (including her mother), as the price of their silence, felt licensed to spend money like water.[9]

In part as a result of state visits abroad (notably to the United Kingdom in 1959 and the United States in 1962), the Pahlavi court became more formal and stiff. In September 1965, to mark the start of Mohammed Reza's twenty-fifth year on the throne, Parliament granted him the title "Aryamehr," a neologism intended to mean "Light of the Aryans." A remnant of the European racial theories of the early twentieth century, the title meant nothing to most Iranians. Photographs of the royal family proliferated in shops and factories and in the newspapers.

Two years later, Mohammed Reza felt confident enough, and his country rich enough, to stage a ceremonial. On October 26, 1967, which was his forty-eighth birthday, at the Golestan Palace, Mohammed Reza was at last crowned Shah. Delayed twenty-six years because, as Mohammed Reza himself said back in 1951, "being king over a distressed, indigent and unhealthy set of people is no honour,"[10] the ceremony resembled to the last detail the coronation of his father back in 1926. General Morteza Yazdanpanah, who had marched with Reza on Tehran in 1921 and was one of the few survivors with Mohammed Reza of the first Pahlavi coronation, was the grizzled master of ceremonies. Once again, a six-year-old crown prince in general's uniform entered the Museum. Once again, the regalia were carried in procession. Once again, the Shah placed on his own head the Pahlavi crown. The difference this time was that Farah kneeled before the Shah, who placed on her head a new crown. The Shah said: "At this time that I wear the crown of the world's oldest monarchy, so for the first time in history a Queen of Iran is also crowned."[11] The word he used for "Queen" was the neologism *shahbanu* or "king-lady."

The malleable Constitution had been altered that August so that, should the Shah die before the crown prince came of age, Farah would act as regent. The queen's coronation was presented as an emancipation of Iranian women. It was a ceremonial counterpart of the Family Protection Act that had passed through Parliament in April and gave married women certain rights in family courts, long established in the West but a novelty in Iran, such as the right to sue for divorce and retain custody of their children.

The ceremony lasted barely half an hour. From exile in Iraq, Khomeini criticized the waste of public property in the "festivities,"[12] but the newsreels do not suggest there was any great outlay. Two glass coaches were built in Vienna, and their teams brought from Hungary. A white silk dress and ermine-lined train were designed for the empress by Marc Bohan of Dior but made at the Officers' Club in Tehran, the only place with tables large enough to spread out the train for the seamstresses.[13] Farah's platinum crown with its emerald green cap was made by Pierre Arpels from loose emeralds, spinels, pearls, rubies, and diamonds in the vaults of the Central Bank.[14] Food for two state dinners was brought from Paris. Impulsive as ever, Mohammed Reza had given just six months' notice to the British and other European royal families, and they all pleaded other engagements. The coronation was a purely domestic affair and cost about £1 million in the money of the time.[15]

Mohammed Reza's government now had a Janus- or two-faced character. There was a public or constitutional face, with a prime minister, cabinet, bicameral Parliament, and a couple of political parties in the American style, specialized ministries, provincial governors, courts of law, and a loyal press. Then there was the covert or unconstitutional face, consisting of Savak and other intelligence services, the armed forces, military tribunals, and the Pahlavi Foundation and other business interests of the court. At the top of both stood the Special Office of the Shah. Each department of state (whether public or secret) was managed as a separate room, with no interconnecting passage but the Shah himself. "I am a great believer in a plurality of administrative channels," he said in *Mission for My Country*.[16] It was an understatement.

Both success and failure brought dismissal. Abolhasan Ebtehaj, the head of the Plan and Budget Organization and a man of such vigor and grasp that a Bank of England official once commented, "I should hope there are not many more intelligent" people in Iran,[17] had been removed in 1959. Hassan Arsanjani, the architect of the Land Reform bills, was packed off in 1963 as ambassador to Italy. The mild and literary Hassan Pakravan was replaced at Savak by the man who had crushed the 1963 riots, General Nassiri. Unlike the nineteenth-century Qajars (or his father), Mohammed Reza did not kill his disgraced favorites. (The exception was Teymour Bakhtiar, who established himself in Iraq, and was killed by Savak there in August 1970.)

After Mansur's assassination, Mohammed Reza appointed as prime minister Amir Abbas Hoveyda. Born into the petty nobility the same year as the Shah, he spent almost all his childhood and youth in Damascus and Beirut, where his father was Iranian envoy. Fluent in French, English, Arabic, and German, he was (like his master) not confident of his literary Persian. His grandfather had leaned toward the Bahais, and that was always held against Amir Abbas. After taking a degree in political science in Brussels during World War II, Hoveyda joined the Iranian Foreign Service and was fortunate to be abroad (with the United Nations in Geneva) during the crisis of 1951–53. He then worked at the National Iranian Oil Company, where he gained a reputation as a capable manager, and later formed with Mansur a circle of modernizing intellectuals, known as the Progressive Circle and later the New Iran Party. He served as finance minister in Mansur's government. A dandy of Mediterranean style, he took two hours each morning to dress.

According to his biographer, Hoveyda believed, like many of the new men who came to the fore after 1963, that the Shah needed them and that the technical demands of modern government would require him to seek support throughout society.[18] If so, Hoveyda was deceived, and his liberalism gave way to an irritable cynicism that, by the time

I was in Iran, had seeped into the higher bureaucracy, foreign service, and press. Yet Hoveyda was just one center of subsidiary power. Alam (who once described his rival as "the Hunchback of Notre Dame")[19] was intent on building up the Ministry of Court as a shadow government. He had also begun to keep a daily journal which, published after the Revolution, casts flashes of light on Mohammed Reza's habits and conversation. Ashraf and Farah promoted their own favorites.

Foreign relations and military affairs Mohammed Reza kept in his own hands. With the country pacified and the Soviet threat in abeyance, Mohammed Reza now saw his principal enemies in Egypt and Iraq, with their modern Soviet military equipment and strident nationalist ideologies. Israel, which had since the early 1950s maintained a discreet representation in Tehran under trade cover, pressed Mohammed Reza to establish full diplomatic relations. He demurred but accepted a mission to Savak from Mossad, the Israeli security service. It was a relationship, as a British official noted in 1963, that "gives each [party] some respite from their sense of isolation."[20] Later, Mohammed Reza was impressed by the performance of the Israeli air and ground forces in the Six-Day War in 1967, and delighted to see Egypt's Abdel Nasser humbled.[21] During the 1973 Arab-Israeli War, when the speaker of Parliament called for solidarity with Iran's Muslim brethren, Mohammed Reza hissed in his ear: " 'Muslim brethren!' They're our greatest enemies!"[22]

The Democratic administration of President John F. Kennedy had little sympathy for Mohammed Reza's fears of republican Iraq, and during the Shah's State visit of April 1962 the president told him that future U.S. aid would be directed to civilian projects and development. For Kennedy, the Shah's military was already too large for border incidents and internal security but still of no use in an all-out conflict. As one of his White House intimates wrote, "His army . . . resembled the proverbial man who was too heavy to do any light work and too light to do any heavy work."[23]

Kennedy's successor, Lyndon B. Johnson, was more sympathetic, and agreed in 1964 to provide credits to buy U.S. weaponry, at first for $200 million, and then after 1966 at $100 million a year at 7.25 percent a year interest. The memorandum of understanding, which coincided with Khomeini's banishment and the Status of Forces Agreement, made the worst possible impression on Iranian public opinion. Since Iran was now creditworthy, the Military Assistance Program was wound down. By 1971, Iran had received more in American weaponry (about $1.4 billion at the prices of the time) than any developing country other than South Vietnam, South Korea, Taiwan, and Turkey.[24]

To mollify the Soviet Union, and to maintain pressure on the Americans, in January 1967 in Moscow Mohammed Reza signed the first of seven agreements with the Soviet Union to purchase arms in return for gas piped from Khuzestan. The equipment—consisting of bread-and-butter military vehicles, antiaircraft artillery, field guns, and RPG-7 antitank rocket launchers—did not require any Soviet technical assistance or the armies of advisers that were established in Egypt, Syria, and Iraq. Savak had enough to do keeping an eye on the foreign technicians at a Soviet-supplied steelworks in Isfahan. Mohammed Reza also bought weaponry on easy terms from Britain, including Hovercraft and other vessels for use in the shallow waters of the Persian Gulf, a missile air-defense system called Rapier, and, in 1971, the most advanced tank in the British armory, the Chieftain.

Developed over the 1960s from the Centurion of World War II, the Chieftain had a low profile, a 120mm howitzer, and advanced ceramic armor, but was for its weight underpowered. For all his misgivings about its engine, nonetheless Mohammed Reza ordered 770 Chieftain tanks and other vehicles on the same chassis in May and June 1971 at a cost of $350 million. The deal was negotiated by Shapoor or Shapour Reporter, the son of an old Zoroastrian newswriter at the British legation. Reporter was nominally a British citizen and a British secret agent, but Sir Denis Wright, by then UK ambassador in Tehran, always thought Reporter was working for Mohammed Reza as well as, naturally, himself.[25] Reporter demanded and received from the British a knighthood and a cut of 1 percent (later 1.5 percent), some or all of which he passed on to Mohammed Reza's Pahlavi Foundation.[26] A second order of 1,450 tanks of an improved version, to be known as Shir Iran (Lion of Iran), would have raised Iran's armored forces beyond those of Britain and given the Shah control of a British manufacturing industry and service. The Revolution intervened before delivery. Marooned on the Tehran boulevards in 1978, the Chieftains became symbols of the Iranian army's musclebound impotence.

Mohammed Reza himself made the purchasing decisions, which were carried out by a procurement department under an air force officer, Hassan Toufanian, and what U.S. officials called "the air force mafia." It was said that the Shah read *Aviation Week* before opening the Iranian newspapers.[27] He astonished Wright's successor as British ambassador, Sir Peter Ramsbotham, by turning to him and asking: "What is the sprocket horsepower of the Chieftain tank, Ambassador?"[28] Mohammed Reza took decisions, the U.S. military noted, that in other armies might be safely left to a lieutenant colonel or colonel.[29] His service commanders reported to him separately, and his minister of war had only routine responsibilities. He ensured that only loyal mediocrities rose to high command. In 1969, he retired all his senior naval commanders.

The overextended British in 1968 announced that by 1971 they would withdraw back to the European theater all their forces "east of Suez," and Mohammed Reza saw a vacuum that Iran—and Iran alone—must fill. Arab nationalism had been weakened by the Israeli defeat of the armies of Egypt, Syria, and Jordan in the Six-Day War of June 1967. In Washington, Richard M. Nixon, who as Eisenhower's vice president had first met Mohammed Reza in December 1953 and, unusually for an American at that period, formed a good impression of him, was elected president of the United States.[30] Nixon and his advisers were at work at what became known that summer as the "Nixon Doctrine," by which the United States, tied down in Vietnam, rather than spread itself ever more thinly would reinforce and supply regional anti-Soviet champions. At the end of March 1969, Mohammed Reza flew to Washington for Eisenhower's funeral and had a long meeting with Nixon at the White House on April 2. Sensing an opportunity, on April 19, Mohammed Reza had Parliament abrogate the old treaty regulating the border with Iraq along the Shatt al-Arab River at the head of the Gulf, which because it ran for much of its way along the Iranian shore he held to be prejudicial to Iranian shipping. He then suborned disaffected Iraqi officers to stage a coup, which was betrayed on January 21, 1970, and caused the Baath to expel the Iranian ambassador.[31]

The Iranian ground forces—which a few years before could barely control internal insurrection and used pack animals and second-hand World War II vehicles and tanks—now consisted of mechanized infantry divisions, the nucleus of an armored force to be based on the Chieftain, more than 1,000 artillery pieces, a transport arm operating Hercules C-130 aircraft, the makings of a combat helicopter park, an air-defense battalion with Hawk missiles, and a household division on the British pattern. Known as the Imperial Guard, it included an elite brigade known as the Immortals or *javidan*, with its headquarters near Niavaran.

The navy, a force of just 1,000 men at the beginning of the 1960s, now had a shallow water fleet of corvettes, Hovercraft, and coastal minesweepers, and had ordered four British destroyer escorts with Seacat antiship missiles. The muddy inlets on the Shatt al-Arab could not accommodate them, and a new base was being built at Bandar Abbas at the mouth of the Persian Gulf.

But the air force was Mohammed Reza's delight. Under Mohammed Khatami, Mohammed Reza's pilot in the flight from Kelardasht in 1953 who was appointed commander in 1958, the Imperial Iranian Air Force went through a breakneck expansion. In the three years after 1965, the force doubled in size. Iran was the first and largest export customer for a supersonic U.S. jet fighter, the Northrop F-5E, receiving 92 aircraft under the grant program and ordering a further 48 on credit. Kermit Roosevelt, now operating in the arms trade, was Northrop's agent. As relations with Iraq deteriorated at the end of the 1960s, Mohammed Reza was permitted to order 32 McDonnell Douglas F-4 Phantom fighter-bombers, and then a further 105. Khatami expanded or built from the stony desert eight air force bases and ten radar stations.

By now, Mohammed Reza was spending about a third of Iran's revenue on the armed forces, or approximately 10 percent of national income from all sources, or gross domestic product. He was driven to seeking advances against oil sales of some $500 million a year from the Consortium oil companies. Iran was some $2 billion in debt to foreign creditors and had to find $204 million a year, or a fifth of its oil royalties, to cover payments of interest and principal.[32] "What can I do when there is no money coming in?" Mohammed Reza snapped one day in 1969 at Alam.[33] Yet he had no intention of letting up. "It is a matter of life or death," he said the following March. "I shall get the money for arms from somewhere or other, even if it means our going hungry."[34]

That was not required.

The tide in the oil market was turning toward the producers. The creation in 1960 of the producers' cartel, the Organization of Petroleum Exporting Countries (OPEC), and the peak in U.S. domestic oil production in 1970 were milestones in the shift to a seller's market. Meanwhile, the decline in the value of the U.S. dollar, which was inflated to finance the war in Indochina, reduced the value to the producers of a commodity billed in dollars. In the first week of February 1971, representatives from the OPEC countries met with those from the oil companies in Tehran to discuss compensation. While Jamshid Amouzegar, the finance minister, handled the negotiations, Mohammed Reza insisted on a hard line. He had lost his fear of the companies, and when Sir Denis Wright (by way of Alam) "strongly advised" caution, the Shah burst out: "I'll fuck his mother so rigid, he'll never advise anybody again."[35]

The result, which was announced on the afternoon of February 14, "broke the global power of the oil industry."[36] The oil companies conceded a 30-cent increase in the price paid per barrel of crude oil from the Persian Gulf basin, rising in five years to 50 cents. With Iranian production also on the increase, the effect of the Tehran Oil-Price Agreement was to double Iran's oil revenue for that year from $1.12 billion to $2.39 billion.[37] The Fourth Development Plan (1968–72), languishing for lack of funds, was revived. Amouzegar received a decoration, and wept. (Characteristically, Mohammed Reza soon demoted him to the Interior Ministry.)

As he set off for St. Moritz by Iran Air charter on February 16, Mohammed Reza was elated. "Presto!" he said to Alam. "The oil problem solved, rain for our crops and Iran's leadership of the whole Middle East acknowledged throughout the world." True to character, he saw the hand of Providence: "I have learned by experience that a tragic end awaits anyone who crosses me. At home or abroad. Take the Kennedy brothers. Nasser and Khrushchev. And at home, Mossadeq. To an extent Qavam. Razmara, who had ill intentions, even Mansur, who was an agent of the Americans and ambitious to the hilt."[38] Now the oil companies were suffering the revenge of Ali and Fatemeh, for presuming to cross their darling. In April, Sir Denis Wright, who had watched Mohammed Reza transformed from the uncertain young man of 1954, wrote a farewell dispatch to London suggesting that "overconfidence" was now the greatest threat to Pahlavi rule.[39] In October, Mohammed Reza staged a pageant at the ancient ruins of Persepolis that came to symbolize his rule.

The celebrations of 2,500 years of Iranian monarchy, held between October 12 and 16, 1971, brought together, as in a cartoon or sketch, the principal themes of the Pahlavi style.

The first was Mohammed Reza's loyalty to monarchy as a form of government. Since coming to the throne, he had seen the ruling houses of Italy (1946), Egypt (1952), Iraq (1958), Greece (1967), and Libya (1969) come to grief, while the previous September the throne of Hussein of Jordan had barely survived an insurrection by the Palestinian population. Islanded in a republican ocean, the Shah was profuse with subsidies or business introductions to the exiled royal families of Italy, Greece, Bulgaria, Egypt, and, after 1973, Afghanistan, and also the ruling houses of Morocco, Jordan, Spain, and the Netherlands.[40] Asadollah Alam's diaries show that Mohammed Reza had no illusions about the virtues of such men as Constantine of Greece. As in the military, it was the commission he saluted, not the officer: the rank, not the man.

The second was the doctrine, sketched out by Mohammed Ali Foroughi at his speech at Reza's coronation in 1926, that it was monarchy rather than the Shia sect of Islam that was the distinctive strength of Iran. Mohammed Reza once said, "Iran's continued existence and its national sovereignty are made possible by the continuation of monarchy."[41] He was "the heir and guardian of a crown and throne of 2,500 years."[42] In a jumble of antiquarian ideas, touched by the traces of a European racialism, it was Iran's ancient dynasties (the Achaemenian, Arsacid, and Sassanian) that revealed the true character of the country, not an alien and Arab Islam.[43] Of the Muslim kings, only the great conqueror, Nader, was honored with a public statue. The ideology took its most lasting form in the Shahyad ("King-Memorial") Monument, designed after a competition by a young architect from a Bahai family, Hossein Amanat, on the freeway into town from Mehrabad Airport. A versatile piece of concrete and marble, the Shahyad later came to symbolize the Revolution; and then, thirty years after that, in 2009, revolt against it.

Although such native history had been taught in Iranian schools since they were built by Reza in the 1920s, few Iranians had much grasp

of the ancient past or much interest in it. Since its excavation by Herz-
feld and Schmidt in the 1930s, the ancient citadel of Parsa (Persepolis
to the Greeks) and its famous Apadana and Hall of a Hundred Columns had been imitated in such buildings as the National Bank, police
headquarters, and Qasr Prison in Tehran, and every type of handicraft,
piece of metalwork, or carpet. Yet for many Iranians, Persepolis was
less the capital of Darius burned by Alexander the Great in 330 BC than
the seat of an Iranian King Arthur, the mythical king Jamshid, who
subdued the demon races.[44] The place was universally known as "the
throne of Jamshid" (*takht-e jamshid*). For the clergy, including Khomeini, the place was tainted with the ancient religion of Iran, Zoroas-
trianism, that Islam had superseded.[45]

Above all, Mohammed Reza wanted his house to be accepted as equal
by the senior royal houses of Europe, especially the house of Windsor.
Like Nassereddin Shah Qajar's three trips to Europe in 1873, 1878,
and 1889, if incomparably less of a financial burden, Persepolis was
designed to establish Iran as a royal power.[46] Success would assuage the
injuries of a hard reign: the rudeness of Churchill and Bullard, Fauzia's
flight home, Maria Gabriella's turned back, and the boycott of the coronation of 1967. (At that time, the court was lobbying for Mohammed
Reza to be admitted, like Nassereddin Shah in 1873, as a knight companion of the senior British order of chivalry, the Garter.)[47]

The idea for a celebration of Iranian monarchy at its most famous
location had surfaced at the end of the 1950s, but had languished in a
committee and in desultory talks with Maison Jansen in Paris through
the unrest and tight budgets of the early 1960s. The coronation, which
at one time was to coincide with the celebration, came and went, taking
with it the 15 million tomans (about $2 million) accrued in the fund
for the celebrations.[48] By midsummer of 1970, the Shah had become
impatient and, in a tussle between the queen (who was nursing Leila)
and Alam for control, the *boulevardier* minister of court emerged
victorious.[49] Doubtful that Jansen could make ready a hotel suitable
for heads of state, on a visit to Paris Alam discussed with the firm the
idea of prefabricated chalets at the ruins. Draped in cloth, they would
have the appearance of some scene of medieval chivalry ("and all the
charm," as the *New York Times* later noted, "of motel rooms everywhere").[50] These were later brought from France to Shiraz in the holds

of Hercules C-130 military transports—at least one hundred flights—and then trucked, with a certain amount of breakage of the bathroom fittings, to Persepolis.[51]

Unwilling to believe that Iranians could cook or serve a banquet for at least thirty heads of state, Alam passed down the rue Royale to No. 6 to visit Maxim's, the Belle Epoque restaurant now somewhat past its best. In the end, either his ministry or the Maison d'Iran under Princess Ashraf's husband brought in the venerable *traiteur* (caterer) Potel et Chabot to supply waiters, Baccarat and Haviland for glass and porcelain, D. Porthault for table linen, the hairdressers Alexandre and the Carita sisters, and Jardineries Truffaut for the roses. There was to be a *son et lumière,* an undemanding historical entertainment that had become popular in France in the 1950s and was now outmoded. When the old court tailor in Sepah Avenue grumbled that he had not the cutters for thirty new civil uniforms for the adjutants, Alam turned to the Paris couture house of Lanvin.[52] The British, notorious in those days for their bad food and poor tables, were consulted on precedence.

On his return from Paris, on October 14, 1970, Alam staged a dry run for the queen's birthday on his ancestral estates at Birjand in the southeast, spending nearly $40,000 on two days of celebrations for the royal family. There were fifty tents and a dinner provided by Maxim's.

Spirits were high at the news of the death of Mohammed Reza's chief rival in the region, the Egyptian president Gamal Abdel Nasser, two weeks earlier. In the light of campfires, first the queen and then her children sprung up to dance with Alam's tenants. A week later, at dinner in Isfahan, when the queen mentioned that a newspaper article had criticized the £200 spent on her birthday cake, Mohammed Reza flew at her: "In Birjand, you wolfed that blasted cake, but as soon as a newspaper writes two words of balls, you come over all remorseful."[53] Even Alam, though he was envious of the queen, felt mortified. It was an omen of what was to come. Nonetheless, Mohammed Reza was horrified by Jansen's quotation for the banqueting tent, and had it reduced to a quarter of the size, and $1 million in cost.[54] Later, when the French menu became a point of contention, the Shah, who never noticed what he ate or where he sat, exclaimed: "What am I supposed to do, give them bread and radishes?"[55]

In the end, not thirty but some sixty-nine heads of state, consorts, or vice presidents accepted, including twenty kings or *emirs* led by one of the only two monarchs senior to Mohammed Reza, Haile Selassie of Ethiopia. Sixteen presidents accepted, including Nikolai Podgorny of the Soviet Union and Marshal Tito of Yugoslavia. Yet it was not as Mohammed Reza had hoped. Fearing that he, and therefore France, might be *mal placé* or seated below the salt, President Pompidou refused. Though he greatly admired Mohammed Reza, President Nixon sent his vice president, Spiro T. Agnew. Queen Juliana of the Netherlands made excuses.

As for Britain, Queen Elizabeth not only sent regrets for herself, on the grounds that she would be on a state visit to Turkey, but said the Prince of Wales could not break off his training in the Royal Navy. The Shah was furious, or as Ambassador Ramsbotham translated into diplomatic language, "a little grumpy."[56] Buckingham Palace insisted that "Her Majesty does not do jamborees," while the British Foreign Office was not inclined to accommodate the Shah because of certain "difficulties" he was making in the Gulf. In its retreat from empire, Britain was trying to disentangle itself from the Arab shore of the Persian Gulf in the face of Iranian claims to the island of Bahrain and three islets in the sea-lanes at the mouth of the Gulf. (At that time, the Shah was saying in private: "I'll take those bloody islands by force and the English and the Arabs can go to hell.")[57]

The Duke of Edinburgh accepted and, like an overgrown schoolboy, raced his aircraft down to Shiraz against Prince Bernhard of the Netherlands and King Hussein of Jordan. He was joined by his daughter, Princess Anne. The ceremonies, including a march past the monumental staircase of Persepolis of fourteen detachments of historical warriors, ending with the Imperial Guard and the literacy corps, passed without a hitch. A half-baked plan by the Islamic left to disrupt the celebrations, by dynamiting the power supply to Tehran, was foiled by Savak.

Instant ceremonial is laughable. The foreign press found Persepolis pompous, shallow, dictatorial, menacing, and *nouveau riche*. Critics questioned why Iran, in debt to foreign creditors to the tune of $2 billion and with a national income of just $500 per capita, should be spending such money. Khomeini called the gathering "a feast of bestial gluttony,"[58] and his break with monarchy as a form of government and, by extension, the Iranian Constitution, can be dated from this time. Abroad, the Confederation of Iranian Students, founded in 1960 in Heidelberg and by now as radical as any student group in the world, made hay. For the student left in Europe, as Marc Kravetz of *Libération* wrote, "Persepolis was where the aristocracy of the world and the jet-set came to flatter Farah Diba while the army cleared out rebellious villages with the machine-gun."[59] As to the Iranian public, who were not invited to attend but watched on television in black and white, they were baffled or indifferent, though Mohammed Reza's oath at the tomb of Cyrus the Great ("Rest in peace, for we are awake") was the subject of ribald comment.

Persepolis introduced an element of the fantastical into the Pahlavi style, as if some toy principality had gained a half-million-man army, or become, as the last British ambassador to the Pahlavi court, Sir Anthony Parsons, put it, "an amalgam of Ruritania and *1984*."[60] It was no better for the French enterprises, such as Maxim's or Jansen's, that never recovered from overtrading on their nonexistent capital or shook off what the world of fashion fears worse than death, which is ridicule. (Maison Jansen, which tried to market a low stool called *Pouf de Persepolis,* went out of business. Maxim's was sold.)

On the defensive, Alam said the celebrations had cost $16.6 million of which $6.3 million was spent on the tent city and $2.3 million on the entertainment. That may just have been the contribution from his ministry.[61] (He had about $1.5 million left over from his budget, which he tried to use to buy a house in town for the Shah—and himself—to take girls. Mohammed Reza, always careful with money, told him to rent and put the money toward a mosque.)[62] There would also have been more or less voluntary contributions from businessmen, from the oil company, and from other ministries for such things as the Shahyad Monument, the new Aryamehr Stadium, a program of school building, and a learned conference. Jansen's claimed that it built the tent city for no more than a luxury hotel at the ruins would have cost.[63]

The queen and her favorites, and Prime Minister Hoveyda, washed their hands of the event, and although Alam continued to call it a "great achievement,"[64] a plan to commemorate it each year lapsed in 1973. Mohammed Reza had other matters on his mind. On November 30, 1971, the day before the expiry of the old British treaties with the Arab

Trucial States, Iranian Hovercraft landed marines on the three islets at the mouth of the Persian Gulf, the Greater and Lesser Tunbs, and Abu Musa. For Ambassador Ramsbotham, the British exchanged "a rock with a few snakes and three Indians with a lighthouse"[65] for a political order on the Arab shore that has survived to this day. Mohammed Reza gave up a weak claim to Bahrain for the first extension of Iranian territory since Turkmanchay. The Arab states, and most particularly Iraq, were angered and alarmed.

CHAPTER 6

The Storm Gathers

◊

And if the Shah says day is night,
Say: "What a moon! And such starlight!"
                                        —Sadi[1]

The Iran I first knew in the 1970s was an uneasy country. It was as if Mohammed Reza's haste to force modernity on Iran was matched by a haste to demolish it, and the conflicts of centuries were being squeezed into half a dozen years.

On February 8, 1971, nine young men armed with light weapons attacked the Gendarmerie post at the village of Siahkal in the Alpine country of Gilan, northwest of Tehran. The assault, by a band of Marxist revolutionaries calling itself the *Jangal* or "Woodland" group, was at first sight a fiasco. With its echoes of the old Communist *Jangalis,* the action was both romantic and antiquarian. As if to confirm one revolutionary's warning that "we are not like fish in the sea, but rather like isolated fish surrounded by crocodiles," the local smallholders and orchard owners sided with the government, the insurgents were rounded up off the hillsides by helicopters, and on March 17, after a trial by military tribunal meeting in camera, thirteen young men were executed. On April 4, the head of Savak's Third Bureau, Parviz Sabeti, appeared on television to describe the operation.

The Siahkal attack caused panic in the radical Islamic Left, lest they be left behind by the secular Marxists. The People's Mojahedin—which had formed in the 1960s under the influence of Third World liberation movements and sought to revise the Shia in the light of international Marxism—decided to stage a series of attacks to coincide with the Persepolis celebrations that autumn, broke cover before they were prepared, and were rounded up by Savak. On May 25, 1972, its entire leadership was shot by firing squad.

Yet, in the hall of mirrors that is revolutionary politics, Siahkal was a success. It disturbed the political calm that had prevailed since the assassination of Prime Minister Mansur and the attempt on Mohammed Reza's life at the Marble Palace in 1965. It showed that for all the reach of Savak, it was possible to organize a clandestine revolutionary group in Iran as in Italy, or West Germany, or among the Irish émigrés in England. After Siahkal, a group calling itself the "Organization of Devoted Guerrillas of the Iranian People,"* or *Fedayan* for short, was formed from the survivors and other revolutionary intellectuals. (They had nothing in common with Navvab Safavi's Fedayan except the name.) Though the Fedayan suffered crippling losses, they could still muster a couple of hundred armed revolutionaries who were on hand at Tehran University, at the climax of the Revolution in February 1979, to do what little fighting there was to be done.

The principal Fedayan theorist, Bizhan Jazani (1937–1975), had been in jail since 1968, where he set an example to other prisoners by his fortitude. With the demolition of the Tudeh in the 1950s and the consolidation of Mohammed Reza's power in 1963, Jazani and others had convinced themselves that armed actions by a "revolutionary vanguard" would waken the phlegmatic Iranian masses to the tyranny of the regime. Siahkal persuaded many people, from Mohammed Reza to the foreign correspondents, that the principal threat to the Pahlavi regime came from this new brand of revolutionary Marxism. Jazani stands out among the failed revolutionaries of that era for his understanding of the religious sentiments of the Iranian "petite bourgeoisie" (bazaar) and Khomeini's potential as a popular and reactionary leader. A Cassandra, Jazani warned the Islamic Left that they were simply playing into the hands of the professional or turbanned clergy, and, like Cassandra, he was proved right.

Under the old revolutionary principle that if your enemy is not repressive, you make him so, Siahkal brought Savak to center stage, increasing its payroll, its standing with Mohammed Reza, its ambition,

---

* *Sazman-e charikhaye fedaiye khalq-e Iran.*

and its savagery. Whereas after 1963 the number of political prisoners had fallen "to a few hundred," according to Pakravan,[2] and certainly only a fraction of those in Egypt and Iraq, political detainees began to fill the new prisons built to replace the old practice of detention in military barracks. In the village of Evin, famous for its ancient walnut orchards, on the site of an estate that had belonged to Sayyid Zia Tabatabai, a U.S.-style jail was completed in 1971 to hold some 1,500 inmates. By the mid-1970s, Savak had filled Evin and new prisons in provincial towns with some 3,000 political prisoners, including such well-known writers as Hushang Golshiri and Gholamhossein Saedi. Savak interfered in the universities, the press, the post and telecommunications, the armed forces, factories, even the retail trade. It was, in the words of Mohammed Reza's last ambassador to London, Parviz Radji, a "state-within-a-state."[3]

For the survivors of a milder age, the new Savak was a disgrace. Fatemeh Pakravan, the head of nursing at the Mossadeq family's charitable hospital and wife of Hassan Pakravan, refused to sit down to dinner with her husband's protégé, Parviz Sabeti.[4] (Sabeti sneered that Hassan Pakravan "should have been a professor at some university.")[5] Mohammed Reza's childhood friend, Hosein Fardoust, who headed a coordination office at the palace called the Special Intelligence Bureau, complained that Savak's Third Bureau (for internal security) had no talent for countersubversion, preferring spectacular actions against accessible targets and the cultivation of a fearsome image.[6] Richard Savin, a British convict in the new prison at Vakilabad, near Mashhad, one day stumbled on the solitary confinement cells for the "politicals." He pulled back a hatch on one door. "It looked like nothing more than a concrete broom cupboard, rough cast, unfinished without windows or shelves or fittings of any kind. The victim stood or more correctly hung with both wrists chained to . . . rings high up on the wall so that his arms hung at full stretch and he looked like a life-sized effigy of the crucifixion."[7]

Abroad, the Confederation of Iranian Students convinced the non-Iranian leftists that Pahlavi Iran was as brutal as the white regime in South Africa or the military junta in Greece. Mohammed Reza's trips to western Europe and the United States were met with hostile demonstrations. On June 2, 1967, while Mohammed Reza was visiting the Western sector of Berlin, German and Iranian students fought with pro-monarchy demonstrators assembled by the Iranian Embassy in Bonn (contemptuously called *Jubelperser* or "Jubilation Iranians"). A police officer shot dead a German student. By the mid-1970s, Savak officers at Iranian embassies abroad were attempting to infiltrate the Iranian students on the foreign campuses.[8] Young Westerners, traveling overland to Afghanistan and India, disliked Iran and brought back tales of the high cost of living, the agitated style of life in Tehran, and, if they were unfortunate enough to be busted for drugs at the frontier, the cement inferno of Vakilabad Prison. Both Mohammed Reza and Princess Ashraf were accused of trafficking in narcotics.[9]

At the universities in Iran, Siahkal inaugurated a period of permanent unrest. For Mohammed Reza, the universities were a conundrum. He saw well enough that they were the key to what he had come to call the "Great Civilization." If Iran was to modernize, to create industries capable of replacing imports and finding markets abroad, and to manage advanced steel furnaces and F-14 Tomcat jet interceptors, he needed college graduates of the first order and plenty of them. In addition to Tehran University, founded by his father Reza in 1934, there were now three other campuses in Tehran, as well as universities in Tabriz, Isfahan, Ahvaz, and Shiraz, and over 100,000 undergraduate students. Another 60,000 were studying abroad.

Yet Mohammed Reza, like many men of his generation, disliked the modern student with his long hair and international poses, and feared the campus as a center of opposition. (When the Paris-based artist Charles Hossein Zenderoudi returned to Tehran for an exhibition in the early 1970s, he was stopped by the police and had his long hair hacked off. The queen erupted and the chief of police was sacked.)[10] By the time I was in Iran, the universities were places of misery, fortified like military barracks, where the best faculty felt themselves crushed between a morose student body and a crude security establishment. Waiting for hours in the scalding sun at the gates of Isfahan University, I felt Savak was an obstacle not just to liberty but to industry.

At a conference on education at Ramsar on September 8, 1973, attended by Mohammed Reza, Alam's deputy Mohammed Baheri submitted a 3,000-page report on higher education, and said that "despite their access to scholarships and other privileges, the university students are indifferent to the condition of their country." Since they were excluded from any say in national or even university affairs, Alam said to himself, what did anybody expect? The government behaved like an occupying power, indifferent to the wishes of the people and aggressively manipulating elections of every type. Was it any wonder that the public responded with indifference?[11]

In the course of the 1960s, new movements had come to birth at a distance from the turbanned clergy among men who, though coming from the religious classes, had adopted civilian clothes and thought not in categories of law but of romance and sentiment. The chief personalities of those movements were the writer Jalal Al-e Ahmad (1923–1969) and the sociologist Ali Shariati (1933–1977). Selecting ideas here and there from the puritan reformers of the interregnum period, and particularly Ahmad Kasravi, and the leftist currents in western Europe, Asia, and Latin America, they captured a generation of young men and women and, long after they could do anything about it, delivered them up to destruction by Khomeini and his movement.

For Al-e Ahmad, as for Kasravi, Iran was "sickened" by Western habits of thought and conduct, and had been since the beginning of the century and the execution of Fazlollah Nuri. In his most famous essay, *Sick from the West*, which saw the light in 1962, he wrote of Nuri: "I look on that great man's body on the gallows as the flag of victory of the Westernisers after two hundred years of struggle." [12] This work, with its hand-me-down theorizing and inky Persian, was set to Oxford University undergraduates. Khomeini was happy to take over Al-e Ahmad's anti-Western rhetoric and became fond of the term *gharbzadeh*, "sick from the West."

Shariati, who was born into a religious family in Khorasan, studied in Paris with the French expert on Islamic mysticism Louis Massignon and the sociologist George Gurvitch, and helped translate into Persian Frantz Fanon's *Les damnés de la terre* (*The Wretched of the Earth*). He received his doctorate from the Sorbonne and later, in the village of Mazinan in Khorasan, the villagers used to bring their sick children to "the Doctor" for treatment. Returning to Iran in 1964, he spent a period in jail before taking a teaching post at Mashhad University, where he attracted a large following while playing cat-and-mouse with the Savak station in Khorasan, the secular intellectuals, and the orthodox clergy. In 1969, his students collected his lectures under the title of *Islamshenasi* (*Islamology*). In this work, which is a sort of sociology of religion, Shariati combined the anticlericalism of Kasravi with the nativism of Fanon. Iran was essentially religious, but the Islam of the Prophet and the Imams—egalitarian, democratic, and free—had been captured since the Safavids by the ruling power and a self-absorbed religious establishment. The Shia clergy, he said, had become a closed monopoly, despotic, stifling, and petrified.[13]

Shariati's vision of the Shia Imams as precocious freedom fighters is true, if at all, only of Imam Hosein and is otherwise unhistorical.[14] What Shariati achieved was to devise a language for revolutionary left-ism without setting off in Muslim houses all the old alarm bells about common property and free love. A sort of Islamic Romance, which only rarely surfaces in Khomeini's writings, is everywhere. Disliking both polygamy and the veil, Shariati offered a vision of femininity—vigorous, loyal, chaste, and companionable—that entranced many Iranian women.

Savak was seeking at this time to use religious intellectuals such as Shariati against the secular left. Its principal officers, Parviz Sabeti and Nasser Moqaddam, decided after a series of interviews, in which Shariati baffled them with high-flown theory, that they could do nothing with him. In September 1971, Savak ordered the university to dismiss him.

Shariati's principal stage now became an extramural institute in Tehran known as the Hoseinieh Ershad, financed by a bazaar merchant in Golhak, the old fief of the British in the foothills of the Elburz. Whereas at the traditional Hoseinieh, the public sat on the floor to hear heartrending stories of the Passion of Hosein, the Third Imam, at the Ershad lecturers spoke from lecterns on points of theology to an audience seated on chairs. Shariati's Frenchified "Islamology" and anticlerical tone (and, no doubt, his popularity) offended the seminary-trained lecturers, such as Motahhari, who withdrew in April 1971 and left Shariati with the place almost to himself.

Under the shadow of Siahkal, and the execution of the Mojahedin leaders, Shariati acquired a large following among young people, with as many as 3,500 registering for a course of his lectures in 1971. He was beset on every side. Savak was willing to tolerate him but only so long, as Sabeti put it in an internal communication, as "he should speak against Marxism and materialism."[15]

The turbanned clergy and popular preachers were snapping at his heels, accusing him of deviation, innovation, Sunnism, an aspiration to Prophethood, and even that bugbear of the early twentieth century, *fokoliyeh* or "Europeanism." As always, sex raised its head. Preachers complained that the female auditors, though seated on a balcony away from the men, did not cover their hair or even, in some cases, their legs. (Once, when a man came up to him after a lecture to complain, Shariati exploded: "If she is wearing a mini-skirt, why the hell are you looking at her!")[16] Then there were the militant students. On May 26, 1972, the day after the Mojahedin leaders were executed, a woman interrupted Shariati's lecture, saying: "With your permission, Professor, the time has come for us to revolt, we can no longer remain subdued. Today, the worthiest children of Iran and the beloved Mojahedin of Islam are being killed one after the other . . ."[17] In exasperation, Shariati said afterwards: "What do you want me to do? Say the things you want me to say and have them close the place down."

Early in the morning of November 17, 1972, the Ershad and its half-built mosque were cordoned off by police. Shariati went into hiding but, after his father was arrested in the summer of 1973, gave himself up to Sabeti. On September 29, 1973, Shariati presented himself at the Komiteh Prison in Army Square. Situated behind the neo-Achaemenian facade of the Public Record Office, the Komiteh was a political prison operated by the Committee Against Sabotage, consisting of Savak, the police, and the armed forces. It was notorious for the mistreatment of inmates. Shariati was held in solitary confinement, but not subject to torture except, as he put it, in being obliged "to engage in scientific discussions and debates with General Zandipur [the Warden], whenever he enters my cell."[18]

While Shariati was in the Komiteh, the poet Khosrow Golesorkhi was put on trial for a nebulous plot to abduct the queen and crown prince at a festival of children's films.[19] His defense before a military court in January 1974 captures the intense atmosphere of that time and the mingling of Messianic Islam and Marxism. Opening his defense with a poem, Golesorkhi then declaimed: "*Verily, Life is belief and struggle!* I begin my statement with a saying of Master Hosein, the great martyr of the Middle Eastern proletariat. Though I am a Marxist-Leninist, I came to social justice through the teachings of Islam and [only] then came to socialism." He then embarked on a historical-materialist analysis of land tenure in Iran, and when reproved by the bench and invited to offer a defense, he sat down and did not speak again.[20] Golesorkhi was shot on February 18, 1974.

Although he disapproved of both armed struggle and the existentialist theorizing of Shariati, Khomeini resisted all calls from Iran that he excommunicate the Mojahedin and Shariati.[21] His principal response to the new challenges from the laity was a set of lectures at Najaf between January 21 and February 8, 1970, which sought to reestablish the primacy of the seminary-trained or turbanned clergy, and then took several steps forward. The boldest of those steps was the doctrine of clerical government or dictatorship, which was not present in his writings or conversation before his move to Iraq in 1965.[22]

In the lectures, entitled *Islamic Government: The Stewardship of the Jurist*, Khomeini asserted that it was the clergy, as heirs to the Prophet and the Imams, who must lead the Muslim community. Since the Koran, together with the Traditions of the Prophet and the Immaculate Ones, are all the law that is needed to govern even a modern state, the sole requirements for the ruler as deputy of the Hidden Imam are "knowledge of the law" and a just character. These two qualities are present in "countless Islamic jurists." They may rule collectively, or authority—and here the reader snaps to attention—may be vested in a single man. "If a worthy individual possessed of those two qualities establishes a government, then he will enjoy the same authority as God's Most Noble Prophet—Bless him!—in the administration of society and it will be the duty of all people to obey him."[23] Yet this would not happen at once, and Khomeini prepared his followers for what revolutionaries of the period used to call (after Mao) the Long March. As with the movement for Constitutional government at the turn of the century, the people had first to be awakened. "The first activity we must undertake is the propagation of our cause; for that is the way of the world and has always been."[24]

It is not for this author to judge whether that is sound theology. Some Iranian theologians say it is not.[25] All the passages in scripture and the Traditions that Khomeini quotes in support of clerical dictatorship have other interpretations. Khomeini's rejection of democracy, and his emphasis on legislative virtue, will be familiar to anybody with knowledge of Plato's *Republic* and Aristotle's *Politics.*

Islamic Government and the doctrine of the "Stewardship of the Jurist" has colonized only part of the Iranian seminary and has found no echo in the other Shia lands, even that most close in temperament to Iran, southern Lebanon. An attempt to impose it on the Shia of Iraq between 1982 and 1988 cost 200,000 Iranian lives. The lectures are shot through with a Navvab-Safavian longing for a simpler world, with "the Islamic judge in each town, assisted by two or three officials and just a pen and inkpot," swiftly resolving disputes between people and sending them about their business.[26]

Khomeini advanced his doctrine a further step in a letter from Najaf on October 31, 1971, in response to the Persepolis celebrations. The letter is addressed not so much at the Iranian public as at the "phoney" clergy of Najaf, and the Muslim governments. It is a typical Khomeini piece from that time, uncompromising in its argument, pungent in its language, credulous of hearsay, and mistaken in matters of fact.[27] What is revolutionary is that Khomeini has turned against monarchical government *in itself*, which he says is abhorrent to the Prophet and the Imams and the source of all Iran's misfortunes for 2,500 years. Khomeini does not mention that the Shia clergy supported Safavids and Qajars, that the Najaf and Qom clergy endorsed Reza's enthronement in 1924, or that he himself acquiesced in Mohammed Reza's restoration in 1953. Instead, Khomeini says: "Islam is fundamentally opposed to monarchy and monarchs and all the Imams put that opposition into practice."[28]

A Scottish philosopher once asked: If a new proposition is self-evident, how come it is new?[29] Reza Hajatpour, a young seminarian who fell afoul of the Qom establishment, put it thus: "Why for centuries did the spiritual classes give their support to kings and princes? If power belongs exclusively to the spiritual classes, how come they have taken so long to recognise it?"[30]

Khomeini was cold-shouldered if not ostracized by the senior clergy in the Holy Thresholds. It was said among the conservative clergy in Najaf that he had ruined one thousand-year-old seminary in Qom, and he was not to be allowed to ruin another. Many of his pupils were in internal exile. One of the most active, Mohammed Reza Saidi, who tried to raise the clergy against a U.S. investment mission led by David Rockefeller of Chase Manhattan in May 1970, died under torture in Qizil Qaleh jail in Tehran. Khomeini's followers in Qom had no press and had to rely on carbon copies of his lectures and statements from Najaf.[31] After Persepolis, Khomeini ceased for several years to comment on developments in Iran and kept aloof from the doctrinal and political battles convulsing Qom. Of one such, which arose over a revisionist biography of the Third Imam, Hosein, *The Eternal Martyr* (1970) by Salehi-Najafabadi, of which Montazeri was the principal champion, Khomeini later said: "For several years, all your strength was dissipated on *The Eternal Martyr*."[32] The quarrel reached a pitch of virulence in 1976 when a Montazeri protégé, Sayyid Mehdi Hashemi, had a clerical opponent of the book in Isfahan garotted. Years later, the echo of that obscure crime was to reach the United States.

The oil market continued to tighten. The international prosperity of the 1960s had brought with it a thirst for every sort of petroleum product. The strain on supply was, at first, concealed from view by the rise in production in eastern Saudi Arabia, then and now the richest oil province in the world. But by 1973 the actual relation of demand and supply was becoming manifest. Mohammed Reza now could achieve through negotiation what Mossadeq had failed to win by force, which was the nationalization of the Iranian oil industry. On March 20, 1973, in a message for the Iranian New Year, Mohammed Reza announced "full and real control" of Iranian oil.[33] The Consortium handed over its remaining operations in Iran to the National Iranian Oil Company (NIOC) and created a contracting company, Oil Service Company of Iran (OSCO), to give technical assistance and financial investment to raise production to as much as 8 million barrels per day, in part through so-called secondary recovery in the mature, even elderly, producing fields. The Consortium was still permitted to purchase Iranian oil at a discount, but in diminishing quantities as NIOC gained experience and customers.

In October came the crisis. In the midst of the Arab-Israeli War, the Arab members of OPEC met in Kuwait and resolved to raise the price of crude oil 70 percent, to $5.11 a barrel, to cut back production,

and to impose an embargo on the United States and the Netherlands for their support to Israel. In the markets for crude oil, there was a scramble for supplies and NIOC auctioned a consignment at $17.34 a barrel. There seemed to be a once-and-for-all shift in the balance of power between the rich countries of the West and Japan and the producers. On December 23, as OPEC ministers in Tehran were about to announce a new "posted" price of $11.65 a barrel, Mohammed Reza, switching between Persian, English, and French, told correspondents at Niavaran, "The industrial world will have to realise that the era of their terrific progress and even more terrific income and wealth based on cheap oil is finished. They will have to tighten their belts. If you want to live as well as now, you will have to work for it." Then, taking aim at the students who made his visits to Europe and the United States such a trial, he said: "Even those children of well-to-do parents who have plenty to eat and are running around throwing bombs here and there—they will have to work, too."[34] For countries instituting gasoline rationing and cuts in electric power, such lectures were infuriating. For Iran, the new price meant Iran's annual oil revenues quadrupled, from $5 billion to $19 billion. For myself, I thought that Iran had become valuable and there would now be a fight for the place.

The question was, what to do with all that money when there was already evidence (in shortages and rising prices) of stresses in the Iranian economy.[35] Even if money was in abundance, other of what economists call "factors" were not, such as skilled laborers, ports, carriage roads and railroads, electricity, water, paper, cement and steel beams and reinforcing bars for building, and farm produce such as bread and meat. There was also, as we shall see, competition for those scarce factors from the spoiled and favored military.

Iran could simply have invested the surplus abroad, and lived on the interest and dividends, and perhaps that would have been better. Mohammed Reza did make loans, grants, and investments abroad of over $2 billion, including a showy loan in July 1974 of $1.2 billion to British public authorities which, because it reversed the historical order, caused satisfaction all over Iran. ("The British Loan" was known about in the Isfahan villages.) Mohammed Reza also bought a 25 percent stake in the steelmaking subsidiary of the West German industrial group Krupp, and a German-British boilermaker, Deutsche Babcock

Wilcox. Negotiations with General Electric, Grumman Aerospace, Union Carbide, and PanAm of the United States came to nothing. The Pahlavi Foundation began building a prestige property in New York, a thirty-six-story granite skyscraper on Fifth Avenue at 52nd Street, now known as 650 Fifth Avenue, at a cost of $42 million. Yet even after paying off old loans, Iran would still have a surplus on its foreign account of $5 billion at the close of the financial year (March 20, 1975).[36]

Instead, Mohammed Reza, backed by his prime minister, Hoveyda, and Abdolmajid Majidi, the director general of the Plan and Budget Organization, decided to spend the windfall in Iran. The Fifth Five-Year Development Plan, which had been in force since March 1973, was expanded out of all recognition. At a meeting at the beginning of August at Ramsar on the Caspian, with Mohammed Reza presiding, it was decided to increase public expenditure over the remaining life of the plan from $36 billion to $69 billion. The economy would grow by a quarter each year, a rate of expansion not matched even by China in our day. No project was too costly. Iran ordered two 1,300-megawatt Siemens nuclear reactors for Bushehr on the Gulf, two further reactors from French industry on the Karun River, a high-speed train network, and three Concorde supersonic airliners.

Majidi, for one, the Central Bank, and even Mohammed Reza himself knew of the risk of inflation, but as the Shah explained to the delegates at Ramsar, it would be "an unforgivable sin" to waste the opportunity. He said: "We should now plan that, in many fields, we will not only have reached the gates of the Great Civilisation in twelve years, but have passed through them."[37] Robert Graham, the *Financial Times* correspondent, wrote: "At the end of the Ramsar meeting, few realised they had just agreed to a 'hyper-boom.'"[38]

Every sector of the Iranian economy, except agriculture, exploded. The ports, with their antiquated handling equipment and inadequate warehousing, became clogged. At Khorramshahr, over two hundred ships were waiting to unload by midsummer 1975 and demurrage— penalties paid to shipowners for delays in unloading—was levied at $1 billion a year.[39] There were not enough trucks or drivers. The old bazaar wholesaling system was overwhelmed. Development land prices, particularly in Tehran, rose to up to ten times the level of the 1960s, showering landowners (including the court) with capital gains but raising

rents and setting off agitation for higher rates of pay. The general price level rose at more than 30 percent a year.

There was a proliferation of private banks. Traffic in Tehran slowed to the walking speed of the nineteenth century. Foreigners poured into Iran, including 25,000 Americans, mostly single males who upset the balance of the sexes and brought a raucousness to such sober cities as Isfahan. In the fog of rising prices, it was no longer possible for business to distinguish a profitable use for capital, and for the public to preserve its old way of life. A dried fruits seller in Chahar Bagh in Isfahan asked me to explain *tavarrom*, the word used in the newspapers to translate "inflation." (I did not know.) In an arid and far-flung country where industrial costs were always high, the rise in wages and rents buried any prospect of export industries (outside the oil sector) and even threatened those, such as hand-loom carpets, that had prospered. Meanwhile, every industrial product imported from abroad included a premium for the petroleum that went into its making. A new petrochemical plant on the mudflats at Bandar Shahpur, which was priced at $600 million, eventually cost $1.8 billion.

Everything and everybody converged on Tehran: migrants, traffic, sewage, factories, banks, hospitals, doctors, civil servants, heroin, divorcées. As the city spread out across the slopes and the desert, lands once thought worthless because they could not be watered created fortunes for landlords and speculators. New industrial families—Khayami, Sabet, Iravani—many of them from unorthodox or Bahai background, came to dominate business. The population, which was 3 million in 1970, was rising at 5 or 6 percent a year. With a million motor vehicles in the capital alone, and haphazard public transport, the streets were clogged with undisciplined and lethal traffic. The telephone exchanges were overloaded. Foreigners hated the place and the hippies, unless they fell afoul of the police, hurried eastwards to the cheap living and narcotics of Afghanistan and India.

The city I knew in 1974 was subject to a sort of gravity, in which to move south was to go downhill and also down the social scale and, in the end, into an inferno. The old highway to the Shemiranat, where Reza himself supervised the planting of the plane trees, was built up on both sides and known as Pahlavi Avenue. At its top, where the air was coolest and cleanest, were the best neighborhoods of Tajrish, Zafaranieh, and Niavaran, and skyscraper hotels full of foreign businessmen. Walking south through the middle-class neighborhoods, one came to a kind of frontier made by Shahreza Street, which the U.S. soldiers in World War II called "Park" and the Islamic Republic *Enqelab* or "Revolution" Street. Here was Tehran University, and attendant bookstores and publishers, bus terminals and the road that led past the Shahyad Monument to the airport.

Further downhill were the scenes of Tehran's tumultuous history become shabby and outmoded: Kakh Street, where both Reza and Mossadeq had lived, Army Square, Lalehzar with its beer bars, the British and Russian embassies, the old Parliament building, the Golestan Palace, and the bazaar. Streets were named after foreign dignitaries who had visited the city, such as Stalin, Churchill, Eisenhower, de Gaulle, and Queen Elizabeth II. At the foot of Pahlavi Avenue, just north of the railway station, was the red-light quarter with the cavernous New Blossom cabaret and the "Fort" or New Town, the walled enclosure where fallen women from the provinces, enslaved for money or heroin to their "masters," sold themselves to laboring men and conscripts in conditions of indescribable wretchedness.[40] It was called the "fortress of the lost."

Southwards, in the old districts long vacated by the respectable middle class for higher up the hill, among the railway lines and around Shush Square and Mowlavi Avenue, the poor and the new arrivals were crammed into alleys, where a single-story brick house of the old-fashioned Iranian type, with its courtyard, porch, and miniature pond, would house a dozen families each to a single room. Water, used a thousand times by the more prosperous citizens uphill, passed down the alley in an open ditch and gave the children somewhere to play. Where the alley met the street, boys congregated, eating cow-lung kebabs from the slaughterhouses, and wasting time, while the girls did their washing in the courtyard.

Beyond spread a saline plain blown over by hot winds, where among the pits and chimneys of the old brickworks were caves and shacks and squatter villages named with that black whimsy that Iranians bring to their affairs: *Muftabad* ("Free-of-charge"), *Zurabad* ("Squatsville"), *Halabiabad* ("Tin-can Town"), or *Hasirabad* ("Mattington").[41] Though opulent by the standards of the slums of Bombay or Manila in those days, the shantytowns were a source of shame to many Iranians. Khomeini (though he is not known to have visited the *gowdals* or pits) raged against them.[42] Two months before the Persepolis celebrations, the court wrote to the mayor of Tehran, Gholam Reza Nikpay, asking him to "take steps" to deal with the shanty dwellers by the Karaj Highway, Kan Street, and Parkvay near the airport because they were in "plain view of the distinguished guests and most undesirable."[43] Pahlavi Iran began to take on a Potemkin character.

In August 1975, the Central Bank attempted to rein in the banks by forcing them to keep higher reserves of capital against their lending. Mohammed Reza ordered a curb on prices and a witch hunt for so-called profiteers, which degenerated into thuggery and Jew- and Bahai-baiting, with thousands of arrests. With the industrial world in recession, oil sales began to fall, and by 1976, Iran had to resort to barter and foreign borrowing. The two-year boom was over. In an interview with the Tehran daily newspaper *Kayhan* to coincide with his birthday in October 1976, and then again in English with *Der Spiegel* the next month, Mohammed Reza admitted that the "orgy of extravagance" had been an error and would come to an end. "Everyone should work harder and be prepared for sacrifices in the service of the nation's progress," he said.[44] He set up an Imperial Commission to investigate how the money had been spent. It was to report not to ministers but directly to himself. As if more were needed to unsettle and terrorize his government, the commission was to include representatives not just of Savak but of a surveillance unit at the palace under Fardoust, the Special Intelligence Bureau.

The story repeated itself in the military. In the early summer of 1972, Nixon and his national security adviser, Henry Kissinger, visited Tehran and crowned Mohammed Reza as the guardian of the Nixon Doctrine in the Middle East. They promised Iran, in the words of a later congressional staff report, "virtually any conventional weapon it wanted."[45] The Shah was offered weapons systems only then reaching the U.S. services, such as the Grumman F-14 Tomcat interceptor, its Phoenix air-to-air missile, and the *Spruance*-class destroyers as the basis of a "blue-water" or open-seas fleet. Richard Helms, ambassador from 1973 to 1976, saw his task as reinforcing the Shah rather than limiting him. An older alumnus of Le Rosey, and a former director of Central Intelligence who had fallen afoul of Nixon, Helms wrote on his arrival in Tehran: "Stability in Iran depends on the survival of the Shah who is the directing force of the Iranian renaissance."[46] In the five years from Nixon's 1972 visit, Mohammed Reza bought more than $10 billion in American-made weapons.[47]

During Nixon and Kissinger's visit, Mohammed Reza complained to the Americans about reconnaissance flights along the border by the high-flying new Soviet fighter, the MiG-25 (known in the West as the "Foxbat"). In the cordial atmosphere, Nixon offered him a choice of two fighter aircraft under development in the United States, the F-15 for the U.S. Air Force and the swing-wing F-14 Tomcat being built by Grumman Aerospace for the U.S. Navy. For all that he possessed no aircraft carrier, Mohammed Reza chose the Navy aircraft for two reasons. It was about a year in advance of the F-15, while its Phoenix missile was capable of dealing not only with Soviet reconnaissance but also the principal Soviet fighter with the Iraqi air force, the MiG-23. Its AWG-9 radar could illuminate or "acquire" a high-flying target 100 miles away. At a fly-off between the two aircraft at Andrews Air Force Base in July 1973, the Grumman test pilots broke every rule of cautious aviation to impress the Shah.[48] Mohammed Reza commissioned 80 Tomcats and 633 Phoenix missiles, at a cost of over $2 billion. Grumman, which had mispriced its U.S. Navy order and was losing about $2 million on each machine it was making at Calverton, Long Island, was on the brink of bankruptcy. Mohammed Reza ordered the Iranian National Bank to provide $75 million in working capital, which saved the company and the U.S. Air Force program.[49]

The best pilots from the active F-4 and F-5 squadrons, young men who had 1,000 or 2,000 hours of flying time, were transferred to the F-14 squadrons at Mehrabad, Isfahan, and Shiraz, which were known to the Americans as the "Persian Cats" (or, in moments of irritation, "Ali Cats"). (The surplus F-5s were sent to Vietnam, or transferred to Mohammed Reza's allies in Jordan.) Yet pilots were only one shortage. The aircraft needed some 6,500 mechanics and technical support staff, at a time when General Mohammed Khatami, the air force commander, also needed to man 32 Hawk ground-to-air missile batteries and a force approaching 500 combat aircraft. In Isfahan, in addition to the F-14 program, Bell Helicopter International of the United States was building from scratch a helicopter force for the Iranian army based on an improved version of the Huey of Vietnam renown, the Bell 214 A/C. Bell brought in about a thousand hard-bitten Vietnam veterans to train the Iranian pilots and ground crew. American officers identified the shortage of technicians as, in the words of a Senate committee report in 1976, "the critical variable."[50]

Khatami's solution had been to create for the F-4 program a new class of technicians or aircraftmen to handle ground operations. Known as *homafaran* (from the mythical Iranian Phoenix or *homa*), they were uniformed civilians mostly from artisanal backgrounds and a traditional upbringing. Though trained in the United States, and well-paid, they had no prospects of promotion to officer rank, and were treated with disdain by some of the pilots and even the American instructors.[51] Numbering some 12,000 men, by the mid-1970s they were already disaffected. The *homafars* were to prove the Achilles heel of the imperial armed forces.[52]

Mohammed Khatami or Khatam was a brilliant figure. The best pilot in Iran, who still flew in the air force display team, he was the star athlete at a court that worshipped physical prowess. He taught the Shah and empress to water-ski and parasail. In 1959, he had married Mohammed Reza's half sister, Princess Fatemeh, and soon had her flying helicopters. Even so, he dared not confront Mohammed Reza about the strains in the air force. In 1974, he confided at a party to Asadollah Alam that there were simply not the pilots or training schools to meet Mohammed Reza's demands. When Alam raised the matter at his daily audience, the Shah brushed it off. "I'm determined that our air force college should train more pilots, even if it means their working round the clock."[53] Since there were already 19,000 students at the Air Training Center at Doshan Teppe in eastern Tehran, that was no small matter.

The U.S. Congress, anxious that the weapons systems were tying the United States into an open-ended relationship with the Pahlavis, had become skeptical. While the arms sales had been a "bonanza" for the U.S. weapons manufacturers and the procurement branches of the services, Nixon's promise of 1972 had taken military sales out of the purview of the Pentagon, the embassy in Tehran, the Military Mission, and the State Department. Once the weapons were delivered, there were "back-end" complexities and commitments of which Iran had not been informed. The Senate, in its staff report of 1976, was blunt: "For at least three years, U.S. arms sales to Iran were out of control and the programs were badly managed."[54] For the diplomat George Ball, Nixon's promise of 1972 was "like giving the keys of the world's largest liquor store to a confirmed alcoholic."[55]

At the British Embassy, Sir Peter Ramsbotham had been promoted to Washington, and was replaced by a man who, with all the traditional diplomatic virtues, was dedicated to British commerce. Sir Anthony Parsons, a former soldier and an Arabist, arrived in April 1974. In the hall of the embassy on Ferdowsi Avenue, which for the latter part of the nineteenth century, and the decade of the 1940s, had given law to Iran, there now stood a display frame with blown-up photographs of British domestic fowls. One caption read: "The Babcock B300 white-egg laying hen averages 265–280 large eggs each year and is consistently successful in comprehensive laying tests."[56] As Alam said of Iran's former tutors and overseers, "Nothing interests them these days save trade and arms sales."[57]

British exports to Iran in 1974 rose by two thirds to £279 million, and by a further three quarters to £495 million in 1975. (Even during the slowdown of 1976, they inched up to £511m and to £655m in 1977.) With the new order for the Shir Iran tank, and for a factory in Isfahan to make tank munitions called "the Military Industrial Complex," Iran was easily the largest foreign market for Britain's defense industry, taking 30 percent of the exports of its arms factories.[58] Iran was also a lifeline for British civil manufacturing, which had a bad reputation for labor troubles and poor quality. The standard Iranian saloon car, the Peykan, was assembled from kits manufactured in Britain. In May 1972, the Anglo-French Concorde stopped in Tehran and Mohammed Reza was invited aboard and for some time took the controls. Because of its noise and expense, the airliner had found no export markets. Iran Air ordered two, with an option on a third.

As Parsons commented in response to a critical British Foreign Office report on his tenure in Iran in 1980: "We must never forget how well we did out of the Shah's regime. . . . British business and industry made an enormous amount of money out of Iran."[59] The British attitude was summed up when the Lord Privy Seal minuted to the prime minister: "The Shah may or may not succeed, but in the short term Iran is going to offer colossal opportunities."[60]

As his military expanded, so Mohammed Reza became tempted to deploy it. On November 30, 1971, as we have seen, Iranian marines occupied the disputed islands of the Greater and Lesser Tunbs and Abu Musa. Iraq responded by re-equipping its armed forces with new Soviet weapons on the basis of a Treaty of Friendship signed with Moscow in 1972. With a renewed revolt of Iraq's Kurds in 1974, Iran supplied artillery and antitank weapons to the rebels, and established long-range fire support from Iranian territory. There were clashes on the border, sniping and kidnappings. In early 1975, Mohammed Reza moved two regiments into Iraq, and positioned a Hawk and a Rapier missile battery to protect the headquarters of the Kurdish rebel leader, Mustafa Barzani. Bloodied by the fight in Iraqi Kurdestan, without Arab support and not ready for all-out war with Iran, the Iraqi strongman Saddam Hussein agreed on March 5, 1975, to an Algerian proposal for a return to the *status quo ante* and an end to hostilities. Mohammed Reza withdrew his air defenses from Iraqi Kurdestan, and the Kurdish revolt collapsed. Alam was startled by his master's ruthlessness. "The Kurds are nothing. They wouldn't have lasted ten days without us," Mohammed Reza said. He was after bigger game. "I wouldn't be surprised if the Iraqis now open up a little to us. They don't want always to be under the thumb of the Soviets," he said.[61] By a treaty signed in June, the border in the Shatt al-Arab was realigned away from the Iranian bank to the deepest part of the channel.[62]

The clearest sign of Mohammed Reza's ambitions was in the Sultanate of Oman, on the southeastern tip of the Arabian Peninsula. In late 1972, he was invited by Sultan Qabus to send troops to fight beside British officers and Omani soldiers against a long-running revolt by tribes in the western province of Dhofar, supported by the Communist government in neighboring South Yemen, or the People's Democratic Republic of Yemen.

Mohammed Reza's purpose was not only to show he was the neighborhood boss but also to give his men battlefield experience. At the height of the fighting, from the autumn of 1974 until the following spring, there were some 4,500 Iranians in Oman, on three months service, supported by helicopters, two squadrons of F-4 Phantoms, and naval vessels. Iranian Special Forces first secured a thirty-mile stretch of road between the Dhofari capital, Salalah, and a forward air base at Thumrait. They then manned a fortified line (named Damavand, after the highest mountain in Iran) across the principal supply lines of the guerrillas to South Yemen. By late 1975, Sultan Qabus's army had pushed the rebels over the border and a truce was concluded the following year. Most of the Iranian forces left Oman early in 1977.

Sir Anthony Parsons, who had served as a soldier, gave the Shah his assessment of the Iranian performance: rigid and unimaginative senior officers, the men tough but not trained for a guerrilla enemy, poor platoon and company tactics, a distaste for nighttime patrols.[63] The three-month rotation dissipated battlefield experience, and because the first hours in combat are generally the most perilous, casualties were higher than they need have been, about three times the 188 dead in the Sultan's army.[64] On the plus side, the tough and lean British contract officers with the Sultan's forces were impressed by the lavish Iranian supply operation and battlefield medicine.

Prime Minister Hoveyda later said that he heard about the Oman deployment only three months after it had begun. Mohammed Reza was no more sparing of the feelings of his officers. Musing on his commanders with Alam in December 1973, Mohammed Reza said: "I don't think for a moment that any of our generals are men of war. They're all poseurs and exhibitionists, except perhaps [General] Azhari, who keeps a low profile, but might be a warrior if put to the test." He reeled off a string of names and dismissed them as worthless. As for Khatami, the head of the air force, he said that he had proved he was a good manager, but how would he fare in war?[65]

Mohammed Reza was never to find out.

After the Persepolis celebrations, Alam had used the surplus in his budget to rent a house for Mohammed Reza to take women. It was not a large house. On their first visit, on December 12, 1972, Alam was obliged to retire to the bathroom with his work, signing a letter to the British queen's cousin, Lord Mountbatten, from the lavatory seat. Coming out into the street, he and Mohammed Reza ran into Farah's mother, Farideh Diba, emerging from a neighbor's garden. That evening, Madame Diba eyed Alam and said: "My! Don't we work hard! I've just seen you with HIM."[66]

She raised the matter again on Christmas Eve. By now there were rumors that the Shah had married a young woman named Gilda—and those rumors had reached Farah's family. Alam wrote in his diary:

"Audience. Reported Madame Farideh's words from last night and, particularly, what she said about her daughter, fortunately, not having been brought up to luxury. In other words, that she might seek a divorce. (Not that she mentioned the word, but that is what she meant.) 'Bollocks!' said HIM. After much debate, it was agreed that bloody little girl has to be found a husband." [67]

Khatami not only took on Gilda but lost his head and heart to her. Alam was able to convince the queen that it was Khatami, not the Shah, who was providing her with motorcycle outriders and helicopter transport. [68] Farah even telephoned Khatami's house. [69] The general's marriage to Princess Fatemeh was said to be on the point of collapse. He was suspected of profiteering on the aircraft contracts. [70] Khatami's associates, not least Mohammed Reza, noticed that he appeared to be in low spirits.

On Thursday, September 11, 1975, Khatami had dinner and played bridge with his closest circle, drank a certain amount, and let fall that on Friday, the Iranian Sunday, he was flying to the Dez Dam in the southwest to try out one of the new-fangled hang gliders just then coming into fashion. Khatami took with him a photographer from *Kayhan,* who photographed him taking off at 11:44 a.m., but not falling to earth ninety seconds later. [71]

At the funeral in Tehran, air force cadets carried Khatami's decorations in procession. His coffin was taken from the Sepahsalar Mosque first on a gun carriage and then in the vehicle which had borne Reza Shah's body to his mausoleum in 1950. The Isfahan air base was renamed after him. An investigation found no evidence of foul play. In Iran, there are no deaths by natural causes and it was rumored Khatami had been killed by the Shah for becoming too closely associated with the United States. [72] In the ensuing weeks, Mohammed Reza told Alam that Khatami had built up a fortune of $100 million which, if found to be illegal, would be confiscated. [73] On September 25, 1975, the Shah revealed to Alam certain "suspicions" about Khatami so secret that the court minister dared not confide them to his diary, but would carry them "as a heavy burden to the grave." [74] Did Mohammed Reza do to Khatami what his father did to Teymourtache? What is strange—or perhaps not strange at all—is that Mohammed Reza showed no regret for the loss of his best and bravest officer. Anyway, Mohammed Reza was forced by lack of revenue to rein in his military spending, cut the U.S. destroyer order from six to four ships, delay construction of the Char Bahar base on the Arabian Sea, and offer oil, instead of cash, for other programs. His goal of an armed strength of 760,000 men, larger than Britain or France could put in the field together, was pushed back to 1982.[75]

At this point, an element of human weakness enters the story. On Monday, April 8, 1974, the fifty-four-year-old Shah attended an exercise on a veteran American aircraft carrier, USS *Kitty Hawk,* in the Sea of Oman and then flew to Kish Island, an old haunt of pirates and date farmers at the mouth of the Persian Gulf that the court had been developing since 1972 as a winter resort for the rich. The next morning, as hot and blue as all the mornings are on Kish, Alam arrived at Mohammed Reza's palace in the best of spirits only to see Dr. Ayadi come out of his apartment.[76] "He took me aside," Alam wrote in his diary, "and said in my ear that we must send for Prof. Jean Bernard, the French blood-specialist, to come and examine the King of Kings. I asked him why, but he would not answer, just said that we must do this. It was as if the world had gone dark before my eyes."

Bernard was the leading hematological oncologist in the world, who had pioneered the treatment of childhood leukemia and identified a hereditary bleeding disorder that now bears his name. He was as well known for the beauty of his character, his work in the Resistance to German wartime occupation, his poetry, and his reasoning in the philosophy of medicine.[77] Back in 1969, one of Bernard's Iranian students, Professor Abbas Safavian, suspecting Alam himself had a form of leukemia, had referred the minister of court to his old teacher at the Paris Medical School.

In the car to the airfield at Kish, things got worse. Chivvying Alam about completing two more hotels on the island, Mohammed Reza said: "Buck up, man! I want them finished in my lifetime." Once seated on the aircraft back to Tehran, Alam gave way to despondency. "What in God's name could this be that should show such sudden symptoms? What will happen to this country if this man is taken from us. Foreigners will descend on us, promote Hoveyda or one of his lot or some General Yes Sir! or groom some bum-boy from Her Majesty's court, and if that's the worst we get we'll thank our lucky stars. Truly, if the

Shah had not been on board, I'd have preferred the airplane to crash just to deliver me from these terrible thoughts about the future."[78]

Bernard was out of town, but flew to Tehran a week later, together with a pupil, Dr. Georges Flandrin. He was not told the identity of his patient. Bernard examined Alam before being told he was to see the Shah at Niavaran. At the consultation, attended by Dr. Ayadi, the Shah told the two Frenchmen that he had noticed on Kish "a few months earlier" a swelling under his left rib cage, and suspected it was an enlarged spleen.[79] (It may have been a relic of his bout of typhoid fever as a child.)

With a needle into the bone, Flandrin withdrew or aspirated a sample of marrow, which under the microscope showed a preponderance of lymphoid cells. The French doctors informed Ayadi that they thought Mohammed Reza had a form of cancer of the lymph cells that resembled early-stage chronic lymphocytic leukemia. For whatever reason, Ayadi begged them not to mention the words "cancer" or "leukemia" to the Shah.[80] In the second week of June, Alam traveled to Paris for his own consultation, where Bernard did not hide his contempt for Ayadi, and said that they "should stop playing around with the Shah's health."[81]

On September 9, the Shah complained to Alam that his spleen was enlarged and he was suffering from a recurring skin rash. It was decided that Bernard should come to Tehran on the pretext of treating Alam.[82] He prescribed a mild anti-cancer drug called Chlorambucil under a false label. It seems that the Shah, who was fond of medicines of every sort ("my candies and sweets," he called them),[83] did not take the pills as prescribed, or Ayadi made a hash of it, and in February 1975 the two Frenchmen were called to Zurich to find the Shah in pain, with his spleen much enlarged. It was decided that the Shah should be examined regularly. When Dr. Flandrin suggested perhaps that Ayadi and Safavian could take the blood sample, they shook their heads. Neither was willing to take responsibility. Between then and early 1979, Flandrin made as many as thirty-five incognito visits to Tehran. So secret was it that in 1978, when the queen mother Taj ol-Moluk was diagnosed with the same condition, her doctors were not given the vital information that the Shah had the illness and the French team did not examine her.[84]

Mohammed Reza put himself in the hands of French doctors in part because of a royal tradition going back to the nineteenth century, but chiefly because he did not trust the British or the Americans or the Iranians. Alam, as we have seen, and possibly also Ayadi, were terrified lest the Anglo-Saxon powers abandon their support for the personal rule of Mohammed Reza and indulge in what was to become known in the United States as "reinsurance." The British foreign secretary, David Owen, himself a medical doctor, later confirmed that they were right. "Had I known," Lord Owen wrote in 2002, "I would have pressed far more vigorously early in 1978, and certainly been adamant in the late summer and autumn of that year, that the Shah should stand down immediately on health grounds."[85] It appears that neither the British nor the Americans received any inkling that the Shah had cancer until his examination in Cuernavaca, Mexico, in October 1980.

How much did Mohammed Reza know of his illness? Perhaps he began to sense that he was mortal and fell prey to his weakness for haste. He told French president Valéry Giscard d'Estaing in St. Moritz in February 1975, "My problem is that I haven't enough time. I intend leaving in seven or eight years. I would prefer to leave earlier, but my son is still too young."[86] Ambassador Ramsbotham, not as close to the Pahlavis as Denis Wright or Percy Loraine but perhaps for that reason dispassionate, felt that Mohammed Reza did not trust Crown Prince Reza or the queen and intended to pass on the throne but maintain some supervisory role away from the center of power.[87] I suspect that is why he was in such a rush to complete the resort on Kish. Above all, if his dynasty was to survive after him, it had to rely for support on a wider franchise than the officer corps, the internal security service, and a vanishing peasantry.

Mohammed Reza was no democrat, any more than Shariati or Jazani or the Khomeini of the *Islamic Government* lectures. With half the population illiterate, he spoke of democracy as a distant prospect, and had done little to prepare for it. On the contrary, his rule had become absolute. Parliament and the Senate, which provided a sort of club for the relics of the period of relatively parliamentary freedom, vied to interpret the "royal pleasure." The two-party system was a source neither of opposition nor debate. One day in cabinet, a minister stood up and said: "Why do we bother to come here if no one discusses anything?" He was ignored.[88]

Even his closest advisers Mohammed Reza treated with disdain. One day in 1975, Alam (who signed letters to the Shah as "Your house-born slave") had an audience with the Shah at his single-story beach house set on stilts at the end of a jetty at Nowshahr on the Caspian. (This was little more than a hut, convenient for water-skiing and parasailing amid the grease left by Soviet ships coming into Nowshahr. "It was . . . far from being the Château de Chambord," Flandrin told his professor after his first visit.)[89]

Alam wrote: "After taking my leave, I had a cup of tea on the jetty. The Shah came outside and, on his own and unoccupied, called me over and there we stood chatting about girls and this and that. I pointed out that the Soviet ships anchored across the harbour were well able to photograph us, or even eavesdrop on our conversation. He shrugged it off, saying that if he needs to hold important discussions or to meet foreign dignitaries he does so not here but at Ramsar. I objected that the Prime Minister and myself are received at Nowshahr. He said: 'Neither of you ever has anything important to say to me.'"[90]

In his first volume of memoirs, back in 1961, Mohammed Reza mused that had he been "a dictator rather than a constitutional monarch, then I might be tempted to sponsor a single dominant party such as Hitler organised or such as you find today in Communist countries."[91] He was baffled by the public's indifference to the material progress under Pahlavi rule, full employment, and the country's new prestige in the world. When Alam suggested that for all the King of Kings' shining achievements and tireless endeavor, the people feel "it has nothing to do with them," he replied, "I've sensed the same thing myself. We have to put some thought into this."[92] He commissioned reports on economic conditions and social attitudes from a group of academics under a liberal Paris-bred economist, Houchang Nahavandi. Nahavandi, who was to become the queen's secretary, found a people frustrated by disappointments rather than pleased with material progress.[93] Farah, who unlike the Shah still traveled on the ground, found "a certain malaise. People still came to me, but they focused on what was wrong rather than what was right." Later, she blamed Hoveyda. "Did he underestimate the importance of the discontent? No doubt."[94]

On February 23, 1975, Alam found Mohammed Reza "drumming his fingers on the desk-top—always a sign that he's lost in thought—

his blessed feet up on the desk." The next day was the same. Later on the 24th, Mohammed Reza telephoned, instructing Alam to call Hoveyda, the speakers of Parliament and Senate, the press, and representatives of the different economic groups to Niavaran on March 2 "to discuss certain issues."[95] At the meeting, Mohammed Reza announced that the two-party system was moribund, and in future there would be just a single political party, where everybody could participate. The new party would be based on the three principles of the 1906–07 Constitution, the White or Shah-People Revolution, and the Pahlavi succession. The party was open to all, and for those who did not want to join, there were two possibilities. Those members of unconstitutional organizations, such as the Tudeh, could select jail or their passports, "and good riddance for they are no Iranians." Those who were loyal to the fatherland, but genuinely wanted no part in the project, would be left in peace, "but we will not tolerate duplicity or the sort of nonsense we have recently seen."[96] Hoveyda was appointed secretary general.

So began the unhappy life of the Rastakhiz or "Resurrection Party of the Iranian Nation," not quite a party and never a movement, ambiguous, disposable, and unsettling.[97] The new Parliament, which opened on September 8, 1975, was divided into two "wings": the "progressive," stressing social equity, and the "constructive," development. One wing was headed by Jamshid Amouzegar, interior minister, and the other by Hushang Ansary, finance minister, the two contenders to succeed Hoveyda as prime minister. Mohammed Reza had in mind a sort of second White Revolution, in which he would reforge his ties with a nation that he had never well understood, depoliticize society, discipline the public administration, and neutralize powerful men. Five more principles, including a national welfare system, were added to the White Revolution. In practice, as Robert Graham of the *Financial Times* wrote, "the party has proved, as all single-party systems under an authoritarian regime, to be just another extension of the executive." The Political Bureau of the party became indistinguishable from the cabinet. Young members were used as a vigilante force to police the antiprofiteering and prices campaign in the summer of 1975, to threaten and bully shopkeepers, and to swell pro-government rallies.

Compared to the essays in social mobilization since the Revolution, such as the Basij militia, the Rastakhiz was nothing much. Yet it did as

Reza Khan as army Commander with the sword of honor awarded him by Ahmad Shah, February 1921.

Reza in 1922 with (from left) Mohammed Reza, Shams, and the forever-unwanted Ashraf.

Mohammed Reza at military school, Tehran, late 1920s.

Mohammed Reza at Le Rosey, after 1931.

"Shah on probation": Mohammed Reza, Fauzia, and the baby Shahnaz at Saadabad, 1942.

Mossadeq on his favorite bedstead in the garden at Kakh Street, 1953.

A newspaper kiosk burns during the royalist coup against Mossadeq, August 19, 1953.

Mohammed Reza and Soraya in their Rome exile, August 19, 1953.

Mohammed Reza returns in triumph to Tehran, August 22, 1953.

The Abadan refinery from the salt marshes, 1956.

Soraya at the New Year reception at the Golestan Palace, March 21, 1956.

Mohammed Reza distributes land deeds in Isfahan, 1962.

Mohammed Reza wearing the Pahlavi crown and seated on the Naderi throne at his belated coronation, October 26, 1967. Farah is beneath him to his right, Crown Prince Reza seated to his left.

The Apadana at Persepolis and, beyond it, Jansen's tent city, October 12, 1971.

The Shahyad under construction, 1971.

Mohammed Reza, impatient as ever, and Farah await the start of a parade in Tehran, 1971.

The Shah at the Haft Tepe cane-sugar scheme in Khuzestan, May 10, 1974. The civilian behind his left elbow is Alam.

Shah's birthday levee at the Golestan Palace, October 26, 1977. Behind the Shah on the left, with white sash, is Hoveyda. Pakravan is at far left.

Shantytown in south Tehran, 1978.

Mohammed Reza besieged at Tabas airport after the earthquake of September 16, 1978.

Soldiers fire baton rounds and tear gas, Tehran, autumn 1978.

much as any of Mohammed Reza's projects to unsettle the population. What seemed to trouble men I knew was that they might no longer live their lives as little touched by the central government as under Nassereddin Shah. There was a sense that Mohammed Reza was out of control, what the Iranians call *bi bar o band*: that, like a refractory donkey, he had shed his load and hobbling string, and bolted into the desert.

On March 21, 1975, which was New Year's Day by the old Iranian calendar, Shariati was released. His detractors in the Islamic Republic claim that he bought his freedom with a more conciliatory line, including two series of articles, published in *Kayhan* newspaper in the first half of 1976, with a conventional anti-Western and anti-Marxist tone.[98] On April 19, Savak agents murdered nine leaders of the radical left, including Bizhan Jazani. The claim that they were shot while trying to escape was not believed, nor was it true. It was Mohammed Reza's most shameful crime. According to one of their killers, speaking at his trial in 1979, the nine were taken by minibus into the hills above Evin, handcuffed and blindfolded, and then shot with a single Uzi machine pistol, the killers taking turns.[99] At his audience on May 2, Alam remonstrated, but Mohammed Reza said: "There was no choice. They were all saboteurs. They would have escaped and that would have been worse."[100] Demonstrations in favor of Khomeini in Qom in June 1975 were crushed and the Faizieh Seminary shut down.

Later that year, the Mojahedin split into Marxist-Leninist and Islamic factions. Ebrahim Yazdi, a cancer specialist at the Veterans Administration Hospital in Houston, Texas, who acted as a liaison between Khomeini and the exiles in Europe and the United States, wrote: "If the Shah's security apparatus had arrested every leader, activist and cadre of the Mojahedin and wiped them out, the effect on the struggle would not have been so severe. The unity of the Islamic forces was shattered and along with it any understanding with the secular groups. The movement had never been weaker."[101] Khomeini's principal pupils—including Montazeri and Hashemi Rafsanjani—were rounded up and imprisoned in Evin, where they kept themselves apart from the leftist prisoners. The historian Abbas Milani remembered how they one day refused to drink from the teakettles he carried to their two cells, on the grounds that as a secular leftist he was unclean.[102] Hashemi Rafsanjani recited the Koran, in a voice that tormented his cell mates, and studied French without gaining mastery of that language. Montazeri picked up some English. On summer nights, the sound of dance music wafted into their cells from the piazza of the Evin Hotel.

Worse was to come in March 1976. To celebrate the fifty-year jubilee of the Pahlavi house, Hoveyda's government replaced the Iranian solar calendar, which took its origin from the start of the Prophet Mohammed's ministry in Medina, with a new Imperial (*shahanshahi*) calendar dated from the enthronement of Cyrus the Great in 559 BC. The year 1355 became the year 2535. The idea had surfaced in the planning for the Persepolis celebrations but fallen away in the bustle and haste. The timing was no better now than then. The Iranian public barely knew of Cyrus the Great and feared that the monarchy was cutting at the Islamic foundation of everyday life. Khomeini, who had returned to commenting on affairs in Iran, criticizing the Rastakhiz and the closing of the Faizieh Seminary the year before, issued a *fatwa* or legal opinion that outlawed the use of the Imperial calendar.[103] He later called it "the worst thing this man has done during his reign, playing games with the dignity of God's prophet, worse even than the massacres."[104] The calendar lasted just over two years.

The atmosphere in Iran was both stagnant and volatile. The themes of recent years—the Great Civilization, the White Revolution, left-wing militancy, clericalism—were exhausted. Business was in retreat, the bazaar surly, and the armed forces decapitated. Everywhere was frustration and doubt. Robert Graham reckoned that as much as $100 million in private capital was leaving the country each month, as if those Iranians who could afford it were "securing a second life for themselves outside Iran." In Vakilabad, the foreign hippies and drug smugglers had long refused to stand for the national anthem when it was played on the television slung from the roof in Block Three, but "by October of '76 the rot had begun to spread into the Iranis. Nobody was getting any backsheesh [prospering], an element of revolt had crept in." The television showed dams and hydro schemes and played fanfares, "but the lights still went out with monotonous regularity and the new generators constantly broke down."[105]

The Swiss government asked the Iranian royal family not to come to St. Moritz because it doubted it could protect them.[106] The following year, Princess Ashraf escaped assassination on the French Riviera. Returning by car in the early hours from the casino in Cannes to her house at Juan-les-Pins, she was overtaken and attacked by two masked gunmen. One of her passengers was killed.

On November 3, 1976, Jimmy Carter, a peanut farmer from the southern state of Georgia, was elected president of the United States on the Democratic ticket. Democratic presidents had never been to Mohammed Reza's taste. Truman had been inclined to do business with Mossadeq, while Kennedy had forced the Shah to accept as premier Ali Amini, whom he distrusted. It was clear to him that the practical, even cynical, foreign policy of Nixon and Kissinger, so successful in its way, would be replaced by one that restricted military sales and emphasized democracy and human rights. Carter, in his speech accepting the nomination at the Democratic National Convention in New York on July 15, 1976, had promised to pursue abroad the ideals of the American founding fathers, and "the unceasing effort to preserve human rights . . . among people everywhere who have become politically more alert, socially more congested, and increasingly impatient with global inequities."[107]

Nonetheless, Mohammed Reza thought he could ride out the storm, as he had done in the early 1960s. Two of his overseas envoys, Hoveyda's brother Fereydoun at the United Nations in New York, and Parviz Radji, a favorite of both Hoveyda and Princess Ashraf, who was ambassador in London, persuaded him that the key to improving Iran's image abroad was "for bureaucratic as much as for moral reasons" to halt the practice of torture.[108] Radji arranged for Martin Ennals, secretary general of Amnesty International, to visit Iran and call on Mohammed Reza. The London-based human rights organization had been publishing estimates from exile sources that there were between 25,000 and 100,000 political prisoners in Iran.[109] (At the time, the entire prison population of England and Wales was 46,000.) After Ennals's visit, Amnesty adopted Savak's figure of 3,200.[110]

A delegation from the International Committee of the Red Cross was invited to inspect twenty Iranian prisons in the spring of 1977. Savin says that the "politicals" in Vakilabad were marched out and replaced by soldiers in civilian clothes in time for the arrival of the Swiss on May 21,[111] but the inspections produced better conditions in prison and an improvement in judicial process.[112] In June, the Red

Cross submitted its report to Mohammed Reza. From his own account (to Alam), the inspectors reported that out of 3,000 political prisoners seen, 900 showed evidence of torture, but that in the recent months rights of appeal had been introduced, prison visits made easier, and signs of torture disappeared.[113]

Civilian society took heart. A former editor of *Kayhan*, Ali Asghar Hajj Sayyid Javadi, took advantage of the more open atmosphere to publish two long letters to the court, written in 1976 or earlier, criticizing arbitrary rule and breaches of the Constitution.[114] The U.S. Embassy translated one of the letters and sent it to Secretary of State Cyrus Vance as a brief for his meeting with Mohammed Reza.[115] Leaders of the old Mossadeqist National Front wrote to the Shah, asking him to "end despotic government, observe the principles of the Constitution and the Universal Declaration of Human Rights, forgo a one-party system, allow a free Press, release political prisoners, permit exiles to return and establish a government based on the representation of the majority." Ambassador Radji in London was astonished: "What's happening in Iran? How can the Shah have changed so much, so fast?"[116]

Under intolerable pressure to cooperate from Savak, Ali Shariati quietly left Iran on May 16, 1977, and found his way to Southampton in southern England, where he roomed with friends in an attic, living on black tea and tobacco, and waited for his wife and family to join him. The soft English summer unmanned him. "How can I think and write about Abu Zarr and the desert," he said to an old colleague from Ershad on June 17, "when I am confronted daily with my green and flowery surroundings."[117] On June 18, as he was about to leave for Heathrow Airport to meet his wife, she called from Iran to say she had been prevented from leaving. That night, at the age of forty-four, Ali Shariati suffered a heart attack and died.[118] Shariati's death was yet another blow to the left, already weakened by factional fighting and the loss of about two hundred young men and women in gun battles or by execution.

In August 1977, Mohammed Reza shuffled his government. He replaced his long-serving prime minister, Hoveyda, with Jamshid Amouzegar, a brusque but experienced and capable manager. Alam was now seriously ill, and on August 4, he received a telephone call from the Shah asking him to retire. Much to his disgust, he was replaced by Hoveyda at the Ministry of Court. Alam made his last entry in his diary at Cap d'Antibes on the Riviera on September 29, heartbroken but still loyal to "my great, beloved King of Kings."[119] (A little later he was admitted to New York Hospital, where he died, fortunate man, on April 13, 1978.)

Soon after the change of ministry, Mohammed Reza summoned General Abbas Gharabaghi, commander of the National Gendarmerie. In order to prepare for an orderly succession to the crown prince, the Shah said, it was necessary that a now literate public should take a greater role in the affairs of the country. Gharabaghi should rest assured that the "policy of liberalization" was "according to Our wish and that we have judged to be necessary." A few days later, Hoveyda and General Gholam Reza Azhari, the army chief of staff, convened a conference of the most senior officers of all the branches, assuring them that "the totality of events. . . . have been well calculated and measured and should give no cause for concern." Gharabaghi, as no doubt other officers, was baffled by this oracular message.[120]

The most striking event of the liberalization was the so-called Ten Nights of lectures and poetry readings held between October 10 and 19, 1977, by the oppositional Writers' Association of Iran at the German Cultural Institute on Pahlavi Avenue, the long, steep boulevard Reza had made and planted with plane trees now almost grown. On the first night, so many came to the Goethe-Institut that the crowd spilled over into neighboring streets, where loudspeakers broadcast the readings. Police and security vehicles were deployed in the back streets but made no attempt to disrupt the readings. Up to 10,000 people attended the first few nights, until rain dampened some of the enthusiasm. There was a sense, according to some who took part, of impunity. All of the speakers called for freedom of expression, the release of their colleagues in jail, and an end to "literature in the shadows."[121]

The clerical opposition also began to mobilize. On October 23, Khomeini's eldest son, Mostafa, had died in Karbala, evidently of a heart attack. As with Shariati in Southampton four months earlier, the death was thought suspicious (though in neither case was there the least evidence of any foul play). Khomeini took the blow with his habitual self-control, repeating the verse from the Koran: "To God we belong and to Him we return."[122] There were memorial services for Mostafa all over Iran, and for the first time in years, Khomeini's name was mentioned (often in circumlocutions) from the pulpit. There was a violent demonstration by students in Qom. In response to a telegram of condolence from Yasser Arafat, chairman of the Palestine Liberation Organization, Khomeini wrote that his pain from losing his son was as nothing to witnessing the crimes of the Pahlavis.[123]

As Mohammed Reza prepared for his first meeting with President Carter in Washington on November 15, Iran seemed to be coming to life. In Washington, he was greeted by a noisy demonstration organized by the Confederation of Iranian Students. Tear gas drifted across the White House South Lawn, and the image of Mohammed Reza with tears in his eyes made magazine covers. The queen, who had distrusted the United States since her first visit in 1962 had been beset by demonstrations, thought there was "a desire on the part of the new administration to embarrass us."[124] Carter himself, a born-again Christian and sometime Sunday School teacher, saw that day as an augury: "The tear gas had created the semblance of grief. Almost two years later . . . there would be real grief in our country because of Iran."[125]

In a private meeting with Mohammed Reza, Carter spoke of the need to honor human rights but, as he reveals in his memoirs, was not insistent. "It soon became obvious that my expression of concern would not change the policies of the Shah in meeting a threat which, I am sure, seemed very real to him."[126] Like so many Americans before him, Carter seems to have fallen prey to Mohammed Reza's charm. On his return from Washington, Mohammed Reza clamped down. Sabeti's men broke up a large meeting of the National Front in a garden in Karaj, northwest of the capital, on November 22. As Robert Graham of the *Financial Times* wrote, the Shah "slammed the door shut at the first available opportunity."[127]

On the eve of the Christian New Year, the Carters stopped on their way to India at Tehran. At a dinner at Niavaran, Carter toasted the Shah in Dom Pérignon champagne, and in front of television cameras spoke of Mohammed Reza with warmth.[128] In his southern accent, he said: "Iran, because of the great leadership of the Shah, is an island of stability in one of the more troubled areas of the world. This is a great tribute to you, Your Majesty, and to your leadership and to the respect and the admiration and love which your people give to you."[129]

The island was soon to be inundated.

CHAPTER 7

The Indian

◆

The Shah was like a man who had lavished everything on a beautiful woman for years only to find she had been unfaithful all along.

—Amir Abbas Hoveyda[1]

The following Saturday, January 7, 1978, at midafternoon, the newspaper *Ettelaat* went out to the street kiosks in Tehran. Those inclined to turn to page seven found an article, in two columns, under the heading: IRAN AND RED-AND-BLACK IMPERIALISM. Beneath the heading was the byline, evidently a pseudonym, "Ahmad Rashidi Motlaq."[2]

Many readers would have skipped. Red-and-black reaction, that is, an alliance between the left and the Shia clergy to arrest Iran's progress, had been a staple of government ideology since the Shah's speech at Qom during the Land Reform agitation back in 1963. Red-and-black *imperialism* was the same conspiracy warmed up to fill a couple of columns and keep the advertisements from touching in a prosperous but news-free newspaper. (You can read this sort of paranoid theorizing in *Ettelaat* today.)

Yet there was something in the article that had troubled the editorial conference at *Ettelaat* on Khayyam Avenue, delayed publication, and in four hundred days would detonate the Pahlavi kingdom.[3] When great interests are at stake, said Aristotle, revolutions are often caused by trifles.[4] It is not just the contingent or accidental that makes history, as Edmund Burke thought, but also the illiterate and deceitful.[5] The *Ettelaat* article had the effect of placing Khomeini at the center of the movement for change in Iran, and then at its head. That may have happened anyway, but this is how it did happen.

The article opened with an appeal to the holy month of Moharram, just coming to an end, and rehearsed the Pahlavi view of recent history: how an alliance of landowners and the left, and the "old" and "new" imperialists—that is, Britain and the United States—had come to grief in the Shah-People Revolution. Therefore, they sought after 1963 to find a spiritual leader to unite their factions, "an opportunist, without beliefs but bound and devoted to the centres of imperialism, and ambitious to the hilt."

Who was that man of the cloth?

> By his own admission, Ruhollah Khomeini had lived in India and there had relations with the centres of English imperialism and for that reasons was known as "the Indian *sayyid*." In his youth, he also wrote love poetry under the *nom de plume* "The Indian" and was called "The Indian." A man of obscure origins, and without standing among the eminent clergy, he seized the opportunity at any price to enter events and make a name for himself. What is clear is that his fame as the chief instigator of the events of 1963 has persisted to this day. Opposed to the [White] Revolution in Iran, he was determined to install a red-and-black imperialism, and unleashed his agents against the Land Reform, women's rights and the nationalisation of forests, shed the blood of innocent people and showed that even today there are people ready loyally to put themselves at the disposal of conspirators and [foreign] national interests. . . . Millions of Iranian Muslims will ponder how Iran's enemies choose their accomplices as need arises, even accomplices dressed in the sacred and honourable cloth of the clergyman.[6]

The article then repeated an old smear about Egyptian involvement in the events of June 1963.

Ettelaat (*Intelligence*) was the oldest newspaper in Iran and had the most conservative readership.[7] The article had been handed to one of its reporters for immediate publication by the minister of information, Daryoush Homayoun, at the congress of the Rastakhiz Party at the Aryamehr Sports Club on January 4, three days after President Carter's departure.

There was nothing unusual in that. Homayoun, who in the late 1960s founded the newspaper *Ayandegan* with Hoveyda's backing, later said he had received it that day in a large white envelope with the seal of Hoveyda's Ministry of Court—again, not unusual—and had not read it, let alone written it.[8]

As to the authors, there are two principal theories. One holds that the Shah, infuriated by recent statements by Khomeini, had asked Savak to grind the article out of its mill.[9] The other is that it was written at the Ministry of Court by a team led by Farhad Nikoukhah, Hoveyda's press adviser.[10] The article, as Homayoun pointed out, had nothing new apart from the Indian innuendos, which were untrue except for the *nom de plume* "The Indian," which meant nothing. Such names are chosen for metrical reasons and used to sign off a poem. With his minute attention to matters of the press, Mohammed Reza was probably the instigator. The language more than echoes his tabletalk as recorded by Alam in his diaries. Parsons, the British ambassador, thought the article would never have been published if Mohammed Reza's old advisers had been living or Alam well enough to restrain him.[11]

At a memorial service in Qom for Mostafa Khomeini back in December, several speakers had called for his father to be permitted to return. No doubt the Shah or his advisers thought they should bring Khomeini down to earth and that, in the altered conditions of Iran in the thirteen years since his exile in 1964, they could get away with it.

Ettelaat thought otherwise. The editor told Homayoun he feared the paper's bureau in Qom might be attacked. The publisher called Prime Minister Amouzegar, who said he knew nothing of the thing, checked with the Ministry of Court, and called back to say the piece must be run and before the Shah's departure for a meeting with his friend Anwar Sadat in Egypt on the 9th.[12] Mohammed Heidari, deputy editor, at home with a cold, advised the news desk to run the piece down-page inside under a twelve-point heading (that is, about the size of the words you are now reading). The article, which should have appeared on January 5, was delayed until January 7, when it ran, dwarfed by an advertisement for Tabriz Machine Tools, at the top of columns four and five of page seven.[13]

Ettelaat arrived in Qom that evening. In summoning up the ghosts of 1963, the court was playing with fire, for it was to resurrect the old controversy over Khomeini's special authority or *marjiyat* that he had acquired in the uprising that year. The next morning, students and student-teachers converged in numbers on the houses of the senior scholars—Golpayegani, Shariatmadari, and Marashi-Najafi—to pressure them to denounce the article for the sake of the sanctity of the turban and, in effect, support Khomeini as they had done in 1963. To a different degree, all did so. There were clashes with the police.

The following day, the 9th, the Qom bazaar was closed, classes at the seminary were suspended, and, in a fight with police in the late afternoon, between five and nine young men were killed.[14] Rumor, then as now the principal carrier of news in Iran, swelled the dead to hundreds. On the 12th, Ayatollah Golpayegani published a letter to a colleague in Tehran, Ayatollah Ahmad Khonsari, which said that "recent newspaper articles and the attack on the holy norms of Islam and the insult to the lofty position of the clergy are a cause of concern, disgust and serious disturbance. Government officials, rather than recognize the justified and reasonable protest of the gentlemen of the seminary and the defenceless people, resorted to firearms in which a number of innocents were killed and a large number wounded and injured."[15] Marashi-Najafi, in a statement published in *Ettelaat* the same day, mentioned Khomeini by name.

There were demonstrations and bazaar strikes in Isfahan and Tehran. A run on the Bank Saderat, then controlled by a Bahai investor, obliged the bank to seek funds from the Central Bank. In riots in Mashhad on the night of the 20th, seventy-three people were arrested and then crammed into a ten-foot-square storeroom at Vakilabad. The next day they were beaten. The British convict Richard Savin wrote in his diary: "Farridooneh [a warder] was working on one and sweating and the doctor's orderly was patching up another against the wall. I think his foot was busted. There was blood in big pools coming out through the door of quarantine and I figure Ferrydouneh [sic] had been working pretty hard."[16] The Rastakhiz organized loyalist counterdemonstrations in Tehran and Qom. As January came to an end, the government believed it had the protest under control. Court Minister Hoveyda told British ambassador Parsons: "We only have to roll a few tanks down the main street of Tehran and it will calm down."[17]

Iran was not the Soviet Union. For all the anticlerical policies of

Reza Pahlavi, the Iranian clergy was not merely intact after fifty years of Pahlavi rule but richer than it had ever been. The rituals of popular religion, the pilgrimages to Mashhad and Karbala and the ceremonies of mourning for the Shia martyrs, had survived in all but the modern quarters of the cities and were cherished by the female half of the population. The queen's Festival of Arts at Shiraz even attempted to revive the Shia Passion Play as folklore. Dispersed through the modern calendar were the "Days of God" (*ayam allah* in Arabic), such as the fasting month of Ramazan; Ashura, the tenth day of the month of Moharram when Hosein was martyred at Karbala; and the fortieth day thereafter (20 Safar or *arbain* in Arabic), where by tradition the women of his family visited his grave. It was the genius of Khomeini's lieutenants, first in 1963 and then again in the course of 1978, to use those red-letter days as occasions for modern street protest and to provoke new instances of suffering and commemoration.[18]

In a sermon in Najaf, distributed by cassette tape to mark the fortieth day after the deaths in Qom, Khomeini cited an old Tradition of the Seventh Imam that knowledge would vanish from the world, like a snake into a hole in the ground, and then reappear in Qom. He gave the Tradition a modern, even leftist, twist. "It is not knowledge alone that spreads out from Qom, but knowledge and action," he said. While appearing to thank the three clerical leaders in the city, in reality he jeered at them for stopping short of criticizing the monarchy. He called on the public to act "like Moses before the Pharaoh of our age, pick up our staffs and oppose this little chap. Nobody should support this regime."[19]

On February 18, there were riots in Tabriz in the northwest. As mourners arrived for a memorial service for the dead of Qom at the Mirza Yusef Aqa Mosque, they found it surrounded by police. According to an eyewitness, a university student named Mohammed Tajali berated the police commander, who shot him dead. The crowd carried his bier through the town, shouting: "Death to the Shah," "Long Live Khomeini," and "O Hosein!," attacking and setting fire to liquor stores, banks supposedly under Bahai control, the Pepsi-Cola factory (owned by a Bahai family), luxury stores, statues, cinemas, and offices of the Rastakhiz.[20] Martial law was declared and, for the first time since 1963, the army was deployed on the streets of an Iranian city. Without baton rounds, tear gas, or horses schooled for crowd control, the army had only live fire.[21] The two days of rioting left six dead and 125 injured while 250 were arrested. Seventy-three bank branches in the city, eight cinemas, and four hotels were burned.[22] Michael Metrinko, the U.S. consul (who was later to spend 444 days as a "guest of the Ayatollah"), reported that the bulk of the rioters were unemployed young men and their targets the symbols of secular society.[23] The queen could understand that the clergy might reject Pahlavi modernity, but found "inexplicable" that the students, opposition, and bazaar should join them.[24] Mohammed Reza sacked the provincial governor and ordered a commission of inquiry.

In a message on the 27th, Khomeini praised the "struggling people of Tabriz . . . for giving the [regime] a smash in the mouth. In every lane and quarter of every town and village, the cry goes up of 'Death to the Shah!'" With the hyperbole that was his favorite species of rhetoric, Khomeini added, "In all the annals of Iranian history, there is nothing to compare with the bloodthirsty massacres of this wild criminal."[25]

At a meeting the same day of the Women's Organization of Iran at Aryamehr Stadium, Mohammed Reza replied in kind. He said: "The pillars of the country, founded on the Shah-People revolution and the Rastakhiz Party of the Nation, are strong and will not be injured by the death throes of an unholy red-black alliance." Then, giving Khomeini an insult quite as good as he had received, Mohammed Reza said: "Let the dog bark: the moon will go on shining."[26] He confided to Sir Anthony Parsons about this time that "his most implacable enemies, and the most powerful, were the mullahs with their hold on the minds of the masses. They could neither be bought nor could they be negotiated into co-operation with a regime which they did not recognise. One side had to lose." Parsons added that the Shah "left me in no doubt that he could not imagine himself losing this battle."[27]

As the days elapsed toward the fortieth after the Tabriz riots, Mohammed Reza gave orders "to avoid bloodshed for the third time at all costs."[28] On March 28, an order for tear gas shells and launchers that had been held up in Washington by the State Department's Human Rights Bureau was forced through by the White House.[29]

On March 30, the fortieth day after Tabriz, there were demonstrations in Tehran and the provincial towns. In Yazd, a desert town east of Isfahan, dogs were driven through the bazaar with placards reading "TOWARDS THE GREAT CIVILIZATION," the title of Mohammed Reza's new book, pinned to their rumps. A militant Khomeini disciple, Ayatollah Mohammed Saduqi, lost control of a mourning march, police fired their weapons, and a score or more people lost their lives.[30] Parsons, touring the old town a couple of days later, was unsettled by the eerie reversion to normality, the textile factories working and the bazaar in business. "It was outside my experience and lulled all of us into a false sense that the situation could not be so bad after all," he wrote. "It was as though each separate incident was a firework which flared up and died down again."[31]

Foreign governments pursued their commercial interests. Fred Mulley, the British defense secretary, visited over the Iranian New Year to try to unfreeze payments for the Shir Iran tank and the Isfahan armaments factory. When Parsons took Mulley down to Kish, where Mohammed Reza was spending the Iranian New Year, the Shah "looked fit and well and was very much in holiday mood." He had just ridden out with King Hussein of Jordan, and the audience took place with dogs and children milling about the room.[32] (A letter of intent was signed in May for the so-called Military Industrial Complex in Isfahan, at a cost of £750m, of which two thirds would be paid in the form of oil to BP.) Margaret Thatcher, leader of the Conservative opposition, came to Iran at the end of April but was deterred by her escort from visiting the Isfahan bazaar. A visit by Queen Elizabeth, no less, was planned for the following spring. Walter Scheel, the West German president, also came to Tehran to seal an order for six Type 209 diesel-electric submarines, to be built at the HDW yards at Kiel and Hamburg, for a total cost of about 1 billion marks. (The Islamic Republic canceled the contract and sought to recover DM231 million in working capital provided by Mohammed Reza, some of which had been used to pay bribes.)[33] Ronald Reagan passed through.

In attempting to bring the economy under control, Prime Minister Amouzegar was pursuing a policy of deflation that discouraged investors and left many people idle. A staged rally organized by the Rastakhiz at the site of the Tabriz riots on April 9, with Amouzegar and most of the cabinet present, was infiltrated by oppositionists and fights kept breaking out. The day before, Rastakhiz agents blew off the doors of apartments belonging to a number of National Front leaders, who had formed a Committee for the Defense of Freedom and Human Rights late in 1977. Messages were pasted on trees and lampposts with the warning: "Gentlemen, these are the first warnings of the Underground Vengeance Organization."[34] A week later bombs were planted in lawyers' offices and one lawyer was beaten up in the street.

One of the targets of the attacks, Mehdi Bazargan, an engineer who formed the principal link between the Mossadeqists and the clerical opposition, said in a foreign radio interview that the Shah "has united every class against him. While His Majesty is in the kingdom, Iran will never know freedom."[35] In London, Ambassador Radji agonized over a dispatch to Hoveyda. In the end, while praising steps "to discard the rigid discipline that, thanks to HIM's revolutionary changes, a society of Iran's present social and intellectual maturity no longer requires," Radji wrote that "if it is intended that, parallel with liberalisation, the Committees of Revenge or National Resistance are to resort to practices that world public opinion must regard as totally unacceptable . . . it would be a thousand times preferable to return to our former ways."[36] In the privacy of his daily journal, Radji wondered whether "the events of the past few weeks will ultimately prove to be a healthy lesson for HIM; [and] whether the casinos and Madame Claude girls can now be regarded as not essential to Iran's forward march; whether less money will be spent on arms; and whether the Rastakhiz Party will be allowed to disappear."[37]

On April 27, 1978, Mohammed Reza received a bad shock. His ally and client in Afghanistan, President Mohammed Daoud Khan, was overthrown and murdered by Communist officers of the Afghan army. So began the Afghan civil war which has lasted, with interruptions, to the time of writing. Apt, like many Iranians then and now, to see all political phenomena as conspiracies of the great powers, Mohammed Reza began to fret that the United States had abandoned the region and that Iran, too, would now fall into the Soviet sphere. "Is it conceivable," he asked his friend Nelson Rockefeller, the former U.S. vice president, "that the Americans and the Russians have divided the world between them?"[38] On a state visit to Hungary on May 13, Mohammed Reza pronounced to reporters, "Iran will not become Iranestan": that is, a Soviet Socialist republic.[39] He also wrote to President Carter saying that he would now need to strengthen Iran's defenses and increase his purchases of arms.[40]

Meanwhile, the religious protest was faltering. The fortieth day after the Yazd killings passed without great incident. Saduqi, the leader of the radicals in Yazd, wrote in exasperation to the leading clergy in Qom and Najaf, complaining of their inaction.[41] While successful in spreading the clerical protest beyond Qom, the demonstrations had never mustered more than a few thousand or gained a firm foothold in the capital. Nobody, except Khomeini and his lieutenants and the shattered remnants of the armed left, expected or wanted revolution. The liberal or secular opposition, including Bazargan and the National Front, while wary and suspicious of Mohammed Reza's sincerity, wished to consolidate the gains already made. Much of the protest now took the form of scattered attacks on Bahai property, cinemas, bars, and restaurants.

In a long dispatch to London on May 10 entitled "What happens if the Shah dies?," Parsons saw the outlook as bleak rather than appalling. The Pahlavi state had slain all the conventional dragons (feudalism, imperialism, and foreign monopolists), but had now lost the initiative. Mohammed Reza's liberalization policy, he wrote, "amounted to a tactic without an overall strategy," and as such was "merely whetting appetites for more." The Rastakhiz was a "fiasco." "Their car has bogged down in the sand," Parsons wrote. Still, the opposition was disunited, the armed forces loyal, and the generals "a mediocre lot." In conclusion, he wrote: "I do not believe there is a serious risk of an overthrow of the regime while the Shah is at the helm."[42] He then left for three and a half months of home leave. The U.S. ambassador, William Healy Sullivan, a veteran of Indochina with a pro-consular notion of his duties, also left on leave to Washington, where he chivvied the State Department to approve sales of tear gas.[43]

At the beginning of June, Mohammed Reza removed General Nassiri as head of Savak. In his place, he appointed not the hard-line Sabeti but Nasser Moqaddam, an officer from military intelligence more in the moderate Pakravan style. Radji predicted he would be "a humanizing influence" at the security service.[44] A little later, Mohammed Reza appointed Dr. Abbas Safavian as his personal physician, in place of the Bahai Dr. Ayadi. On July 5, Hoveyda made public a stricter code of conduct for members of the royal family in business affairs. In the atmosphere of relative calm, with the schools and universities shut and the forty-day demonstration a quiet affair on June 17, Mohammed Reza took himself to his beach house at Nowshahr, where he brooded.

In a speech on August 5, the seventy-second anniversary of the granting of the Constitution in 1906, Mohammed Reza announced the age of "responsible democracy" in Iran: freedom of association and speech and the press within the Constitution, and elections for the next Parliament in June 1979 that would not be confined to candidates of the Rastakhiz, but open to all. The unhappy two-year experiment with a one-party state was over. He said: "I can absolutely assure you that the elections must be one hundred per cent free: that is, everyone may cast his vote and have his vote counted."[45]

In private, Hoveyda told Ambassador Radji (who was visiting from London) that the court should be able to control 120 seats in the new House. It was a matter of negotiating Ramazan, due to begin on the morrow, and the mourning rites of Ashura in December. Ever sanguine, Hoveyda was confident of "manipulating" the elections.[46] Radji called on Princess Ashraf, his former lover, at her newly decorated house at Saadabad. "Well, is this what you wanted?" she asked. "Are you happy now?" With as much delicacy and tenderness as he could muster, Radji advised her to go abroad for a while, "until things cool down." On August 8, he was driven down the jetty at Nowshahr to call on Mohammed Reza. For all the gossip, the Shah looked "well, if a little thinner." He had evidently been brooding, for he asked: "Do our Western friends also have a hand in the current disturbances?" When Radji proposed a scheme to split the religious opposition, by lending support, funds, and publicity to a moderate such as Ayatollah Shariatmadari, Mohammed Reza answered: "On all this, people are now working." The audience went so well that Radji forgot to put across his chief proposal: that the Shah withdraw from all but the military and foreign policy aspects of government.[47]

With the opening of Ramazan, the radical clergy reverted to a more traditional style of protest. When a leading clergyman of Isfahan, Jalaleddin Taheri, was arrested for criticizing the monarchy from the pulpit, there was a strike in the famous handicrafts bazaar and a *bast* or sit-in at the house of his more conservative colleague, Mohammed Khademi. On the evening of August 10, violence broke out, and on

August 11 martial law was declared. Chieftain tanks, with their barrels wrapped in canvas and the crews in open turrets, were parked at intersections.[48] According to the martial law administrator, six persons were killed. In an analysis of the security situation at this time, the CIA station declared that Iran "is not in a revolutionary or even a pre-revolutionary situation."[49] Then, on August 19, an event occurred which shattered all illusions and drove Iran over the edge.

That Saturday, at about ten o'clock in the evening, four young men set fire to a ramshackle cinema in the old British oil town of Abadan in the southwest. In under five minutes, more men, women, and children died in pain than in all the prisons and torture chambers of the Pahlavis in half a century. The death toll was put first at 377, then raised to 430, and then again to 470. (The sextons at Abadan Cemetery spoke of 600 corpses, and the cinema cashier, who had counted the takings for the last show of the day and gone home, said he had sold 650 tickets.)[50] I thought at the time that Khomeini's people were desperadoes beyond all my experience and Mohammed Reza should book his suite at the Excelsior in Rome. In a year marked by caution and restraint on both sides, the Abadan fire was the exception.

Khomeini and the liberal opposition immediately blamed the court, which was so divided and demoralized it could not respond. Foreign correspondents reported that the Rex Cinema fire was the work of Savak provocateurs bent on smearing the Muslim opposition, or on scaring the neutral public into rallying round the regime.[51] Many Iranians and, notably, many Iranian women abandoned the monarchy.[52] The oil industry, on which the Pahlavi state depended for its revenue and credit, turned against the regime and shut down.[53]

That false version of events has survived to this day and would survive for all time but for two contingencies. History sometimes comes down to a few wretched individuals and, at rare moments, to a single one.

The families of the victims refused to keep silent for the good of the Revolution but rather demanded justice. Much later, after Mohammed Reza had gone, they staged a sit-down strike in the heart of Abadan and then in the cemetery where their parents and children lay. They were repeatedly attacked by revolutionary militiamen. After 106 days, the strike was broken up by Revolutionary Guards.[54] At last, in the summer of 1980, the families were granted a form of a public trial in the Taj or Crown Cinema, built by Anglo-Iranian in the 1940s, and renamed after the Revolution the Naft or Oil Cinema.[55] The victims' families, numbering some seven hundred people, filed past marines and Revolutionary Guards into the building, gave up their matches and cigarette lighters, and heard what they had always known: that the fire had been set by religious radicals.

The chief perpetrator was tormented by conscience. He admitted the crime to his friends and his mother. Traveling by bus the length of Iran, he tried to confess his guilt, but could find no one to listen. At the Alavi School in Tehran, he could not press through the crowds to reach Khomeini. He was sent away by the revolutionary interior minister. He sat for hours in the waiting rooms of the great divines of Isfahan, but they drew in their skirts and told him it was not their business. Portrayed as a Savak agent, expelled from all society, he was not molested, for he had on him the mark of Cain.[56] At the hearing in the Naft Cinema, for all the attempts of the public prosecutor to mitigate his guilt, the judge to blame the "satanic Pahlavis and their Israeli and American overlords," and the screams of his mother outside the door, he wept and confessed.[57] At dawn on September 4, 1980, the Islamic Republic gave him the bullet he craved and, like a wounded animal, put him out of his misery.[58]

CHAPTER 8

The Burnt Cinema

◇

So We ordained for the sons of Israel that whoever
took one life (except in retribution or for wickedness on
earth), it would be as if he murdered the whole world.

—Koran[1]

Hosain Takbalizadeh was a junkie and a drifter. Trained as a welder, he
lived with his mother and her second husband, who sold cold drinks
from a pavement stand, in one of the streets or as they were called in
Anglo-Indian fashion "Lines" in the shadow of the refinery at Abadan.
Unemployed, he hung out with his friends on the corner and dealt heroin and hashish.[2] He had been in and out of jail since 1975 for theft,
armed assault, and affray.[3]

Abadan was a town unlike any in Iran. An alluvial island, about
forty miles by as little as two miles wide, bounded by rivers on all sides,
with temperatures in summer of 125 degrees and 99 percent humidity,
it was a place of palm groves and scattered hamlets until Anglo-Persian
built its refinery, which became the world's largest. The town drew in
laborers from Kurdestan and the Arab districts, and a population of
60,000 in the 1920s had become 300,000 by the mid-1970s. The transfer of the crude oil terminal to Kharg Island in the Gulf, and refinery
exports to Bandar Shahpur, was partly made up for by a petrochemicals
industry producing polyvinyl chloride (PVC), dodecyl benzene deter-
gent, and caustic soda, and an international airport. Managers lived
in the old British garden suburbs of Bawarda, Park, and Braim, while
laborers, the unemployed, and shopkeepers clustered in the bazaar of

Abadan City in shabby streets interrupted by pipework and stinking of hydrogen sulphide.

The segregation evident in Inge Morath's photographs of the Consortium era—the foreigners on stools in a half-timbered pub downstairs, the Iranians on the floor round the samovar on the roof[4]—had vanished but had left Abadan with schools, hospitals, tennis and boat clubs, parks and welfare institutions that could compare with those of the capital. "Don't speak of Abadan, but speak of Paris," went the local song.[5] Abadan played no part in the disturbances of the first half of 1978 and the refinery and petrochemical industry were working as normal.

The public prosecutor made much of Hosain's sad family circumstance. At some point, Takbalizadeh was introduced by a certain Asghar Nowruzi to religion, studied the Koran, and gravitated toward a religious institute in Abadan called the Hoseinieh of the Isfahanians. He made friends with three men, described by the court as "good lads from a moral point of view": Farajallah Bazarkar, who ran a radio repair shop in the bazaar, and two others named in court only as Yadollah and Fallah. (They are presumed to have perished in the fire.)[6] Takbalizadeh was sent to Isfahan to cure his addiction but soon tired of the treatment and returned to his old habits in that town.[7] After the riots and deaths in Qom at the beginning of January 1978, his new friends searched him out in Isfahan and forced him to undergo in-patient treatment in the Tavanbakshi hospital. Takbalizadeh returned by bus to Abadan on August 18 with a stack of clandestine religious literature and tapes, alighting on the edge of town and walking home. His friends found him that evening at his mother's and said to him: "We want to set fire to a cinema."[8]

Khomeini loathed cinemas, and applauded attacks on them. Though there is no report of his ever having entered one himself, he believed that the West employed feature films to distract the Iranian public from its religion, traditions, and duty, and he did not like the promiscuous mingling of the sexes in the darkened auditorium.[9] By the middle of Ramazan and August, some two dozen cinemas across Iran had been burned. On August 9, 1978, the mob had attacked the Shah Abbas Hotel in Isfahan, a restored caravanserai that was the finest hotel in Iran, and on the 11th crowds set fire to cinemas and liquor stores in the *grande allée* in the town, known as Char Bagh or "The Four Gardens." Martial law was imposed and there was a sit-in at the house of an elderly religious scholar, Khademi. On the 13th, arsonists attacked a restaurant in Tehran popular with foreigners, the Khansalar, where ten Americans were among the forty injured. The unrest spread to Shiraz, and on the 16th, the Queen's Shiraz Festival was canceled. Sobbing, Takbalizadeh told the court amid the screaming of the women: "I am not a criminal and a murderer, but I wanted by this means to come close to the people making the revolution but in my ignorance I made a great mistake." [10]

That evening the friends filled four small drink bottles with solvent (*thiner* in the anglicized Persian of the town) and poured it over the lobby of the Soheila Cinema, where it did not catch. [11] They decided they needed to stabilize the solvent. [12] The next day, August 19, was the anniversary, by the Iranian solar calendar, of the *coup d'état* that toppled Mossadeq in 1953. At the head of the "Line" in which his mother's house stood, Takbalizadeh met his friend Farajallah or Faraj, who said, "Let's do it tonight." They ate a liver kebab at their usual stand, while Farajallah returned to his shop to mix the solvent with vegetable oil and poured the mixture into four soft-drink bottles. By now it was eight o'clock. They took a taxi to the Soheila, but found the ticket office shut. Returning downtown, opposite the Municipality they saw the Rex Cinema, and Faraj jumped out and bought four tickets. [13]

The Rex was on the second floor of a building on a shopping arcade, opening onto Municipality Street. Downstairs in an old shopfront was the ticket office, and then customers climbed the stairs to an L-shaped corridor that ran down one side and the back of the auditorium, with three sets of doors to the theater, a door to the projection room, and, at the end, a small snack bar or buffet. In addition, there were emergency exits to fire escapes each side of the screen that were either locked or, fatally, opened inwards. This being Abadan, the wooden walls of the auditorium were clad in PVC.

That evening the cinema was showing an Iranian film, *The Deer,* which the young men had seen before. It had already started. Takbalizadeh, Farajallah, Yadollah, and Fallah carried in the bottles of thinner in bags of juice and pistachio nuts, went into the four-toman balcony auditorium, and sat on a single seat. About fifteen minutes later, Farajallah slipped out to the lavatory at the head of the stairs, found nobody about, and returned. A little later, about halfway through the film, they went out into the lobby. There was nobody in the corridor, or at the water fountains, and the buffet was closed. Now sobbing uncontrollably, Takbalizadeh told the court: "Faraj and I poured the stuff on the back wall and chairs of the buffet, while the others spread it where the corridor met the main stairs."

He struck a match and a wall of flame engulfed the corridor; and then, astonishingly, he went back into the auditorium, and sat down with Faraj and Yadollah (Fallah had disappeared). Perhaps, the prosecutor suggested, he had just wanted to play the hero, and warn the people, but Takbalizadeh demurred. He said: "I wanted to say something, but I did not have the strength. Then somebody from behind screamed, 'The cinema is on fire!'" The film stopped. The lights came on, and then went off again. With the main doors on fire, people scrambled down through the three-toman seats to the doors by the screen, but these were either locked or the crush was too great to allow them to be opened. Many died in their seats, evidently choked by the gases from the burning PVC. Takbalizadeh escaped by the main stairs. The janitor and an employee ran up the stairs from the street and attempted to work the fire extinguishers but were baffled by them and the smoke and made their escape. Firefighters tried to break down the west wall of the cinema, but were unsuccessful.

In Tehran the following evening, Sunday, Mohammed Reza had come back from Nowshahr to attend the garden party always held at the queen mother's palace at Saadabad to celebrate his return in triumph from Rome in 1953. Official celebrations had been canceled, but Taj ol-Moluk was not to be gainsaid, and the cream of Tehran society collected under the old planes and pine trees, the women in full *décolleté* or plunging necklines and the men in dinner jackets. It was to be the last reception at the Iranian Imperial Court.

To one of the guests, Mohammed Reza, sitting beside his mother on the verandah, looked aged, downcast, and worn out. He seemed to have lost weight. "The whole evening he did not move from his seat for a second and stuck close to his mother like a helpless child," she wrote. After dinner, Prime Minister Amouzegar appeared on the verandah and whispered into the Shah's ear. "Whatever it was that he said, it made the Shah so angry that he pushed his Prime Minister violently away from him," she wrote.[14] No doubt, Amouzegar was attempting to resign.

Rumors spread as fast as the flames. It was said that General Reza Razmi, the Qom police chief who had been transferred to Abadan after the January riots in the seminary town, had ordered the doors to be chained so that nobody could escape; that the city fire trucks had no water; and that the police hindered the Abadan Fire Department's work. There is no evidence for any of that. On the contrary, the fire department had tried to smash down one wall of the auditorium. (As the most combustible town in Iran, Abadan probably had the best-trained civilian fire brigade in Iran.) A woman who managed to escape told the court she saw no chain over the main door. Nonetheless, Judge Musavi-Tabrizi in 1980 condemned to death—along with Takbaliza-deh—the elderly owner of the Rex (who had been away in Tehran), the cinema manager, the Abadan antiterrorist chief and investigating officer, an off-duty policeman, and a Savak officer who had just been transferred to Abadan but had not started duty. Others, including fire-fighters, were condemned to jail.

In a message to the people of Abadan on August 22, the day of the funeral for the victims of the fire, Khomeini treated the rumors as fact. "Only the authorities," he said, "could have lit the ring of fire round the cinema, and ordered the cinema staff to lock the doors." Deploying a syllogism, he said: "This inhuman act is contrary to the laws of Islam, and therefore cannot have been committed by the opponents of the Shah, who have risked their lives and property for the sake of Islam and Iran."[15] He continued: "This heart-breaking tragedy is the work of the Shah, his masterpiece, and designed as grist to his vast propaganda mills both at home and abroad."[16] Nonetheless, Khomeini continued to rail against cinemas. In an interview with French television in Najaf on September 14, he said that movie theaters were places of corruption which the public, spontaneously and without direction from the clergy, had decided must be destroyed. The Rex fire, however, was the work of the Shah's agents.[17] (He was still claiming that a year later.) The National Front, as opportunistic as the clerical opposition, in a statement on August 24 likened the Rex fire to the burning of the Reichstag in Berlin on February 27, 1933, which allowed Hitler to impose a state of emergency and destroy his left-wing opponents.[18] Parsons later reported to London that although the fire was "almost certainly the work of opposition extremists," the rumors of government agents "showed, dramatically, the latent hostility of popular opinion."[19]

Government and court were paralyzed. Daryoush Homayoun, the minister of information, said the fire broke the spirit of the Shah, and caused him to become uncertain.[20] In an outburst in front of Ambassador William Sullivan, just returned from leave, Mohammed Reza accused the British and CIA of orchestrating the unrest. Why was the CIA suddenly turning against him?[21]

Nobody was willing to provoke the religious opposition. Queen Farah was dissuaded by Amouzegar from visiting the families of the victims. "I felt that he had lost confidence, confidence in the king and myself as symbols of strength and harmony in the country," she wrote. "I felt that he no longer had the same image of me, the image that had allowed me to talk freely and sincerely with all Iranians over the last twenty years."[22] All around her, she sensed a changed attitude. A former minister sent her a Koran.[23] As the British chargé d'affaires commented to London on August 29, the government's "hopes of turning the ghastly Abadan fire to advantage were dashed."[24] Takbalizadeh sat at home with his mother until months later, on December 26, he was arrested for affray and consigned to prison, but not brought to trial. There he would stay until the prisons were opened on February 12, 1979.[25]

Mohammed Reza put his faith in the Qom establishment and their fear and distrust of Khomeini. It was too late. The three leading scholars in Qom announced they were sending a delegation to Abadan to investigate the Rex fire but, for reasons that can well be imagined, it never reported and probably never set out.[26] Through interlocutors including General Nasser Moqaddam of Savak and Farah's secretary, Houchang Nahavandi, Shariatmadari was calling on Mohammed Reza to do something "spectacular."[27] Whatever the Delphic words from Qom meant, the Shah decided to let go the honest and surly Amouzegar, a decision that he came to regret.[28] Three governments came and went, each weaker than the last and more ready to make concessions to the liberal opposition and Khomeini. Old scores were settled, and many men, and some women, who had enjoyed the Pahlavi sunshine found themselves in prison. Like scorpions within a ring of burning petrol, the Pahlavi court stung itself to death.

Amouzegar's replacement on August 27, Jafar Sharif-Emami, received from Mohammed Reza a promise of full executive power. Born into a clerical family in 1910, Sharif-Emami had studied on a railway scholarship in Germany and Sweden, and had been arrested and imprisoned for a year in a purge by the British and Soviets of supposed German sympathizers at the Trans-Iranian Railway in 1943. He had served a brief stint as prime minister in 1960–61, until a teachers' strike in which a man was killed by police caused Mohammed Reza to demand his resignation. Nonetheless, he was elected president of the Senate and served for fifteen years as director general of the Pahlavi Foundation, where charitable works were inextricably intertwined with Mohammed Reza's investments.

Sharif-Emami was principally known as Grand Master of the Grand Lodge of Iran, which had been founded with pomp in 1969 in affiliation with the French, German, and Scottish Crafts. Freemasonry had appealed to the Iranian nobility and secretarial class since the first informal lodge, known as *faramushkhaneh* or "The House of Forgetting," was set up in the 1850s. But it was a source of suspicion to society at large, to the clergy and to such non-Masons as the Pahlavis, father and son. It is not beyond conjecture that Mohammed Reza, who exaggerated the influence of the Freemasons in both Iran and abroad as he did all secret societies, hoped to enlist the Brotherhood to his aid.[29] (Later, after Sharif-Emami's flight, the Grand Lodge's records in his house fell into the hands of revolutionaries, who used them as dossiers to persecute the remaining Masons.)

Bald and ponderous, Sharif-Emami had no more of a political following than Amouzegar, but lacked his honesty and grasp of detail. The queen had tried to secure the post for her chief secretary, Nahavandi, a French-trained economist and liberal, who met Mohammed Reza on the 22nd.[30] On the 25th, Nahavandi and Moqaddam of Savak pleaded with her to block the appointment of Sharif-Emami. "He will lead us straight into the abyss," Moqaddam said. The queen called her husband on the telephone, listened for a moment, then replaced the receiver. "Unfortunately," she said, "there is nothing to be done about it."[31]

Sharif-Emami announced his government of "National Reconciliation" on August 27. In his first communiqué, he rescinded the Imperial calendar and closed the cabarets and the casinos on the Caspian (which were owned by the Pahlavi Foundation and had been established under his management). He allowed a number of clergymen to return from their uncomfortable rural exiles. The press and universities were freed and political parties, other than the Rastakhiz, were permitted. The U.S. Embassy dubbed his policy of concessions to all wings of the opposition "feeding the crocodiles." [32]

At his first cabinet that morning, Sharif-Emami opened with a prayer and then asked his ministers, including Nahavandi, who had reluctantly agreed to serve as minister of higher education, for their plans. It was clear, said Nahavandi, "he did not have the faintest idea of what to do." [33] The next day, for the first time, there were pictures of the exiled Khomeini in the newspapers. On August 29, Chairman Hua of the People's Republic of China arrived, leading a delegation of forty-two officials, for a four-day visit. What might in other circumstances have marked the triumph of Mohammed Reza's anti-Soviet diplomacy and forward alliances seemed empty and interminable.

Ramazan was drawing to an end. The festival that concludes it, known as the Feast of Fast-Breaking, revealed to Iran and the world the change in sentiment wrought by the Rex Cinema fire. The Tehran clergy applied for and received permission for a prayer gathering at the Musalla, a dusty vacant lot in northwest Tehran where years later Khomeini was to lie in state. At the end of the service, they were joined by tens of thousands of demonstrators in a march from Tajrish through the center of Tehran to the railway station in the popular quarters of the south. Tehran had never seen such numbers in the streets. Among them, for the first time, were large numbers of women in the black wrapper worn to the mosque and cemetery, known as the "prayer chador." Some of them were new to that costume, but wore it to advertise their rejection of Western dress and the paraphernalia of fashion and commerce that came with it, and their identity or alliance with the poor. The marchers called for the release of political prisoners, most notably Montazeri and the popular and respected Ayatollah Taleqani, and for the first time threw flowers at the soldiers deployed in trucks at the intersections, crying: "Brother soldier, why do you kill your brother?" [34]

Another large demonstration took place at the close of the festival on Thursday, September 7, this time without permission and in a grimmer mood. According to that afternoon's newspapers, enjoying a freedom they had not known since the 1950s, some 100,000 people took part in a march to the Shahyad Monument or "King-Memorial," which was renamed by the speakers the Freedom Memorial. That was ten times the numbers of even the Isfahan demonstrations of August. From the sidewalks, the marchers were sprinkled with rosewater while market trucks distributed fruit.[35] Placards called for "Islamic Government."

That day (or possibly on the 4th), Mohammed Reza flew over the crowds in a helicopter. In the days after, he kept repeating to visitors: "What have I done to them?"[36] Reports that the Shah's morale was low rang alarm bells in London and Washington.[37] His twin, as ever, had the opposite reaction. Arriving at Mehrabad on the 7th from a conference of the World Health Organization in Alma-Ata in Soviet Kazakhstan, Princess Ashraf was told that the road to her house in Saadabad was blocked by the demonstrators at the Shahyad. As a helicopter took her over the monument, she saw that one corner was "completely dark. I realised this black mass was a mass of Iranian women, in the mournful black *chador* their grandmothers had worn. My God, I thought, is this how it ends?" The next morning, she called on Mohammed Reza, who ordered her out of the country. "For the first time in our adult lives, he raised his voice to me: 'I am telling you that for my peace of mind, you must go.'"[38] Princess Shams also left Iran at this time.

Encouraged by the display of numbers, Khomeini and his advisers made an adjustment in strategy to ensure that momentum was not, as in the late spring, lost. In a message of congratulation to the "brave Muslim people of Iran" on the occasion of the festival, he called for a widening of the protest beyond the "Days of God." "Let nobody imagine that with the passing of the blessed month of Ramazan, his religious duties are in abeyance. These demonstrations against tyranny and in promotion of Islam are a form of worship that is not confined to only certain months or days."[39] On the 7th, Yahya Nuri, who administered a mosque and Hoseinieh in the district of Zhaleh Square about a mile to the east of the Parliament house, called on the people to demonstrate the next day, a Friday. "People were so fired up," the man who was to become revolutionary interior minister, Mohammed Reza Mahda-vi-Kani, recalled, "they did not care who had called the demonstration, and that none of the orthodox clergy was present."[40] In the changed circumstances since the Rex fire and the mass demonstrations of the festival, that was perilous.

Zhaleh Square—"Dew Square," or as it was already known, "Martyrs' Square"—was no Alexanderplatz or Tahrir Square, but a traffic-tormented circle about half the size of an American football field where Farahabad Avenue met the north-south Shahbaz Avenue.[41] In old Reza's time it marked the eastern city limit. Beyond it the road ran eastward past a power station, the "machine-gun factory" where rifles were assembled under license from the West German arms industry, a vast military airfield, and a barracks of the Imperial Guard, to the Tehran racetrack at Farahabad. In the explosion of the city after World War II, the desert had filled up with the streets and houses of a lower middle class.

Sharif-Emami was frantic to break the cycle of demonstrations. At a meeting of his security council that Thursday evening at 7:30 p.m., he reported that "His Majesty is deeply uneasy."[42] Though it was already 10:30 p.m., desperately late in the day, he decided to impose martial law for twenty-four hours in the capital and eleven other cities.[43] The announcement of martial law, banning gatherings of more than four persons, went out on the radio the next morning at 6 a.m., by which time the people had already begun to gather in Zhaleh Square and Farahabad Avenue. "Black Friday" had dawned.

Mohammed Shanehchi, a well-known middleman in the bazaar who like a million other Iranians was to find his way into exile, later recalled:

I rose at six to say my prayers. I turned on the radio and heard that there was martial law today. It had been arranged that the people would collect in Zhaleh Square. I was anxious and frightened. A little after seven, I got to Zhaleh Square and immediately heard the sound of gun shots. The people had collected there early in the morning and the order to shoot had been given. The people were trying to demonstrate, sh slogans and make speeches when the order to shoot was giv . in the first bout of firing, ten or twenty or thirty people fell. The pe e formed ranks, and pressed forwards, shouting slogans, and were met by fire. Four or five people were hit. The people scattered into the sidestreets. Whenever the shooting diminished, the people came forward. The firing and the running battles lasted until about four in the afternoon when the soldiers began to withdraw.[44]

George Chalmers, the British chargé d'affaires while Sir Anthony Parsons was on leave, cabled London that an eyewitness had told him that crowds collected at about 0800, and by 0845 had reached some 10,000 people, "shouting slogans for the removal of the Shah and the government, and in support of Ayatollah Khomeini." The crowd dispersed, but regrouped at about 0915, when the army shot into the air. "When this was ignored, our informant says that troops then fired into the crowd, killing a number of people. Our informant saw six people shot down." On the dispatch, a Downing Street official noted: "After months on the brink, this situation is turning very sour and dangerous."[45]

A set of photographs by Abbas Maleki, published in *Kayhan* on the second anniversary of the killings, shows more clearly than the spoken accounts what happened. In one image, five solders are crouched down at three-yard intervals between the broken white traffic lines of the roadway. They are without protection but for their rifles. Beside one is what appears to be a block of concrete or detached piece of paving. In front of them is a crowd of men and women carrying a banner on which the name KHOMEINI can be read, some people standing, some seated. None is obviously carrying a weapon.

There appears to be a standoff, calm and good-natured, but for three young men in front with their mouths open and arms raised. The next picture, taken an instant later, shows the young men in front spread-eagled on the ground, two or three more down in the crowd, and people rising like a wave from the seated position, still smiling.[46] In Bulletin No. 4, issued that evening, the Tehran Martial Law administrator, General Gholam Ali Oveissi, said that the army had come under attack from Molotov cocktails, firearms, and knives, and many soldiers had been wounded. Despite warnings to disperse, the crowd was reinforced and the soldiers obliged to respond. Unfortunately, based on hospital reports, by 5:30 p.m. there were 58 dead and 205 injured.[47] In addition, the Cyrus the Great department store in Farahabad Avenue was burned. At the $60 million Farahabad racetrack, opened by an Australian and Hong Kong company in June with thoroughbred and Turkoman races and totalizator or pari-mutuel betting, the meet went ahead, though racegoers were advised to avoid "bad traffic" in midtown. In the restaurant on the upper floor, waiters padded over the soft Isfahan and Nain carpets with caviar and champagne, while gunfire rattled away all afternoon, helicopters passed overhead, and the crowd approached the gates of the racetrack. The meet was called off. To at least one of the racecourse's employees, the contradictions of Pahlavi rule had come home to roost.[48] On September 14, at a ceremony of remembrance for the dead of Zhaleh at the cemetery of Behesht Zahra, there were cries of "Khomeini is our Leader."

Zhaleh Square confirmed in Iran the impression of the Rex fire, which was that the monarchy was bent on murdering the people. Rumor, the principal weapon of an unarmed people, put the number of dead as high as 3,000, then 10,000, and even, in an echo or rhyme of Khomeini's figure for the dead of 1963, 15,000.[49] General Oveissi was said to have blocked the entrances to the square, deployed Israeli snipers on rooftops, machine-gunned the crowd from helicopters. Those tales found their way into the foreign press and diplomatic and intelligence reports.[50]

In contrast, the reputable sources concur that the demonstration in Zhaleh Square and the surrounding streets went on all day, which would not have happened if thousands had been massacred in the morning. Recent writing, based on the unpublished analysis of the Islamic Republic's Martyrs' Foundation (which pays pensions to the families of Muslims fallen in the Revolution), gives a figure of sixty-four dead in the square, including a woman and a young girl, and twenty-four elsewhere in Tehran that day.[51] That is not far from the figure of eighty-six dead in Tehran on Black Friday provided by the Martial Law Authority to Mohammed Reza.[52]

If Oveissi wanted to terrorize South Tehran, he succeeded, but he also terrified the north. Issues of live rounds to soldiers were restricted, and from that week the Chieftain tanks carried no heavy munitions lest, as in 1953, a tank crew should go over to the people and attack Niavaran or the Supreme Commander's Staff.[53] Tight rules of engagement obliged the men on the street to submit to fraternization from the crowds and the officers to insults and abuse. As one minister later put it, "Mohammed Reza Pahlavi was emotionally wrecked, if not psychologically broken, by the events of Black Friday."[54] The next day, Mohammed Reza dismissed as minister of court Amir Abbas Hoveyda, for years his faithful prime minister but now seen as an obstacle to any reconciliation. Three former ministers were arrested on charges of corruption. Dr. Ali Qoli Ardalan, the new minister of court, announced new regulations for the activities of the royal family and their business ventures.

Hoveyda's dismissal coincided with the visit from Washington of his old enemy, Ardeshir Zahedi. Bellicose and self-advertising, Zahedi had served as foreign minister and then ambassador to Washington where he perfected, according to Hoveyda, *la diplomatie du caviar, des montres et des putes* (the diplomacy of caviar, gift watches and call girls).[55] Zahedi believed that he could do as his father had done in 1953 and save the Pahlavis, and he had found a ready listener in Carter's national security adviser, Zbigniew Brzezinski, who felt that any successor regime would be unfavorable to U.S. interests. For Iranians, with their long and cloudy memories, Tehran began to smell of 1953.

William Sullivan, anxious after Mohammed Reza's outburst over the CIA about "the very apparent despondency of Shah," urged President Carter to call the Shah by telephone. When he told Mohammed Reza of the plan on September 10, the Shah's "chin moved up from his knees to at least his chest."[56] Though Carter was busy at Camp David supervising peace talks between Egypt and Israel, they spoke for half an hour that evening. (Mohammed Reza claims the call was never made.)[57] On the 16th, a message was delivered from British prime minister James Callaghan in support of both liberalization and Mohammed Reza's throne. "Your declared intention to hold free elections next year found a ready echo among the many well-wishers of Iran in this country," Callaghan wrote.[58]

Sir Anthony Parsons, who had returned to Tehran during the night of the 13th, delivered the prime minister's message on the morning of the Saturday, the 16th. He was shocked by the Shah's appearance. He "looked exhausted and spiritless."[59] Mohammed Reza asked if Britain had any influence with the religious classes. Parsons answered that "thanks to his own suspicions of our . . . involvement with the mullahs, I and my predecessor had made a point of severing all connexion with the religious classes."[60] Parsons sent Peter Westmacott, second secretary, to see Ayatollah Shariatmadari in Qom at the end of the month. He did tell Mohammed Reza about it. He also developed contacts with the National Front.

Mohammed Reza said to Parsons that any regime in Iran other than his own rule would be worse for British interests. The British ambassador replied that "We were not hedging our bets, nor were we seeking reinsurance with any of the opposition elements."[61] Foreign Secretary David Owen, who disliked Mohammed Reza and the Pahlavi monarchy, minuted that the Shah's "passivity and depression is disturbing." Prime Minister Callaghan retorted: "Yes, but he can come back!" The British sent some riot-control equipment and a small military mission to train the army in tactics developed in Northern Ireland over the past eight years.

That evening, September 16, 1978, at half past seven in the evening, an earthquake measured at 7.8 on the Richter scale demolished Tabas, an ancient oasis town in Khorasan, killing 11,000 people, and another 9,000 in fifty villages. Over the objections of Sharif-Emami, the queen flew to Tabas "with a heavy heart,"[62] only to find that the Isfahan bazaar had organized relief and she was met with discontent and "even the anger of these suffering people." There were rumors that the Americans had been staging underground bomb tests in the desert. Iranians, who for centuries had relied on local saints to protect them from earthquakes, saw in the tremor God's displeasure with Iranian society. "I had the physical sensation of staggering under these blows," the queen wrote.[63] (The newspapers carried a picture of Mohammed Reza at the wheel of a vehicle at Tabas Airport, but he does not appear to have driven into town.) Mohammed Reza did open the International Trade Fair in Tehran on the 19th.

Stunned by the Zhaleh killings, the opposition withdrew from the streets to regroup. The initiative passed to the left. Wild-cat strikes broke out at the National Iranian Oil Company refinery at Abadan, the telephone company, the Central Bank and National Bank, the water board, the Isfahan steelworks, and the engineering industries in Arak and Tabriz. The strikers demanded increases in pay to compensate for soaring prices which, at an annual rate of 30 percent, were set to double in three years. Sharif-Emami conceded pay rises of 25 percent and more, at an annual cost thought to be more than $1.7 billion, which could only be financed by savings on capital projects, especially armaments. Parsons, who was nothing if not experienced, noted on October 3 that industrial unrest "could turn out to be a much more sophisticated way of embarrassing the government and one which the martial law authorities will find it very difficult to counter." [64] That is what was to happen.

Sharif-Emami then made an error. He pressed the Baath government of Iraq, under the good-neighborly provisions of the 1975 Algiers Agreement, to silence Khomeini. Saddam Hussein needed little encouragement to repress the Shia. On September 24, Iraqi agents surrounded Khomeini's house in Najaf and placed limits on his movement and his visitors. The blockade was lifted two days later, but Khomeini had lost patience and decided that he could no longer remain in "the nest of snakes." He applied for a visa for Kuwait. That threw the Sharif-Emami government into a dilemma. Sharif-Emami was alarmed lest Khomeini turn up in Iran for the Moharram mourning ceremonies in December. His following was now so great that his organization in Iran was dispensing monthly allowances or stipends to students of 10,000 rials or $125 per person, five times what Shariatmadari was paying. [65]

On October 2, Sharif-Emami summoned Parsons and Sullivan and asked whether they could press the Soviets to persuade the Iraqis to control Khomeini. Neither man was about to permit the Soviet Union a way into the crisis, and they rejected what Parsons called "a crude and inappropriate proposal."

Khomeini's lieutenants abroad began scouting locations. Not short of money, Sadeq Qotbzadeh flew to Syria and Algeria. Montazeri's son Mohammed ("Ringo"), who had connections with radicals in Lebanon, suggested Khomeini should seek the protection of the Palestinian militia in the Bekaa Valley in Lebanon. ("The Palestinians can't even protect themselves" was the retort from Khomeini's entourage.) [66] The search was complicated by the disappearance in Libya of Moussa al-Sadr, a pupil of Khomeini's in Qom who had been invited to Lebanon in 1960 and emerged in short order as the leader of the Shia in the south of the country. He was last seen on August 31, at his hotel in Tripoli, on his way to a meeting with the Libyan leader, Muammar Gaddafi.[67] They quarreled and reports filtered out that Gaddafi had had him murdered. (The Islamic Republic later launched an investigation, but then needed Gaddafi's help in the war.) Ebrahim Yazdi, the Houston surgeon who was also a U.S. citizen, insisted the Muslim world was not safe for Khomeini and he was able to win over Mostafa Chamran. Khomeini must go to Europe.

Parsons took to calling on the Shah at Niavaran every week to ten days. To present a united front, and because they got on together, he generally came with Sullivan. Parsons had nothing to convey from the Callaghan government and, in giving advice, he generally insisted it was his own opinion. He supported liberalization, though it now consisted in the imposition of religious orthodoxy, and opposed a military crackdown which, since the strikes, he thought unlikely to succeed.

By now, Parsons had concluded that the old "monolithic regime headed by the Shah . . . no longer exists." What had replaced it was a sort of triangle: the Shah at Niavaran talking to every sort of politician behind his prime minister's back, including those such as Ali Amini, prime minister in the early 1960s, who had been out of favor since 1963; Sharif-Emami at the prime ministry dismantling the Pahlavi state; and the generals, increasingly restive at the prime minister's conciliatory policies.[68] In a message to David Owen on October 9, Parsons wrote: "Popular support for Khomeini has reached the point where any agreement with the more moderate clergy may not be enough." On it, the prime minister minuted: "I think Dr. Owen should start thinking of reinsuring."[69] The Middle East Department of the Foreign Office in London, always more gloomy than Parsons, reported that on present trends, "the dynasty would be lucky to survive until Christmas."[70]

On October 11, the main newspapers went on strike in protest at General Oveissi's attempt to impose direct censorship. Sharif-Emami intervened and guaranteed their freedom. The prisons were emptying. Released without warning from Vakilabad Prison, Richard Savin found himself footloose and stoned in a bloody insurrection in Mashhad. Old M47 Patton medium tanks with rubber track masks prowled the city, and the evening was punctuated by machine-gun fire. That night two soldiers, a lieutenant and sergeant, became detached from their unit and tanks and, in desperation, fired into the crowd. Savin came upon their bodies in the bazaar, nailed to planks of timber and then dowsed with petrol. "They left the soldiers propped up in a doorway, faceless scarecrows with glazed blisters for eyes, soot black teeth grinning from mouthless caverns, and in the air that unmistakable acrid tinge of singed hair mingled with the sweetness of cooked flesh."[71]

Even the queen ("a tower of strength" to Parsons, "the one with guts" for Hoveyda) had her bad moments. She wrote in her diary: "I have the feeling there is no hope anymore."[72] Then she pulled herself together. "I have to stay strong; it's the only way to keep going."

CHAPTER 9

The Junction

◊

A sovereign may not save his throne by shedding his countrymen's blood.

—Mohammed Reza Pahlavi[1]

On Thursday, October 5, 1978, Khomeini left Najaf with four companions and an entourage of well-wishers for the Kuwait border. His intention was to spend seven or eight days as a guest of the Shia clergy in Kuwait, then travel to Syria. Arriving at noon at the Kuwaiti border post of Abdali, the party was kept waiting for half an hour and then denied entry. Turning back toward Iraqi territory, they were held in the Iraqi Security Service post at Safwan. Caught in a stateless no-man's-land, Dr. Ebrahim Yazdi managed to convey a plea for help to the U.S. administration in Washington, but it fell on deaf ears.[2] Finally, at about midnight, the Iranians were taken under escort to Basra, the principal city in southern Iraq.

In their enforced idleness, Yazdi pressed the case for Paris. Always concerned about his rank and dignity, Khomeini could not imagine a senior Shia clergyman residing "so to speak, among heathens," and he feared he might be drawn into *émigré* politics. He had, in addition, heard that French bread was made with pig fat.[3] Yazdi had two arguments in favor of Paris: air and telephone communications were excellent and Iranian citizens needed no visa. Yazdi was held overnight at the border, but when he arrived at the hotel in Basra on the morning of the 6th, Ahmad Khomeini told him that his father was persuaded.

The Iraqis were delighted to be rid of their troublesome guest. Embittered by the Algiers Agreement of 1975, Saddam Hussein was nonetheless not strong enough to provoke Iran. Khomeini's attacks on the Shah's regime were a source of friction between two countries that did not trust or like each other. The Iraqi government agreed to let Khomeini and his party travel to Paris, but on condition that they use the national airline, Iraqi Airways. The Iranians feared that the Iraqis were preparing either to do them in, or at best to deliver them to Tehran. They were haunted by the fate of Khomeini's old pupil Moussa al-Sadr, who had disappeared without trace in Libya. In reality, Saddam did not wish the French to have advance warning of their distinguished visitor and send him back to Baghdad. In secrecy, the Iranians were brought up by air from Basra and taken to the Dar-es-Salaam Hotel in Baghdad.

At Baghdad Airport the other passengers were boarded and the bulkhead curtains drawn, before the Iranian party, consisting of Khomeini, his son Ahmad, two members of his staff, and Dr. Yazdi, were prodded up a spiral staircase into the first-class lounge, which in a Boeing 747 occupies a hump-shaped upper deck. The only other passenger in the upper cabin was an armed Iraqi air marshal, who prevented them from descending to the main passenger deck.

It was not until they landed for a layover at Geneva that Yazdi was able to push past the marshal and call his associates in Paris from the terminal. At Orly-Sud, the party split into two and passed in "five or six minutes" through passport control. Once in the arrivals hall, they were greeted by a discreet welcoming committee, including Sadeq Qotbzadeh and Abol Hassan Bani-Sadr. They were taken to a fourth-floor apartment belonging to Bani-Sadr's friend Ahmad Ghazanfarpour, in the district of Cachan, in the southern suburbs beyond the Paris beltway known as the Boulevard Périphérique.[4]

Khomeini had insisted that he not be attached to any particular exile group, and was not pleased. As it turned out, the stream of visitors to the fourth-floor flat caused the neighbors to grumble, and after three days Khomeini moved to a shabby villa owned by a certain Mehdi Asghari in the overgrown village of Neauphle-le-Château, some twenty miles further to the southwest. The village was known, if at all, as the home of the orange liqueur Grand Marnier and, more recently, the novelist and screenwriter Marguerite Duras. The house, on the corner of the route de Chevreuse and the sentier des Jardins, became a sort of Qom translated to the frosty Ile-de-France.

As Khomeini sat under his apple tree at Neauphle-le-Château, his enemies destroyed one another. Britain discouraged Mohammed Reza from using force to suppress the protests. In Washington, civilian rivalry and an inexperienced president hindered policy, while the U.S. ambassador in Tehran, William Sullivan, pursued a line of his own devising. By January 1979, relations between Washington and its Tehran embassy had broken down, and Sullivan was insulting the president. The most decisive U.S. action was to warn the Soviet Union, which was attracted to Khomeini's anti-American rhetoric, against interference. Carter wrote in strong language to Communist Party secretary Leonid Brezhnev on November 21.[5] The revolutionaries could pursue their aims more or less unhindered from abroad.

Mohammed Reza himself, by his intrigues in November and December and then his departure in January, demoralized the Iranian officer corps. The general staff looked for direction from the U.S. military, but General Robert E. "Dutch" Huyser's mission in January, with badly drafted orders, succeeded only in preserving the leading officers for the firing squad. Providence itself could not have managed affairs more favorably to Khomeini. Many of the plans laid in Paris (for a shadow oil industry or military training in Lebanon) were overtaken by events. "We had no idea it would be so easy," one of the party later said. "We were planning for years of struggle. The Shah's fall took everybody by surprise."[6] Granted three months' residence in France, Khomeini received an extension on or just before January 2.

When President Giscard d'Estaing, who was on a visit to Brazil, was told of Khomeini's arrival in Paris, he was faced by unpalatable choices. He could allow the old man to stay, or send him back to his place of origin (Iraq), or to his homeland (Iran).[7] He had asked through French representatives in Tehran back on October 15 if Mohammed Reza would have any objections to Khomeini's "change in venue." The Shah did not, believing, in his own words, that Khomeini "could do as much damage from Hamburg or Zürich as he could from Paris." Mohammed Reza did not wish to provoke European public opinion by bullying "a frail and crazy old man."[8] In other words, he did not want Khomeini back in Iran and was confident (as he told Sir Anthony Parsons on October 10) that the French would "prevent Khomeini indulging in political activity."[9] Sharif-Emami thought Khomeini had made an error in going to a Christian country, which was also the headquarters abroad of the Communist Tudeh Party.[10] The British let out a sigh of relief. David Owen, the foreign secretary, had been advised that, in the most unlikely event of Khomeini seeking to come to Britain, "we would have to let him in."[11] (In fact, Khomeini's entourage rejected London because of the superstition, dating from the Constitutional Revolution of 1905–11, that Britain exercised an influence over the Shia clergy.)[12]

The move to Paris was, in Ebrahim Yazdi's phrase, a "turning-point." Khomeini now had at his disposal the engines of world publicity, and he worked them as once the clergy of the Constitutional Revolution had used the new media of lithography and the telegraph. In the space of 118 days, Khomeini gave several hundred print and broadcast interviews. Reminded by the French Interior Ministry both in Cachan and Neauphle that he must abstain from politics, he did nothing of the sort. Qotbzadeh arranged for the conservative newspaper Le Figaro, which supported the Giscard government, to interview Khomeini. After that, it was not easy for the French authorities to bar the world's press from flocking to Neauphle. Until Khomeini began to call for Iranian army troops to desert, the French were content to enjoy their fickle popularity in Iran. A bazaar merchant bought up all the spear lilies (gladioli) in Tehran and had them delivered to the French Embassy on what was then called France Boulevard and is now Nofeloshato. Air France and other French institutions were spared the violence against foreign property in Tehran that autumn.

For Ebrahim Yazdi, speaking long after his disgrace, Neauphle showed for the first time that royal government, which had survived, like many crueller, more incompetent, and more unpopular institutions for lack of alternative, now had that. Here was an "equation" anybody could understand: Shah out, Khomeini in.[13] Khomeini in France reinforced in Iranians a notion of themselves that was both vulnerable and precious. Instructed for half a century that they must put aside their old character, with its cramped houses and shabby dress and elaborate rituals, Iranians now saw that character paraded through Paris, capital of the world. They saw an Iranian acting in the fashion of approximately 1911, a man such as Fazlollah Nuri might have recognized. They chose to ignore the modernity that kept him there: the volunteers copying tape cassettes, the interpreters and spin doctors, the direct distance dial telephones and teletype, and more money in a day than Fazlollah saw in his lifetime.[14]

The villa soon proved too small, and the party rented a larger property across the road, where Khomeini and his son Ahmad moved. They were soon joined by his wife and their son-in-law Shahabuddin Eshraqi, who took charge of domestic arrangements and the feeding of the visitors. In the garden was the apple tree, somewhat in need of pruning, under which Khomeini liked to sit. Later, when the weather turned cold and wet, a tent was put up in the garden as for festivals at his house in Qom. The Iranians took over the Hôtel Verbois in the village. Life settled into a pattern set at an angle to or athwart the French civilization round about. Khomeini rose an hour before dawn, said his prayers, rested a little, received a digest of news from Yazdi, then walked in the empty lanes. Once he made an excursion to Louis XIV's palace at Versailles, scene of great events in another revolution. In the afternoon, he would preach a sermon in the garden or under the tent, and in a style more informal than his cold and harsh statements to the press.

Iranians are adept at close-quarters living, but there were tensions between the lay émigrés, many of them long resident in Europe or the United States, and the Najaf party. "I have no spokesman," Khomeini said, and a notice to that effect was pinned up, taken down by Yazdi, and then pinned up again.[15] The volunteers resented the delicacy of the visiting clergymen and their refusal, like spoiled women, "to put their hand to black or white" (pots and dishes). When his loyal disciple Sadeq Khalkhali came into the kitchen and started bawling orders, the young man at the sink (who was a doctoral student in chemistry in the Netherlands) said: "I am a volunteer here, and you can bloody get it yourself."[16] As for the laymen, Baqer Moin, the editor of the BBC Persian Service, captured them in a vignette from December: "Bani-Sadr stood in the street with the mien of someone who took himself too seriously. Ebrahim Yazdi, who was thought to be always up to something, was taking journalists aside and briefing them about the 'Imam's movement.' The gregarious Qotbzadeh on the other hand mingled with everybody, laughing, joking and exchanging pleasantries."[17] All three were to come bitterly to grief.

The press interviews were managed down to the commas. Khomeini received the journalists kneeling on the ground, either under the apple tree or in the tent. He did not rise to greet them or bid them goodbye. He answered only questions submitted in writing, and then on lines discussed with his staff.[18] He was, in the words of John Simpson of the BBC, "cold and fierce." He made no small talk. According to Yazdi, if Khomeini veered from the script, it did not matter, because the interpreter gave the prepared answer.[19]

Reporters, as unused to the Iranian practice of religious dissimulation (*taqieh* or *ketman*) as to sitting on the ground, found that Khomeini was a man like themselves. "I don't want to have the power or the government in my hand. I am not interested in personal power," he told a *Guardian* reporter on November 16. "After the Shah's departure from Iran, I will not become a president nor accept any other leadership role. Just as before, I limit my activities only to guiding and directing the people," he told *Le Monde* on January 9. As for the role of women in Islamic Iran, an issue of interest and not just to the women reporters, he said on November 6 (again to the *Guardian*): "Women are free in the Islamic Republic in the selection of their activities and their future and their clothing." None of this interpreter-speak was borne out by events.

Even those with more experience were misled. To the U.S.-based scholar Said Amir Arjomand, who saw him on January 2, 1979, Khomeini appeared wedded to Nuri's policies of seventy years before. Parliament should be restricted to small executive business, such as urban planning and traffic regulations, "that are not related to the [Holy] Law, and it is beneath the dignity of Islam to concern itself with them."[20] Arjomand came away thinking that the Islamic Republic would be a transient affair, the state would wither away, and God (or rather His lieutenants) would rule. (Arjomand underestimated the siren call, even to elderly clergymen, of the powerful, well-armed state.) In the first draft of the Constitution of the Islamic Republic that was prepared in France, according to Yazdi, Khomeini himself crossed out all references to the clerical dictatorship or "Stewardship of the Jurist" of his Najaf lectures.[21] A clergyman who gave a lecture in Paris on the topic was snubbed by Khomeini in public.[22]

By the end of October 1979, it was Khomeini, not Sharif-Emami or Mohammed Reza, who radiated power. It was as if some figure of fathomless authority had appeared and with a single glare brought modernity, like the flirtations and theatricals of *Mansfield Park*, to an end. A stream of men came to pay their respects or take instructions: his pupils Montazeri, Motahhari, and Mohammed Beheshti; the pious engineer Mehdi Bazargan, leader of a small group called the Iran Freedom Movement; Karim Sanjabi and Dariush Forouhar of Mossadeq's old National Front; and even, in the end, emissaries of the United States. As one British diplomat, schooled like so many of his type in the Persian lyric poetry of the Middle Ages, wrote: "The moths were drawn towards the brightest light."[23] Khomeini's intransigence, his refusal to alter his habits to suit his new domicile or the rules of diplomacy, seemed to cow and unsettle them. He had, more than any man of his generation, a talent for sitting still.

Now seventy-one years old, Mehdi Bazargan had been active in politics since the 1950s. Dispatched by Mossadeq to take over the oil company in 1951, he had passed the years of Mohammed Reza's autocracy as an engineer in private practice or in prison. Pious without fanaticism, honest without priggishness, he served as a bridge between the Mossadeqists and Khomeini's clerical followers. He wore a broad necktie of 1960s fashion. From his years in France, he had formed an attachment to parliamentary government. Cautious by nature, he felt the movement must come to some accommodation with the Iranian army and its chief supplier, the United States. At his two meetings with Khomeini at Neauphle on October 22 and 24, the first since the tumult of 1962, he was "struck dumb" by Khomeini's simplicity and optimism, and "his absolute refusal to take any account of the existence or influence of the United States."

Bazargan said: "We are not in Najaf or Qom now where our word is law."

Khomeini replied: "We will sell America oil at the market rate and buy from them, instead of arms, agricultural machinery. How can they object?"[24]

To gain control of the movement and to prevent a repetition of Zhaleh Square, Bazargan persuaded Khomeini to form a Revolutionary Council in Tehran which became active only in December and was revealed to the public in January 1979. Consisting of clergymen, Bazarganists, and a couple of dissident military officers, the Council always had, as Bazargan put it, a "turbanned" majority. The principal members were Bazargan himself and Mohammed Beheshti, a worldly and political cleric who had studied at Tübingen in West Germany and spent the second half of the 1960s as director of the Shia mosque in Hamburg. Mohammed Reza's last prime minister, Chapour Bakhtiar, called him a "Rasputin with two foreign languages," but that did no justice to the man's vision and capacity for organization. The Revolutionary Council permitted Khomeini, without rising from the ground, to sound out William Sullivan and to open contact with the officer corps. By December, Sullivan was astonished that the "liberation movement knew quite explicitly the attitudes and operations of the various military officials."[25]

Khomeini's departure for Paris set off a new wave of strikes. Schools, ministries, the railway, and Tehran Airport were all affected. A work slowdown began at the Abadan refinery on October 14, and two days later the technical staffs walked out. When the refinery guards moved in, the strike spread to the loading terminal on Kharg Island in the Persian Gulf and the production fields, the petrochemical industry, and the gas-gathering plants. That these strikes were occurring not in the bazaar and traditional trades but in the modern economy of Pahlavi creation was universally remarked.

At Niavaran, Mohammed Reza's choices were falling away. Relations had broken down between Sharif-Emami and the army, the oil fields were crippled, and the schools and universities in turmoil, with the Tehran University campus under student occupation. Mohammed Reza saw only two possibilities: a military government or a coalition government formed about some distinguished figure who might unite the "Constitutional" forces (that is, those willing to preserve the monarchy) against the Khomeinists and the hard left.

As to the first, Mohammed Reza said he was under pressure from his senior officers "to allow them to save the country."[26] When Colonel Colin Powell, a U.S. Army officer who was to reach high office under the Reagan and Bush administrations, visited the Officers' Club in Tehran on October 23, he found morale high. From a reviewing stand, he watched a parade of the brigade of royal guards, known as the *Javidan* or Immortals, "in tailored uniforms, berets, and gleaming ladder-laced boots, who performed with much shouting and martial flair. The Iranian officer next to me explained, 'Their loyalty is total. The Immortals will fight to the last man to protect the Shah.'"[27] In contrast, Mohammed Reza feared that a military government might provoke a general strike.[28] Both ambassadors supported him.

As for the second, a string of elderly politicians such as Abdullah Entezam, Ali Amini, and Mohammed Sururi paraded through his office at the Niavaran Palace. They needed to be old, as the Shah confessed, to be untainted by the autocratic government after 1963.[29] Entezam was stone-deaf but, as Mohammed Reza commented with more spirit now he was up to his old games, "still seems able to walk straight." Amini, in contrast, was "only 74."[30] Amini had served as prime minister in 1961–62, but Mohammed Reza had thought him merely the long arm of the Kennedys, and dismissed him as soon as he was able. It was a sign of desperation that he was toying with an Amini government. Parsons advised him on October 10 against changing the ministry, and said the government should "keep their nerve" until the opposition "exhausted itself."[31] He found the Shah "haggard" but calm and objective. Parliamentary elections now seemed a long way away. Looming over everything was the mourning month of Moharram, due to begin on the evening of December 1. It was a matter of surviving that. The lack of respect for Mohammed Reza at all levels "has become alarming," Parsons wrote.[32] The Shah had few visitors and one, the Tehran professor Ehsan Naraghi, found in the end he had to hitchhike to Niavaran because of the strikes. The palace administration was beginning to break down and William Sullivan once called to find nobody about, until he barged into the queen.[33]

Evin, as it emptied of prisoners, was thinking of the post-Pahlavi era. On October 25, 1978, the eve of Mohammed Reza's fifty-eighth birthday, the doors connecting the different blocks or *bands* were opened and Hosein Ali Montazeri received a visit. The Mojahedin leader, Masoud Rajavi, and about twenty other Mojahedin prisoners entered his cell and sat down. Rajavi said: "Mr. Khomeini has gone to Paris and it looks like the revolution will be victorious. What is he going to do? Whom will he select to run the government? Iran needs a force that is disciplined, experienced and prepared and the only group that is righteous, organised and capable of administering the country is us. You have some influence with Khomeini, so please pass him a message that the organisation that can run the country, achieve his objectives and is also correct in its religious observances is the Brigade of Mojahedin."

Constrained by Iranian and prison etiquette, Montazeri was dreading the return visit, but the next day the passage doors were bolted, and on the 30th both he and Ayatollah Taleqani (who was in the prison hospital at the Qasr) were released. Taken by car to the Savak headquarters at Sultanatabad, Montazeri was received by General Moqaddam himself and showered with apologies. According to Montazeri's account, the Savak chief maintained that he had no idea that he and Mr. Taleqani were in jail, had gone at once to His Majesty, saying that they were distinguished men, the country needed them.[34] The two clergymen were among 1,126 political prisoners released in the birthday amnesty, bringing the total to more than 2,700 freed since 1977.[35] There remained approximately 900 political prisoners, mostly of the left, who were released in the New Year by Chapour Bakhtiar.[36]

At the end of the month, there was a flicker of hope that even leaders of the National Front might take office in a coalition government under Abdullah Entezam. It was immediately extinguished. Karim Sanjabi of the National Front, who had served as minister of education under Mossadeq, had been invited to the Socialist International in Vancouver, and decided to break his journey in Paris. At their first meeting on October 28, Khomeini treated him with disdain. When Sanjabi attempted to speak privately, Khomeini ordered him to speak to the room. Khomeini refused to receive his visitor again until he had renounced the monarchy. Sanjabi canceled his trip to Canada. After cooling his heels in Paris for several days, he composed and Khomeini accepted a declaration which called for the abolition of the "illegal and unconstitutional monarchy" in favor of a new form of government on "the principles of Islam, democracy and independence," to be decided by referendum. That may not have mattered much for the few troops the Front could bring but it was the death knell for Iranian constitutionalism in its last bastion.[37] The National Front, active in politics since the 1940s and still lit by the faint nimbus of Mossadeq, could not afford to differ from an elderly jurist in exile. On his return to Tehran, Sanjabi was arrested by the military authorities and then, at Mohammed Reza's intervention, released. Sanjabi, the Shah noted, "is obviously hand in glove with Khomeini."[38]

On October 30, the oil workers once again came out on strike. Production of crude oil fell from 6 million barrels a day to 1.5 million and the throughput at the Abadan refinery from 600,000 to 200,000 barrels a day, which was not enough to supply the Iranian public over the coming winter. Gas supplies to the Soviet Union were cut and immense crude-oil tankers cluttered the shallow waters around Kharg Island. The revenues that underpinned Iranian credit, and hence all its international commerce, vanished. The bazaar reported an increase in remittances abroad, sales of gold jewelry and bullion, and a 10 percent rise in bank notes in circulation. "We are melting away like snow in water," Mohammed Reza told the two ambassadors the next day. He also said, in the manner of an aside, that the former Savak chief, General Nematollah Nassiri, would have to go to jail, and "probably, Hoveyda as well." [39]

On November 4, the occupation of Tehran University turned violent when students pulled down the statue of Reza Shah at the main gate. (Months later, it could still be seen lying, headless, with its stone belt, cartridge pockets and cape, among the weeds.) The army detachment at the gate fired through the railings, killing at least one student and wounding others. As news spread and film of the shooting was aired on television, there was uproar in Parliament and clashes across the city. At their meeting that evening, Mohammed Reza told the British and American ambassadors that Brzezinski had telephoned him the day before, offering strong U.S. support either for the formation of a coalition government or a military government. Though himself as skeptical as Parsons about the value of brute force, he understood Brzezinski to mean that he should "establish law and order first, and only then continue our democratization program." [40] Parsons, who believed that Mohammed Reza had made up his mind for a military government, returned to the British Embassy through the wreckage of burnt-out vehicles "with considerable foreboding." [41]

The next day, as Parsons put it, "the balloon went up."* On Sunday, November 5, Tehran burned. Banks, liquor stores, airline offices, hotels, a portion of the British Embassy, and other symbols of Pahlavism, for-

---

* In World War I, British artillerymen sent up balloons to signal to their own trenches the imminent start of firing.

eign influence, and modernity were set on fire. In Lalehzar, the stench of alcohol from the torched bars and restaurants caused even a KGB officer to swoon. Melted beer cans had fused into a sheet of metal on the asphalt.[42] In the ebb and flow of crowd action, and the bank notes and ticker tape fluttering in the air above Ferdowsi Square, there was a shift in the order of battle. The disparate forces making up the protest, whether those were college and high school students and young people, the bazaar, or the hard-left guerrilla groups, "effected a junction" (as they say in the military).

Along the boulevards laid out by Reza beside the university, free-thinking North Tehran and religious South Tehran, for the first time in the Pahlavi era or even since the Constitutional Revolution, combined and fraternized. A well-organized march in celebration of Ayatollah Taleqani's release from prison came up from the south of town into the bourgeois streets and joined forces with the students and their supporters.

Trevor Mostyn, a British Persianist on business in Tehran selling educational books, heard through the door of a bookshop opposite the university gates the shout, "The bazaris are coming!" He wrote: "At about 4.20 a huge, orderly procession bearing hundreds of portraits of Khomeini appeared through the smoke on our left [south]. The two masses gradually approached each other. When the two crowds came together, their very mass in unity was frightening. They spread through each other with huge cheers, and a ripple of embraces."

Through the smoke of the burning Pahlavi Foundation bank, the Omran Bank, and the drift of tear gas, an immense gun barrel appeared and then the entire Chieftain tank "rolled into full view and the crowd began to edge away, as if from some hellish beast," wrote Mostyn. "But then, but then—was that a flicker of a smile on a pale soldier's face?—a thunderous roar of joy burst from the crowd. Demonstrators leapt on the tank, hugging and kissing the soldiers until it became a moving bundle of cloth and flesh and pretty girls. 'Soldiers, you are our brothers!' filled the air and lily-white flowers seemed to bloom from their rifles."[43] The crowd did not know that the tank carried no heavy ordnance.

That day, along with all the cinemas downtown and midtown, liquor stores, insurance offices, and state companies, about four hundred bank branches were set on fire. The rumor of the day was that it was the work of *agents provocateurs* and Savakis, to show, as Trevor Mostyn put it, "what anarchy really meant." It is hard to imagine that Moqaddam of Savak would have been so reckless. The attacks of November 5 were, as a Central Bank vice governor put it the following week, "a determined and organised effort to break the banking system."[44] With the Central Bank paralyzed, and the Ministry of Finance on strike up to the level of director general, the National Bank found itself the only source of funds for the banks, and came close to failing. Over the next weeks, the old Imperial Bank, now known as the British Bank of Iran and the Middle East, had to restrict withdrawals to 5,000 rials. Foreign exchange was provided by the Central Bank only to the limit of 200,000 rials per person. Four banks, including Saderat, ran out of funds and had to be propped up.

There was no looting of the banks and few, or possibly no, casualties in the arson. Sir Anthony Parsons concluded that it was the work of the Mojahedin, with or without involvement of the secular Fedayan and the Communist Party.[45] As for the army, Parsons was puzzled by its inaction. The arsonists had been few in number and could easily have been dispersed. He was soon to have his answer.

In the late afternoon, a group of men broke into the British Embassy in Ferdowsi Street, and finding a consignment of bottled methane gas, set fire to the Chancery building and a guardhouse, and knocked out the telephone exchange and cipher room. (In London, Prime Minister Callaghan was woken by the duty clerk.) Held up by the Taleqani procession, Parsons finally made it back to the embassy to find crowds throwing stones up at the windows, and, at the back, a platoon of infantry with an armored car "standing there taking absolutely no notice of what was going on." From the nearby French Embassy, Parsons reached General Gholam Reza Azhari, chief of staff, on the telephone and gave full vent to his temper. "It is all your fault," Azhari replied. "You have been persuading His Majesty for too long to stop us from intervening and restoring the situation."[46]

Night had fallen, there was no electric power, and as he stood in the darkness, Parsons received a summons to the Niavaran Palace. Saying he would come only when he had done a roll call of his staff, Parsons at last set off in an army vehicle, escorted by two armored cars, through scenes of devastation that reminded him of the closing days of World War II. "I saw multi-storey office buildings which had completely collapsed, liquor stores still blazing, smouldering debris everywhere, the skeletons of cars and buses overturned and abandoned," he later wrote.[47] At the palace, among the soft-footed servants in their tail coats, and the deferential *aides-de-camp*, Parsons entered a different world. After a testy exchange, Mohammed Reza said that he had no alternative but to choose a military government and had ordered that Azhari's appointment as prime minister be announced the next day. On their way down, Parsons and Sullivan met Azhari, looking forlorn as he climbed the stairs.[48]

Parsons came away with the paradox that both sets of extremists had had a good day. The armed forces, in making "no attempt to prevent the wholesale destruction,"[49] had forced military government on the Shah, while the opposition, in bringing an end to civil government, had extinguished "all hope of a valid political solution which would have left the Shah's regime *in situ*."[50] Parsons was convinced that the Shah had "done everything to avoid the military option and that he was left with no alternative."[51] Even so, he did much to limit its freedom of action.

Azhari was no Oveissi, the burly Tehran martial law administrator and so-called butcher of Zhaleh. "Shrewd, humane and respected" (Parsons),[52] Azhari was not, in William Sullivan's view, the sort of "fierce military commander one might expect to find in a regime based so heavily on military support."[53] Chief of staff since 1971, he was efficient and undemonstrative. Mohammed Reza also believed that, alone of his generals, Azhari might be a fighter.[54]

Azhari could find only five other military men to serve as ministers in his cabinet, and since those continued with their military duties, much of the work was delegated to what was left of their civilian staffs. Even if Azhari had been inclined to clamp down, Mohammed Reza forestalled him in a broadcast at two o'clock in the afternoon of November 6. One passage stuck in the minds of everybody, friend and foe: "I, too, have heard the message of the revolution of you, the Iranian people. I am the guardian of the constitutional monarchy which is the divine duty entrusted the Shah by the people. After all the sacrifices that you have made, I pledge that in future the Iranian government will be founded in the Basic Law, social justice and the people's will and know nothing of despotism, tyranny and corruption." In other words, the Pahlavi monarchy would be what it had never been, a Constitutional monarchy.

Mohammed Reza then appealed to the clergy, to parents, young people and teenagers, politicians, factory workers and villagers to unite for the good of the country not behind him but, this time, alongside him. "You should know that in the revolution of the Iranian people against colonialism, tyranny and corruption, I am beside you; and in the defence of our territorial integrity, national unity and Islamic religious observances, in the establishment of basic freedoms and the realisation of the wishes and ideals of the Iranian people, I will be by your side."[55]

It was not a bad speech. Parsons found it "an impressive performance."[56] Had Mohammed Reza delivered it at the peak of his power, looking sovereign and confident, it might have had some effect. He did not. He looked contrite.[57] He was promising to withdraw from active government, and to restore the Constitutional monarchy of 1906, but why should anybody believe him? How could he promise liberties while appointing soldiers to govern under martial law? Anyway, the Constitution had been interred without obsequy by Khomeini and the National Front at Neauphle. It was a mistake to use and therefore authorize the word "Revolution."

In his sermon to staff and visitors in the French villa garden on the evening of November 7, Khomeini spoke with a levity familiar only to his intimates. Knowing more words of French than he would admit, Khomeini turned Shah into *chat*. He spoke of the famous cat of Kerman, known to all Iranians from a fourteenth-century verse satire, who kills a mouse and then repairs to the congregational mosque, weeping and calling on God for forgiveness, and distributing alms. A mouse hiding below the pulpit witnesses these scenes and spreads the good news that the cat has become "devout, a believer, a MUSLIM!" In their simplicity and good nature, the mice bring the cat presents of choice food and drink, at which he kills five of them, one with each paw and the fifth in his teeth. Khomeini addressed the Shah: "We know your contrition. It is the contrition of the cat."[58]

Daryoush Homayoun, the sometime minister of information, was lunching with friends when Mohammed Reza came on television. He later wrote: "We sat with our eyes fixed on the screen at the Shah's image, thin and broken down, reading with difficulty from the page. While the announcement of the military cabinet had shaken the opposition, the Shah was begging people to be kind enough to let him fight along with them against the corruption and bombast of his own absolute rule. He was saying that they had nothing to fear from military government. Bewildered, we said our goodbyes and went home. At one o'clock in the morning, our servant knocked at the bedroom door, saying that there were men at the door who wanted to see the master of the house." [59] He was taken to the Military Police headquarters at the Jamshidabad (or Jamshidieh) barracks. His arrest saved his life.

Detained with him were eleven ex-officials of the royal regime, including General Nassiri, the director of Savak, who had been summoned back from the Iranian Embassy in Islamabad in Pakistan, and Gholam Reza Nikpay, the former mayor of Tehran, who had applied for the 1984 Olympic Games. On the morning of November 7, General Ali Mohammed Khademi, the longtime president of Iran Air and architect of its brilliant success, who had been forced to resign in September, died from three gunshot wounds. It was said that he had killed himself to escape arrest, though his family and former staff always claimed there had been foul play. A Bahai, and a member of what the U.S. Embassy used to call the "aviation mafia," he had enemies. Rumor sped about town that Azhari intended to arrest Hoveyda. At his audience that day Parsons threw caution to the winds, warning Mohammed Reza that "to arrest [Hoveyda] would be to arrest the Shah." Mohammed Reza changed the subject. In his furious mood, Parsons went on to criticize the royal family, and said it would be a "fatal mistake" if they used the cover of military government to return from their retreats abroad. He singled out Princesses Ashraf and Shams, their children, and the Shah's half brothers Abdolreza, Gholamreza, and Mahmoud Reza. The Shah "took this blast surprisingly well." He said that only Abdolreza was in Iran. "The rest would not return: he would see to that." [60]

The following morning, Parsons telephoned Hoveyda at the flat he shared with his mother in North Tehran, and urged him to "run for it." Down the line, Hoveyda laughed: "My dear Tony, I have done nothing I am ashamed of. If it comes to a trial I shall have plenty to say. In any case I have a lot of detective stories to read." [61] They never spoke again.

At a meeting at Niavaran that morning, not one of Mohammed Reza's advisers spoke up for Hoveyda, not even the queen, though she later said it "broke her heart." Hoveyda was to be the scapegoat, to be loaded with the errors and sins of the court and sent out into the wilderness. In the course of the meeting, Savak chief Moqaddam telephoned and said that Hoveyda's arrest was "more important than our daily bread." [62] Early in the afternoon, Mohammed Reza called his faithful minister to say that he was to be moved to a secure location "for his own safety." About three hours later, two senior officers arrived and, after a tongue-lashing from Hoveyda's ex-wife, Laila, took Hoveyda away to a Savak safe house in Fereshteh Street. [63]

The supporters of the regime, disgusted by the flight abroad of men such as Parviz Sabeti of Savak and ex–Finance Minister Hushang Ansary, were frightened. On the 26th, a group calling itself the "Staff Society" of the Central Bank published a broadside listing those Iranians who had transferred abroad over 10 million tomans each ($1.25 million) in the two months up to October 22. The 144 persons named included such men as General Toufanian (280m tomans), the prime minister (421m), Prince Shahriar, the son of Princess Ashraf (370m), and even the governor of the Central Bank, Yusef Khoshkish (31m). Precise, topical, comprehensive, and plausible, the list was obviously a fake, but with the main newspapers on strike, there was no attempt to examine or verify it. "The List has the upper classes in jitters," a British banker wrote in his diary on the 29th, "even though people see it is a fake." [64] In one of those misfortunes that had dogged the court since August, when the acting governor of the Central Bank was due to go on television to refute the list, the electricity workers cut the power and he was heard only by those with battery radios. [65]

Azhari saw it as "his first duty to produce calm," then to restart the economy and pursue the anticorruption drive. [66] In the first shock of military government, he had some success. By a mixture of carrot and stick, raising wages by nearly a quarter and arresting the entire strike committee at the refinery, Azhari managed to restore oil production to about 60 percent of its pre-crisis level. [67] With the assistance of navy technicians and the foreign staff of the Consortium's Oil Service Company of Iran, production inched up by November 13 to 2.6 million barrels a day and then, by the 20th, to 4 million. In an omen of the intimidation that was to come, a bomb was detonated in the car of the OSCO general manager.

Azhari failed to bring under control the strike-bound ministries or the universities and high schools. Rather than submit to military censorship, the press went on strike and none of the chief newspapers appeared until January. To fill the void, Iranians listened to the BBC Persian Service, which Mohammed Reza had distrusted since its foundation in 1940. Customs officers ceased to clear goods at the borders, and with the Central Bank on strike, no cash was reaching the provinces. There were nightly power cuts. Fighting flared up in the streets. Without non-lethal equipment, the army attempted to disperse the rioters by firing into the air until, at the point of being overwhelmed, they lowered their gun barrels. In the first two weeks of military government, some forty people were killed by the army.[68] As the mourning month of Moharram loomed in the calendar, much of the shrine towns of Qom and Mashhad passed under the control of the religious opposition. In Isfahan, army officers and other ranks in civilian clothes applauded a *sayyid* who called for the Shah's execution.[69] Constantly on the telephone to local governors and military commanders, Mohammed Reza says he gave the same order: "Do the impossible to avoid bloodshed."[70]

In the memoir from Mexico, *Answer to History*, Mohammed Reza justified those orders. He wrote: "A sovereign may not save his throne by shedding his countrymen's blood. A dictator can, for he acts in the name of an ideology and believes it must triumph no matter what the cost. A dictator has nothing to bestow for power resides in him alone. A sovereign is given a crown and must bequeath it to the next generation."[71] Mohammed Reza had spilled blood, but he had no appetite for it, and his enemies knew it.

CHAPTER 10

A Box of Earth

◇

I have done more for Iran than any Shah for 2,000 years.
—Mohammed Reza Pahlavi[1]

It is hard to say at what moment it became clear that Mohammed Reza would go. With the center of his regime disintegrated, both extremes of it required him off the stage: whether for a civilian government headed by an elder statesman or moderate oppositionist, or so the army could in the manner of 1953 "rectify the situation."[2] Few knew of the Shah's illness, but he appeared to be badly in need of rest on the Caspian, or on Kish Island or at Bandar Abbas where, as Mohammed Reza put it later, he could "visit his navy."

An early hint came at a meeting with U.S. Ambassador Sullivan on November 1, 1978, when Mohammed Reza said he would "rather leave the country than submit" to the referendum on the monarchy, agreed by Khomeini and Karim Sanjabi of the National Front.[3] On November 11, Mohammed Reza told British ambassador Parsons that "if he thought it would benefit the country, he would leave next day."[4] A week later, Mohammed Reza raised the question of abdication and the formation of a regency council to be headed by the queen. He said he was ready to leave "tomorrow," but "his was the sole authority which could control the armed forces, keep them united and obedient and out of factional politics." Livening, he told of the calls he was receiving from the United States, including a sepulchral voice purporting to be Senator Edward Kennedy, intoning: "Mohammed, abdicate!"[5] Parsons continued to believe that the Shah should stay to maintain the unity of the army and prevent anarchy. He felt that the queen would not command

195

the same loyalty. As for the chances of a coalition government, it was hard to imagine unless "the opposite pole to the Shah, Ayatollah Khomeini, had somehow in the interim period been neutralised."[6]

Britain was about to be engulfed by the industrial strife known as "the winter of discontent," and ministers were losing their relish for Parsons's long reports. Foreign Secretary Owen had spoken up for Mohammed Reza on British television on October 22, but his remarks were received badly in both Britain and Iran. On the 27th, Prime Minister Callaghan ordered that there should be no further public expressions of support for the Shah, "which are not, in any case, advantageous to the [British] Government in domestic political terms."[7] Speaking in the House of Commons on November 6, the foreign secretary said it was "for the Iranian people to determine the Government under which they live."[8] Defense Secretary Fred Mulley told Callaghan on the 13th that the loss of the Shir Iran tank contract would cost 10,000 British jobs and jeopardize the development of the next British battle tank set for introduction in the mid-1980s, now known as the Challenger.[9] Iran had in any case stopped making payments on the tank and the Military Industrial Complex ammunition factory. The UK government concluded there was little it could do to protect its economic interests, except ensure the safety of the 10,000-odd British subjects in Iran.

Parsons continued to see Mohammed Reza every two or three days, but could only advise the Shah to stay the course, not to abdicate, and not to unleash the military (in which Parsons had little faith). Britain was lowering the curtain on nearly two centuries of close attention to Iran. At the close of the month, Parsons was informed that he had been promoted to a desk job in London. Anxious about its relations with other traditional rulers such as the house of Saud, Britain never advised the Shah to leave. On December 20, Foreign Secretary Owen recommended British neutrality.

Sullivan had his own ideas. On the strength of his staff's contacts with the National Front and Khomeini's as-yet-secret Revolutionary Council, including Mehdi Bazargan and Mohammed Beheshti, on November 9 Sullivan sent to the U.S. State Department a long cable entitled "Thinking the Unthinkable." In it, he relegated Mohammed Reza to the side and proposed that an accommodation between the military and the religious forces might be "essentially satisfactory" to the United States. Khomeini would hold a "Gandhi-like" position and appoint to senior office only men who were acceptable to the pro-Western military, such as Bazargan, rather than the "Nasser-Qadhafi" type he might prefer. Such an accommodation would, he wrote, "avoid chaos, ensure the continued integrity of the country, preclude a radical leadership and effectively block Soviet domination of the Persian Gulf." [10] It was also unlikely to come about and did not come about.

President Carter, who believed that U.S. policy was to stand by the Shah, was not ready to think the unthinkable, and ordered Secretary of State Vance to bring the envoy into line. [11] Sullivan took no notice and together with John Stempel, his chief political officer, was by December meeting Bazargan and his advisers as often as four or five times a week. [12] Not only Carter but his national security adviser, Zbigniew Brzezinski, lost confidence in Sullivan and dispatched envoys to Tehran to second-guess him. In Washington, George Ball, an experienced ex–foreign service officer, wrote a report on U.S. options for the president and urged him, at a meeting at the White House on December 14, to advise the Shah to withdraw from active government and transfer power. [13] Carter was unwilling to "tell another head of state what to do," and the Ball report was stillborn.

Ardeshir Zahedi, the Iranian ambassador in Washington, returned to Tehran, having told Carter and Brzezinski in the Oval Office on November 21 that Mohammed Reza was eager for him to serve as prime minister or minister of court. Carter knew from other sources that was untrue. [14] Zahedi's main contacts were with Brzezinski in Washington and the hard-line officers Mohammed Reza had overlooked in appointing Azhari. Tehran rang with the echoes of 1953: the Shah dejected and sidelined, sustained by his wife; a Zahedi "intriguing furiously" (Parsons); [15] military messes alive with talk of a *coup d'état*. Yet beneath the swagger, there was anxiety. Amir Hosein Rabii, commander of the air force, was heard to say: "I will bomb Najaf if the Majesty orders me to," but also talked of joining his family in Florida. [16]

In comparison, dealing with Moscow was simplicity itself. The Soviet Union was slow to react to the crisis in Iran, and found the religious nature of the protest hard to comprehend. On October 31, the Communist Party newspaper *Pravda* published a letter of birthday greeting to the Shah from the party secretary, Leonid Brezhnev. By November 19, the Soviets had become alarmed that the United States intended to intervene. That day, *Pravda* published a statement from Brezhnev which warned that "any, and particularly military interference in the affairs of Iran, a state bordering directly on the Soviet Union, would be regarded by the Soviet Union as affecting its security interests."[17] That last was a reference to the Soviet-Persian Friendship Treaty of 1921, which gave Moscow the right, in the case of military intervention by a third party, "to advance its troops into the Persian interior."

Carter sent a protest to Moscow. "I trust," he wrote, "it was not your intention to suggest that the incorrect reports to which you refer might be used to justify Soviet interference in Iranian affairs. I am sure you appreciate that any such interference would be a matter of the utmost gravity to us."[18] British prime minister Jim Callaghan wrote to the president on December 2 to say that, though there was no evidence of any active Soviet role, "it was essential that Brezhnev should be warned . . . of the consequences of rashness." He added, with justice as it turned out, that "the Soviet leader will not want their actions to cause serious problems with the US." By now, officials were working on a French suggestion of a summit meeting, possibly on French territory in the West Indies. Callaghan minuted: "This is a matter for Martinique—tho' the Shah may be gone by then."[19]

As the month of Moharram approached, the atmosphere became suffocating. Few doubted that the days of mourning, and particularly the ninth and tenth days of the month, would see the trial of strength that would bring both the military government and the monarchy down. Yet Khomeini's message, when it came on November 23, was more deliberate and less insurrectionary than expected. The protest he called for was to be religious in character and a defiance of the military government. "Dear people, hold your gatherings without referring to the authorities. If you are prevented, gather in the squares and streets and proclaim the sufferings of the Muslims and the treachery of the Shah's regime."[20] He ordered seminarians into the villages, to publicize the crimes of the regime and to reassure the villagers that Islamic government would not bring back the landlords. Ayatollah Abdol Qasim Khoy in Najaf, who had received the queen on November 18 and given her a carnelian ring engraved with prayers for Mohammed Reza,[21] and

Ayatollah Shariatmadari in Qom also called on Iranians to remember the religious character of the festival.

Moharram began at sundown on Friday, December 1. At 9 p.m., when the curfew came into force, crowds gathered in the dark streets and on the rooftops. Shouts and whoops of "God is Great!"—*Allahu akbar!* in Arabic—reverberated through the autumn night, punctuated by gunshots and the howling of dogs. Young men raced through the blackout shouting, "Death to the Shah!" Firing continued until about 3:30 a.m., with at least seven dead (according to the military authorities), though the next day knots of boys carried bloodstained shoes and shirts through the streets, shouting, "Three thousand dead, three thousand dead."[22] For Parsons, it was the first sign that the military was losing control of Tehran. "The people have successfully and massively defied the edicts of the military authorities," he cabled to London on December 3.[23]

It was the shouting that was so shattering to the nerves. A mile to the west of Niavaran, Desmond Harney, a Persian-speaking British banker, was called out by his servant into the cool garden. "A great beat of sound in the distance came to my ears. Tens of thousands of voices were shouting 'God is great,' ceaselessly punctuated by the rattle of gunfire and crackle of shots. On, on, unbroken, '*Allah-u Akbar, Allah . . .*' Dogs barked."[24] The firing was into the air but that did not make sleep any easier. "Then the crack, and then another, and then a short burst of automatic fire only a few hundred yards away. Who is stalking whom? The lights snuff out at 10 p.m. Grope again for the candles and the Camping Gaz burner," Harney wrote in his diary on the 3rd. At the Soviet Embassy in Churchill Street, intelligence officers heard the familiar crackle of the Kalashnikov semi-automatic rifle, which was not issued to men in the Iranian army. They concluded that a fight was on the way. The Savak surveillance post, established in a soft-drink stand before the main gate since time out of mind, vanished.[25]

In their jangled state, foreigners thought to detect a breakdown in the famous Iranian hospitality. The land that many had loved, the place of roses and nightingales, skiing at Dizfin and fly-fishing in the river Lar, was revealing its shadow side. Less given to literary culture, the American ex-military men in Isfahan said they always knew Iran could never attain an American civilization and, in a favorite phrase, "these people will never make it." Pamphlets appeared on the eve of Moharram calling on all foreigners, except the news correspondents and the darling French, to leave Iran. The American School in Tehran was shut and the U.S. Embassy encouraged the 12,000 or so Americans still in the country to "think in terms of long Christmas holidays."[26] In London, Callaghan approved proposals for joint evacuation planning with the United States, France, and West Germany.[27] The departure lounge of Mehrabad Airport was pandemonium. Sullivan was inundated with requests from senior officers in the Iranian military for U.S. visas.[28]

Word spread of immense marches for the Tassua and Ashura on December 10 and 11. Nobody doubted that, as Harney wrote, "on Sunday and Monday if the army is asked to fire, it will break up."[29] General Oveissi, the martial law commander, was for a show of force, but Azhari persuaded Mohammed Reza to overrule him. In negotiations conducted by Moqaddam of Savak and General Gharabaghi, the interior minister, with the Tehran clergy, General Azhari pledged to withdraw his men and tanks from the streets in return for restraint in the slogans and no attacks on public buildings. Ashura was reinstated as a public holiday.

From the windows of the British Embassy, between 9 a.m. and 12 noon on both mornings, Anthony Parsons watched the stream of humanity passing north up Ferdowsi Street in ranks from sidewalk to sidewalk for four hours. "This was no half-starved rabble from the shanty towns," he wrote. "Well dressed, healthy, the women carrying babies or leading children by the hand, the backbone of traditional, urban Iranian society passed before our eyes in their thousands."[30] The Tehran clergy kept its word. At Shahreza Street, rather than continue north to the prosperous quarters, the General Staff headquarters, and the Niavaran Palace, the march turned west past the university and out through the western suburbs to the Shahyad Monument. The army, deployed north of Shahreza, was out of sight, and the crowd policed itself.[31] Foreign correspondents computed that as many as 2 million took part each day.

Even if the numbers were half that, it was a powerful demonstration in favor of an Islamic Republic, and a tribute to the organizing power of Beheshti and the Tehran clergy. Fear had evaporated and unattached people, concerned up to then with their private affairs, gave in to the fundamental impulse to be seen on the side of the victors. Khomeini called it a "nationwide referendum." The lesson was directed not just at the beleaguered court and the armed forces, but at modern Iranian society. The Fedayan and Mojahedin marched under their own banners but were engulfed. At the Shahyad, the leaders of the march presented a joint declaration of seventeen points. Point One was: "Ayatollah Khomeini is our leader." The second day was more vicious, with militant banners calling for "Death to the Butcher Shah" and "Yankee Go Home." In Isfahan, after the mourning ceremonies were over, militants tore down the statues of Mohammed Reza and his father and attacked the Savak headquarters, where they were with difficulty repelled.[32] In Mashhad, the Hyatt Hotel was burned. Once again missing the point, *Tass,* the Soviet news agency, commented: "The demonstrations are mostly of a political character . . . although Tehran radio tries to portray them as religious processions."[33]

General Oveissi was heard to say that such hesitation would never have occurred under the Shah's father, but Azhari had earned his pay and expenses. He had little time to congratulate himself. At about 4:30 p.m., two young soldiers, one a conscript, opened fire with automatic weapons on officers in the mess hall of the Imperial Guard garrison at Lavizan, just east of the palace, killing seven officers and wounding fifty.[34] The next day in Isfahan, royalists staged a march and were addressed by the military governor, General Reza Naji. Backed up by armed soldiers who shot the locks off shuttered shops, they went on the rampage, stopping traffic and forcing drivers at gunpoint to shout "Long live the Shah" and display Mohammed Reza's portrait. When a man of seventy either refused or did not understand, his car was shot up from behind. According to the city hospitals, twenty-five people were killed, almost all with shots to the back, and there may have been others not brought to the hospital. A saloon car careened into the crowd of donors at an emergency blood bank. Similar scenes, on a smaller scale, played out in Montazeri's hometown of Najafabad, twenty-five miles away.[35]

When he called on Azhari on December 18, Ambassador Parsons found the general "tired and dispirited" by the insubordination of the local commanders. He had recalled General Naji. Parsons came away anxious about divisions opening in the armed forces, and more than ever convinced that the Shah must not leave.[36] Meanwhile, as the price of preserving Tehran north of Shahreza Street, the army had given up the south and east of the town, leaving their bases (notably the airfield at Doshan Teppe and a nearby arms factory) isolated and difficult to reinforce other than by air. The security men at the U.S. Military Mission code-named Doshan Teppe "Little Bighorn," and so it was to be.[37]

Day by day, the country slipped out of government control. Walking his dog in Darrakeh, one of the old villages of Shemiran, the banker Desmond Harney found himself in the Islamic Republic, the walls stenciled with portraits of a beetle-browed Khomeini, the children singing "Death to the Shah!" On the path used by hikers out of the village, a dead donkey lay amid its excrement, a skewer driven through its bloated stomach and tied to it a piece of paper with a single word: SHAH.[38] Small towns, such as Saveh or Najafabad, were taken over by self-styled *komitehs,* while in the cities troops provoked beyond endurance fired into crowds or, in the case of Mashhad on December 14, burst into a hospital and attacked the medical staff.

At Niavaran, Mohammed Reza was, in Parsons's words, "chasing shadows." Old Ali Amini was advising him to retire to Bandar Abbas, and hand over to a regency council which would fulfill all the Shah's functions but that of commander in chief, and to a national government to supervise elections.[39] Mohammed Reza was also talking to a National Front veteran, Gholam Hosein Sadeghi, who had served as interior minister under Mossadeq. The army was pleading for him to stay, warning that it would disintegrate. On December 21, Sullivan called at the prime minister's office and found Azhari in a darkened room by his office, lying on an army cot under an army blanket beside a cylinder of oxygen. He had suffered a heart attack on the 19th. The prime minister told Sullivan that the talks with Sadeghi had destroyed the morale of his cabinet. After ten months in the streets, restricted in their rules of engagement to firing into the air, the soldiers were demoralized. Raising himself onto his elbow, he said: "You must know this and you must tell it to your government. This country is lost because the king cannot make up his mind."[40] The next day, Mohammed Reza told Sullivan and Parsons that Sadeghi had until the 25th to form a government. If he failed to restore control, the Shah would retire to Bandar Abbas to "visit his navy" and allow the army to "crack down."[41]

It was too late. On the morning of Saturday, December 23, Paul E. Grimm, the acting manager of the Oil Service Company of Iran, which managed the oil industry on behalf of the Iranian state, was assassinated in Ahvaz. As he drove to work at the OSCO headquarters on the left bank of the Karun, three gunmen attacked his car in the Kourosh district and fired repeatedly through the windows. Grimm collapsed onto his gas pedal and crashed through the main city intersection. Almost simultaneously, across the river in Kian Pars, his Iranian colleague Malek Borujerdi was shot with a single bullet to the chest. There were reports that an Iranian laborer at Gachsaran had also been murdered for strikebreaking.

There had been warnings. Six weeks before, Grimm's superior George Link had escaped a car bomb. For weeks, Americans and Europeans in the south had received threatening letters. Just days before, Grimm had shown reporters a page torn from a school exercise book that he found one morning on his desk: "You have been warned to return to your country. There will be no more warnings." Grimm, an experienced oilman, laughed it off as a "practical joke" by employees.[42]

The assassinations caused a flight of foreigners from the fields. Dogs and cats were put down or sedated and bundled into baskets for the drive to the international airport at Abadan. The elementary school in Ahvaz closed, the snowflakes on the windows and Christmas decorations in the classrooms still gathering dust months later. The strike at Iran Air, and the shortage of motor fuel, compounded the panic. Gulf Air pilots ran shuttles to carry some 1,200 foreigners from Abadan International Airport to Bahrain.[43] The local staff were no less intimidated. "The Iranians are just as scared as the foreigners," the *New York Times* was told.[44] Crude oil production fell to the levels of the early 1950s, or 600,000 barrels a day, all but a fraction of it going to the Abadan refinery for gas and kerosene. To compound the tension and irritation in Tehran, drivers there waited for hours in mile-long lines at the gas stations.

On December 24, the Marine guards at the U.S. Embassy on Takht-e Jamshid Street used tear gas to repel an attack by college and high school students. The demonstrators broke down the gate and threw burning tires into the compound for an hour before military reinforcements arrived. There were attacks on the offices of the British Council (the British cultural service) in Ahvaz, Shiraz, and Mashhad. The British, U.S., Canadian, Danish, Italian, Belgian, and Irish ministers advised all their subjects or citizens who had no important business to leave. London dispatched two Hercules C-130 transports to Bahrain and a Royal Navy survey ship to evacuate Britons from the naval base at Bandar Abbas. On December 27, the *Kitty Hawk*–class aircraft carrier USS *Constellation* was ordered from the Philippines to a station southeast of Singapore and instructed to prepare for deployment in the Arabian Sea. In addition, to reassure the Saudi royal family, a squadron of American F-15s was dispatched to Riyadh.

Bazargan feared events were running out of control. He told Khomeini's staff in Paris by telephone on the 30th that the oil field strikes were a "two-edged" sword, for while they denied fuel to the military they also were creating hardship for the public, and particularly the poor, who depended on kerosene to cook food and heat their houses. If the left became entrenched in the oil industry, it might be difficult to dislodge them and thus to finance the Islamic Republic. Montazeri carried a similar message from General Moqaddam of Savak.[45]

Armed with Khomeini's commission, Bazargan and Hashemi Rafsanjani traveled to Ahvaz and Abadan on the 31st and, with difficulty, persuaded the strikers to run a minimum of 600,000 barrels a day through the refinery for domestic consumption. In a blandishment to the military, Bazargan proposed that the army and air force would be supplied with gasoline and aviation spirit to the extent of their routine or pre-crisis needs. As Bazargan pointed out, it was the first occasion where Khomeini had given a direct order for the management of affairs of state and showed that the "ruler of the country was Khomeini."[46] Even so, it would take two weeks to restore the flow of petroleum products to the capital. Rather than wait all day amid the gunfire at gas stations, families roped together their plastic jerrycans on the pavement. After filling one, the pump attendant pulled the rope and brought the next one forward and the people returned in the afternoon to claim their fuel. The weather had been mild but on January 9, 1979, it turned cold, and winter at last set in. There was no fuel to heat the barracks, and the disgraced ex-ministers at Jamshidabad walked round to keep warm.

When Parsons took his leave of the queen on December 24, he found her brittle and detached. She described the burning of the city on November 5 as "a little *feu de joie* by the people." He asked her if he might say goodbye to Hoveyda in prison, but she appeared uninterested, and he let the matter drop.[47] On the 27th, at the request of the palace, the U.S. Consulate issued visas to the queen mother, Taj ol-Moluk, and her companions, and they left on or around the 30th to join Princess Shams at her house in Santa Monica, California.[48] Either then or on a separate transport, Mohammed Reza sent away his father's remains from the mausoleum at Shah Abdolazim, and those of his brother Alireza. When Dr. Flandrin examined the Shah the next day, he found him "visibly suffering from apparently dreadful tension. He could not stop listening to the news while I examined him."[49] The queen suggested that she remain alone at Niavaran, as "a symbol" of her husband, but Mohammed Reza asked her to stay at his side.[50]

At this point, an element of the fantastical enters the story. Sadeghi had ruled himself out when, on December 28, he asked for another six weeks to form his government. Azhari resigned and was allowed to leave the country for medical treatment. Yet in all places and at all times, a man can be found with the audacity to try where everybody else has failed, and that man was Chapour Bakhtiar. Introduced to Mohammed Reza by way of Moqaddam and the queen, Bakhtiar agreed the next day to try to form a government. He accepted that, once his cabinet had been endorsed by Parliament, Mohammed Reza might leave the country for a rest. When Amir Khosrow Afshar, the foreign minister, expressed doubt, Mohammed Reza threw up his hands and said: "Who else is there?"[51] That day, Sir Anthony Parsons too gave up hope, saying that "the only thing that is likely to restore calm and economic and administrative activity is the Shah's departure."[52]

Chapour Bakhtiar had led an adventurous life. The son of a Bakhtiari khan murdered by Reza in 1933, and grandson of a prime minister, he had been a classmate of Hoveyda in Beirut. World War II had found him a student in France, where he enlisted in the French army and then, after the French capitulation, by his own account, ran messages for the Resistance between Paris and Brittany. Married to a Frenchwoman, devoted to French literature, he dressed and behaved like a French gentleman, and (like Mohammed Reza) preferred to speak

French. According to his memoirs, Bakhtiar rebuffed an approach by Mohammed Reza on his return to Iran in 1946, but was drawn to Mossadeq and served as deputy labor minister in his second government. As one of the leaders of the revived National Front coalition in the 1960s, he spent some five and a half years in Mohammed Reza's jails. He despised the Pahlavis as shallow and illiterate, but did not hate them: indeed, he quite liked them in a mild sort of way.[53]

In taking the job, Bakhtiar showed he had Bakhtiari guts. While to others he was no more than a "fig leaf" (in Sullivan's words) to permit Mohammed Reza to leave the country with a scrap of constitutional modesty, he saw himself as the heir of Mossadeq and the last bastion of democracy in Iran, who would somehow "steal the revolution away" from the barbarian Khomeinists and the left.[54] Soon after being nominated, he paid a visit of homage to the farm at Ahmad Abad where Mossadeq lies buried under the dining-room floor.[55] For Bakhtiar, the premiership was no more than his due, and not before time. Yet amid his vanity, he had a streak of intelligent caution and that almost saved his life.

He told Parsons on December 30 that the Shah had agreed to go abroad for rest or medical treatment, would appoint a regent or regency council (not including the queen), and would leave the country just as soon as the cabinet was presented to Parliament. The armed forces would answer to the prime minister.[56] On January 1, 1979, in an interview with Iranian television, Bakhtiar played his only card. He was, he said, the heir to Mossadeq, who had "preferred imprisonment to the prevailing corruption." At his press conference on the 3rd, Bakhtiar said in French that the Shah was "irrevocably" resolved to take a rest and vacation, and that it would be a "signal honor" for Khomeini to return to his homeland.

As if the scene needed another note of farce, Mohammed Reza made up his mind to leave only after a visit by Lord George-Brown, a former British foreign secretary and notorious drunkard.[57] To the exasperation of Parsons, George-Brown arrived at Tehran by a charter flight from Kuwait, arranged by the British businessman and former intelligence officer John Cuckney, on January 3. He saw Mohammed Reza the following day and reported that the Shah would leave as soon as Parliament had approved the Bakhtiar government.[58] It seems there was to be no scamper as in 1953, the Beechcraft cabin littered with discarded clothes. The question was: Where to go? Mohammed Reza owned houses in St. Moritz and in Surrey, England, but the first (in the grounds of the Hôtel Suvretta House) was insecure and the second (which he had never visited) was bound to be damp as well as unsafe.[59] On January 3, President Carter confirmed in a message by way of his ambassador that the Shah would be welcome in the United States and would receive protective security.

The administration in Washington was pulling in three directions. As Peter Jay, Callaghan's son-in-law and British ambassador, cabled on January 2, there were three principal impulses: the State Department and George Ball, who favored a civilian coalition; Brzezinski, who wanted "firmness" whether civil or military; and the president, who covered inaction by public support for the Shah. As Jay reported, the third had prevailed, but with enough of the first two "to give grist to the Russian propaganda mill and some encouragement to the Iranian military."[60] Only Brzezinski was thinking of military government "with the wraps off":[61] that is, without the restrictive rules of engagement imposed by Mohammed Reza the previous September.

Jay was surprised the next day to receive a visit from Gary Sick, of the White House staff, to ask a favor of the British in exploring the "thinking" of General Fereydoun Djam, a respected military officer once married to Princess Shams who had fallen afoul of Mohammed Reza and was now living in London. Sick did not wish to use the U.S. Embassy in London and suggested that the old Iran hand Sir Denis Wright might take to General Djam a list of questions, one of which has been blacked out in the British archives. It was presumably to lead a 1953-style military coup. The British responded in the outraged tone of reformed libertines. Foreign Secretary Owen wrote to the prime minister that the Foreign and Commonwealth Office was recommending Britain have nothing to do with the plan. Callaghan minuted: "Quite right!"[62] As it turned out, Djam refused to serve in Bakhtiar's government.

In Tehran, William Sullivan was pressing "that we go directly to Khomeini in Paris to evolve some working arrangement with him."[63] He had no confidence in Bakhtiar or the armed forces. His meetings with Bazargan and Beheshti's emissaries, shivering in greatcoats in blacked-out CIA safe houses, had passed beyond the generalities of the "Unthinkable" cable. His idea was to "skip the Bakhtiar interlude and move on to a Bazargan government."[64] In other words, he wanted to use American influence to bring about an accommodation between the armed forces and the Bazargan group, and bring to power without bloodshed a moderate leadership with both civil and military obligations to the United States. Bazargan's staff gave him a list of over a hundred senior military officers expected to stay true to their oaths.[65] These would receive, along with the Shah, safe-conduct out of Iran. Yet the safe-conduct depended on the acquiescence of Khomeini, and that in short order. As Gary Sick put it, Sullivan "had to have time to find room on the shah's plane for a hundred Iranian officers."[66]

In discussions with the State Department in Washington, it was resolved that a Persian-speaking foreign service officer, Theodore L. Eliot, Jr., would travel to Paris to try to fashion an arrangement with Khomeini that would transfer power with a minimum of bloodshed. Brzezinski insisted that Sullivan first consult the Shah, no doubt hoping that Mohammed Reza would oppose direct contact. In fact, he listened to Sullivan "without enthusiasm" but voiced no objections.[67]

Carter hesitated, and early on January 5, Sullivan (according to his own recollection) was woken by the duty officer and handed a cable informing him that the Eliot mission was off. Furious, Sullivan fired off a message to Vance saying that he thought the president had made a "gross mistake" and "irretrievable error."[68] Carter (who says the cable, "bordering on insolence," was actually sent on January 10) ordered Sullivan withdrawn from Tehran. Secretary Vance, unwilling to dispatch a new man into the maelstrom, dissuaded the president. Henceforth, Sullivan was sidelined and Carter relied "primarily," and possibly entirely, on General Huyser.[69]

"Dutch" Huyser, a burly and straightforward airman who was the deputy commander of U.S. forces in Europe and had long experience of the Iranian military, arrived from Stuttgart in the cockpit of a C-141 transport carrying fuel to Tehran on the afternoon of January 4, clad in civilian clothes. He did not recognize the city: not a car, bus, or motorcycle in sight, sidewalks deserted, gas stations chained shut or beset by long lines of people carrying jerrycans, in every other window a portrait of Khomeini. As night fell, the bursts of automatic gunfire took him back to the front line in Korea.[70] His presence in Tehran was known within hours and was soon picked up by Soviet commentators, who portrayed him as an American proconsul or "military governor" and dusted off the military provisions of the 1921 treaty.[71] In Sofia on the 13th, Soviet party secretary Brezhnev told the Bulgarian leader, Todor Zhivkov, that the Americans had made a mistake in supporting Mohammed Reza so long and events had gained a "strong anti-American and not just anti-Shah character."[72]

As might be expected from the disunity in Washington, Huyser's orders from there were all things to all men. He was to urge the senior Iranian officers to support a "strong and stable government," to remain cohesive and to work closely together. No Iranian military leaders should leave the country. The president and the U.S. military were strongly behind them and would continue to provide military supplies and training. As to the government they should support, "a civilian government appears to be the most likely prospect at present." As Huyser interpreted the message, Brzezinski "wanted it to convey to the Iranian military a green light to stage a military coup and considered that it did so. President Carter intended it to convey such a meaning only as a last resort."[73] The orders were refined over the next week into three options: to encourage the Iranian military (a) to support Bakhtiar, (b) to take action to bolster the civilian regime, for example in the oil fields, and (c) to take power if civil order collapsed.[74] The orders were immediately countermanded by Secretary Vance, and then the next day reinstated.

Huyser found the senior officers in a "totally helpless state."[75] Hassan Toufanian, the head of military procurement, was desperate to resign and leave the country, as were General Gharabaghi of the Gendarmerie and Amir Hosein Rabii of the air force. They could not understand why the United States could not restrain Khomeini or silence the Persian broadcasts of the BBC. Huyser met daily with five senior officers, whom he called "the Group," with Moqaddam sometimes joining them, listening but saying nothing. Rabii, a friend whom he visited at his headquarters at Doshan Teppe on the 6th, mentioned an entity called "the Board," consisting of himself, Toufanian, Admiral Kamaleddin Habibollahi of the navy, and, at some point, Manuchehr Khosrowdad of army aviation, which had discussed a military takeover but made no preparations nor stockpiled war reserves. That should have been no surprise, for such preparations with Mohammed Reza still in power might have cost them their lives. Mohammed Reza himself told Huyser that the staff "hadn't given internal threats a second thought, and their war reserves were quite inadequate for an internal operation."[76]

Some of General Huyser's time was taken up in finding an Iranian signature to release the U.S. government from its liabilities to U.S. defense contractors if the new government (as seemed likely) canceled $6 billion in government-to-government supply contracts. He was also under instructions to protect advanced U.S. military technology, notably the Phoenix air-to-air missile and its supporting equipment. That caused some officers, notably Toufanian, to suspect American purposes were principally selfish. Nonetheless, apart from Oveissi, who had been allowed to leave Iran on the 4th, the general officers stayed at their posts and went with fortitude to their deaths. The immediate effect of the Huyser mission was to destroy the last shred of Mohammed Reza's morale. He concluded that the United States now intended to "neutralize" his army and to cause his generals to abandon their oaths.[77]

At about the time Huyser landed at Tehran, President Carter arrived on the French Caribbean island of Guadeloupe for his summit meeting with the leaders of France, West Germany, and the United Kingdom. He found that his three colleagues had abandoned Mohammed Reza and believed the Shah should leave as soon as possible. The French and West Germans had commissioned position papers from Neauphle by Sadeq Qotbzadeh (for the French) and Sadeq Tabatabai (for the Germans). President Giscard had also sent his personal ambassador, the former interior minister Michel Poniatowski, to call on Mohammed Reza at Niavaran on December 27. Poniatowski reported that the Shah was determined not to employ force and asked of his allies at Guadeloupe only that they restrain the Soviets. As for Khomeini, Mohammed Reza said that expelling him would have "the most grave consequences" not only for himself but for France, and "it would in the end be better to do nothing." Khomeini's residence permit, due to expire on January 5, was renewed.[78] Giscard did agree at Guadeloupe to carry a message from the United States to Khomeini that would ask him, in confidence and without prejudice, to support Bakhtiar and warn him of unrest in the armed forces.

According to Ebrahim Yazdi, two French Foreign Ministry officials called on Khomeini at Neauphle-le-Château on January 8. The old man answered his French visitors with civility, and said he respected the wish of both Carter and Giscard for secrecy, but his answer to Bakhtiar was no. As to the Iranian armed forces, Khomeini took President Carter to be threatening a *coup d'état* and counter-threatened that should that occur, he would order a mass uprising or Holy War (*jihad-e moqaddas*). Carter should have no fear of communism in Iran or any other "deviant ideology," for Iran would submit neither to East nor West. Most striking of all, in the light of what was to happen later that year, Khomeini asked President Carter to give the Shah asylum: "If Mr. Carter wishes to display his good will, ensure calm and prevent bloodshed, he should take the Shah away."[79]

Yazdi does not mention it, but he also had six meetings with a U.S. official, the political counselor at the U.S. Embassy in Paris, Warren Zimmerman, at a discreet distance from Neauphle and its swarm of reporters. Although the slightest contact with the United States was enough to destroy a career in the Islamic Republic (and did destroy Yazdi's career), there can be no doubt that Khomeini gave his permission. These meetings took place on January 15, 16, 18, 19, 24, and 27. Zimmerman told Yazdi that the military had considered taking power by force, had deferred their plans at the urging of General Huyser, but might act if Khomeini were suddenly to return to Iran. Yazdi said that the fault lay with Bakhtiar and the machinations of the military, and only Khomeini could bring stability. He also said that, if the United States ceased meddling in Iranian affairs, friendly future relations were possible.[80]

On January 6, Bakhtiar, dressed in a democratic suit in substitute for the morning coat of despotism,[81] presented his cabinet to Mohammed Reza and was, for his pains, expelled from the National Front. In the drama in which he was both player and audience, the Iranian Constitution was at last to come into force. He wrote: "August 5, 1906 to January 6, 1979. What palavers, battles, riots and blood have passed to get from there to here!"[82] He lifted press censorship, and that afternoon the newspapers were back on the streets, splashed with pictures of Khomeini and obituaries for the dead of the last two months. In the course of his short administration, Bakhtiar announced the dissolution of Savak, freed the last nine hundred political prisoners, outlawed sales of oil to Israel and the white regime in South Africa, and announced that Iran would pull out of the old defense pact, CENTO.

On the 8th, Sir Anthony Parsons called on Mohammed Reza to say goodbye. Unusually for an Englishman of his formation, Parsons could not restrain his tears. He asked that they part without further discussion. The Shah put his hand on Parsons's arm and said: "Never mind, I know how you feel. But we must have one last talk." He returned to the question that had haunted him since August. After all that he had done for them, why had the Iranian people turned against him? Parsons murmured about the Tobacco Protest of 1891 and the Constitutional Revolution of 1906. The same alliance of mollas, bazaar, and intelligentsia that had humbled Nassereddin and Muzaffareddin Qajar had brought Mohammed Reza Shah to grief. The Shah bristled at the comparison: "I have done more for Iran than any Shah for 2,000 years; you cannot compare me to those people."[83] That night it snowed, and winter at last set in.

On the morning of January 11, Sullivan brought General Huyser to call on Mohammed Reza and passed on an invitation from the U.S. president to stay at a ranch belonging to Walter Annenberg, a newspaper proprietor and Nixon's ambassador to London, near Palm Springs in Southern California. Mohammed Reza accepted. The day after, Mohammed Reza summoned the senior generals and ordered them to support the Bakhtiar government. They were on no account to attempt to contact him abroad. When Gharabaghi, who had been appointed chief of staff, pressed him for orders should Bakhtiar fail—"if unforeseen events occur contrary to the Constitution"—Mohammed Reza was silent and then said: "Do what you and the other force commanders consider opportune."[84] He had lost interest even in his armed forces.

A council of regency was named under the chairmanship of one Sayyid Jalaleddin Tehrani, and on the 15th, the Shah's two youngest children, Ali-Reza and Leila, left in a C-130 transport for the United States, where they joined Crown Prince Reza at Reese Air Force Base, in Lubbock, Texas. That evening in Tehran, reports spread that the Shah would leave the next day for the United States by way of Aswan in Egypt, where he would stay for a few days with President Sadat, and the holy cities of Mecca and Karbala. The moon was just past the full in the cold, clear night and, all over Iran, people thought to see Khomeini's face in it. The more sophisticated said the image had been projected by the Americans.[85]

The next day was bitterly cold. At 12:30 p.m. at Niavaran, the palace servants lined up along the route between the door and the helicopters in camouflage waiting on the launching pad. When Mohammed Reza and Farah emerged, he in a dark suit, both wrapped up in coats, the servants beat their heads and chests or threw themselves at Mohammed Reza's feet. He tried to console them: "We are leaving for a long-needed rest and shall soon return."[86] Amid their luggage was a tiny box of Iranian soil.[87]

Their route took them over the headquarters of the Supreme Commander's Staff, and the officers came out onto the balcony to watch them pass over. At the royal pavilion at Mehrabad Airport ten minutes later, there was no official delegation to meet them and no guard of honor, only a detachment of Imperial Guards at ease. Mohammed Reza, anxious as in 1953 to respect dead constitutional niceties, waited for Bakhtiar, who was at that moment subject to the vote of confidence in Parliament. The royal party looked over the field scattered with strike-bound aircraft. At last Bakhtiar arrived, looking pleased with himself, having secured 149 votes in favor, 43 against, and 13 abstentions. With him was the parliamentary speaker. "You're twenty minutes late," said Mohammed Reza.

In a short statement, Mohammed Reza said: "The economy must be revived and people return to their normal lives." When asked when he would return, he answered: "That depends on the state of my health on which I cannot now say anything definite."[88] Pressed one final time by a frantic Gharabaghi to allow the general staff to contact him, Mohammed Reza replied with some heat: "No."[89]

When two guards officers fell at his feet, begging him to stay, Mohammed Reza stooped to lift them and, as he stood, tears showed in his eyes. A Koran had been brought on a silver tray, and the couple walked under it toward the silver-and-blue royal flight Boeing 727, known as *Shahbaz* or Falcon. (Rabii, commander of the air force, had ordered the aircraft test-hopped that morning.) Bakhtiar accompanied the Shah into the cabin, kissed his hand and descended the steps. Mohammed Reza then took the pilot's seat and, at 1:24 p.m., the aircraft took off.[90] An hour later over the Persian Gulf, having left Iranian airspace, Mohammed Reza returned to the passenger cabin and asked for lunch to be served. The revolutionary *komiteh* that now controlled the airport had not permitted any supplies to be loaded.[91] The royal family shared their bodyguards' rice and beans.

When news reached Tehran a quarter of an hour later, the city took to the streets. People shouted, "The Shah has gone," and held up bank notes with the Shah's portrait defaced or cut out. With difficulty, cables were attached to the statue of Reza in Army Square and, as in 1953, it was pulled down under a blizzard of ticker tape from the windows of the Central Post Office. Cars, with their lights burning and horns blaring, formed interminable traffic jams. Driving through town, Desmond Harney found troops at Tajrish Square, smashing with staves the windshields of cars with their lights on or with portraits of Khomeini. He passed Niavaran Palace, still flying the blue Imperial standard, and then plunged out of the Imperial Guard precincts back into old Tehran, "alive with kids and teenagers jumping on garden walls, piling high on the roofs of vans, shouting their heads off, brandishing carnations and gladioli or portraits of Khomeini, showering sweets on passing cars."[92]

Amid the tumult and euphoria, a local reporter noted the slogan: "Now the Shah is gone, America is next."[93]

CHAPTER 11

God Is Great

◊

If God's Prophet were here now, He'd say, "Why did you give My son three hosannas, and Me only one?"
—Mehdi Bazargan[1]

On the television in Gharabaghi's office at the Supreme Commander's Staff compound in North Tehran, the Iranian and U.S. officers watched Mohammed Reza depart. One officer laid his head on General Huyser's shoulder and wept. Admiral Habibollahi, the commander of the navy, attempted a locker-room suavity: "When rape is inevitable, relax and enjoy it."[2]

There was talk of seizing power, that very night, at 2:30 a.m., but Huyser brought the officers down to earth. He knew the staff had made no preparations, nor identified the installations—such as the television station and power plants—to be occupied. The forces were short of winter clothes and depended on diesel and motor gasoline brought in from Saudi Arabia in converted C-130 transports. "Do you fully realize we do not have the planning to the point where we could achieve success?" Huyser asked. Gharabaghi, who had returned from the airport encouraged by the conduct of the Imperial Guard, astonished Huyser by saying: "The Shah told us to trust you, to listen to you, to obey you."[3] After seven and a half hours, the group broke up.

For Huyser, the Iranian General Staff had come through the ordeal. The officers had not left en masse for Mehrabad and scrambled onto Mohammed Reza's aircraft. Always more sanguine than Ambassador Sullivan, Huyser believed the Iranian armed forces could retain their cohesion in support of the Bakhtiar government. After nearly a year on

215

the streets, exposed to insults, threats, and bouquets thrust down their rifle muzzles, and restricted in how they could retaliate, the ground army under General Abdol Ali Badrei was troubled and introspective. Yet Huyser believed that desertions of perhaps 100 per day were manageable in a force of 480,000, three quarters of them professionals.[4] Anyway, he thought a coup would require scarcely more than 20,000 men, who could be supplied by the Imperial Guard.

In contrast, Sullivan believed that the army should simply step aside, and the two envoys, as they sat each night back-to-back in the secure communications room at the U.S. Embassy, were speaking to Washington at cross-purposes. (When Huyser reported their differences in person to the president at the White House on February 5, Carter was furious at their disunity. "The President looked as grimly angry as I had ever seen him," noted Gary Sick of the National Security Council staff.)[5] By then, the U.S. Embassy was writing that Khomeini's movement was "better organized, enlightened and able to resist communism than its detractors lead us to believe."

In support of what was known in Washington as "Plan B," Huyser had urged the staff to devise a maneuver for troops to take over the food supply, water, power, and communications, and the oil fields. Iranian currency was printed in the United Kingdom and used to pay the troops. To test the mettle of the senior officers, and to stiffen their morale, Huyser had proposed two exercises. The first was to offload diesel and gasoline for the ground forces from a tanker that he had asked the U.S. Defense Department to dispatch to Abadan. Since Abadan was an export terminal, the fuel would have to be reverse-pumped into the storage tanks and those defended, but that was within the capacity of the Iranian navy. Yet though the vessel at least three times steamed up the Shatt, it was turned back by the National Iranian Oil Company and never docked.

The second was to take control of the twenty-six border crossings and customs posts where the strike at the customs had choked off vital supplies. At the Bazargan crossing with Turkey, some 750 heavy trucks were held up.[6] The border posts were mostly well away from towns and the action could be portrayed as humanitarian. In reality, the purpose was not just to alleviate the shortages of food and medicine but to stem the flow of propaganda books and cassette tapes and also small arms, principally from a Lebanon racked by civil war, into the mosques. That plan was also not carried out, and Huyser came to suspect Gharabaghi of lacking guts and the staff of double-crossing him.[7] In reality, they humored him.

Mohammed Reza, in his memoir from Mexico, accused his two five-star generals or field marshals, Hosein Fardoust and Abbas Gharabaghi, of being "traitors."[8] The two men survived the holocaust on the roof of the Refah School, and for many royalists, safe in Paris or Los Angeles, that constitutes a fault. It is pleasant from safety to call on others to make the supreme sacrifice.

Mohammed Reza's friend from childhood, Le Rosey, and the officers' school, where he graduated second in the crown prince's class, Fardoust had served as deputy director of Savak and then as head of the Special Intelligence Bureau, a sort of anti-Savak set up by Mohammed Reza to spy on his administration. A relic of the court and kitchen government of the 1940s, Fardoust always had Mohammed Reza's ear, but his influence was never great and, by his own account, he spent much of the last years of Pahlavi rule playing bridge and rummy at the Young Iran club. After the Revolution, he lay low for four years, moving between different addresses in Tehran, but was picked up in 1983 and died, probably of natural causes, at the age of seventy in 1987. In the course of those eight years, he wrote a memoir which was published in 1990 by the revolutionary successor to Savak, the Ministry of Intelligence. Amid his fantastic conspiracy theories, it appears from this work that Fardoust considered himself released from his oath of the Shah's departure on January 16 and thenceforth proceeded with an almost English indifference.

Abbas Gharabaghi was an officer of the old school, who had graduated third in Mohammed Reza's class, and went on to the French military academy at Saint-Cyr, then at its old location near Paris. He was not happy speaking English and, as commander of the Gendarmerie or rural patrol, had had little contact with the U.S. Military Mission. He was suspicious of foreigners. He served as interior minister under both Sharif-Emami and the military government of General Azhari, and had come to see the limits of what the military could achieve. Always close to Mohammed Reza, he was appointed chief of staff on January 6, 1979 (which gave Oveissi, the martial law commander, the pretext of pique in leaving the country and, for a while, saved his life).

In his own memoir, published in Paris in 1985, Gharabaghi appears to be describing a victory. There is no hint that he fell short in the smallest article of his duty. Unsuited to supreme command, up to the last moment he pleaded with Mohammed Reza not to leave. He tried to obey the Shah's last orders, to support Bakhtiar, to avoid bloodshed, and "warn the commanders not to do anything crazy" (*ne fasse une folie*). As instructed, he held a press conference on the 14th to insist that "there will be no coup d'etat."[9] When on January 18 soldiers and royalist toughs or "club wielders" went on a rampage against the religious opposition in the oil town of Ahvaz, he ordered the army to suppress them.

Yet as the days elapsed after Mohammed Reza's departure, Gharabaghi came to doubt Bakhtiar's loyalty to the monarchy, was demoralized by Sullivan's contacts with the opposition, and disgusted that Khomeini might be permitted to return. To carry out Mohammed Reza's orders to cooperate, Gharabaghi formed a council of senior officers, which met four times at the Supreme Commander's Staff, beginning on "D-Day minus one" (January 15, the day before "Departure"). Huyser did not attend the Higher Commanders' Council meetings, and the minutes, which were published in 1987, make no mention of him. Here there is none of the bluster reported by Huyser, only perpetual complaint about morale, supplies, and communications. There is no hint of a plan to go to war with the popular movement. (The commander of army aviation, General Manuchehr Khosrowdad, had been heard to say on the eve of Mohammed Reza's departure that, given the "unreliability" of the rank and file, a coup would probably fail.)[10] The arrival of a U.S. Defense Department civilian, Erich von Marbod, on January 18 to renegotiate the U.S. military supply contracts, a Derringer pistol strapped to his leg, caused them to question American priorities. The oldest of the senior officers, Hassan Toufanian, is noted as saying: "American support of the Iranian army is nothing but a lot of hot air." The fault of Gharabaghi and the other officers was not treachery but incompetence. In trying to preserve the monarchy, which was already lost, they failed to save the army, and that was to have consequences, not just for Iran.

On January 19, 1979, the fortieth day after Ashura and the great mourning procession of December 11, the opposition staged a mass march to call for the return of Khomeini to his homeland. Under rules agreed between Moqaddam of Savak and Khomeini's Revolutionary Council, the march passed without any outright challenge to the government or the military. That day, Bakhtiar approved the plan to take over the customs posts, and Huyser reported back to Defense Secretary Harold Brown that evening with some satisfaction.

When he called at Gharabaghi's office the next morning, Huyser "nearly went into a state of shock."[11] The strikers at the customs had allowed the trucks from Turkey through, and the plan had been called off. Whether the plan leaked or was deliberately revealed to the opposition, Huyser was more than ever doubtful Gharabaghi would act. Later that morning, he learned from a distraught Toufanian and Rabii that Gharabaghi had resigned as chief of staff. At a meeting that night with Bakhtiar and Sullivan, the chief of staff was persuaded to withdraw his resignation papers on the promise that Khomeini would not be permitted to return.[12] A man who resigns once will resign again, and here Bakhtiar and Sullivan made an error. Bakhtiar's sole card, which was the threat of military dictatorship if he failed, was beginning to look like a bluff.

On January 21, a Sunday, *Kayhan* ran the banner: "Imam Khomeini will lead the Prayers this Friday!" That was too soon for Mehdi Bazargan of the Revolutionary Council. He needed more time to work on the army, on the parliamentary deputies, and, above all, on Bakhtiar. Colleagues in Mossadeq's government in the early 1950s, and from the revived National Front of the early 1960s, the two men were fond of each other. Bazargan suggested to Khomeini that Bakhtiar, who held his commission from the old regime, should travel to France and tender his resignation to Khomeini, at which point he would be named provisional prime minister until a referendum on the form of the new government. They were, as Bazargan put it, in Bakhtiar's debt for having persuaded Mohammed Reza to leave the country. At a meeting on January 23, a resignation letter and a letter of appointment were drafted by Bazargan's associate, Abbas Amir Entezam, and accepted, with some alterations, by Bakhtiar. The "formula" was conveyed by telephone to Khomeini, who agreed to consider it.[13]

This project, so rich in opportunities for treachery, failed. Three days earlier, Bakhtiar had sent Sayyid Jalaleddin Tehrani, the chairman of the Regency Council, to Paris to talk to Khomeini and to warn him that his movement risked being captured by the hard left. Sayyid Jalaleddin was a court cleric who, back in 1963, had worked with Pakravan of Savak to effect Khomeini's release from detention. "At least he could understand that bloke's [Khomeini's] language whereas we collar-and-tie men were at sea," Bakhtiar said later.[14] Khomeini refused to receive Sayyid Jalaleddin unless he first resigned, which the poor man immediately did, declaring that the Regency Council was unconstitutional.[15] Supported by the Tehran clergy, Khomeini insisted on the same terms for Bakhtiar.[16]

Bakhtiar, made of altogether stiffer fiber than Sayyid Jalaleddin, canceled his trip to Paris and ordered the general staff to close Mehrabad Airport to inbound flights on the 24th. There were considerations of safety. With the air traffic controllers on strike, the air force personnel in the tower at Mehrabad could control only such aircraft as they could see, and a Pan American pilot had reported a near miss on approach. It was agreed by the general staff that if Khomeini attempted to return, his aircraft would be diverted to Kish Island, the luxury resort at the mouth of the Persian Gulf. Desmond Harney the banker noted in his diary on the 26th: "Incredible that a modern state can play cat and mouse with thousands of legitimate travellers as part of a checkmate with a political opponent."[17] In a letter on the 27th to Khomeini, the prime minister's elaborate courtesy could not conceal his habitual impudence. He advised Khomeini "to accept a delay in your return to Iran."

Meanwhile, Mohammed Reza dallied. At the Oberoi Hotel on Elephantine Island just downstream from the first cataract on the Nile, which had been cleared of its three hundred guests, he sat silently, as the queen put it, "dumbfounded and deep in thought." When Dr. Flandrin came from Paris to perform his medical examination, Mohammed Reza's face lit up as if he feared "that his doctors might also abandon him." It is possible that he still dreamed he could repeat the comeback of 1953, from Aswan rather than Baghdad, and that is why he delayed. Sadat tried to persuade him that "Egypt was closer to Iran for setting up the resistance he had in mind," and even offered a refuge for the Imperial Iranian Air Force (IIAF). Mohammed Reza said merely: "The air force belongs to Iran." Farah believed that, too proud to act himself, her husband would return only if "the people called him back."

General Huyser's arrival had destroyed his faith in the United States. Farah had never been comfortable there. The children were now cooped up at Reese Air Force Base in Texas, and Farahnaz called to say: "Don't come here. It's not safe."[18] Whatever the cause, the delay was fateful for Mohammed Reza and the United States. On January 22, anxious not to impose on the Sadats' hospitality, they flew to Morocco as guests of their old pensioner, King Hassan. While Mohammed Reza had no contact with his army, Farah was speaking to General Ali Neshat of the Imperial Guard every day. A "Constitutionalist" demonstration on the 25th, in which the families of military men were allowed by Gharabaghi to take part, raised Farah's hopes and even brought a smile to the Shah's exhausted face.[19] On January 31, Mohammed Reza sent back both the Falcon airliner and the IIAF aircraft that had taken the children to the United States, paying the $14,777 for fuel with a personal check.[20] In the tension in Tehran, punctuated by mass rallies and scuffles with the army, Mohammed Reza's presence in Morocco kept alive the rumors of a military *coup d'état*. *Kayhan* newspaper ran a series on Mossadeq.

The opposition increased the pressure on Bakhtiar. The leading clergy, led by Montazeri, staged a sit-in at Tehran University. At a demonstration in front of the university on the 26th, a crowd armed with sticks and knives (but not, according to the *New York Times,* with firearms) clashed with the army. When shots in the air failed to disperse the people, the soldiers fired into the crowd and even into side streets and doorways, killing fifteen.[21] There was a four-hour bloody fight at nearby 24 Esfand Square on the 28th, and the following day the Fedayan led an attack on the Gendarmerie headquarters there. A crowd surrounded the Mercedes carrying a Gendarmerie officer, General Taqi Latifi, and beat him up. As he lay on the ground, bleeding, he was stabbed in the side. (Montazeri's disturbed son, Mohammed, known to the foreign correspondents as "Ayatollah Ringo," used to show off the sidearm he had taken from Latifi until the Revolution finished him off also.)[22] At least seven people were killed. A shaken Gharabaghi blamed General Huyser for the bloodshed. The same day, workers in the armaments industry, including the so-called machine-gun factory near Zhaleh Square, scene of the Black Friday killings, marched in support of Khomeini's return to his homeland.

Gharabaghi was anxious about inroads by the opposition among the air force contract technicians known as *homafars*, qualified engineers who resented the privileges of the commissioned men, and in the army aviation wing. At Khatami Air Force Base outside Isfahan, the sixteen F-14 aircraft from the United States were placed under special guard and the "black box" missile guidance systems removed.[23] Believing that the United States was about to withdraw the F-14s and other advanced equipment, the *homafars* marched on the Isfahan and Shiraz air bases, causing Grumman to order its staff out of the country. The IIAF commander, Amir Hosein Rabii, sent two detachments of special forces to Isfahan. On the 27th, about 4,000 *homafars* were locked out of the helicopter training school in Isfahan and then fought with army troops. Huyser began to suspect that, as he put it, "we could be heading for a fire-fight."[24] Some 160 *homafars* were arrested or cashiered. To quell the rumors that the aircraft had been taken out of the country, Rabii staged a fly-past over Tehran on the 29th, involving more than a hundred aircraft and five F-14s. Huyser was impressed.

At the third meeting of the Higher Commanders' Council on January 28, the staff faced a grim reality. The armed forces had little fuel, electricity, or money, and quite soon might not have food. As Gharabaghi said, summing up: "Military action is neither expedient nor possible." That evening, at Bakhtiar's request and with his permission, Gharabaghi received Bazargan at his own house.[25] Nasser Moqaddam of Savak was also present. According to his own account, Gharabaghi repeated that the armed forces had sworn oaths to sustain the Constitution and the legal government. The meeting broke up evidently without progress.

Bowing to the inevitable, and apparently without consulting the general staff, Bakhtiar announced on the 29th that the airport would be opened and "no obstacle placed in the way of His Eminence's return." He told a furious Gharabaghi not to worry, for he had "the matter in hand."[26] No doubt, he expected something to turn up.

Khomeini's return to his country after fourteen years of exile was set for February 1, 1979. While Khomeini himself said, "I am just a seminary student, do not overdo the ceremony," his supporters in Iran intended a show of popular strength that would amount to a "referendum" in favor of an Islamic Republic. People would be bused in from the other provincial towns. From the airport at Mehrabad, Khomeini would pass east along what was still called Shahreza Street to Tehran University; turn south down Pahlavi Avenue to the railway station; east along Shush Avenue and then south again to the Behesht-e Zahra, "the Paradise of Fatemeh the Radiant," a windblown cemetery on the west side of the Qom highway which had grown since the 1950s in mournful step with the city of the living.* The dead of Zhaleh Square and other clashes with the army were buried at a section called Lot 17. As in the great demonstrations of Moharram in December, the army would withdraw but be ready if assistance in managing the crowds was required.

The streets, littered with rubbish from the garbage workers' strike, were cleaned by volunteers. The airport terminal was swept and armed men placed on the roof. On the afternoon of the 29th, the red-light quarter north of the railway station and just to the west of Khomeini's route down by Pahlavi Avenue was attacked by a downtown mob and burned. The Shams brewery, the New Blossom cabaret and dance hall, dozens of bars and liquor stores, and the "Fort" or New Town were razed to the ground. The women of the fort were beaten and mistreated, and according to eyewitnesses, at least two were killed.[27] It was the first arson since the day the banks burned on November 5. The columns of smoke were visible from Shemiran.

The U.S. Embassy now believed that, on Khomeini's return, as much as 80 percent of the armed forces would defect.[28] Mohammed Beheshti, one of Khomeini's chief organizers in Tehran, had boasted to an embassy officer: "We control everyone below the rank of major."[29] The general staff feared that an attempt on Khomeini's life would provoke a civil war, in which the armed forces would find themselves immobile for lack of fuel.[30] As a show of strength, on January 31 the land forces moved an entire division through the streets of the capital, a column of trucks and armor stretching more than two miles and including twelve Chieftains and six Scorpion light tanks.[31]

Khomeini's circle had hoped to use an Iran Air jet airliner, to be

---

* Behesht-e Zahra is now the principal shrine of the Islamic Republic, and famous for its Martyrs' Fountain of red-tinted water.

called "Flight Revolution," but Bakhtiar refused permission. Instead, the Tehran merchants put up 400,000 tomans ($50,000) to lease an Air France 747B-100 with a full crew. Air France insisted that, just in case permission to land was refused, the machine carry enough fuel for the return journey. Restricted to a maximum takeoff weight of 300 tons, AF-4721 could carry only half its complement of passengers.

All the Iranians in Neauphle were to travel except, for reasons of modesty, Khomeini's wife. Her son-in-law, Shahabuddin Eshraqi, would accompany her home. In addition, places were offered to some 120 journalists, for reasons of publicity, as "a form of insurance" against attack and even, to the German reporter Peter Scholl-Latour, "as hostages."[32] On departure from Neauphle, the village _curé_ made a farewell speech, causing Khomeini to mutter to his son Ahmad's brother-in-law, Tabatabai, "Their men of God are as talkative as ours."[33] At Charles de Gaulle Airport, Ebrahim Yazdi read a statement from Khomeini in English, thanking the French for their hospitality and "their conception of freedom."

The first-class lounge, up a spiral stair, was reserved for Khomeini to rest. In the economy cabin, the reporters grumbled at the want of their customary fuel, wine and tobacco. In contrast, the Iranians feared they might be attacked, refused permission to land, or diverted to some desert air strip and there arrested. The famous Iranian politeness became frayed. When John Simpson of the BBC asked Khomeini in Persian for a comment, "he just looked out of the window." Simpson concluded: "We had served our purpose during all the interviews he gave before leaving France."[34] Peter Jennings of ABC News fared little better. When he asked Khomeini what he felt about returning to his homeland, he replied: "Nothing" (_hich_ or, possibly, _hichi_, "nothing at all"). No doubt, Khomeini was weary of reporters: he was to receive only two or three more foreign journalists in his life. The royalists and liberals were disgusted at his lack of heart. His supporters saw in that single word something unfathomably profound, as if, as the philosopher Mehdi Haeri-Yazdi put it, Khomeini had reached that point in his spiritual ascent where he could regard all earthly phenomena with the boundless indifference of God.[35]

That is as may be. Dr. Yazdi's wife, Sourour (Sarah), had sent from the United States three bulletproof vests: one for Khomeini; one for his son Ahmad; and one for her husband. Just before dawn, when Kho-meini went up to the first-class lounge to say his prayers on a check-ered brown Air France blanket, Yazdi followed him and, as sun lit the snowy mountaintops of Kurdestan, persuaded him to take off his robe and cloak and put on the vest.[36] That is why, in the photographs and film of Khomeini descending the gangway, he appears so bulky and the Air France flight attendant supporting his arm must descend shoul-der-first. Khomeini is also wearing the vest at Behesht-e Zahra.

At last, after circling for twenty minutes to burn fuel in order to reduce the landing weight, the captain received permission to land. He made a low-level pass to ensure the runway was clear of obstacles, then brought the machine down just after 9 a.m. local time on Febru-ary 1. The reporters disembarked. To suppress the squabbling among the clergy, it was resolved that the Air France *chef de cabine* (the chief flight attendant or purser) should help the old man down the gang-way. Khomeini, frail and wrapped up thick against the cold (as people thought), descended on his arm. Looking from the top of the gangway, Abol Hassan Bani-Sadr knew that he had lost Khomeini. "The clerics had abducted him,"[37] he wrote later. The army had not permitted the public to come nearer to the airport than the Shahyad Monument, but even so the terminal was milling with more than a thousand clergy-men and bazaar supporters. There was no representative of the Bakh-tiar government. In the crush, the foreign correspondents could not make out Khomeini's short statement. They picked up from their local stringers his last phrase: "I pray to God Almighty to cut short the hands of foreigners."[38]

Mohsen Rafiqdoust, a bazaar militant appointed by Beheshti and the Welcome Committee to take charge of security for Khomeini, had brought an armored blue-and-white Chevrolet Blazer with lead panels and a bulletproof glass cabin. As it turned out, on the route to Behesht-e Zahra Khomeini elected to ride in front beside Rafiqdoust, and Ahmad Khomeini rode in the back. The doors were held shut by crook-locks. Two young men rode shotgun on the roof, and were scolded by Kho-meini for showing the crowd the soles of their feet. As the convoy of eight vehicles and ten motorcycle outriders approached Shahyad Square, the exiles came upon a scene without Iranian precedent. Num-berless people filled the streets, packed roofs and windows, dangled from fences, stood on the pillions of motorcycles. The BBC and other observers reckoned there were 3 million on the streets that morning. Rafiqdoust, as he peered through the windshield, said 6 million. An unbroken mass of humanity filled Shahreza and Pahlavi Avenue and all the twenty miles to the cemetery. Some cried out the half-line from the poet Hafez: "When the demon goes, the angel takes his place." [39]

This was not, as the foreign correspondents thought as they scrabbled to make the scene comprehensible, Charles de Gaulle returning to Paris in 1944 through bursts of gunfire. This was not a mere exile come home after fourteen years, but a messiah. All the centuries of waiting for the Hidden Imam had been their own kind of inferno, and the Iranians would take what they could in the here and now. Or perhaps, as Bakhtiar put it, Khomeini had simply made donkeys of an entire nation. [40] As the red-and-white Blazer crept westward, flowers and candy raining on the roof, Khomeini kept asking his son Ahmad behind him the names of the streets.

Within 150 yards, the marshals lost control. The crowd broke between the Blazer and its escort vehicles, which became entangled and forced to halt. Outside the university, Rafiqdoust at the wheel found for the first time that it was the crowd moving the vehicle, rocking it from side to side, and he had no control. "I felt my hands were on the wheel, but cut off from my body," he said years later. (A plan to meet parents of the dead at Tehran University was out of the question, to the relief of many since the campus was dominated by the hard left and the Mojahedin.)

At the foot of Pahlavi Avenue, at the traffic circle known as Gomrok-Amiriyeh, the crowd became all but impassable. As the correspondent of *Kayhan* put it before he too was engulfed, the square in front of the railway station, Shush Avenue, and the Yadavaran road to the cemetery were "an ocean of humanity. If you had thrown a needle in the air it would not have touched the ground." Here were people who had been passive up to that moment, the villagers and denizens of the shantytowns, and their understanding of what was happening was more straightforward than in the uptown districts and incomparably more profound. The boundary between politics and religion, never fixed or set in Iran, had vanished. God, state, and people were one.

On Yadavaran, among the old brick pits and shantytowns, the Blazer gave up the ghost. The air conditioning, the weight of the armorplate, and the constant stopping and starting caused the engine or gearbox to fail. The steering jammed to the right. Inside, it was black as night. Rafiqdoust was on the point of fainting. Suffocating, Khomeini demanded to leave the vehicle, which would have cost him his life. Five hundred yards away, Rafiqdoust saw a helicopter. (Huyser says Rabii had sent his best crew in a UH-1 "Huey.") The crowd tried to push the Blazer, but it merely turned a circle to the right, and so they carried it, all 1.5 tons of it, inch-by-inch to the machine. Rafiqdoust saw Khomeini and his son boarded, and then he passed out.

The helicopter landed at the entrance to the cemetery, but again no vehicle could pass through the crowd, and Khomeini returned to the aircraft. At Lot 17, the marshals formed a human chain to clear a circular space just large enough for the helicopter to come down. The down draft from the rotors blew the weedy saplings and scattered clouds of sand. As Khomeini made his way to the podium, he was jostled and for a moment lost his black *sayyid*'s turban.

He spoke in his habitual fierce monotone. Mohammed Reza Pahlavi, "that vile traitor," had departed, leaving a thoroughly ruined land where "only the cemeteries had prospered." There remained only Bakhtiar, "the feeble last gasp of the Shah's regime," and the armed forces command. "I will decide the government," he said. "To oppose it is to deny God as well as the will of the people." As for the armed forces, he praised the *homafars* and called on the commanders to abandon both Bakhtiar and their American advisers. "I want the army to be independent. Mr. Field Marshal, and you, Mr. Major-General, do you not want to be independent? Do you want to go on being a servant? Come to the bosom of the nation. Let that man [Bakhtiar] go."

Then came what sounded like a pleasantry: "Do not imagine, if you let him go, that we will string you up on the gallows." [41]

The crowd was now packed so tight at the tribune that there were fears Khomeini might be crushed. He was taken to the press tent and, as a ruse to disperse the crowd, the Huey started its engines. Young men pressed in under the turning rotors, clambered onto the landing skids, and clung to the airframe. With great care, the crew lifted off, hovered at fifteen feet as the young men dropped and tumbled back to earth, then set off. The crowd was uncertain and stayed where it was.

Finally, Khomeini left in an ambulance and was picked up by helicopter some distance from the cemetery.[42]

Khomeini had asked to be lodged in South Tehran and as guest neither of the government nor a particular individual. The reception committee had chosen the Refah, a traditionalist girls' primary school built with charitable donations in a lane in the old-fashioned quarter off Ain od-Dowleh Street, just to the east of the Parliament building. There the Revolutionary Council had been meeting since its foundation. In preparation, the large courtyard or playground was spread with rugs. Before that, he was to visit the wounded from the demonstrations in the venerable teaching hospital known as the "Thousand-Bed" just north of the main Tehran University campus. It seems he was too exhausted to do so. From the hospital car park, Khomeini drove with his son to his elder brother Pasandideh's house. The general staff did not know where Khomeini was and became frantic that he might have come to some harm. It was as if, as Gharabaghi noted, they were protecting the opposition rather than the legally constituted government.[43]

The Refah School proved too cramped, and the next day Khomeini moved his residence next door to the allied Alavi No. 1 School on Iran Avenue, where he occupied two tiny rooms overlooking the court. Alavi had the virtue of two entrances, which eased the crowd of people flooding in to offer their allegiance. It was also entirely under clerical control. "In reality this was a coup d'etat, which saved the Imam from the clutches of Bazargan's Freedom Movement and the National Front," Khalkhali later wrote.[44] Khomeini's close associate, Morteza Motahhari, said: "I felt that these people were crowding the Imam and trying to control him."[45] The sexes were segregated, men calling in the morning, women in the afternoon. When someone grumbled at the women visitors' sometimes cute Islamic dress, Khomeini shook his head, as if to say, Pardon them for once. The learned Montazeri reminded them that when Ali had been at last named Caliph in Medina in Year 35 (AD 656), women had run bare-breasted to give their allegiance.[46] Such was the sense among those men that Shia history, after more than a thousand years of wandering, had come full circle.

Tehran was now too hot for General Huyser. He was under unremitting assault in the Soviet press, which warned on January 30 of a "creeping military coup as a result of the crude and overt U.S. interference in Iran's internal affairs."[47] He was receiving threats to his life even on the military telephone network. Someone had scrawled DEATH TO HUYSER in red paint on the compound wall of the Supreme Commander's Staff. "Having hundreds of thousands of people chanting 'Death' at you really did bring a conclusive feeling of being unwanted," he later wrote.[48] In bidding farewell to the Iranian officers on February 3, he let fly at Gharabaghi, saying he lacked the will or guts to do what was needed. Huyser was hoping to provoke him, but Gharabaghi just sat in silence. "Well," said Huyser, "it appears to me that it is a lost cause, as none of you want to face the realities of life." As he stood up to leave, Rabii blurted out: "My brother, if it's necessary to save the country, I will do the necessary things and take charge."[49] It is an Iranian custom to spare the feelings of guests.

"Dutch" Huyser left as quietly as he arrived, boarding a C-130 at Mehrabad just after nightfall that Saturday evening. That meant flying through the air defenses around Mehrabad, but Huyser had confidence that the antiaircraft units were loyal to IIAF commander Rabii. As the aircraft crossed the Turkish border, the crew broke into a roar of applause.[50] Meanwhile, Erich von Marbod of the Pentagon had finally extracted a signature—either Bakhtiar's or Toufanian's, the sources disagree—to cancel the orders for F-16s, AWACs reconnaissance aircraft, and *Spruance*-class destroyers. "Whatever the U.S. Government was paying Eric Von Marbod," Gary Sick wrote, "it got its money's worth."[51]

At a press conference at the Alavi School on the 5th, Khomeini presented his provisional government. Bazargan stood beside him in a flared tweed jacket and kipper tie and put the correspondents at their ease.[52] Then Khomeini began to speak: "By the authority delegated to me by the Holy Law, I hereby pronounce this man as ruler and since I have appointed him he must be obeyed. This is not an ordinary government. This is government by Holy Law. Opposition to this government means opposition to the Holy Law and that entails a heavy punishment."[53] Though few of the foreign correspondents had heard of the Najaf lectures or the "Stewardship of the Jurist," they thought to detect a new tone. Baqer Moin, of the BBC Persian Service and a former seminarian who knew both, saw an absolutism of which the Pahlavis could not have dreamed. "Having emerged from arbitrary imperial rule," he wrote, "Iran was, it seemed, set to experience a new autocracy, divinely inspired."[54] In place of democracy was the oath of allegiance. When asked about the provisional government, Bakhtiar said he would "tolerate it as a joke."[55]

On February 8, a group of *homafars* and uniformed non-commissioned officers came to the Alavi School to make their obeisance. *Kayhan* splashed a picture of them across eight columns, showing a sea of military caps and hands raised in salute, but from behind, so they could not be identified. The photograph, with its warring perspectives and unnatural patterns of light, was doctored, but that did nothing to reassure the commanders at their meeting that day. Deserters arriving at the school were given civilian clothes.[56]

That evening, at 7 p.m., five men gathered in the office of the prime minister to settle the fate of the country. They were Bakhtiar, and Generals Gharabaghi and Moqaddam on the one side and, on the other, Bazargan's two lieutenants, Abbas Amir Entezam and Yadollah Sahabi. According to Amir Entezam's account, Sahabi began by praising Chapour Bakhtiar's long struggle in opposition politics, which greatly affected the participants. An eloquent man, Sahabi turned to the officers and said: "Every person killed, every building reduced to ruins, is a loss to Iran. You, too, are Iranian. You love your country and are its pride and glory. You must put a stop to this slaughter. History will record both our services and our derelictions."[57] Gharabaghi once more reassured them that no coup was in the planning. Bakhtiar himself barely spoke. Amir Entezam took away the impression that the man was isolated. After three hours, it was decided to meet again at 4 p.m. on Saturday, February 10, but that meeting was overtaken by events. Gharabaghi delayed so long that the army disintegrated under him, and in the end he had nothing to offer the provisional government but himself, in civilian clothes, and nothing to preserve but his life.[58]

In an interview with *Kayhan* on February 9, Bakhtiar said the armed forces would accept a republic, but only if it was brought about in "calm and peaceful fashion."[59] Bakhtiar was not ready to step down, nor Gharabaghi to join the Revolution, nor Khomeini to call for insurrection. It was necessary that there should be a fight. The spark that set it off on the evening of Friday, February 9, is presented in all the eyewitness accounts as a happenstance. If so, it occurred at precisely the place where, from a strategic view, the armed forces were at their most vulnerable: Doshan Teppe, "Hare Hill," or what the Americans called "Little Bighorn."

Doshan Teppe Air Force Base had its origins in the 1930s, when the British company Hawker Siddeley established a factory making military biplanes for Reza. It had spread out to cover a shallow valley, approximately three miles by two, and comprised a runway and taxiways, Rabii's staff headquarters, a maintenance base, radar station, and the Air Training Center, which on the eve of revolution had 23,000 cadets. With the sprawl of the city eastward in the 1950s and 1960s, the air base had become islanded in a teeming neighborhood and commanded from the roofs of buildings on all sides. An insurrection there could be more easily reinforced from the streets than at the provincial air force bases, such as Isfahan and Shiraz. Since the disturbances in January, a unit of the Immortals of the Imperial Guard had been stationed at the base.

Just to the west of Doshan Teppe, on the north side of Farahabad Avenue (now Victory Avenue), was the 50-acre arms-manufacturing complex known in Tehran as the "machine-gun factory." Established before World War II beyond the city limits at Zhaleh Square, for years it had turned out the Iranian military and sporting rifle known as the *berno* (after the Czech city of Brno), but its machinery had by now been replaced by the West German arms industry to produce 30,000 G-3 rifles and 5,000 MG-1 machine guns annually. It was solidly built and garrisoned, but not invulnerable. The third strategic happenstance was a conference and show of force called for February 8 by the Fedayan at Tehran University to mark the eighth anniversary of their attack on the police post at Siahkal in 1971. The newspapers reported that as many as 20,000 people attended.[60] It also meant that some hundred professional revolutionaries, including many just released from prison in the Bakhtiar amnesties, were gathered in one place and could direct reinforcements for the battle in the east of town.[61]

At about 9 p.m. on that Friday evening, February 9, Iranian television again broadcast a collage of scenes from Khomeini's return.[62] In the common room of the warrant officers' mess at Doshan Teppe, a group of *homafars* and air force cadets began to chant hosannas (the salutes to the Prophet and his descendants known as *salavat*). The din infuriated some of the commissioned officers. A shouting match broke out, shots were fired, and the Military Police called for support from the Third Brigade of the Imperial Guard nearby. One report has the Immortals bringing their armor right up to the windows of the mess, another speaks of hauling out airmen onto the parade ground and shooting them.[63] In the streets outside, the arrival of the Guard units caused a rumor there was to be a general massacre of the technicians and cadets, and people began throwing up barricades and setting fires. The airmen barricaded themselves into the Air Training Center, next to the Air Force Staff headquarters, and by midnight there was an impasse and the shooting died down. When Gharabaghi called the air force commander at 1 a.m. to find out what was happening, Rabii played down the disturbances and denied that shots had been fired. "They have all gone to sleep," Gharabaghi reports him as saying.[64]

Early the next morning, the 10th, the fighting flared up. Either in the night or at first light, reinforcements were brought down from the Imperial Guard base at Lavizan. An airman told James Allan of the *Daily Telegraph*: "This morning the guards sent for reinforcements, who arrived in tanks, armoured cars and lorries. Hundreds of airmen decided to leave the base but as they walked towards the main gate they were told to stop by the commander of the guards who was using a loud hailer. They kept walking towards the gates calling out that they were unarmed. The guards' commander ordered a soldier on gate duty to shoot at the airmen but he refused and was shot dead by the guards. They then opened fire on the airmen who scattered in all directions. Some even stood there throwing stones at the soldiers as they were firing at them."[65] The airmen stormed the base armory, shot the sentry, and started distributing weapons to the cadets and supporters outside.[66] A group of U.S. newspapermen arrived at the main gate soon after 6 a.m. and found a crowd of demonstrators and the Guard firing over their heads. They took refuge on the second floor of an apartment building, where Joe Alex Morris, an experienced reporter with the *Los Angeles Times,* took a round in the chest. He was carried over the heads of the crowd into Doshan Teppe, but was dead before he reached the base hospital.

By 10 a.m., the city was in full insurrection. At Tehran University, there was controlled pandemonium, as loudspeakers called for volunteers, and young men peeled off commandeering vehicles and motorbikes, waving automatic weapons. Some wore armbands showing their allegiance to the Fedayan or Mojahedin. They surged eastward, drawing crowds with them. Along the leafless boulevards to Doshan Teppe, buses were overturned and set alight and barricades put up of sandbags, metal gates, bedsteads, hat stands, and "every sort of possible material that could be scavenged from building sites and burnt-out cinemas."[67] The barricades would not have caused a Chieftain tank even to slow. Newsreel of the day shows a masked professional revolutionary and an exasperated air force non-com instructing the people in how to man the barricades and to shoot automatic weapons. Someone shouts, "Do not fire in the air!" On the lampposts and trees are makeshift signs, saying: "Support your air force brothers!"[68]

In a maneuver that does credit to the strategic instincts of the Tehran crowd, the Immortals at the base were now invested: the besiegers besieged. All round the perimeter of the base, airmen and civilians had thrown up earth emplacements on balconies and roofs, pouring fire into the base from AK-47 and M-16 rifles, machine guns and tear gas launchers. Sullivan could not understand why the Imperial Guards were not using the 120mm howitzers on the Chieftain, but we now know they had been issued no heavy ordnance. With Molotov cocktails, the insurgents disabled trucks, armored personnel carriers, and five tanks: one at Fauzia Square, and four on Damavand Avenue.[69] A Guard helicopter was brought down or crashed. By early afternoon, some 4,000 armed insurgents had control of East Tehran and were spreading out and attacking police stations. At 2 p.m., the police precinct at New Tehran just east of the base fell.

Bakhtiar ordered a curfew and martial law, ostensibly because of the Fedayan Congress. At 2 p.m., communiqué No. 40 of the military government moved the curfew forward from midnight to 4:30 p.m., ordered martial law to be rigorously enforced, and instructed the army and air force to support the military governor in crushing insurrection at the cadet school. Many felt that was a prelude to a coup. Some at the Alavi School, such as Ayatollah Mahmoud Taleqani, were for observing the curfew to prevent bloodshed, but Khomeini was implacable. He recorded a statement which was broadcast from a short-wave transmitter at the school with a range of four miles. He said: "I have not given the orders for Holy War, and I still wish for matters to be settled peacefully. I issue a solemn warning that if the Imperial Guard does not desist from its fratricide and return to barracks, I will take my final decision. Responsibility for what follows shall lie with those shameless aggressors. As for the declaration of martial law, the people should pay it not the slightest attention." [70]

They did not. All over town, police precincts were evacuated or overrun. Small groups of airmen or armed leftists stormed the precincts, cleared out the defenders, and then moved on to the next, while unarmed boys, some as young as fourteen, pillaged the buildings, setting fire to furniture, records, doors, and window frames, and reducing them to smoking hulks. The police withdrew in disorder to the Gendarmerie School in the Vanak district in the north of town, where they sowed panic among their colleagues. Ambulances weaved between the barricades, carrying the wounded. By nightfall, all but the police headquarters were in the insurgents' hands.

At 6 p.m., at the insistence of Gharabaghi and the military governor of Tehran, General Mehdi Rahimi, Bakhtiar convened the National Security Council at his office. The officers arrived by helicopter as the sun was setting through the smoke, and fell to blaming one another. Bakhtiar interrupted and ordered that the crowds had to be dispersed, and the Air Training Center relieved. General Badrei, the army commander, said he had ordered an infantry battalion from Qazvin, a hundred miles to the west, as reinforcement. Moqaddam of Savak was told to arrest a list of persons that almost certainly included Khomeini and Bazargan. Since Savak had disintegrated, along with the police, Badrei said that special forces of the Imperial Guard would be made available to Moqaddam.

In the tumult, two men were calm. Hosein Fardoust was not a man to change his habits. All that winter, he had passed each evening at cards at the Young Iran club off Takht-e Jamshid Street, though the company diminished as more and more members went abroad until, in the end, he was alone. That evening, he found the door locked from the inside, but the doorman opened it and the club secretary made him supper. Then General Fardoust, head of the Special Bureau of Intelligence, sat down before the television. That is how the Pahlavis came to an end: the tyrant fled and his special friend, amid the motor horns and the gunfire, watching television. [71]

As the noise of battle approached the Alavi School, and tracer fire crisscrossed the night sky, Khomeini was pressed by his son-in-law Eshraqi to move. Everybody knew his precise coordinates, and an artilleryman with a single shell could flatten the school and wipe out the clerical leadership. The sole defense was a heavy machine gun on the roof. Khomeini refused even to change rooms and went to bed at his usual hour. At about 3 a.m., the faithful Khalkhali, who was sleeping by the door of Khomeini's room, saw the old man fumbling to read the time by the faint glow of his nightlight. "Master, couldn't you sleep?" Khalkhali said. Khomeini replied: "Like you I am not so young as I was." Khomeini rose, washed, and said the night prayer.[72]

At staff headquarters, Gharabaghi pressed General Badrei for news of the battalion from Qazvin, but it had passed out of communication. At 10 p.m., an armored column rumbled past the Supreme Commander's Staff toward its barracks at the Qasr and filled him with foreboding. Just before midnight, General Toufanian called to say that the machine-gun factory at Zhaleh Square was under heavy fire and the garrison urgently needed reinforcement. Gharabaghi called Badrei to hear that the battalion from Qazvin had been stopped at Karavansara Sangi, fifteen miles west of the city, and disarmed. Some sixty trucks, along with jeeps, ambulances, arms, and ammunition, had passed to the insurgents. He called General Neshat, commander of the Imperial Guard, but he refused to act, saying the Immortals were on a special mission for the Shah.

Gharabaghi then tried Manuchehr Khosrowdad of army aviation. He could not reach him, but told his deputy, General Ismail Atabaki, to dispatch commandos to the factory by helicopter. Atabaki said that there was complete disorder, that he could not reach Khosrowdad and his orders were not being obeyed.[73] A column of tanks, under the command of General Riahi, was being prepared at the Imperial Guard headquarters at Lavizan to retake the air base, but was held up for lack of heavy ordnance for the 120mm guns. At the Qasr barracks, men were throwing down their weapons on their bunks and deserting en masse. Meanwhile, IIAF commander Rabii was calling from Doshan Teppe: Where are the tanks?

Thirty tanks finally set off at 3 a.m., but advanced scarcely more than a mile before, in the new housing development of Tehran Pars, they were ambushed. Riahi was killed and several tanks were burned. The remainder either turned back to base or chose to fraternize. That was the last throw. Some time before 6 a.m., Bakhtiar ordered the aerial bombing of both the cadet school and the machine-gun factory, but he was told by Rabii that was impossible.[74] Around 8 a.m., under the cover of relentless fire and torrential rain, a crowd with pickaxes and bayonets broke through the walls of the machine-gun factory at five points, and started assembling and passing out machine guns, rifles, and tear gas launchers which were sped through the morning streets to Khomeini's headquarters at Ain od-Dowleh and the university.[75] Gharabaghi took stock. The army was in disorder, the army air force in utter indiscipline, the military governor had lost touch with district commanders, command posts were not functioning, Neshat had disobeyed orders, Khosrowdad could not be found, and Moqaddam had not been provided with forces to make arrests. The police headquarters in Army Square was about to be overrun. At that moment, the logistical adjutant of the army called.

"I believe it to be my duty to inform you, General, not to rely on the ground army."

"That is very unfortunate."

"Indeed." [76]

Gharabaghi called a meeting of all the commanders of the armed forces and other military establishments at the Supreme Commander's Staff for 10:30 a.m. The armed forces at least still controlled the air, though Gharabaghi's own helicopter had twice been hit by small arms. When Chapour Bakhtiar called at 9 a.m., summoning him and Rahimi to the prime minister's office, he pleaded the prior engagement. As if on cue, Kazem Jafroudi, a senator and friend of both Bakhtiar and Bazargan, rang to confirm that both men had agreed to meet at his house in Shemiran at 4 p.m. and they would expect Gharabaghi also. As he turned for the conference room, he heard that the police headquarters had been overrun and that the barracks at Eshratabad (where Khomeini had been held in 1963) was under attack. The hospitals were reporting a death toll, by the dawn of that day, of 175 and some 659 wounded.[77]

Twenty-seven officers gathered in the conference room of the Supreme Commander's Staff headquarters. They comprised all the service chiefs and their deputies, the defense minister and his deputy, the heads of bureaus for personnel, intelligence, operations, logistics, planning, and training, and the chief counsel and financial inspector. All but Fardoust were in uniform. There were more general officers than chairs and four or five of them, including Khosrowdad, who had now surfaced, were required to stand. Fardoust whispered to Badrei beside him, "How many men have you at your disposal?" The army commander replied that he would be hard-pressed to defend even the barracks.[78]

Gharabaghi opened with a general account of the battle. Moqaddam was next, saying that Bakhtiar had effectively disbanded Savak, the stations in Tehran and the major towns had been overrun and burned, and he had ordered his officers to retreat with their records and weapons to the barracks of the police and Gendarmerie. They had been admitted only after direct orders from the chief of staff, but their families were exposed to attack from the public. Otherwise, he had no information. Then Badrei, the army commander, spoke of Neshat's refusal to act, the loss of contact with the Qazvin battlalion, the ambush of the armored column at Tehran Pars and the death of Riahi, and the disorderly retreat of units to barracks, creating terror and disorder. He concluded: "The situation is such that the Ground Forces can do no more."[79] Other officers gave devastating accounts of the state of the air force, Gendarmerie, and police. At that point, Gharabaghi was called out to speak by telephone to Bakhtiar, but again refused to come to the prime minister.

On his return to the room, General Hushang Hatam, deputy chief of staff, proposed that since His Majesty had left the country, and it had become a discussion over what form of republic should be established, the army should support the people but "withdraw from the field of political conflict."[80] Gharabaghi reminded the generals that Mohammed Reza had ordered him both to avoid bloodshed and to conserve the unity and integrity of the Imperial Armed Forces. The men looked to Fardoust, as Mohammed Reza's friend, but he merely said: "I approve the Hatam proposition. In my opinion it may be too late."[81]

The discussion came down to alternatives: to ally with the popular forces, or to declare neutrality. Neutrality won. Hatam's draft was read out, altered in some small points, and unanimously approved. It read:

Army Order, 22/11/1357

The Iranian Army is duty bound to defend the independence and integrity of our dear country. Up to now, in the midst of the internal disturbances, it has endeavoured to the best of its ability to fulfill this duty in support of the legal governments. In light of the latest developments in the country, the High Council of the Army convened today the 22nd Bahman 1357 at 10.30 a.m. where it was unanimously resolved that to avoid chaos and greater bloodshed it should declare its neutrality. Orders have been given to military units to return to their bases. The Iranian Army has always been the support of the noble and patriotic people of Iran and always will be. It will support with all its forces the wishes of the noble people of Iran.[82]

All the officers signed, although the defense minister, General Jafar Shafaqat, on the grounds that he was a minister, crossed his name out. It was 1 p.m. Gharabaghi informed Bakhtiar and the order was broadcast at 1:15 p.m. on February 11, 1979.

In his memoirs, written in Paris, Chapour Bakhtiar railed against Gharabaghi's "treachery" and dereliction of duty and the rank absurdity of a "neutral" national army.[83] The order was also, like all the actions of the general staff in those days, without effect. The insurrection was not to be stopped. At Tehran University, now in warm sunshine, captured trucks and jeeps and commandeered buses were hauling the weapons from Zhaleh. The cries went up: "Reinforcements to Eshratabad!" "Eshratabad needs ammunition!" The poet Reza Baraheni, just three weeks returned from exile, asked a young man how to fire an automatic weapon. "It's simple," the young man said as the crowd made a ring around him, "you fit the magazine in the magazine well, like this; pull back the bolt; move this little thing you see here to 'Burst'; and pull the trigger." Where could they find weapons? "From the Master [Khomeini]. You get them from the Master's house."[84] By then, both schools were piled to the rafters with plundered weapons.

Then a wailing ambulance parted the crowd, and someone shouted: "Eshratabad is taken!" There was a burst of firing in the air in celebration, but just as soon, someone else was shouting: "The Citadel needs reinforcement. Get your weapons. Go to the Citadel. The Citadel needs help."

"They've surrounded the Komiteh. The Komiteh is about to fall!"

"To the Bagh-e Shah! The Guard is landing helicopters!"

At the prime minister's office, Bakhtiar was sitting at his desk, his lunch half-eaten before him. Bullets were slapping into the walls from a fight at the Marble Palace. There was a knock on the door, and without waiting for an answer, two men, a policeman and a Savak officer, entered.

"Prime Minister, the situation is deteriorating."

"I know. I will leave when it is time to leave." At the cadet college, a helicopter was waiting for him, and he passed out of view.[85]

The battle surged northward up Pahlavi Avenue and one by one the bases were overrun or surrendered. The Qasr and Evin prisons were opened, as empty of political prisoners as the Bastille in 1789. The radio station fell to the insurgents and those with sets heard the announcement: "This is the voice of the revolution." Heavy earth-moving equipment was seen battering the base perimeters. By midafternoon, the Supreme Commander's Staff was under fire from tank crews that had changed their allegiance. The staff and the members of the U.S. Military Mission took refuge in a bunker underground.

Even at this late moment, when he was desperately trying to reach Ebrahim Yazdi to extract the U.S. officers, Ambassador Sullivan was pestered by calls from Washington about the prospects of a military takeover. Sullivan, as he later recalled, made "a scurrilous suggestion for Brzezinski" and then, for good measure, offered to say it in Polish. Sullivan did manage to get through to General Philip Gast, the U.S. Military Mission chief. Though under fire, Gast gave a professional assessment of the chances of a successful military coup in Iran: one in twenty.[86] Those were generous odds. (Yazdi and a clergyman named Mahdavi-Kermani with great difficulty extracted the U.S. officers and brought them in military vehicles to the rear entrance of the U.S. Embassy compound in the small hours of the following morning, Monday, February 12.)

In Stuttgart, Huyser received a call from Deputy Defense Secretary Charles Duncan and Brzezinski, asking if he would return to Tehran to lead a military takeover. Huyser replied that he would return on the following conditions: unlimited funds; the pick of ten to twelve U.S. generals; 10,000 of the best U.S. troops; and undivided popular American support. In a word: No. He later wrote, "I didn't think the people I was talking to were ready for that type of action, nor did I believe the American people would give their support. Therefore, the answer was obvious—it was not feasible."[87]

At 5 p.m., Gharabaghi and Moqaddam slipped out the back entrance of the staff headquarters, and made their way to Engineer Jafroudi's house. What had been intended as a parley was now an act of surrender. Gharabaghi begged Bazargan to issue a communiqué asking the people to halt their attacks on the barracks and bases. That he promised to do. Bakhtiar was nowhere to be seen, but at one point, Jafroudi brought in a sheet of paper and showed it to Bazargan. It was evidently Bakhtiar's letter of resignation. The last prime minister of Imperial Iran was not seen again until, at the end of March, he was reported to be staying near the pleasant French Alpine town of Mégève.[88] He had left Iran with his usual aplomb, traveling first class with Air France, in dark glasses and with a small beard behind a copy of Le Monde, and disguised, though it was no effort for him, as a French businessman.[89] Gharabaghi also made his way to Paris and for a while the two men bawled "Treason!" at each other across the indifferent arrondissements.

General Hatam surrendered staff headquarters at evening. At naval headquarters, Admiral Shoa Majidi, who had long seen which way the wind was blowing, ordered his men not to return fire.[90] Both Sultanata-bad, where Savak had its headquarters, and Lavizan held out until the next day, when Badrei was killed, possibly by his own men.[91] General Mohammed Ali Beglari, the loyalist deputy commander of the Guard, also fell. In the provinces, the army garrisons surrendered or were simply abandoned by their defenders.[92]

So ended the Pahlavi army in a defeat so rapid and comprehensive, one searches in vain for its like whether in modern or ancient history. Its conquerors were men and women many of whom had never picked up a weapon, and some who never did so again. In truth, the Pahlavi army had nothing to fight for, except its honor, and in the course of those two days honor came to seem a small thing. The soldiers were defeated because, unlike their young adversaries, they could not imagine victory. "The modern tradition of defeat" mentioned by the U.S. officer back in 1953 weighed like a nightmare on their backs. It is a military axiom that there are no bad soldiers, only bad officers; and none worse than Second Lieutenant Pahlavi, who left the field.

At the Jamshidabad barracks, the disgraced ministers heard the approaching tumult. By afternoon, the buildings were under fire from the apartment blocks across the street. Standing on a radiator, one of their number saw a crowd hanging up a sign reading: THE ISLAMIC BARRACKS OF JAMSHIDABAD. At 6 p.m., the few remaining soldiers threw open the cell doors. Daryoush Homayoun, the former information minister, who had grown a beard in his three-month captivity, stepped out into the headlights. Someone shouted: "Is Hoveyda here?" Nobody recognized Homayoun and he passed into a side street. Nassiri of Savak and Nikpay, the former Tehran mayor, either stayed where they were or were detained. They paid with their lives. Sheikholislami Zadeh, the former minister of health, stayed to treat the wounded soldiers, and was imprisoned for his pains. The streets were full of trucks and cars, with young people firing into the air. "It is the end of us," thought Homayoun, "and the beginning of their end." At the Tajrish Bridge, he was picked up by a car with two young men, one cradling an Uzi machine pistol for the fight that was about to begin. "We got this baby at Eshratabad," he said.[93]

At the safe house in Shian, just south of Niavaran, Hoveyda's Savak guards heard the army broadcast and decided to leave. They urged Hoveyda to make his escape and left behind a vehicle with keys and a pistol. Hoveyda was still intent on defending his record. He asked his friend, the doctor Fereshteh Ensha, to convey his surrender to the provisional government. After some delay, she reached Dariush Forouhar, the National Front stalwart and Bazargan's labor minister. A posse consisting of a clergyman, an armed guard, and Madame Ensha commandeered an ambulance, threaded their way through the roadblocks, and found Hoveyda, alone and unguarded, on the house porch. Even with the siren running, they were shot at at a checkpoint and the driver hurt. Forouhar received Hoveyda kindly, but dispatched him to the Refah. It had begun to snow and the ambulance picked its way with agonising slowness through the crowd. Hoveyda was led upstairs and locked in a small room, its windows blacked out by newspapers. As Dr. Ensha left, she heard a hubbub in the crowd: "They just brought in Hoveyda."[94]

So many prisoners were brought in that Eshraqi announced that

Refah was only accepting senior military officers and high servants of the regime.

Of the fall of Niavaran early on Monday afternoon, there are two principal accounts. The truth lies somewhere between them. According to *Kayhan*, the Imperial Guard raised white flags on the building and their vehicles, received money and clothes from the crowd, and went, weeping, on their way. Sayyid Hassan Mostafavi, minister of the Niavaran congregation, took charge of the building and ensured nothing was taken or damaged.[95] Today, you can wander round the palace and marvel at Mohammed Reza's home movie theater and other superannuated luxuries.

According to a royalist account, the Guard commander found he was losing his men. One said his son's school was under fire. Another had a stomach upset. The officer was unable to get through to General Beglari at Lavizan. The crowd was massing at the gates. Deciding, as so many on those two days, that discretion was the better part of valor, he asked the palace operator to put him through to the Alavi School. Taleqani answered and welcomed him to Islam. The officer said: "I am a *sayyid* and I have been a devoted Muslim all my life. I don't need to come to Islam, but I need someone to come here so I can surrender the palace."

A low-grade molla or *akhund* was prodded to the front of the crowd. The officer handed him the keys to the palace and an inventory. For a moment, he thought of the Shah with his entourage, the parade of visitors, and all the power and ceremony of those years; and now "this dusty *akhund*, from some village, ugly and malnourished, is taking the key to his palace. Truly, God is Great."[96]

CHAPTER 12

Dog Wedding

◇

The dead donkey is a wedding-feast for dogs.
—Proverb

Sadeq Khalkhali was a farmer's son from the country near Khalkhal in Azerbaijan in the northwest of Iran. He was born in 1926. He came to the seminary in Qom in 1943, where he was a classmate of Khomeini's son Mostafa, and soon fell under the spell of Navvab Safavi and the Terrorists of the *fedayan-e islam*.[1] By his own account, he and his friends planned to disrupt Reza Shah's cortège on its passage back from Egypt in May 1950, but were unable to act either at the Qom railway station or as the body lay in state in the shrine of the Immaculate Lady. With the defeat of the Islamic Fedayan five years later, Khalkhali made himself useful to Khomeini, and when the royalist provocateurs infiltrated Khomeini's house on March 22, 1963, it was Khalkhali who took the microphone to shout them down.

Khalkhali was imprisoned that June, and passed a portion of the 1960s and 1970s in internal exile. Small and roly-poly, with pebble spectacles and a shrill laugh, Khalkhali was vain of many things but above all of his wit. When at his trial the scholarly Hassan Pakravan inquired what, precisely, was "corruption on earth," Khalkhali shot back: "What you're guilty of!"[2] When he came upon Hoveyda in the Qasr toying with his final meal of rice and broad beans, Khalkhali said: "Would you like a bottle of spirituous liquor to help it down, Mr. Hoveyda?"[3] Like the Qajar executioners, the "lords of wrath" in their blood red shirts, Khalkhali played to the gallery.

It is a curiosity of scholastic Iran that the more learned the religious jurist, the less ready he is ever to preside over a court of law. Khalkhali has been accused of many things, but only once of religious learning. On February 24, 1979, two weeks after the surrender of the army, Khomeini summoned Khalkhali to the Alavi School and gave him a letter appointing him judge of the revolutionary courts.

"There'll be blood in this," Khalkhali said, "and hard labour."[4] Khomeini knew how to flatter. "I heard from my late son Mostafa that you worked on the commentary on the *Arveh* and are licensed to exercise judgment on matters of law as a *mojtahed*."[5] That was all that was needed. Khalkhali later said: "Let that whore Ashraf and her friends know that those who made the revolution with their bare hands now have weapons at their disposal."[6] Bani-Sadr had dreamed of a Golden Age where there would be "no more hostility, nor oppression, inequality or sorrow, old age or death, winter cold or summer heat."[7] The reality was altogether more commonplace.

On Monday, February 12, royalist prisoners were brought out under the television lights. First to be led in was the former prime minister, Amir Abbas Hoveyda, leaning on a cane, but in good spirits and more than able to hold his own under Ebrahim Yazdi's hectoring. Hoveyda said he had not attempted to escape and that he looked forward to a fair trial. "I take responsibility for my actions and am not afraid because I believe in God," he said. Amir Hosein Rabii, commander of the air force, who had given himself up that morning, was still the debonair aviator. Others appeared shaken to the core, and of a group of men blindfolded in the courtyard, many were badly injured. (They were evidently Savakis who had taken refuge in the Bagh-e Shah barracks.) General Nassiri of Savak, who was beaten up and bayoneted in the neck at his arrest at Jamshidabad, was not presented, but he appeared that night on television, his head and neck wrapped in stained bandages.[8]

Just before midnight of Thursday, February 15, Nassiri, Manuchehr Khosrowdad of the paratroopers, and the military governors of Tehran and Isfahan, Rahimi and Naji, were shot on the roof of the Refah School. Khalkhali and two other judges, along with some "seven to fifteen" jurors, found them guilty of "torture, massacre, treason and corruption on earth." Khalkhali had wanted to execute twenty-four men that night. Each was photographed on the same straight-backed school chair, his name on a handwritten placard hanging from his neck. Behind the chair was a dais covered in village carpets and a blackboard of Koranic verses written in chalk, including that quoted at the opening of chapter 8: "Whoever took one life, it would be as if he murdered the whole world." Yazdi kept finding reasons to delay. Losing patience, Khalkhali bustled round to the Alavi School, arriving out of breath, and received Khomeini's permission to execute that night four or five prisoners. They could not agree on the fifth, so the four generals were led up to the roof, blindfolded, and their hands tied. A young man stepped behind them and shot them in the neck with a pistol.[9] As they lay on the ground, the bodies were shot again.[10] Flashlight pictures of the victims in pools of blood were splashed across the next afternoon's newspapers.

So began a Terror which was to last, with intermissions, for almost ten years. In its first phase, the principal victims were royalists, including ex-Prime Minister Hoveyda; six cabinet members, including the only woman minister, Farrokhrou Parsa; senior officials and members of Parliament; thirty-five generals including Rabii, Neshat, and Atabaki; some fifty field-rank officers; Savak officials including General Moqaddam, who came to Amir Entezam's office on February 14 or 15 to place the organization's files and operations at the disposal of the prime minister, but was arrested by the *komiteh* in the corridor outside; the mayor of Tehran; three Freemasons; a Jewish businessman; and thirty or more Bahais.[11] In the provinces, where the first trials took place on March 1 and possibly before, many of the victims were common soldiers and low-ranking police officers known to local people. Before that, many were simply lynched, like the six Savak agents at the fall of the station at Rasht in Gilan on February 12.[12]

Khalkhali wrote: "Lately, I have been thinking how few people I killed. There were just so many ripe for execution who escaped me: the likes of the Shah, Farah, Ashraf Pahlavi, Sharif-Emami, Gharabaghi, Fardoust. I could go on."[13] Even so, the royalist purges were without precedent. To find their like, one would have to go back to the executions of Tudeh military officers in 1954 or the Babi pogrom of 1852, but the dead then were reckoned in dozens. As Montesquieu wrote in the eighteenth century, popular governments are always more vindictive than monarchies.[14]

The country wanted revenge for the casualties of the past twelve months. The crowds had shouted at Khomeini's cavalcade on February 1: "In the dawn of victory, the place of the martyrs is empty." Though the deaths by violence of the Revolution year are now known not to have exceeded 3,000, those losses were many times the death toll of the insurrections of 1953 and 1963. When Radio Tehran announced the killing of the generals at 7 a.m. on the 16th, the poet Reza Baraheni was drinking the first tea of the day with a school headmaster in Javadieh. The teacher said: "Thank God! Those bastards have shed blood in every family in the land." [15] The public had gained a taste for excitement, and did not want the Revolution to end. The radio said: "The execution of these executioners is not only to console those who have suffered. It is to infuse new blood into the veins of the revolution." [16]

The revolutionary courts were established to impose the authority of the turbanned clergy and to recover prestige lost to the left, which had done much of the fighting that destroyed the imperial regime and was gaining adherents. It was the left, after all, not the seminary, which had suffered in the Savak torture chambers. *Ettelaat* reported that the decision to execute the four generals was taken when an "armed group" arrived at the Refah and demanded the prisoners be handed over. [17] The trials were the first engagement in a struggle for power between the radical clergy, with Khomeini at their back, and the moderate religious such as Ayatollah Shariatmadari, the provisional government under Bazargan, the returning émigrés such as Bani-Sadr, and the hard left.

What concerned Khalkhali's critics was not the death sentences but his slapdash and indolent way of working. [18] Charges were vague, unsubstantiated, sometimes mere gossip, [19] sometimes the capital crimes listed in the fifth chapter of the Koran, "corruption on earth" and "war against God." No evidence was presented nor witnesses called. Some but not all defendants were informed beforehand of their charges and allowed to write a short defense. They were permitted no counsel. There was no appeal against sentence. Most of the trials were held in camera, and many at night. There was no consistency in sentencing, except a bias toward the death penalty. Bazargan called the trials "a scandal." Bani-Sadr saw Khalkhali making a farce of his project to put on trial, before Iran and the court of world opinion, the Pahlavi regime. The trials dispelled what little goodwill the Revolution enjoyed in Europe and North America. Bani-Sadr's friend Ahmad Salamatian, taxed by the *Libération* correspondent with Khalkhali's theatrics, could only bluster: "What good fortune for the West! He is doing you good service, Khalkhali. If he had not existed, you would have had to invent him."[20]

After midnight on March 14, Hoveyda was woken in his cell at the Qasr prison and called without warning to a makeshift courtroom. Befuddled by a sleeping pill that he had been prescribed by the prison doctor, he struggled to make sense of the indictment. It comprised sixteen counts of corruption on earth, war against God, espionage, foreign borrowing, ruining agriculture and forestry, heading the Rastakhiz Party, Freemasonry, granting capitulatory rights to Americans, misinformation, and smuggling heroin. Unshaven, and gaunt from four months in prison, Hoveyda asked for time to prepare a defense. Khalkhali ignored him. At or before 3 a.m., Prime Minister Bazargan telephoned and ordered that the trial be adjourned. With a referendum looming on the establishment of an Islamic Republic, he had prevailed on Khomeini to suspend the revolutionary courts until new regulations were drawn up. "I knew they wanted to get Hoveyda away from us," Khalkhali wrote.[21] Hoveyda's friends in France were mobilizing and four former UK prime ministers (Macmillan, Home, Wilson, and Heath) petitioned the provisional government for clemency.

Bani-Sadr continued to press for a show trial that would, he said, display to the youth of Iran and world opinion "the nature of the *ancien régime* and how the United States came to dominate Iran."[22] Together with Asadollah Mobasheri, the minister of justice in Bazargan's provisional government, Bani-Sadr flew by helicopter to Qom where, since March 1, Khomeini had been in residence. They had with them documents and a handwritten letter from Hoveyda. "We can make of this process a trial of the Shah's regime and thus inform the world of his [Mohammed Reza's] misdeeds," Mobasheri said.[23] Bani-Sadr says Khomeini agreed to a public trial that might last up to a month.

Demanding that the trials resume, the Revolutionary Guards and warders at the Qasr sent a mission to Qom to warn that they would take matters into their own hands. In a statement on April 1, Khomeini sided with Khalkhali: "There can be no objection to the trial of these people. They are criminals and it is known that they are criminals. All this about a lawyer being present, and a right to appeal. These are not people charged with crimes. They are criminals."[24] The new regulations, which merely endorsed Khalkhali's practices, were published on April 5. On the 7th, Khalkhali traveled to Qom and heard from the old man: "Don't listen to the Bazargans of this world."[25]

Khalkhali drove straight from his audience back to Tehran and the Qasr where, as he came in the gate, the thousand or more royalist prisoners began to stamp their feet and beat on the walls and doors of their cells, shouting: "Bloody Khalkhali has returned!" He gave orders that nobody was to leave the prison, disconnected the telephones, and locked the handsets in an ice chest.[26] At 3 p.m., Hoveyda was brought into the stifling courtroom. His devoted friend, Dr. Fereshteh Ensha, had been permitted to send him some clothes, and he was dressed in a dark blue shirt under a fawn polo-neck sweater and brown trousers. Seated close beside him on his right was a man in a white turban and aviator sunglasses, who unsettled him—and with good reason.[27]

The charges were repeated. Khalkhali then spoke, by his own account, for half to three quarters of an hour about the crimes of the Pahlavi regime and Hoveyda's hand in them. Hoveyda's defense, such as it was, was unlikely to persuade such a prosecutor-judge. He said that he, like all the Pahlavi prime ministers except Mossadeq, was the servant of a "system" in which foreign policy, the armed forces, Savak, the oil company, and other important departments of state were managed by Mohammed Reza as reserved domains. It was, Hoveyda said, recovering the shadow of his old poise, as if he had been a constitutional monarch and Mohammed Reza the prime minister. Hoveyda said that his vision for the country was just and progressive and he had failed only for lack of time. Khalkhali became impatient and told him not to go into detail.

Then: "You are repeating yourself, Mr. Hoveyda."

Again: "You are repeating yourself."[28]

Hoveyda fell silent. Two hours had passed. Khalkhali announced his verdict and pronounced sentence. He said: "You are found to be a corrupter on earth. You are condemned to death." White as paper, Hoveyda asked for a month's reprieve so he might write the history of the past twenty years. Khalkhali demurred. The prisoner was led down the corridor toward the prison yard. As Hoveyda stepped out into the hot dusk, the man in the white turban drew out from his gown a machine pistol and shot him twice in the nape of the neck. Spreadeagled on the ground, Hoveyda begged for a *coup de grâce*. His last words were: "It wasn't supposed to end like this."[29] In the week that followed, Rabii of the air force and the elderly former Savak head, Pakravan, who had both done Khomeini service, were shot. Later, Khomeini was heard to say: "I regarded Pakravan as a reasonable and law-abiding person."[30] Khalkhali decided that, having killed the other surviving Savak chiefs, it would be more pleasing to God to do the whole lot.[31]

The revolutionary courts were only one of Mehdi Bazargan's headaches. Cautious, deliberate, and humane, the engineer was unsuited to the revolutionary turmoil and once said that the day he resigned would be to him "a second wedding day."[32] His government, comprised of mosque-going professional men from his Freedom Movement or the National Front, had no control over the *komitehs*, armed to the teeth and numbering over a thousand in the capital alone; nor over the new Corps of Guards of the Revolution, created by Khomeini in a decree of May 5 as a counterweight to the leftist militias and responsible not to the provisional government but the Revolutionary Council. (Beheshti, among others, was for allowing the regular armed forces to wither away.) Bazargan was criticized in public by Khomeini in Qom over matters ranging from the dress of women public servants to aping the manners of the West. "You are weak, sir, you are weak, and so long as you are weak, you will be the prey of the strong," Khomeini said in Qom on March 7.[33]

Meanwhile, in the proliferation of new political parties and newspapers, the Khomeinist clergymen on the Revolutionary Council, led by Beheshti, formed the Islamic Republican Party (IRP). It drew on the organization of mosque, bazaar, and lane that had assembled the great crowds of December and January. In echoes of conditions in Germany in the later 1920s, the IRP deployed its own militia, known as *hezbollahis* or "God's partisans" or, after the bands of roughs retained by the nineteenth-century clergy, *chomaqdaran* or "club wielders." Under Hadi Ghaffari, the son of a clergyman who had died in Mohammed Reza's prison in 1974, the *hezbollahis* terrorized the university campuses, broke up rival party meetings, and even attacked demonstrations in Tehran early in March by professional women alarmed by the prospect of compulsory Islamic dress, the retirement of female judges, and the repeal of the Family Protection Act. An advertising executive, pressing an icepack to her swollen forehead after the women's demonstration on March 10, told the *New York Times*: "They fooled us. This is no revolution. This is a mullah's game. It's nothing more than a mullah's game."[34] Old Reza's nightmare of the 1940s—*akhundbazi* in Persian—had passed into daylight.

On the extreme left, the Tudeh leaders returned from their exile in East Germany, profuse in their support for Khomeini while expecting (in the leftist jargon of the day) that such a creature of the "superstructure" would be swept away by the logic of class war. A new First Secretary, Nureddin Kianuri, a grandson of the anti-Constitutional divine Fazlollah Nuri, no less, won a power struggle on January 14. He insisted that what appeared to his predecessor as reactionary obscurantism was, to a more profound analysis, "objectively progressive."[35] Like the Fedayan, the Tudeh thought the women's cause a mere distraction and an issue of interest only to "ladies of leisure" (*zanan bi dard*). At another extreme were the fundamentalists of the *Forqan*, an Arabic word meaning "touchstone" that is applied to the Koran. Founded at the time of the Mojahedin schism in 1975 by a seminary dropout from Luristan, Akbar Gudarzi, the group derived from a reading of the Koran an ideology that was murderously anticlerical. On April 23, they assassinated General Mohammed Qarani, the new chief of staff, and then late in the evening of May 1, to the great sorrow of Khomeini, his former pupil Ayatollah Motahhari. In all, the group staged some twenty successful or frustrated assassinations before being broken up early in 1980. (Gudarzi and six others were shot in January 1981.)

The provisional government was not entirely ineffective. The oil industry was started up, and the first export tonnages were lifted on March 5. By midsummer of 1979 Iran was producing 3.9 million barrels per day at prices as high as $40 a barrel. Money the country had, with revenue of over $1 billion a month, and could easily pay for imports of food and the expenses of its retainers. Yet Iran was at a standstill. The banking system was insolvent on both sides of the balance sheet, its deposits vanished and many of its debtors unreachable abroad. There was no civil building or investment. Mohammed Reza's military programs had been abandoned and many industrial businesses, their owners fled or denounced as profiteers of a *taghouti* or idolatrous regime, had been taken over by the new Foundation for the Oppressed (or Foundation of the Weak). A new source of clerical patronage, the foundation continued to pay wages in idle factories and hotels and soon had debts of the equivalent of $3–$4 billion and all but worthless assets.[36] The building cranes on the northern skyline of Tehran were motionless. In the automobile showrooms, the foreign limousines found no buyers. The hairdressers and beauty parlors were empty. The provisional government lured public servants back to work with pay rises of as much as 400 percent, but there was little to do, and anyway revolution was more appealing than office drudgery. "After you've brought down the Shah," a professor at Tehran University told the *New York Times*, "going back to a factory job or a classroom is going to be unbearably boring."[37] In truth, Iran has never recovered the busy, almost Protestant, character of the last Pahlavi years, which now seems an aberration.

In the countryside, the perennial hunger for land and water erupted into disputes and seizures. Impressed by Khomeini's promises to revive agriculture, small proprietors and the landless seized disputed ground or broke up the consolidated estates that had grown up on the ruins of Mohammed Reza's Land Reform. In the Turkoman Steppe abutting the Soviet Union, where large cotton and wheat farms had existed since the 1930s, these disputes over land were fanned by the Fedayan and were to burst out into open insurrection. In the outlying regions, such as Kurdestan, Baluchestan, among the Arabs of Khuzestan, and the Qashqai tribes of Fars, the breakdown of the Pahlavi state revived faded dreams of local autonomy. By August, Kurdestan was in uproar, and Khomeini ordered assaults by both the army and the inexperienced Revolutionary Guards Corps, outfitted by the Palestinian resistance with the standard Beirut armament of AK-47 automatic rifle and RPG-7 grenade launcher. Khalkhali was conducting traveling assizes to execute the rebels.

Meanwhile, Iran became an Islamic Republic. In Neauphle back in November 1978, Khomeini had permitted Karim Sanjabi of the National Front to call for a popular vote to establish "a government on the principles of Islam and democracy." With the defeat of the royalist forces, the words "Islam" and "democracy" became, as for the

Nurists and the democrats in 1907, banners or badges of allegiance. For Khomeini, the word "republic" was alien enough. On his return to Qom on March 1, Khomeini told a crowd at the Faizieh Seminary: "Do not employ the word 'democratic.' That is Westernism. The nation wants an Islamic republic [Cheers]; not merely a republic, nor a democratic republic, nor a democratic Islamic, but an Islamic republic."[38] To ensure as large a turnout as possible, the voting age was lowered from eighteen to sixteen years, and on March 30 and 31, 1979, some 18 million Iranians were presented with a single question: whether to replace the monarchy with an Islamic Republic. The "Yes" portion was colored Islamic green. The Fedayan called for a boycott, while in the restive regions, such as Kurdestan and the Turkoman Steppe, there was little or no voting.[39] The provisional government announced that 98.2 percent of those voting had voted "Yes," almost the same majority as for Mohammed Reza's Land Reform and other measures in January 1963.

Attention now turned to the constitution of the new Islamic Republic. Khomeini's Najaf lectures were philosophical in character and had little to say about the form of God's government. Anyway, since the Koran and the conduct of the Prophet and the Imams gave law for all time, there was no need for a legislature or any judicial paraphernalia, while Islamic charity would supply the revenues of a welfare state. The collapse of the monarchy had given the exiles in Paris small leisure to develop those notions, and the draft constitution given on the Air France 747 for safekeeping to Peter Scholl-Latour of the West German television station ZDF filled a single yellow folder.[40] The challenge now was to resist or neutralize theories of government from the allies in the fight against royal government, including parliamentary democrats, Marxists, Shariatists, and Shia extremists, at a time of violence and bloodshed.

The draft, written principally by Bazargan's allies, was published on June 14.[41] Its 151 articles were based on the 1907 Supplement to the Iranian Constitution, with the difference that sovereignty rested with the people, and was not entrusted by the people to a monarch. In place of old Nuri's committee of five religious lawyers to oversee legislation was a Guardian Council—the name a distant echo from Plato's *Republic*[42]—but with a restricted veto and a majority of lay judges. As might be expected from a draft inaugurated in Paris, the principal feature was an executive presidency in the fashion of the French Fifth Republic. Men and women were equal before the law, and Zoroastrians, Jews, and Christians (but not Bahais) were guaranteed freedom of worship. There was no reference to the "Stewardship of the Jurist."

The draft was approved in short order by Bazargan's cabinet, the Revolutionary Council, and Khomeini, who made some small alterations. Irritated by the slowness of the provisional government, Khomeini proposed an immediate referendum on the draft.[43] The secular parties and the regions, especially Sunni Kurdestan, that feared a strong presidency, demanded an elected constituent assembly with powers to revise the draft, on the pattern set at the dawn of modern constitutional government in France in 1789. It was a demand they came to regret. Bani-Sadr reports Hashemi Rafsanjani saying to him: "Who do you think will be elected to a constituent assembly? A fistful of fundamentalists and ignorant fanatics that will do such harm that you will regret ever having convened them."[44]

No constituent assembly was summoned. Instead, at a meeting in Qom on June 18 or 19, the four leading seminary jurists—Khomeini, Shariatmadari, Golpayegani, and Marashi-Najafi—agreed instead to an elected Assembly of Experts of seventy-three members. Of those successful at the elections on August 3, fifty-five were clergymen, leaving the National Front, Bazargan's Freedom Movement, the Paris émigrés, and the left with just ten seats. Their consolation was that Khalkhali was not returned.

The Assembly of Experts convened in the Senate chamber on August 19, 1979, the Mossadeq anniversary, amid the fighting in Kurdestan and the closure of several leftish newspapers, attacks by *hezbollahis* on the headquarters of the Fedayan and the Tudeh, and a protest led by Mossadeq's grandson at the football ground of Tehran University. The Kurdish delegate did not take his seat. It was Ramazan, and the delegates worked through the day and broke their fast at sundown. A message from Khomeini was read out, stating that "the Basic Law of this republic must be founded, one hundred percent, in Islam."[45] Montazeri was preferred to Taleqani as chairman, but it was Mohammed Beheshti, as deputy chairman, who directed the meetings with his habitual skill and tact. For Beheshti, modern societies divided into two classes: those that drew their coherence from territory, the past, or nationality (such as France and Germany), and those "ideological societies" that had formed about a shared thought or belief (such as the Communist states). The new Iran would fall into the second group, promoting a unity of thought like a Marxist state, yet without compulsion and open to the world.[46]

It soon became clear that there was a majority among the delegates for clerical government on the basis of Khomeini's "Stewardship of the Jurist," and in the course of the sittings, six days a week—not without debate and protest—both the draft and the Constitution of 1906–07 were bent and shaped to accommodate Khomeini in both person and theory. Attempts by the provisional government to arrest the fall into theocracy received short shrift from Qom. By then, Taleqani had died of a heart attack and Bazargan lost his only supporter in the clerical leadership.

The provisional government's draft was no longer recognizable. In the hole left by the removal of the monarch from the 1906–07 Constitution was now the Jurist or Leader, endowed with more extensive powers than a mere king. The laws of the land were now those of the Shia schools, which converted the liberties of the citizen into duties. Yet amid those novelties, the 12 chapters and 175 articles of the Basic Law preserved such elements of European (and American) origin as Parliament, elections, the separation of powers, and *habeas corpus,* as well as the international leftist and nativist language of that era. Sovereignty emanated from God and was delegated to his Steward (Articles 2 and 5), and also, at the same time, to an enfranchised people (Articles 6 and 56). It is that ambiguity that troubled opponents of the Constitution at the time, notably Shariatmadari, and gives Iranian politics its special character. The Basic Law of 1979 would make legitimate both clerical domination in Iran and also, in a sort of undercurrent, objection to it. Nonetheless, the Constitution has survived, with one substantial revision in 1989, to the time of writing.

The Preamble gives some history in the turgid or inflated style that had come into fashion. The Revolution had succeeded, where the movements of 1905–06 and 1953 had failed, because of its "pious* and Islamic character" and the leadership of a single man, Khomeini. It was

---

* *Maktabi,* which literally means "of or pertaining to the religious primary school."

the "Imam," as he is called throughout, who raised the people against the American conspiracy known as the White Revolution in 1963, and, at the height of royal repression, wrote the plan for Islamic government on the principle of the "Stewardship of the Jurist." The *Ettelaat* libel of January 7, 1978, is mentioned, then the seven- and forty-day mourning marches, and the violence of the regime which cost some 60,000 dead and 100,000 wounded.[47] (Those numbers are fanciful.) The Preamble says: "Women were conspicuous in every theatre of this great struggle. The sight of mothers with infants in their arms hastening to the scene of battle and towards the mouths of machine-guns showed the decisive part played in the struggle by that substantial section of society."

By means of the Revolution, the Iranian people purified itself of a godless past and foreign ideological influence, returned to the authentic traditions of Islam, and could now establish a model society at home and then "a single community worldwide . . . within this century" (that is, before 2021). For this purpose an ideological army, the Corps of Guardians of the Islamic Revolution, was established, alongside a judiciary and mass media conforming to Islamic norms, and a government unencumbered with bureaucracy. The Preamble ends with another paean to women in their character as mothers.

The pivot or linchpin of the Constitution (and, in the way of mechanics, its point of greatest stress) is the Leader or Jurist. He is introduced in the Preamble, and then described in Articles 5 and 107–12. Article 5 reads: "While the Lord of the Age is beyond perception, Stewardship and the Imamate of the community devolve upon the just and pious Jurist, who is acquainted with the conditions of his age; brave, resourceful, and possessed of administrative ability; and recognized and accepted as leader by the majority of the people." Article 107 specifies that the Jurist should be a "Source of Imitation" or a model for a "decisive majority of the people."

In the event that no single man is so recognized by the majority of the people, a council of jurists will assume the Leader's powers. Those include appointing the chief of staff and service commanders of the regular armed forces and the Revolutionary Guards, the higher judges, the clerical members of the Guardian Council, and the head of state television and radio; the vetting and confirmation of the president and his dismissal after a parliamentary vote of no confidence; and the declaration of war and peace. Leader or leadership council are selected by an elected Assembly of Experts, which may also dismiss them if incapacitated or otherwise incompetent.

The democrats still had their president, elected by popular franchise, though most of his powers had now passed to the Leader; a cabinet headed by a prime minister appointed by the president and confirmed by Parliament; and a single-chamber legislature with wide powers to make laws, but subject to the control of the Guardian Council. That body now consisted of six laymen and six specialists in religious law with the power to veto all and any parliamentary legislation. Article 4 reads: "All civil, penal, financial, economic, administrative, cultural, military, political and other laws and regulations must be based on Islamic criteria." The Constitution was thus overcrowded at the top with both men and offices and rich in opportunities for conflict.

Articles 23–28 provide for freedom of speech, association, assembly, the press, communication, and occupation but, as was already evident on the streets, within Islamic norms. Both torture (Article 38) and martial law (Article 79) are outlawed. The commercial and economic chapters favor distribution and a welfare state while stressing the sanctity of private property. The most important article is a limitation on commercial and military contracts with foreigners (Article 153), which was to hinder attempts to attract foreign investment to the ravaged oil and gas industry after the war. The environment is to be protected. Apart from a section on provincial councils, which was never enacted, there is no mention of devolution of power to the regions.[48]

The delegates emerged from their labors on November 15, 1979, to find a world altered out of recognition. On November 4, there occurred an event which was to criminalize Iranian society, isolate the Islamic Republic from the course of world affairs over the next thirty years, and may yet prove fatal to it. For Jimmy Carter, woken from his Sunday sleep by Brzezinski on the telephone, that November 4 was "a date I will never forget."[49]

At ten thirty that Sunday morning, some three or four hundred young Iranians scaled the walls of the U.S. Embassy in Takht-e Jamshid Street, and broke into the ground floor and basement of the Chancery building. The embassy staff barricaded themselves behind the steel doors of the Chancery and a few held out for three hours. They were then rounded up, blindfolded, and handcuffed. Meanwhile, Bruce Laingen, the chargé d'affaires, and two colleagues were visiting Ebrahim Yazdi at the Foreign Ministry and were to be held there, as prisoners in all but name, for 444 days.

The hostage-taking destroyed the Bazargan government, and brought the Iranian Revolution, which up to then had been a local affair, to the attention of the world. By the time the hostages were released, Iran was at war, clerical government entrenched, and the opposition to it under pressure. Khomeini was to call it "the Second Revolution." In countless conversations in Iran, I never heard anybody regret the hostage-taking, recognize the injury done to the United States, or rue that country's enduring resentment.

To some authors, the hostage-taking was the second phase in a clerical *coup d'état* of which the first was the Constitution drafted by the Assembly of Experts.[50] In a tactic that was adopted by the extremist Sunni Muslims such as Osama bin Laden in the 1990s, but was then a novelty, the Iranians chose to tackle not local divisions such as rebellious Kurds or women in undress but evil itself in the form of the Great Satan, the United States. For only Satan himself, in his uniform of Stars and Stripes, could be an adversary worthy of the epic Iranian Revolution.

In reality, the occupation of the U.S. Embassy arose in the student politics of the Tehran universities and the wanderings of Mohammed Reza in foreign lands. It was limited in its conception and, in its execution, haphazard. Most of the hostage-takers—Abbas Abdi, Ebrahim Asgharzadeh, Massoumeh Ebtekar—later moved into the democratic camp and became sticklers for the Law of Nations. Even Mohammed Mousavi-Khoeiniha, the clerical *éminence grise* behind the occupation, said in 2000 that, if called to repeat the hostage-taking, he and his friends would not do so.[51] When Griboyedov was cut to pieces in 1829, Fath Ali Shah sent what became known as the Shah Diamond to assuage Russian anger. In 1924, when U.S. Vice-Consul Robert Imbrie was murdered in an anti-Bahai riot, Reza paid $110,000 for his body to be transported home in the USS *Trenton* and gave $60,000 in blood money to his widow.[52] Khomeini was content this time to let events take their course and see what opportunities might arise.

The diplomatic missions, established in the nineteenth century in the northern suburbs, were now in the heart of midtown. They were seen by less traveled Iranians as lairs of bribery and espionage. The British Embassy in Ferdowsi Street was attacked on November 5, 1978, and the U.S. diplomatic compound in Takht-e Jamshid partially overrun that Christmas Eve. On February 12 or 13, 1979, the Israeli mission was captured and handed over, with some fanfare, to the Palestine Liberation Organization. (The thirty-three staff had gone into hiding and were evacuated by Sullivan.)[53]

On February 14, St. Valentine's Day, with Niavaran and the army bases captured, the Fedayan and others attempted to carry the fight to the United States. At 10:30 a.m., the twenty-three-acre U.S. Embassy compound came under machine-gun fire and some seventy-five attackers broke in and captured William Sullivan and his staff. Yazdi and a clergyman from Ain od-Dowleh Street, backed up by air force mutineers and *komiteh* gunmen, negotiated their release. A young *luti,* armed in the style of that week only with a beard and a bayonet blade, took it upon himself to protect the ambassador. The provisional government also helped Sullivan extract a group of U.S. servicemen held by air force mutineers at a joint post that monitored Soviet missile tests at Kapkan, near the border of Soviet Turkmenistan. Sullivan saved his own life, if not his career, slipping out of the country by way of Mehrabad in the small hours of April 6. A staff of approximately sixty persons remained. The consulates in Tabriz, Shiraz, and Isfahan were closed. Sullivan had already sent the bulk of the confidential files back to the United States. As for the British, all through 1979 they were alert to the possibility of attack, consulting with their new ambassador in Tehran, Sir John Graham, before admitting Chapour Bakhtiar and Princess Ashraf for flying visits to London.[54]

Meanwhile, in Morocco, Mohammed Reza had outstayed his welcome. King Hassan sought help from Paris and a former French intelligence officer well known to the Shah, Alexandre de Marenches, called on him in Marrakesh and told him, as the queen wrote, "the risks our host . . . was facing because of us."[55] Dejected by the executions in Tehran, Mohammed Reza sent word to the U.S. Embassy in Rabat on February 22 that he had now decided to travel to the United States and enquired about arrangements for his reception. With the St. Valentine's Day attack and the Kapkan incident, the United States now wanted to place the invitation on hold. Sullivan warned from Tehran on the 26th that a renewed invitation would "confirm the worst suspicions of those Iranian revolutionaries who assumed that the U.S. was plotting to restore the shah to power." (He says that he began to warn, "in more explicit terms," that American diplomats might be taken hostage.)[56] On the 27th, President Carter angrily told Brzezinski that he "did not want the shah in the United States playing tennis while Americans in Tehran were kidnapped and killed."[57]

An indirect approach on February 28 to the British Embassy in Rabat, that Mohammed Reza wished to visit his house, Stilemans, near Godalming in Surrey, received a discouraging reply.[58] France was out of the question. In the end, Mohammed Reza's friends in America, principally David Rockefeller, the chairman of Chase Manhattan Bank, and Nixon's national security adviser Henry Kissinger, were able to exert pressure on the Bahamas, the British ex-colony in the Caribbean that made a good living from tourism, casino gambling, tax evasion, and the narcotics trade, to accept Mohammed Reza on a three-month visa. The Labour government in Britain had lost a vote of confidence in the House of Commons on March 28 and it was likely that a Conservative government would come to power at elections on May 3. The Conservative leader, Margaret Thatcher, had given private assurances that she would then admit Mohammed Reza.[59]

On March 30, the royal family, Mrs. Diba (Farah's mother), nine staff and bodyguards, and the family dogs left Rabat on an airliner provided by King Hassan for Nassau, the capital of the Bahamas. On Paradise Island, across a small bridge from the capital, the Shah and queen were put up in a small bungalow. It was no bigger than the beach house at Nowshahr. Their luggage, consisting of fifteen cases, was stored under a tarpaulin in the yard. The others made shift in bungalows or hotel rooms elsewhere on the island, which had been developed as a resort by the U.S. casino operator Resorts International.

The next ten weeks were, as the queen wrote, "among the darkest times of my life."[60] Surrounded by barbed wire and patrolled by American securitymen, the beach house was open to the view of the curious, and both oppressive and insecure. It was also expensive. Mohammed Reza had lost his property and assets in Iran, and access to the Pahlavi Foundation. Though a rich man by the standards of that era, he was spending tens of thousands of dollars a week. "The Shah was so outrageously overcharged that he very quickly wanted to find an alternative place," Rockefeller said.[61]

It was in Nassau that they received the news of Hoveyda's death. Unable to control his tears, Mohammed Reza left the room. A day or two later, they received a letter from Saideh Pakravan, upbraiding them for sunning themselves while her father gave his life for them. As his supporters were daily cut down by bullets, Mohammed Reza was more than ever concerned to keep his illness secret. With the curtains drawn, and only the queen as nurse, Dr. Flandrin began administering the first of three courses of chemotherapy.[62]

On May 20, Mohammed Reza received a visit from a gentleman in dark glasses, traveling on a passport in the name of Edward Wilson. It was Sir Denis Wright, incognito, persuaded out of retirement by Sir Anthony Parsons to inform Mohammed Reza that so long as the provisional government was not in control of Iran, the United Kingdom could not, after all, offer him asylum.[63] The queen claims that Wright sported a mustache and a hat, but the mission was farce enough without such embellishments. She blamed Parsons, but in truth the "Iron Lady" had bent. According to Wright, Mrs. Thatcher brushed aside the Foreign Office's commercial and security arguments, but not their warnings about another attack on the Tehran Embassy. "The third argument was: Are you then prepared either to see the Ambassador shot or surrender and hand over the Shah. And that was what made Mrs. Thatcher flinch, as it were," Wright said.[64] A couple of days later, the Bahamian government told the Iranians that their visas would not be renewed despite, as Mohammed Reza put it, "the enormous sums I spent there."[65]

With three weeks of their residence left, they received an invitation to move to Mexico. Kissinger had persuaded President José López-Portillo to issue it. Rockefeller's staff found a walled house in a quiet cul-de-sac in Cuernavaca, a town south of the capital favored by North American bohemians, and they left Paradise Island with relief on June 10. In Cuernavaca, "concealed among the nightingales and bougainvillea," as García Márquez described the house,[66] Mohammed Reza began work on the justificatory memoir later published in English as *Answer to History*. Chapour Bakhtiar, organizing resistance from Paris, telephoned, but Mohammed Reza would not speak to him. Farah began looking for a house "with the prospect of staying some time."

Then Mohammed Reza fell ill. Flandrin was in Paris, so the queen called a local doctor, who diagnosed malaria. The treatment produced no improvement and Rockefeller's man, a young public relations executive named Robert Armao, lost patience and summoned Dr. Benjamin Kean, a specialist in tropical diseases at New York Hospital. Kean saw that Mohammed Reza was ill, and not with malaria. His patient made no mention of cancer, and refused a blood test, but the fabric of secrecy began to collapse.

On October 1, President Carter was told that the Shah was ill and might need treatment in the United States.[67] On October 18, Flandrin met Kean in Cuernavaca and gave him the history of the Shah's lymphoma. In a scene reminiscent of the "royal consultation" at Muzaffareddin's bedside in 1906, Flandrin, Kean, and the Mexican doctors examined Mohammed Reza together. They diagnosed obstructive jaundice, probably caused by gallstones blocking the bile duct. The spleen was again swollen. Over Flandrin's protests, Armao and Dr. Kean insisted that the Shah go for diagnosis and treatment not to Mexico City but to New York Hospital. (Dr. Kean later conceded that the equipment required was available in Mexico City.)[68] Overwhelmed by the combined weight of the Rockefeller organization and competitive New York medicine, Flandrin was discharged with the present of an engraved silver cup.[69] Mohammed Reza passed into the glare of American publicity.

President Carter was briefed that evening. Mohammed Reza was not coming to the United States to play tennis. At breakfast the next morning, the president gave conditional approval for treatment in New York but, turning to his advisers, said: "What are you guys going to advise me to do if they overrun our embassy and take our people hostage?"[70] Bruce Laingen in Tehran was told to inform the provisional government of the Shah's condition, tell of the plans to treat him in the United States and, as Carter put it, "seek their assistance." Laingen, accompanied by Henry Precht, an Iran specialist at the State Department, called on Bazargan and Yazdi on October 21. Like everybody else, their hosts had no inkling of Mohammed Reza's lymphoma and were suspicious. Yazdi maintains that he said, "You are opening Pandora's box." In his element as a physician, he asked for an examination by Iranian doctors and suggested two names, which the Americans agreed to pass on. (The Iranian examination never took place.) Laingen requested additional protection for the embassy, and the next day extra police were in evidence. Secretary of State Cyrus Vance told the president that "the Iranian Government reacted with moderation when informed by us that the Shah will visit the United States for medical reasons."[71]

That evening, Mohammed Reza set off for New York in a Gulfstream aircraft and was admitted to New York Hospital early the next morning, Tuesday, October 23. Amid the jeers and shouts of demonstrators outside, surgeons performed two operations to remove the gallstones but dared not, for risk of infection, remove his swollen spleen. He was also wheeled, in the small hours, down a subterranean passage littered with trash and dirty linen, to the Memorial Sloan-Kettering Cancer Hospital for chemotherapy.

On the day that Mohammed Reza entered the United States, five students gathered for a meeting in the Islamic Students' Union in the northwest corner of 24 Esfand (now Revolution) Square opposite Tehran University. They comprised the central committee of the Office for the Consolidation of Unity, a circle of Khomeinist students founded in September to liaise with Khomeini's staff in Qom and take on the leftists on the campuses. All were from technical and engineering colleges, where most of the students were from middle-class or artisanal families, with small relish for the leftist jargon flying about the halls of Tehran University.

To protest against Mohammed Reza's admission to New York, Ebrahim Asgharzadeh (of Aryamehr Technical College) proposed a sit-in or occupation at the U.S. Embassy for "a maximum of two–three days." To distinguish them from the leftists, they would be unmasked and unarmed. He was supported by Mohsen Mirdamad of the Polytechnic and Habibollah Bitaraf (Faculty of Engineering), but opposed by two conservatives on the central committee. Mohammed Ali Seyyid Nejad (Teacher Training College) said the sit-in was illegal under Islamic law, and Mahmoud Ahmadinejad (University of Science and Technology), who would go on to be a two-term president of the Islamic Republic, said an assault on U.S. property would strengthen the Marxist groups. Anyway, according to Asgharzadeh, Ahmadinejad "viewed the Soviet

Union to be a much more serious threat."[72] The meeting broke up and the majority trio resolved to pursue the plan on their own.

In secrecy, lest the armed campus groups forestall them, they sought legal backing from a leftist clergyman, Mohammed Mousavi-Khoeiniha. Born in Qazvin, northwest of the capital, in 1937, Mousavi-Khoeiniha had joined Khomeini's circle in Qom, where he had become friendly with Ahmad Khomeini, and done a spell in prison. He was now ensconced as an adviser at the state broadcaster. He later said that the group feared the provisional government was drifting closer to the United States and that the Shah's arrival on U.S. soil was an element in an American conspiracy to "destroy the Islamic Revolution" and turn Iran into a "U.S. puppet."[73]

The conspirators called on Mousavi-Khoeiniha at his office on an upper floor of the television center. A "clever" man (according to Asgharzadeh), Mousavi-Khoeiniha told them Khomeini could not openly overrule the provisional government and Revolutionary Council he had appointed. He would inform Khomeini in his own time. Meanwhile, he said, "Go and tell the students that the Leader is aware of the plan." Abbas Abdi of the Polytechnic confirms that Mousavi-Khoeiniha "was opposed to requesting an opinion from the Imam saying that, although he approves, he will not be able openly to express his consent."[74] On Friday, the 26th, the sabbath in Iran, the organizers arranged an excursion in the stony foothills above Evin to discuss the plan with an expanded group of about eighty students.

On November 1, finding themselves in Algiers for the celebration of the twenty-fifth anniversary of the uprising against French colonial rule in 1954, Prime Minister Bazargan, Foreign Minister Yazdi, and Mostafa Chamran, the defense minister in the provisional government, held a private meeting lasting one hour and a quarter with Zbigniew Brzezinski. The meeting had been cleared with Khomeini,[75] and built on talks Yazdi had held with Cyrus Vance at the UN General Assembly in New York on October 3 on such Iranian grievances as the missing F-14 black boxes and the Iranian credit with the Pentagon.

That November 1, a demonstration took place outside the U.S. Embassy, but although the staff were dispersed to other embassies in Tehran, and only the Marine Guards and security remained, police diverted the march and held the crowd at bay. On November 3, Khomeini issued a statement calling on students and seminarians "to broaden their attacks on the United States and Israel, so that they may force the U.S. to return the criminal and deposed Shah."[76] Asgharzadeh said, "We took this as a sign that the Leader was aware of our plan." Anxious at all times to show unquestioning loyalty to Qom, they made plastic badges of Khomeini and pinned them to their shirts and chadors. They were no party or political sect but "Students who Follow the Line of the Imam." They staked out the embassy compound from surrounding buildings and passing motorbikes, bought bolt-cutters in the bazaar to cut the chain on the main gate, and organized a small truck to haul off the embassy files.

At 10:30 a.m. on that rainy morning of the 4th, which was the anniversary of the killings at Tehran University in 1978, about three hundred young people broke from the main demonstration and ran toward the U.S. Embassy compound. A young woman produced the bolt-cutters from under her chador while other students scaled the wall. The Marine Guards, under standing orders from Bruce Laingen not to use firearms, spread tear gas and fell back on the Chancery building. There the iron window-grilles and steel doors were, as Gary Sick put it, adequate to hold out "for two or three hours until help could arrive. It worked exactly as planned with only one crucial exception—help never came."[77] Students broke through the bars on a basement window in the northwest corner, and by 1:30 p.m. the building was occupied apart from the secure area, behind a combination lock, where embassy staff continued to shred confidential files until late afternoon. Asgharzadeh cursed himself for not cutting off the power supply.

Long before then, he had set up headquarters in one of the outlying buildings. His first action was to call Mousavi-Khoeiniha, who arrived, to the relief of the occupiers, within forty minutes. Whether then or later that day, Mousavi-Khoeiniha called Khomeini's house in Qom and spoke to Ahmad Khomeini. According to Asgharzadeh, the message from Qom was: "You have taken over a good place. Do not be anxious but hold it tightly, for we have work to do there." A delegation set off to the Senate to justify the occupation to Montazeri, Beheshti, and the Assembly of Experts. Then they waited for the provisional government to expel them (as on February 14) or otherwise respond. Mohammed Reza Mahdavi-Kani, who had been appointed back in May to bring some order to the *komitehs*, twice telephoned threatening Mousavi-Khoeiniha that his men would throw them all out by force if they had not left the site by nightfall.

Instead, soon after the 2 p.m. news bulletin, thousands of people converged on the embassy, shouting: "Death to the Shah." "We could not believe it ourselves," Asgharzadeh said. A young man named Akbar told the *New York Times*: "We realized our action was something great! Yes, something really great! It was like a bomb burst, and we realized then that we had to keep going."[78] The public support seems to have been decisive in swaying Qom. For Bani-Sadr, it was an instance of Khomeini's fatal tendency to "act by reaction" to events.[79]

It was Khomeini's habit, after the midday prayer and a frugal luncheon, to rest away the afternoon. Sadeq Tabatabai, the provisional government spokesman and a favorite of Khomeini, was dispatched by Bazargan to inform the old man that unless he ordered the students out, the provisional government would resign. By the time he arrived by helicopter, Mousavi-Khoeiniha had "contacted the Imam" and Khomeini was content to accept the government's resignation. Mahdavi-Kani, whose *komiteh* at the embassy had been overrun, corroborates this account. Incensed with Mousavi-Khoeiniha, he telephoned Ahmad Khomeini, who chuckled and said: "The Imam is content with the situation and you should keep out of it."[80] By late afternoon, Asgharzadeh had what he called "a sustainable situation." He called a press conference. Photographs and film of bound and blindfolded American public servants were broadcast round the world. (Asgharzadeh now concedes the press conference was an error, but not the blindfolds.) The occupiers demanded the return of the Shah and his fortune; an apology by the United States for its crimes against the Iranian people; and a pledge not to interfere in Iranian affairs.

Just after 9 a.m. the next morning, the British Embassy telexed London that the Revolution was "taking another lurch towards extremism."[81] In his statement to students of November 3, Khomeini had, in a moment of confusion, accused Britain (rather than France) of giving asylum to Bakhtiar. The embassy was expecting the worst, and did not have long to wait.

At the cabinet meeting later that morning, complaining of the "interferences, obstacles, opposition and differences of opinion," Mehdi

Bazargan tendered his resignation to Khomeini.[82] Ahmad Khomeini visited the occupied embassy, both to endorse the occupation and to discourage a general attack on the legations. Tabatabai returned to Qom, this time in a red Mercedes 280, with his friend Peter Scholl-Latour. The German reporter squatted on the large machine-made carpet in the reception room, while Khomeini talked down to his pet, "like a stern father to an obedient son." Khomeini was not in the best of moods. Turning to Scholl-Latour, he said: "I regard the occupation of the American Embassy as a spontaneous and justified retaliation of our people."[83]

At 5:40 p.m., attackers scaled the wall of the British Embassy at several points, rounded up the staff and their families, took over the Chancery, and demanded access to the secure zone where the confidential files and ciphers were stored. The embassy staff saw that while the most radical of the attackers claimed to be "Students who Follow the Line of the Imam," there were also armed Revolutionary Guards and the *komiteh* gunmen who up to that time had been part of the expanded security for the embassy. The embassy staff concluded that "the religious leadership" had decided one hostage-taking was enough and that the Guards were there to ensure nobody remained overnight. The attackers were taken away by bus at 10:30 p.m.[84] In thirty-six hours, the occupation of the U.S. Embassy and the imprisonment of its staff had become an institution of state. "We no longer defined the rules of the game," Asgharzadeh said.

The occupiers dug in for the long haul. Each noon, they lined up in ranks in the car park inside the gates to pray. The boys and girls prayed apart, dressed in a composite new style they made fashionable: on one side, beards and olive-drab combat jackets, on the other thick scarfs in dusky colors framing cloister-pale faces, a tentlike chador, jeans, and sneakers. They called one another "Brother" and "Sister." Outside the gates, reporters and the curious gathered, and carts sold soft drinks and steamed sugar beets. The American TV network sound engineers liked to play snatches of the third-act opening of Wagner's *Die Walküre,* the sound track to the helicopter assault in the new hit movie, *Apocalypse Now.*[85]

The files were trucked back, and "because we had nothing else to do,"[86] as Asgharzadeh remembered, the occupiers studied the documents. Young women, whose grandmothers had knotted carpets in the

1920s, pasted together the filaments of shredded copy paper and even attempted to reconstitute burned microfilm. Published as "Documents from the Nest of Spies" in sixty-six volumes, the embassy papers were of small general interest. ("Nest of Spies" was the term coined by Ali Dashti for the Anglo-Iranian Oil Company in the 1950s.) Mahdavi-Kani found the spying allegations puerile. "All embassies do this sort of thing, and the great powers more than most," he said.[87] Instead, the students released fragments at critical moments to embarrass those known as the Liberals (*liberalha*) and moderate clergymen and to manipulate the presidential and parliamentary elections. "We determined the order of exposure," wrote Massoumeh Ebtekar of the Polytechnic, "by the significance of the document, which in turn was closely related to the turbulent political and economic situation in the country."[88] Like the witnesses at the Salem trials, they were both credulous and spiteful.

In the witch hunt, in which any contact with Sullivan or, later, Laingen was enough to ruin a man, the students destroyed Abbas Amir Entezam but not, for example, Beheshti. (At the time of writing, Amir Entezam has been thirty years in prison.) Like the student Red Guards of that other septuagenarian, Mao Zedong, in 1966, the occupiers saw themselves as the purge of a society putrid with individualism and foreign habits of thought. The republic had been made, as Saint-Just said of the first French Republic, by a people "stained with the trash and crimes of the monarchy." It was a matter of teaching them virtue![89] Massoumeh Ebtekar, who had grown up in the United States, made up for it by fasting two days a week. She grated on the nerves of the hostages.

In this atmosphere of competitive piety, the Council of Experts approved the articles (107–12) that defined clerical Leadership and completed their work. Despite opposition from the left, the lawyers' association, the Sunni minorities, and Turkish-speaking Azerbaijan, the new Constitution was approved by referendum on December 2 and 3. In the Tehran shantytown known as *Halabiabad* ("Tin-can Town"), a woman greengrocer named Massoumeh Akbarzadeh told the *New York Times*: "We have done as he [Khomeini] has asked us—we have voted for his constitution. Now will he give us what we want—a more decent life?"[90]

The moderate Ayatollah Shariatmadari had reservations about the role of the Jurist, and warned on December 3 of the contradiction in the new Constitution between popular sovereignty and the rights of the Leader. When his house in Qom was attacked, and a guard on the roof shot in the back, supporters in his hometown of Tabriz and the Islamic People's Republican Party seized the governor's office and the television station. It seemed for a moment that Iran's second city would once again, as in 1907, come to the rescue of democracy. Revolutionary Guards retook the station, the IRP organized counterdemonstrations, Shariatmadari shrank from bloodshed, and the revolt in miniature collapsed. On January 8, 1980, Shariatmadari forbade his followers to use his "name or portrait or in any way weaken the Islamic Republic or its achievements."[91] The Islamic People's Republican Party was disbanded and Khomeini's sole rival in the seminary was neutralized. (By a selective use of Savak files, publicists of the new regime blackened his character, and in 1982, Shariatmadari was stripped of his clerical honors and placed under house arrest.)

At the end of January, Abol Hassan Bani-Sadr, universally regarded as a favorite of Khomeini, was elected president in a landslide, receiving 75 percent of the votes. Khomeini had banned clergymen from standing, and the IRP was unable to put up a credible lay candidate.

With his mustache and horn-rimmed spectacles, and his delight in his own voice, the new president was to Bakhtiar "the eternal student." He had spent the 1960s in Paris and like Shariati drunk the strong waters of French sociology. He dabbled with a doctoral thesis that he never completed. Exhilarated by the student uprising in Paris of May 1968, he valued above all "popular effervescence" and spontaneity. For Bani-Sadr, "revolution was the most beautiful work a generation can conceive or realise."[92] Except for his clerical breeding, he was not unlike the anarchistical *Spontis* of the European New Left, such as Daniel Cohn-Bendit or Joschka Fischer, but breeding was all. Ever since 1964, he had idolized Khomeini. In 1972, at his father's funeral in Najaf, Bani-Sadr met his hero and adopted him as a sort of godfather. At Neauphle, they became close. His later recollections from exile carry a refrain that is repeated over and over again. The Leader had ceased to be "the Khomeini of Paris."[93]

Planning to restore order and repair the armed forces, Bani-Sadr was instead engulfed in the hostage crisis. For the next three months, Bani-Sadr and Sadeq Qotbzadeh, his foreign minister, attempted to

Khomeini under his apple tree at Neauphle, October 1978.

Khomeini's portrait held aloft at a rally at Tehran University.

An Imperial Guardsman kneels at Mohammed Reza's feet at Mehrabad airport as he leaves Iran for his second exile, January 16, 1979.

Mohammed Reza's fallen statue near the Alavi School.

Khomeini is helped down the stairs from the aircraft that brought him from Paris, February 1, 1979. At the left in the black turban is Ahmad Khomeini.

The helicopter carrying Khomeini lands at Behesht-e Zahra cemetery, February 1, 1979.

Bakhtiar at his last press conference as Prime Minister, February 8, 1979.

Bazargan, center, with his Cabinet. On his left is Forouhar, assassinated in 1998, and on his right, Amir Entezam, still in prison after twenty-five years.

Khomeini at the
Alavi School,
February 2, 1979.

Barricades on
Farahabad Avenue,
February 10, 1979.

The fight for
Eshratabad,
February 11, 1979.

Masked *komiteh* gunmen at a street barricade, Tehran, 1979.

American hostage paraded at the occupied U.S. Embassy, November 4, 1979.

Montazeri, holding G3 rifle and bayonet, addresses a rally at Tehran University, November 23, 1979.

Bani-Sadr is mobbed by supporters during the presidential campaign, January 1980.

The incinerated wreck of the US C-130 Hercules transport and Sea Stallion helicopter in the desert after the failure of Eagle Claw, April 27, 1980.

Volunteers, with belongings and shrouds, mustered at Azadi Stadium in Tehran for the 1985 offensive.

Fallen Iranian soldiers in the Hoveizeh marshes, March 20, 1985.

Women in black prayer chadors gathered for Khomeini's funeral rites in Tehran, June 6, 1989. The podium is made of shipping containers.

gain custody of the hostages. The two men acted not out of scruple, but because they feared the crisis had captured the Revolution, hobbled government, and obscured Iran's actual grievances. Bani-Sadr was also concerned to re-equip the armed forces.

By now, Mohammed Reza had left the United States. On November 29, Mexico withdrew its promise to allow the Shah to return and, on December 2, he was moved to Lackland Air Force Base, near San Antonio, Texas, where at first he was placed in a windowless room in the psychiatric block. Hamilton Jordan, the White House chief of staff, persuaded General Omar Torrijos, the military leader and *supremo* of Panama, to renew his invitation to the Shah. Robert Armao, who had no confidence in either Torrijos or the medical care available in the Isthmus, was overruled by Mohammed Reza, who had been shaken (and the queen frightened) by their reception in the United States. They left on December 15 for the island of Contadora, thirty miles out in the Gulf of Panama on the Pacific side of the Isthmus, where once again they were fleeced.

President Carter sought a diplomatic solution to the crisis, while preparing plans for both a rescue mission and, if the hostages were harmed, military retribution. On November 14, he signed an order to prevent Iran from drawing on some $6 billion in deposits at U.S. banks and their branches in foreign jurisdictions.[94] He also barred all arms shipments to Iran. As he told Mrs. Thatcher and President Giscard (who was visiting her in London) by telephone on November 19, "there is no way that we can permit the blackmail to work and send the Shah back to Iran. That is completely out of the question."[95] He attempted to collect favors from Muslim countries that might influence Iran, and on November 19, recorded his first success. The Palestine Liberation Organization, embarked on its long struggle to gain recognition from Washington, persuaded Khomeini's circle to order the students to release the African-American and women hostages. With bad grace, the occupiers released thirteen people, leaving fifty-two men and women still in captivity. The PLO found itself out of its depth in Qom, and attempted no further mediation.[96] A mission to Tehran by Kurt Waldheim, the UN secretary-general, was a fiasco and he was fortunate to escape in one piece. Washington sought a UN Security Council resolution to impose sanctions on Iran, but the proposal was vetoed by the Soviet Union on January 13, 1980. At the end of that month, six of the embassy staff, who had slipped out of the back gate on November 4, left Iran on Canadian passports.

Qotbzadeh loved all things subtle, elaborate, and delinquent. Unable himself to deal with the United States, he authorized two of his companions from Paris days, the human rights lawyer Christian Bourguet and an Argentinian named Héctor Villalón, to negotiate. They led State Department officials down a succession of winding alleys that were supposed to ensure the transfer of the hostages to the Revolutionary Council. Their plans included both extradition proceedings in Panama and an international commission to investigate Iranian grievances. In February, Khomeini was treated in hospital for heart trouble, and during that time those discussions seemed to be gaining shape and substance, but on the 23rd he was well enough to announce that the fate of the hostages would be decided by Parliament, which was not yet elected. Carter began to lose patience.

On Contadora, the royal family became suspicious. In part as a result of Dr. Kean's tactlessness, relations had broken down between Mohammed Reza's American physicians and the Panamanian authorities. At her wit's end, the queen telephoned Jehan Sadat, the half-English wife of the Egyptian president, who said they had always been welcome and that the American doctors could perform the splenectomy in Cairo.[97] On March 23, over protests from the State Department, they left Panama for Egypt. Despite a last-minute attempt by Bourguet to halt the aircraft in the Azores, they reached Cairo and were lodged at the Kubbeh Palace, where Mohammed Reza had stayed before his marriage to Fauzia all those years before. Mohammed Reza's wanderings among the barbarians were over. He was immediately transferred to the Maadi military hospital where, on March 28, the Lebanese-American Michael DeBakey and a team of Egyptian surgeons removed the swollen spleen. It weighed over four pounds. Dr. Flandrin, who was back in medical favor, believed they had left behind an abscess.

In protest at Mohammed Reza's return to Egypt, Khalkhali demolished Reza's mausoleum at Shah Abdolazim. Tehran was treated to the spectacle of Revolutionary Guards and shrine loafers with picks and spades trying to break up a monument built to last a thousand years. "You have no idea just how solidly built it was," Khalkhali wrote. Bani-

Sadr ordered him to stop, but, in the pattern established at the U.S. Embassy, Ahmad Khomeini visited the scene, and that decided it. In the end, Khalkhali brought up heavy demolition equipment and explosives and, after three weeks, leveled the mausoleum.[98]

The hot weather was coming on, and the nights shortening. The window for an American rescue mission was closing. On April 16, Carter approved a plan for which U.S. Special Forces had been training in the deserts of the western United States for five months. "Operation Eagle Claw," as it was known, was more challenging than the successful operations by Israeli commandos at Entebbe, Uganda, in 1976 and at Mogadishu, Somalia, by a special unit of the West German border force the following year. There the hostages had been held at airfields. The plan devised by the U.S. Joint Chiefs was complex and demanding of both men and, more especially, machines. Under cover of darkness, helicopters, military transports, and fuel tankers would fly beneath the Iranian radar to rendezvous in the desert, where the helicopters would refuel and embark the commandos and their equipment brought in by the transports. The helicopters would deliver the men to a point southeast of Tehran, then both would lay up until an assault on the embassy the following night. Iran's desolate geography and harsh climate, which had so often protected the state and would do so again, brought both the plan and, as Carter came to believe, his presidency to grief.

At nightfall on April 24, 1980, which was 10:30 a.m. in Washington, after five and a half months of planning and training, eight RH-53 "Sea Stallion" helicopters from a minesweeping squadron took off from the nuclear-powered aircraft carrier USS *Nimitz,* in the Gulf of Oman. Their destination was 600 nautical miles away, the refueling site, codenamed "Desert One," straddling the long-distance motor road between the towns of Yazd and Tabas. Eight C-130 Hercules transporters, carrying ninety Delta Force commandos and fuel in giant bladders for the helicopters, set off from Masira Island in Oman. Flying low and in radio silence, the helicopters evaded detection, but about two hours into the flight, cockpit instruments on helicopter No. 6 diagnosed a crack in a rotor blade. The helicopter was abandoned in the desert, and its crew carried on by helicopter No. 8.

An hour later, the formation flew into a thick cloud of dust and fine sand, known in Arabic as a *habub,* and then into a second. In zero visibility, a second helicopter (No. 5) suffered damage to its navigation and flight instruments, and returned to the *Nimitz.* Six helicopters arrived at the rendezvous, but between fifty and eighty-five minutes after schedule. A third helicopter (No. 2), which had limped in with a faulty hydraulic pump, was deemed unusable.

With the helicopter force down to just five airworthy machines and dawn approaching, the operation commander, Colonel Charles A. Beckwith, decided to abort the mission. President Carter agreed. By then, Carter's "seldom-used country road nearby"[99] had been quite busy. The U.S. forces had shot up a fuel tanker, and stopped a long-distance bus and impounded its forty-four passengers. In maneuvering under power to refuel for the flight out, one of the helicopters (No. 4) collided with the C-130 tanker, setting both aircraft ablaze and causing ammunition to explode. Eight Americans lost their lives, and all the helicopters were abandoned. The commandos and air crew then left the site and Iranian airspace without at any point being detected by Iranian military forces.

The failure of the mission, announced by President Carter at 1 a.m. Washington time, was a dividend that the student occupiers of the U.S. Embassy could not have imagined. Khomeini compared it to the miraculous destruction by stone-throwing birds of a Christian expedition against Mecca, described in the chapter of the Koran called "The Elephant" and its commentaries.[100] Carter spoke of a "strange series of mishaps, almost completely unpredictable."[101] The Joint Chiefs, in investigating the disaster, dispensed with the supernatural and pointed out deficiencies in planning and preparation: inadequate weather data, too few helicopters, no complete and full-scale training exercise, and a landing site bisected by a motor road. Even if Colonel Beckwith had decided to proceed, the mission was running late. Meanwhile, the burned-out oil truck, empty bus, and abandoned RH-53 (No. 2) might have alerted the local military long before the rescue itself could be mounted on the second night.[102]

The hostages were moved from the embassy compound and dispersed about the city and the provincial towns. A couple were put up in the old royalist Lubyanka, the Komiteh Prison. Back on February 12, 1979, the morning after its capture, a visitor had proposed that the

Komiteh, with its cells radiating from a circular well, be preserved as a "museum to the sufferings visited on our youth."[103] It was too useful a place for that.

The ease with which the Americans had come and gone played on suspicions of the loyalty of the armed forces, which was compounded when the Iranian air force bombed the abandoned U.S. aircraft. General Bahman Bagheri, the air force commander, was dismissed and then arrested. Khomeini had always hated the standing army as the instrument of Pahlavi modernism and foreign influence. Confined to barracks, without exercises or maneuvers, and expecting soon to be disbanded, the regular armed forces were at low ebb. There were rumors of plots and at least one attempted *coup d'état*, in which paratroopers planned to capture the Shahrokhi air base just north of Hamadan in Kurdestan, which had been renamed "Martyr Nozheh" after a pilot killed in action against the rebels the previous August. From there, serving or cashiered pilots arriving by road from Tehran would launch F-4 sorties against such targets as Revolutionary Guards bases, the IRP headquarters, and even the house in the northern suburbs where Khomeini was wont to spend the hot months.

According to the American historian Mark Gasiorowski, who later interviewed some of the conspirators in exile, the plot had financial backing from Bakhtiar and Princess Ashraf, whose son Shahriar had been assassinated by Iranian agents in Paris back in December.[104] As recounted to Gasiorowski, the plot made Eagle Claw seem like simplicity itself. It was compromised and the paratroopers were rounded up in the night of July 9 before they could mount the attack, the pilots ambushed, and six of them killed.[105] The "Nozheh *coup d'état*" unleashed a new witch hunt, and in the end some 144 officers, non-commissioned officers, and civilians were executed.[106] Twelve thousand men were purged from the armed forces. On July 18, a squad of five men led by a Lebanese Shia convert, Anis Naccache, using false press credentials, attempted to take revenge on Bakhtiar at his flat on Boulevard Bineau in the district of Neuilly in Paris, but succeeded only in killing a neighbor and a police officer, and wounding a second officer.[107] (Naccache was sentenced to life imprisonment but exchanged for French hostages held in Lebanon in 1990. Bakhtiar was finally assassinated by Iranian agents on August 6 of the following year.)

In the fevered atmosphere, the last piece of the constitutional jigsaw fell into place. At parliamentary elections held in two phases, Beheshti's IRP and its allies won a majority of the 247 seats contested. (There were no elections in Kurdestan and Baluchestan, and five seats were allocated to the religious minorities.) On May 29, Ali Akbar Hashemi Rafsanjani, a pistachio farmer from the southeast and former student of Khomeini, was elected speaker. The IRP majority in Parliament forced on Bani-Sadr as prime minister Mohammed Ali Rajai, the very essence of the pious or *maktabi* bazaar layman and sometime principal of the Refah School whom the president treated with disdain. In a pattern of rivalry between Parliament and president that was to continue to the time of writing, the two men quarreled for months over the composition of the cabinet. With Rafsanjani speaker and Beheshti chief justice, the IRP controlled the levers of power.

At ten o'clock in the morning of July 27, 1980, after a succession of operations by feuding physicians, Mohammed Reza breathed his last with the box of Iranian soil beneath his pillow. His virtues were love of country, a good mind, pleasant manners, industry. His faults were variations on a single fault, which was distrust. He did not trust his advisers, his people, his son, his wives, his doctors, nor even, in the end, himself. President Sadat gave him a state funeral. Mohammed Reza lies buried, for the present at least, beside his father in the Rifai Mosque in Cairo.

The death of the tyrant did not help the hostages, or staunch the effusion of blood. According to Amnesty International, "a minimum" of seven hundred people were executed in the year to April 1981.[108] With the royalists out of the way, the new victims were principally drug addicts and traffickers, those accused of crimes against sexual morality, and Bahais or Jews caught up in the spy fever. In May 1981, Bani-Sadr appointed Khalkhali to head a campaign to eradicate the narcotics that had bedeviled Iranian life for a century. Khalkhali set about the task with vigor, erecting gallows in the Tehran streets and dispatching some two hundred victims. He later claimed (quite falsely) "to have almost entirely dismantled the drugs trade in Iran."[109] His chaotic working habits betrayed him when he was unable to account for the equivalent of some $10 million in money and goods confiscated. He resigned in December.

On the campuses, the secular left was cleared out. On April 19, the Revolutionary Council announced that the universities would be closed at midsummer. The leftists were given three days to close their campus offices. On the 21st, the *hezbollahis* went on the rampage in both the Tehran colleges and the provincial universities. Bani-Sadr disgusted his leftist supporters by leading a mob onto the campus of Tehran University and joining the call for "cultural revolution." From his house in northern Tehran, Khomeini told the crowd that most of the college faculty "are in the service of the West and have brainwashed our children. I do not fear economic blockade or military incursion. What I fear is cultural dependence and colonial universities."[110] There were dead and many broken heads. The universities would not open again for two years. The Mojahedin and majority Fedayan, which had by now infiltrated many of the institutions of the Revolution, went underground.

When Khomeini complained that the civil service was still using Pahlavi stationery and postage stamps, "purification committees" dismissed thousands of teachers, foreign office officials, and military officers. Women in the civil service were obliged to cover their hair and mask their silhouette in the shapeless wrapper known (from French) as the *manto*. On July 6, the Revolutionary Council forbade women to enter public buildings (even post offices) unless wearing "Islamic Dress."[111] Many women accepted this belated enforcement of Reza's dress reforms of the 1930s as the price for working outside the household. Others, both men and women, despaired at the mixture of idleness and violence that was Islamic government and, if they were able, emigrated. By the early years of the war, hundreds of thousands of professional people had left Iran for Turkey, Continental Europe, Britain, Canada, and the United States. Most intended to return, but the war just went on and on.[112] They included as much as a third of the tenured university staff, the physicians, and the dentists.

Absorbed in its Festival of Revolution, Iran had little thought to spare for its neighbors. On December 27, 1979, Soviet troops invaded Afghanistan to prop up the unpopular Communist government that had seized power in April 1978. "Had I remained in power," Mohammed Reza wrote, "the Russians would not have dared invade Afghanistan."[113] There is, indeed, some evidence that the Soviet Union felt emboldened by the Iranian Revolution. "The Iranian Revolution has undercut the military alliance between Iran and the USA," Brezhnev had told the East German leader, Erich Honecker, in Berlin in October.[114] Recognizing that a U.S. attack might cause the Soviet Union to invoke its rights to intervene under Articles V and VI of the 1921 Friendship Treaty, the Revolutionary Council on January 22, 1980, abrogated those articles and annulled its 1959 cooperation agreement with the United States. There were two attacks on the Soviet Embassy (on January 1 and April 27) but, again, no attempt to take hostages. More trouble was in store on Iran's western border.

Saddam Hussein was born of peasant stock in 1937 on the upper Tigris. He belonged to the Sunni minority in Iraq. A village hoodlum, he gravitated toward the Baath or Renaissance Party, which combined a populist Pan-Arabism with a cult of violence. Saddam came to prominence when he was picked by the Baath as part of a four-man team to assassinate the Iraqi president, Abdul Karim Qassim, in Baghdad's main street, but he succeeded only in wounding him. Himself hit in the leg, he escaped back to his home territory (as he was to do when the U.S. Army overran Baghdad in 2003). Three years' exile in Syria and Egypt widened his horizons. In 1968, together with his cousin, Ahmed Hassan al-Bakr, and other clansmen, he seized power. By the mid-1970s, with the nation prospering from its oil revenues, he became the most powerful man in Iraq, and the most feared. When Sadat of Egypt began to negotiate a peace treaty with Israel, under President Carter's sponsorship, Saddam summoned the Arab states to a summit meeting in Baghdad and bullied and cajoled them into expelling Egypt from the Arab League. He saw Iraq as displacing Egypt as the leading power in the Arab world. In July 1979, he pushed his cousin aside and, in a bloodbath, seized the presidency.

Saddam had two pieces of business with Iran. He resented the Algiers Agreement of 1975, which aligned the southern border between the two countries along the deepwater channel of the Shatt al-Arab. Documents and recordings of his tabletalk, captured by U.S. armed forces in 2003, show that he regarded the agreement as an insult and a humiliation, and believed the Iranians had not kept their part of the bargain. At first, he was cautious. As he told his ministers a week after the collapse of the Iranian army on February 20, 1979: "We are not worried about the current state of Iran, but rather the unpredictable outcome of the different phases [of revolution] in Iran. . . . We can destroy them, not with boastfulness, but with rational calculations and justifications."[115]

Saddam also feared that Iran would sow dissension, either directly or through example, among the majority Shia in the shrine towns, the teeming Baghdad slum known as Thawra (now Sadr City), and Iraq's second city, Basra. After Shia militants made an attempt on the life of the foreign minister, Tariq Aziz, in Baghdad on April 1, 1980, Saddam expelled many Iraqis of Iranian origin and executed the jurist and philosopher Mohammed Baqer al-Sadr and his sister, Amina, representatives of the most distinguished clerical dynasty at Najaf. (In recordings of Saddam's execution in 2006, the guards or spectators can be heard shouting: "Long Live Mohammed Baqer!")

Saddam began to probe Iran's defenses with long-range artillery along the 900-mile frontier and also in faraway London. On April 30, six men, who had traveled to London on Iraqi passports and received automatic weapons and grenades brought in the Iraqi diplomatic bag, attacked the Iranian Embassy, which occupied a five-story building at No. 16, Princes Gate, looking onto Hyde Park. For six days, they held twenty-six people hostage, chiefly Iranian diplomats but also journalists and visa applicants, and a police officer, PC Trevor Lock, who managed to keep his sidearm concealed throughout the siege.

Iranian Arabs from Khuzestan—or Arabestan, as it was known under the Qajars—the six claimed to represent a group called the Democratic Revolutionary Front for the Liberation of Arabestan. Their leader, Awn Ali Mohammed, demanded the release of Khuzestan separatists imprisoned in Iran and the intercession of an Arab delegation to negotiate their safe departure from the United Kingdom. Saddam's purpose was to publicize his quarrel with Iran among the Arab states. Of the Arab regimes, Mrs. Thatcher trusted only the Jordanians, and when they refused to take part, the initiative collapsed. The embassy was not a free-standing building but part of a row built in the 1850s. Working from the neighboring building, the police inserted listening devices, the sound masked by a sudden access of roadworks and an alteration in the flight path for airliners descending to Heathrow Airport.

By the evening of May 3, the Special Air Service Corps, a troop of special forces founded originally in World War II, had attached abseil ropes to the chimneystacks of No. 16 and unlocked a skylight. On May 5, an exasperated and frightened Awn shot Abbas Lavasani, the press officer at the embassy, and dropped his body on the step outside. Mrs. Thatcher, who was returning to London by car, pulled off the road and, using her car telephone, ordered an assault. Just after 7 p.m., in the full view of spectators and watchers on television, between thirty and thirty-five men of the 22 SAS Regiment dropped a stun grenade through the skylight, smashed through the upper windows, and stormed the building, killing all the terrorists except one who hid among the hostages. One embassy employee was killed. PC Lock tackled Awn to the ground, and was awarded the United Kingdom's highest medal for civilian gallantry. With no thought to spare from the quarrel with the United States, the response in Iran was muted and suspicious. Hoping to assist Carter, Mrs. Thatcher wrote to Bani-Sadr on May 6. The letter, drafted and delivered by Sir John Graham, asked that "the Imam should order the release of the American hostages as a gesture of goodwill to the brave men who risked their lives to free the Iranian hostages and give thanks to God for their safety." It seems to have gone unanswered.[116]

At midsummer, Iraqi Military Intelligence submitted to Saddam a report on Iran's weaknesses. Those were its bad foreign relations, the political division between Beheshti and the Banisadrists, separatism in Kurdestan, Khuzestan, and the Turkoman Steppe, disorder on the roads, a collapse in oil production and revenue, money inflation, unemployment, weak leadership in an army demoralized by favoritism to the Corps of Guards, units 50 percent under strength, a militia of no operational value, and an air force stripped of its foreign technicians. The report, which was among documents captured by the U.S. Army in 2003, stated that "Iran has no power to launch wide offensive operations against Iraq or to defend on a large scale." It predicted a "further deterioration of the general situation in Iran's fighting capability."[117] On July 7, commanders were ordered to prepare for war with Iran.[118] When one senior officer said the armed forces would need at least two years to come up to strength and train, he was silenced.[119]

By September, Saddam was convinced that the opportunity would never be better to recover the losses of 1975, to unite and militarize

Iraqi society, and to enhance Iraq's standing in the Arab world. Beyond that, opportunities might arise for the overthrow of the regime and the capture of the Iranian oil province, Khuzestan. The border clashes increased in number and intensity, with a heavy bombardment by Iranian artillery and air force on September 4. By the 11th, the Iranian border town of Qasr-e Shirin had been abandoned by its residents, its famous date palms reduced to matchwood.[120] On the 13th, an Iraqi MiG-21 was shot down, apparently by an F-14 Phoenix missile.[121] "Geography was against us," a senior official of the Iraqi Baath Party later told me. "We have major cities within one hundred kilometers of the border. If we had waited, those cities would have been destroyed. The war began on September 4." [122]

Saddam was prepared for Iranian resistance. "Once a warplane attacks Baghdad, then that's it. With a single telephone call, we will come down like lightning on their heads," he told the Revolutionary Command Council on the 16th.[123] The next day, Saddam abrogated the Algiers treaty and ordered all foreign vessels in the Shatt to take on an Iraqi pilot and fly the Iraqi flag. Bani-Sadr ordered Iranian mobilization. Five days later, precisely at noon on September 22, 1980, nearly two hundred Iraqi aircraft took off on missions to bomb air bases in western and central Iran, including the two Tehran bases on the south side of Mehrabad Airport and Doshan Teppe. The towns of Abadan and Khorramshahr came under artillery bombardment, and Iraqi infantry and tanks crossed the frontier at nine points along the border between the Shatt and the mountains of Kurdestan. The world watched to see of what stuff the Iranian Revolution was made.

CHAPTER 13

The Scent of Watermelon

◆

*A few green Revolutionary Guards turned the sweet
dreams of America into a nightmare.* [1]

In the summer of 1982, elated by the victories of the spring that had
driven the Iraqi army from the deserts, marshes, and palm orchards of
southwestern Iran, the Political Office of the Corps of Guards of the
Islamic Revolution published a book entitled *Two Years of War* to celebrate the "secret evidences of God's providence" in the "war imposed
on us." [2]

The war, the Political Office said, had revealed to the world the novelty and force of Iran's revolution. Under the Prophetlike leadership of
the Jurist-Steward of the Age, the armies of Islam had struck fear into
the bullies of West and East, the capitalists and the liars of the Ham-
mer and Sickle, the quisling Saddam Hussein, the fat boys of the Persian Gulf, the usurpers of the Holy Places (the Saudi royal family), and
the despoilers of Jerusalem (Israel), and shown the so-called liberation
movements the way to wage war.

"The bully-boys had hoped for a Six-Day War which would set up
their lackey Saddam as a new Israel on the Persian Gulf, but the people
of Iran and a few green Guardsmen turned the sweet dreams of America into a nightmare." Iran had devised a new style of warfare, which
deployed not alien and costly armaments but a light infantry equipped
with a trust in God and a devotion to self-sacrifice. In the tempest of
war, where only the Ark of the Noah of the Age would be saved, Bani-
Sadr, the Hypocrites (Mojahedin), and the liberals had foundered in

the flood.[3] Although the Political Office did not say this, it is evident that of all God's blessings, the greatest was the creation of the Corps of Guards of the Islamic Revolution.

Two Years of War commemorates the braggadocio of that summer in Iran and helps us understand why, in July 1982, Khomeini rejected an Iraqi offer of armistice and chose to pursue the war onto Iraqi territory. With that decision, he transformed victory into defeat. Yet the Iranian ideology accommodates both. The revolutionaries retired into a corner for twenty years, sustained by the consciousness that they had been stabbed in the back.

As a civilian, Saddam Hussein knew nothing of arms and had no clear idea of what he wanted to achieve with them. To launch a surprise attack to adjust a border breaks ancient rules of war. Yet a force of nine small divisions, with three divisions in reserve, was too small to capture and hold much of the far-flung territory of Iran.

Had Saddam been serious about dismembering Khuzestan, he might have followed General William Slim in 1941 and occupied the two principal passes of the Zagros, the Paitak and Dezful, to cut off reinforcement from Tehran and the northeast. At least since the days of the Baghdad Pact and CENTO in the 1950s, Iraqi doctrine had planned for paratroopers to hold those passes against a Soviet attack through Iran.[4] Saddam ended up with a war of attrition against an adversary with three times the population and five times the land area. By choosing to fight his main campaign along the Shatt al-Arab, Iraq's principal outlet to the sea, Saddam cut his own throat.

With the air attacks of September 22, 1980, he hoped to emulate the Israeli destruction of the Egyptian air force on the ground on June 5, 1967. They were a failure, and for almost twenty-four hours, the Iranians were not aware they were engaged in all-out war. Operating at long range, with only two days' preparation and no exercises, the Soviet-made Iraqi MiG, Sukhoi, and Tupolev bombers could inflict little damage. From beyond the grave, General Mohammed Khatami earned his pay and expenses when the Iraqi bombs failed to penetrate the reinforced aircraft shelters he had built to NATO standards. The bases were ringed by antiaircraft artillery and Hawk surface-to-air missile batteries. "Each air base was like a ball of fire," said one of the Iraqi wing commanders.[5]

At the military sector on the south side of Mehrabad Airport, the MiG-23s hit a single F-4 Phantom undergoing repair, a Boeing 707, and a C-130 transport. A second wave at midafternoon was no more effective and damage to the runway was slight. By early evening, flights of up to six Iranian F-4 Phantom fighter-bombers and F-5 Tiger interceptors slipped through Iraqi radar and missile air defenses and attacked air bases and industrial plants. Working all night, the *homafars* prepared and armed two hundred fighter-bombers and support aircraft. Racing with the dawn behind them, they were low over Baghdad at first light and attacked every air base in eastern Iraq, destroying twenty aircraft on the ground, damaging the main bridge over the Shatt, and setting the Basra oil refinery on fire.

Because of the damage to the airfields and their defenses, Saddam dispatched as many as a hundred combat aircraft to airfields in Oman, North Yemen, Jordan, and Saudi Arabia, where they were unwelcome. Transports were flown to Amman, and King Hussein of Jordan had to inform Israel (by way of the United States) that he harbored no aggressive intentions toward the Jewish state. Gaining in confidence, the Iranian airmen pursued the retreating Iraqi aircraft, and then, as the Iraqi missile air-defense batteries held fire, broke off to strike industrial targets. They had learned from their U.S. instructors to turn toward an incoming missile. Often, the Phantom pilots flew so low that their bombs came in at too shallow a trajectory and did not detonate. On September 30, two Phantoms attacked the Iraqi nuclear power station at Tuwaitha, just to the south of the capital, but their bombs bounced off the dome of the 70-megawatt reactor (known as Osirak or Tammuz-1) and fell unexploded to ground. A furious Saddam compared the Iranian aircraft to the shared or "service" taxis that ply fixed routes between Arab cities.[6] In the air, before the wear and tear on men and machines began to tell, the Iranian air force had the upper hand and an F-14 emptied the sky for days. On the water, Iranian gunboats bottled up the Iraqi navy in port. Two floating batteries had to be shipped overland to the small port of Umm Qasr, the other side of the Fao peninsula.

On the ground, there were three principal axes of the Iraqi attack. In the mountainous Zagros, where the Iraqi aim was to establish a forward line to prevent an Iranian descent on the Mesopotamian plain, armor and infantry captured the border town of Qasr-e Shirin but were halted before the Paitak Pass and the town of Kermanshah beyond. They also overran the town of Mehran in the Posht-e Kuh ("Beyond the Mountains") to the south.

Those were sideshows to the main advance into the oil province of Khuzestan. Here the terrain favored armored cavalry. Bounded on the north by the foothills of the Zagros, the land is an extension of the Mesopotamian plain, flat, gravelly, and marked by fan-shaped alluvial sands brought down by the rivers. Running from west to east, those rivers are the Karkheh, which runs south only to turn west and lose itself in the Hoveizeh Marshes; the Dez; and the Karun, the only navigable river in Iran, which flows through the provincial capital of Ahvaz down to the port of Khorramshahr. There it divides with one branch, known as the Bahmanshir, running southeast through palm gardens and the other issuing into the Shatt. On the island between the two branches stood the town, oil-export terminal, refinery, and tank farm of Abadan. Soft and sodden in winter, much of the ground dries in summer into salt flats that support the weight of a tank.[7]

What was designed as a *Blitzkrieg* ("lightning war") of German or Israeli character within two days had become bogged down. There was no coordination between the different Iraqi units, or any strategic plan, and the divisions ground to a halt when they reached the end of their supplies or, as in Khorramshahr, met spirited resistance. As Izzat al-Douri, the vice chairman of the Revolutionary Command Council, had warned at the meeting in Baghdad on the 16th, stocks of munitions ran down and resupply from the Soviet Union (by way of Jordan) was to prove difficult. There were insufficient armed reserves to continue the attack.

Though men in the Arab headcloth known as the *keffiyeh* were shown to foreign reporters at the border crossing of Shalamcheh, there was no Arab uprising in Khuzestan. None of the "counterrevolutionary forces" hoisted colors. Instead, after the first shock, the Iranian army regrouped at defensible positions while the Corps of Guards redeployed from their Kurdish wars and volunteers, arriving in minibuses or even taxis, poured into the province. There was a call for Land Rovers, an elementary British farm vehicle assembled from kits in Iran and favored by the tribes.

In the north, the Iraqis advanced thirty miles but were held by the depleted Iranian 92nd Armored Division before the town of Dezful, where the principal road, railway line, and oil pipelines link Khuzestan with the north. The Iranians defended a bridgehead on the west or right bank of the Karkheh and protected the sprawling Vahdati air force base. In revenge, Iraqi artillery demolished the town. The Iraqi 5th Mechanized Division advanced by road and was at the outskirts of Ahvaz by September 27, but could not enter the city without infantry support. Spread out across the desert, it busied itself with building roads and waited for reinforcements. Between the two, battle raged for a week in front of the small town of Susangard, but the Iranian armor, supported by helicopters, held. Army and power company engineers broke the levees on a tributary of the Karkheh, turning the ground to mud and preventing a linkup with the Ahvaz column. It was the first instance of the hydraulic warfare that was to play such a role in the next eight years.

From the border crossing at Shalamcheh, the Iraqi 3rd Armored Division advanced into the northern suburbs of Khorramshahr but, untrained for close-quarters combat, could not negotiate streets turned to rubble by the bombardment from Tanuma across the Shatt. The inhabitants, rather than welcoming the invader, decamped to Shiraz, while a company of Chieftain tanks, marines, Gendarmerie, and Guards operating out of the city's Friday Mosque ambushed the Iraqi tanks with shoulder-fired grenades and petrol bombs. The smoke from the burning refinery at Abadan draped a pall of darkness over the ruins, and the town stank like a filling station. The Reuters correspondent, brought into the town by way of Abadan, was shown by the Iranians the remains of a Soviet tank and fifteen armored personnel carriers destroyed in a six-hour battle for the port and customshouse on the Shatt on October 5. Morale was high, he reported.[8] Baghdad radio claimed the town had fallen but, in reality, Iranian snipers held out in the port for weeks as warehouses and stranded vessels were pounded to scrap about them. From the south or left bank of the Karun, snipers and mortar teams prevented Iraqi vehicles from crossing the suspension bridge onto Abadan Island. In Tehran, Abadan was renamed *Khuninshahr,* or "City of Blood."

On October 4, Iraqi officers were told to destroy the old border posts and fences in preparation for a unilateral cease-fire at the new advanced positions the next day. The cease-fire was immediately rejected. Iran's conditions for ending the war were a total Iraqi withdrawal, $150 billion in reparations, an international commission to determine which side had been the aggressor, and the repatriation of refugees who had fled to Iran.

Ordered not to cede an inch of ground, on pain of drumhead execution, the Iraqi commanders dug in their tanks, hull-down, behind fifteen-foot earth berms, without any regard for the vulnerabilities of the position. In one case, at Allahu Akbar ("God is Great") Hill, a tank battalion of the 39th Armored Brigade entrenched itself without infantry protection on top of a hill. (It was destroyed in a night attack by the Revolutionary Guards the following May, with the loss of thirty tanks and all but nine men.) The Iraqis made only intermittent attempts to break up the rear areas. One of the features of the war was that Iran could mass 100,000-man volunteer armies from Tehran and the plateau and dispatch them by bus to the front. Soldiers and Guardsmen were inundated with gifts of food, candy, blankets, and bottled water.

Checked in the City of Blood, unable to clear the town or cross the suspension bridge, the Iraqi command attempted a flanking operation. On the evening of October 9, advance parties of the Iraqi 3rd Armored Division crossed the Karun at Mared, some fifteen miles north of Khorramshahr. Engineers laid Soviet PMP heavy floating pontoon or "ribbon" bridges, such as the Egyptian army had used to cross the Suez Canal in the October 1973 war, at Salmaniyeh and Darkhovein.[9] The first tanks crossed on Friday, October 10, and ambushed a supply column on the main Ahvaz-Abadan highway. The force established a bridgehead on the east side of between three and five miles and cut the highway. Moving at about one mile per day, the tanks reached the northern outskirts of Abadan on October 18 but were held by irregulars at the bridge over the Bahmanshir and in the part of the suburbs known as Zolfiqar. The town was not fully invested, as supplies could be brought up by Hovercraft and boat through the marsh at the south of the island.

In Khorramshahr, after an intense training course in urban warfare, Iraqi commandos and special forces fought their way to the Friday Mosque and captured the bridge on October 26. The main Iranian force withdrew, but volunteers and irregulars remained, and on October 30, near the railway station, a fourteen-year-old boy from Qom named Mohammed Fahmideh, who had been wounded, strapped grenades to his waist and detonated himself under an Iraqi tank.[10] He was to become the poster boy of the Iranian volunteer militia.

By the end of November 1980, the war of movement was over. The invasion force was at its furthest limit, in a series of vulnerable salients, across about 4,000 square miles of Iranian territory. At that point, rain and exhaustion brought a halt to campaigning, though the airwaves continued to resound with accusations. Each side called the other Zionist lackeys. The Iranian newspapers daily reported whole Iraqi divisions destroyed in the Zagros and mayhem by small teams of Revolutionary Guards deep in Iraqi territory.

In the lull, which was to last eighteen months, the Islamic Republic freed the American diplomatic hostages, established its legal code, extirpated its enemies, and covered up its women. The last of Khomeini's companions from Paris, Bani-Sadr and Qotbzadeh, were destroyed. By October 1981, all the principal offices of state with the exception of the prime ministry were in the hands of Khomeini's pupils from the Qom Seminary. They stayed in place until the end of the war. As Bani-Sadr's friend Ahmad Salamatian commented, "As regards the commanding heights of the *nomenklatura*, from 1981 to 1988 Iran enjoyed a relative stability."[11]

Iran was exporting little oil, gasoline and kerosene were rationed, and foreign currency reserves were adequate for no more than one month's civilian imports, let alone weapons and military replacement parts. The country needed to recover the money frozen in foreign bank accounts by President Carter back in November 1979. The Iranian public had lost interest in the hostages.[12] "We have reaped all the fruits of our undertaking," Mousavi-Khoeiniha told the *New York Times*. "We defeated the attempt by the Liberals to take control of the machinery of government. We have demonstrated . . . that we have the weapons not only to resist but also to defeat the all-powerful United States."[13]

Sadeq Tabatabai, Khomeini's favorite, had been working on a solution through his contacts in West Germany. On September 12, 1980, in a speech to Iranians traveling on the pilgrimage to Mecca, Khomeini declared four conditions for the release of the U.S. hostages: the return of Mohammed Reza's fortune to Iran; the cancelation of all claims against Iran; a pledge of U.S. military and political non-interference; and the unfreezing of Iranian financial assets. In a debate on November 2 that for heat would not have shamed the House of Commons, Parliament approved the four conditions set by Khomeini. It appointed a commission of seven deputies led by a radical militant, Behzad Nabavi, but forbade them to deal directly with the United States. The Algerian government, which was trusted by both sides, acted as broker.

President Bani-Sadr was left on the sidelines. The hostages were brought to Saadabad. After many twists and turns, the so-called Algiers Accords were signed on January 19, 1981. According to Massoumeh Ebtekar, the hostage-takers were not consulted at any point, and when Behzad Nabavi came to explain the agreement, they did not comment.[14] The students dissolved their ranks. Some had already gone to the front and were butchered in the premature offensive of January 5.[15] As far as I can tell, none of the leaders of the occupation of the U.S. Embassy fell in the war.

The United States agreed to lift trade sanctions imposed the April before, to drop its litigation in the International Court, and to release the blocked financial assets. Some $7.95 billion in gold bullion and securities was to pass to an escrow account, "Dollar Account One," at the Bank of England. Of that, $3.67 billion would be placed at the New York Federal Reserve to cover Iran's liabilities to U.S. banks and corporations on pre-revolutionary loans and contracts. A further $1.4 billion of Iranian money would fund an international tribunal for the arbitration of commercial claims and counterclaims. The clerical government, as innocent in matters of money as Reza Pahlavi in 1933 and Mossadeq in 1952, would receive in cash just $2.88 billion. It was now clear who was hostage and who hostage-taker.

The United States promised "not to intervene, directly or indirectly, politically or militarily, in Iran's internal affairs"; extracted pledges from the hostages and their families not to sue their captors or the Iranian government; and promised to enforce any judgement in U.S. courts that attached the Pahlavi family's wealth. The Iranians claimed that amounted to $56.5 billion. Since that was half of Iran's entire revenue from Reza's accession in 1926 to Mohammed Reza's exile in 1979, the United States treated the demand as infantile and ignored it.[16] (The Islamic Republic never produced evidence for the figure nor ever persuaded a foreign court of its claims against the Pahlavis.) Anyway, as Farah pointed out, "not a penny" of the Shah's fortune was held in the United States.[17]

Two days before the inauguration of President-elect Ronald Reagan, Parliament in Tehran approved the Algiers Accords. At 10:18 a.m. GMT on January 20, 1981, the Bank of England confirmed it was in funds and the fifty-two hostages were taken by bus to Mehrabad. Within the hour after the inauguration, three Algerian aircraft took the hostages out of Iran and their ordeal ended. As they told their stories, it emerged that they had not been as well treated as Massoumeh Ebtekar and others claimed. They had come out alive.

Now Bani-Sadr spoke up. The deal brought nothing for the Islamic Republic. Where was the U.S. apology for its support for the Pahlavis? Where was the Shah's fortune? Where were the spare parts and supplies for the army and air force? The first country ever to repay its foreign debt in wartime, Iran had no hope of new loans. He told Khomeini that Prime Minister Rajai and Behzad Nabavi should be put on trial for giving away "the public wealth to the United States."[18]

The sniping over the hostages was just one skirmish in the fight between Bani-Sadr and his allies, which included the remains of the National Front, the quietist clergy, and even some of Khomeini's household, versus the Islamic Republican Party. In the slogan of the day, it was a battle between "Liberalism" and the "Line of the Imam." "Liberalism" did not mean European liberalism, of which the clerical party knew little. It was an insult word of obscure origin and forgotten meaning, like "Whig" or "Tory." The Line of the Imam was a doctrine of allegiance and submission, somewhat similar to the *Fuehrerprinzip* of the Third Reich, but of course not like it at all. In truth, this was a war of the schools: between the Koran school, representing *faqahat* or (approximately) Scholasticism, and the modern universities, above all those abroad. It was the old war of the turban and the collar-and-tie.

It was also a dispute between military forces. Bani-Sadr and the army command hoped to hold the Iraqi attack, and exploit foreign alliances and diplomacy to end the war. In contrast, those following the Line of the Imam wanted to press the war and use it to purify Iranian society and expand Iranian influence. While at the front, regular soldiers and Guardsmen fought together, in Tehran there was no compromise. In a long conversation on the evening of April 18, 1981, Hashemi Rafsanjani was candid to Bazargan. He said: "Until we had our people in place, we were ready to tolerate [other] gentlemen on the stage. Once Parliament was constituted, hard-line forces were no longer prepared to act with circumspection and accept Liberals in key posts or, indeed, any faction in the Islamic Government but that of the Line of the Imam. The revolutionary institutions, the Parliament, the Supreme Court and the *Hezbollah* [storm troops] will not tolerate Liberals."[19]

What was the Line of the Imam? What did Khomeini want? His vision of Islamic government did not allow for disagreement, let alone the poisonous daily exchanges in the press and on television. He liked Bani-Sadr and was grateful for his help in France. Yet by experience and temperament, his loyalty was to the seminary clergy of Qom and to the propagation of the Shia. If he agreed to an armistice, he told Hashemi Rafsanjani, how could Iran help the Iraqi people overthrow Saddam?[20] The IRP told him that Bani-Sadr was moving closer to the Mojahedin, whom he distrusted and feared, and building support among the unpolitical clergy in Tabriz and Mashhad.

Deprived of power, at loggerheads with his prime minister, the house speaker, and the chief justice, refusing (in a phrase Salamatian took from de Gaulle) "to inaugurate the chrysanthemums," Bani-Sadr spent most of his time at the front, racing between headquarters in a Range Rover camouflaged with dried mud. His newspaper, *Islamic Revolution,* carried on its front page a daily diary and photographs of the president sharing rice and the discomforts of war with common soldiers. (The IRP said he lolled in a Pahlavi-era palace in Andimeshk.) He became popular with the public and later claimed that Khomeini became jealous of him. Ever the footloose journalist, he poured ink across his newspaper, railing against the IRP monopoly of power, the hostage settlement, the suppression of freedom of speech and assembly and—a sensitive point—the revival of torture in the prisons. (It was now known as "discretionary punishment" or *tazir.*)

To break out of his isolation, and under pressure from public opinion and what he called the "sanguinary clowns" of the IRP, Bani-Sadr approved a premature offensive. On January 5, 1981, with regular army units still at half-strength, inadequate reserves, and no preliminary training, he launched "Operation Victory" to recapture Susangard. It was nearly a catastrophe. A brigade of the 16th Armored Division was caught in an enveloping operation and mauled, losing as many as sixty Chieftains. A second brigade was sent in to a hopeless situation. The Iranians had to withdraw to close the opening to Ahvaz. An attempt to relieve the pressure on Abadan five days later was no more successful.[21] President and general staff lost prestige in Tehran and Qom.

On March 5, when *hezbollahis* tried to disrupt a rally at Tehran University called by Bani-Sadr to commemorate Mossadeq's death, they were roughed up (possibly by Mojahedin) and handed over to the police. Parliament was outraged at the turning of the tables. An exasperated Khomeini called the country's leaders to his house on March 15.

Bani-Sadr came alone. He sat down beside his old master, with Bazargan and Ahmad Khomeini as moral support. Ranged in front of them on the floor were the leaders of what Bani-Sadr called the *mollariat*: the IRP secretary general and chief justice, Mohammed Beheshti; Hashemi Rafsanjani, the speaker of Parliament; Mohammed Ali Rajai, the prime minister; Ali Khamenei, who had been defense minister and was now supervisor of the Revolutionary Guards; and Abdol Karim Musavi-Ardebili, the prosecutor general. Khomeini, who appears in Bani-Sadr's account angry and bewildered, demanded of them all: "Do you intend to annihilate the Islamic Republic?"[22] Bani-Sadr accused the IRP men of knowing nothing of the religious law and said that the institutions they represented were illegitimate. Beheshti retorted that the president boasted of "the most luminous intellect of the century" while accusing all those who opposed him of lacking intelligence and principle. Hashemi Rafsanjani demanded that Bani-Sadr cede his position as commander in chief. Bazargan, pouring oil on troubled waters, proposed that a three-man committee be appointed to adjudicate differences between the president and the other officers of state. Khomeini accepted his proposal but, in the widening conflict, it had no effect. For reasons not entirely clear to me, Ahmad Khomeini, who controlled access to his father, abandoned the president.

Hashemi Rafsanjani visited the Abadan front in late March, where he was fascinated by the low-level helicopter flight but suffered from diarrhea. He brought back to Khomeini complaints that the regular army was inactive. Ali Khamenei pressed Khomeini to involve himself in war operations.[23] By early April, Khomeini was questioning Bani-

Sadr why 175mm self-propelled artillery, of which Iran had about 1,000 pieces, were not being dispatched to the Abadan front.[24] The IRP bloc in Parliament opposed Bani-Sadr's appointments to ministries, cut off funds for the president's office, and chipped at his powers. Bani-Sadr responded by appealing to the people, in his newspaper and in speeches and rallies up and down the country. On June 7, both *Islamic Revolution* and the newspaper of Bazargan's Freedom Movement were closed for publishing inflammatory articles.[25] Bani-Sadr responded by issuing a broadside on the streets, entitled *The Message of the President of the Republic,* calling for "resistance and uprising." Neither in Tehran, nor in his hometown of Hamadan where he took refuge, was there an answer. In a fierce speech, Khomeini threatened to do to him what he had done to the Shah.[26]

On June 10, Khomeini dismissed Bani-Sadr as commander in chief. (In celebration, the Revolutionary Guards launched an offensive, code-named "Commander in chief Khomeini, Spirit of God," against the northern sector of the Karun salient, but could not progress.) Bani-Sadr returned to Tehran that evening and vanished from public view. Hashemi Rafsanjani was for letting him leave the country, "where he will be lost among the royalists and Bakhtiarites."[27] One hundred and seven deputies signed a motion to impeach the president on the ground of political incompetence. Khomeini, who still believed that Bani-Sadr could be brought round, instructed Hashemi Rafsanjani to delay.

On June 15, the National Front and opposition attempted to stage a show of strength in midtown but were overwhelmed by an IRP countermarch of 500,000 from the southern districts. In a broadcast, Khomeini ordered Bani-Sadr to appear on television and "repent" of his call to insurrection. The president still believed that the old man loved him and that something remained of the "Khomeini of Paris." In a letter to Khomeini that day, he wrote like a dutiful son: "However you behave, I will not violate my responsibility to you. However angry you are, my devotion to you will not be diminished." Yet he repeated his complaints that the government was unconstitutional and liberty was being suppressed.[28] Khomeini, exasperated by the "arrogance" of the letter, that evening ordered Hashemi Rafsanjani to table the impeachment motion.[29] The Guards were ordered to arrest the president, but he had passed underground.

The debate on the motion opened on June 20. The Mojahedin, who had held onto the arms captured in the fight at the machine-gun factory and the barracks back in February 1979, staged a mass demonstration which erupted into armed clashes with the Guards. At least sixteen people were killed. The sound of gunfire and the roars of the *hezbollahis* penetrated the chamber. Early the next morning, June 21, fifteen "counterrevolutionaries" were shot in Evin, and Khalkhali told deputies that thirty-five more would die by nightfall.

Deputy after deputy charged that the president was guilty of insubordination to the Imam, creating faction, negligence as a military commander, and disgracing the Islamic Republic with his allegations of torture. One hundred and seventy-seven votes were cast to impeach him, with just one vote against and twelve abstentions or absences.[30] With the votes counted, Hashemi Rafsanjani, Khalkhali, and Hadi Ghaffari emerged onto the balcony of the Parliament to roars of "Bani-Sadr to hang!" Hashemi Rafsanjani said: "From this moment, Bani-Sadr is eliminated from the Islamic Republic. Switch your slogans to America." The obedient crowd complied and cries of "Death to America" filled the square.[31]

The Mojahedin, who had dreamed of armed insurrection since the 1960s, went into battle. On the 27th, a booby-trapped tape recorder exploded while Ali Khamenei was preaching at the Abu Zarr Mosque, depriving him of the use of his right arm. On the 28th, at 8:50 p.m., a bomb went off in a rubbish bin by the stage at the IRP headquarters, killing Beheshti, the secretary general, who was speaking at the time, as well as four cabinet ministers, six deputy ministers, twenty other members of Parliament, and dozens of party and government officers, including Montazeri's son, "Ayatollah Ringo." The explosion, which caused the building to collapse, was heard all over the capital.[32] While Beheshti was torn limb from limb, most of the others died in the falling concrete and timbers. For some time there were cries for help, but the emergency services lacked the training and equipment to rescue them.[33] The full death toll was never computed but set at seventy-two.

The Mojahedin have never claimed or refused responsibility, but the trail led to a jobbing electricity student named Mohammed Reza Kolahi, who had left the building ten minutes before Beheshti's speech on the pretext of buying ice creams.[34] His student report showed a connection with the Mojahedin. Amidst panic in the clerical camp, Khomeini displayed his habitual composure. "I have asked revolutionary courts to use decisive Islamic justice to deal with corrupt individuals," he stated on July 9. "Any leniency will be like showing mercy to the sharp-toothed tiger."[35]

On July 29, Bani-Sadr and Masoud Rajavi of the Mojahedin slipped out of the country in a Boeing 707 military tanker. The pilot was Colonel Behzad Moezzi, who had been in the cockpit with Mohammed Reza in the flight to Aswan back in 1979. He had been imprisoned after the Nozheh coup and then released at the outbreak of war. He had filed a flight plan for a routine night exercise, but then told Mehrabad of an emergency, and flew low and fast into Turkish airspace. Once in Paris, Bani-Sadr and Rajavi announced the formation of a National Council of Resistance to overthrow the clerical government.

On August 30, just after 2:30 p.m., an incendiary bomb destroyed the prime minister's office during the weekly meeting of the National Security Council. It incinerated Rajai, who was standing in as president of the republic; Mohammed Javed Bahonar, his replacement as prime minister; and the chief of police. Suspicion fell on Masoud Kahsmiri, the secretary of the council, a Mojahedin *tavab* or "repenter" who habitually placed his briefcase under the oval table at which the council sat, and a tape recorder on top. What were thought to be the ashes of his carbonized body had lain in state in the Parliament building, but then his house was searched and his parents found to have vanished. Mohammed Reza Mahdavi-Kani, the interior minister, who had overslept his siesta by five minutes and thus saved his life, was named temporary prime minister.[36] A week later, the revolutionary prosecutor general was blown to pieces. In that evil summer of 1981, assassins killed the Friday prayer leaders in Tabriz, Kerman, Shiraz, and Yazd, as well as other "Pulpit Martyrs," the warden of Evin Prison, revolutionary court judges, and members of Parliament. Government buildings became strongholds, lit all night by halogen lights, and officials rode in armored vehicles. Asadollah Lajevardi, the prosecutor general, who liked to be known as Hajji Aqa (approximately, "Boss"), lived for his own safety in Evin. The Mojahedin turned to killing minor officials, Guardsmen, and prison warders. The other left-wing groups, apart from the Tudeh, took up arms.

Ehsan Naraghi, who had already served two terms in prison as a royalist, the last in relative comfort, was arrested again on July 1, this time as Bani-Sadr's former professor at Tehran University. The prison where he had walked with his friends in the courtyard, discussing literature and the shortcomings of Pahlavi rule, he found transformed into a concentration camp. When his guard left him for a moment outside the courtroom, he pushed up the edge of his blindfold to see a sight that caused him to swoon: "Fifty or more young men and girls, blindfolded, were crammed into the corridor, powerless and utterly submissive. At regular intervals, a warder passed in front of us, shouting: 'Blindfolds down! Knees into your chest!'"[37]

A prison, built by Mohammed Reza to hold fifteen hundred prisoners, by late summer held eight or even ten times that number. In the cells, approximately six yards by six, as many as seventy young people slept head to foot. They were arranged each night by a "sleep architect." At mealtimes, a "mayor" was elected to cut pieces of white cheese with the back of a teaspoon into helpings as small as a quarter of an ounce, according to age and state of health. Delicacies such as bread or dates were set aside for those returning from interrogation or the tribunal. Each night, after midnight, they listened to the crash of heavy machine-gun fire from the courtyard. Lying on the floor, holding their breath, they counted the single-shot *coups de grâce*. One night, Naraghi counted eighty executions in Evin.

For lack of solitary confinement cells, the prisoners were held for hours in so-called coffins, four and a half feet by three feet by twenty inches, in which according to Amir Entezam many lost their minds.[38] As the assaults outside on the Guards and warders increased through September, there were rumors of a general massacre of the prisoners. Amnesty International reported 1,600 executions in the three months after Bani-Sadr's impeachment, including 300 over the weekend of September 18–20.[39] The Mojahedin said that they lost 6,000 members either in prison or in battles with the Revolutionary Guards. In the women's or "sisters" block, now swelled to about 350 prisoners, Shahrnush Parsipur, a writer incarcerated with her mother, reckoned the average age of her cellmates was nineteen.[40] A rumor passed through the country that, to sidestep a ban on killing unmarried girls, female prisoners were being forcibly married (that is, raped) before execution.

Montazeri, who was trying to halt the execution of girls and women except in case of murder, denied it, but to no effect, and many families that were able sent their headstrong daughters abroad.[41] (Marjane Satrapi, who later became celebrated as a graphic novelist, was dispatched to Vienna at the age of fourteen, where she was soon destitute.)[42] On September 20, 1981, Lajevardi said: "Even if a twelve-year-old is found participating in an armed demonstration, he will be shot. The age doesn't matter."[43]

From September, prisoners were encouraged to gather in the prison sports hall to hear repentant colleagues confess, and those debates and confessions were televised. On Thursday nights, loudspeakers blasted out the old Shia Komeil prayer through all the prison blocks. Outside the prisons, the threat from the Mojahedin justified a new conformity. Guards and the *komitehs* harassed women unless they covered their hair. Sadeq Qotbzadeh was arrested in April 1982 on suspicion of plotting to bomb Khomeini's house. Before he was shot, he implicated Shariatmadari, who was stripped of his clerical honors and confined to his house. Secular judges were forced into retirement, and ancient punishments, such as the stoning of women for adultery and the amputation of hands for theft, were incorporated into the penal code.

By the end of 1982, after over 5,000 young people had perished on the revolutionary gallows, the back of the revolt was broken.[44] The Mojahedin survived abroad, notably in France, until Masoud Rajavi and other leaders were expelled in 1986 and took refuge in Saddam Hussein's Iraq. In Iran, the crisis left behind institutions for repression that have proved impossible to dismantle. At its leisure, the clerical party then demolished the Tudeh and a conservative religious grouping known as the Hojjatieh. On May 1, 1983, Tudeh party secretary Nureddin Kianuri appeared on television and, combining Islamic and Marxist-Leninist traditions of self-criticism, recounted the "treason" of the left in the years since the Constitutional Revolution at the beginning of the century. He thanked his jailers for the opportunity they had given him to study Iranian history. (In the surviving film of his confession, he appears like an automaton; later he told a UN delegation visiting Evin that he had been tortured.)[45] A year afterward the Tudeh ideologue Ehsan Tabari regretted in public that he had devoted his life to Marx rather than to Motahhari.

By then, the tide had long turned on the battlefield. Though isolated by sanctions going back to the U.S. Embassy takeover, Iran was able to replenish its munitions on the international market. Syria, whose Baathist government was in family feud with the Iraqi Baath, made available a transit base at Damascus Airport. The Soviet Union, despite its support for Iraq, also allowed its weaponry to pass to Iran from Bulgaria and North Korea.[46] "Shame that North Korea is part of the Eastern bloc," Hashemi Rafsanjani mused in his diary. "What with our No-East-No-West policy and all." For spares for the Phantoms and other U.S.-made equipment, Iran bought through third parties surplus inventory from its blood enemy, Israel, and even Ethiopia. Iran was fleeced. In one deal that came to light, the middleman absconded with $56 million. Equipment became miscellaneous and ammunition analysis a military specialty. Soldiers at the front found themselves unpacking eastern European RPG-7 grenades from boxes marked in English "Typewriters" or "Tractor Parts."[47]

In the summer of 1981, Khomeini demanded that the siege of Abadan be broken. The city was surviving on supplies brought up by water under fire from the western shore of the Shatt, but in the autumn engineers from the 77th Khorasan Division completed a new road, the Unity road, to supply the town. In the small hours of September 27, army and Guards units supported by helicopters attacked the Karun salient. In two days of hard fighting they pushed the Iraqis back over the Karun and poured into Abadan. The victory in "Operation Eighth Imam" was a boost to morale and convinced the Iranian command that it could now conduct large-scale operations.[48] The triumph was dimmed by the loss on the 29th of a C-130 Hercules carrying the defense minister and four senior commanders as well as thirty-four other men. Colonel Ali Sayyad Shirazi, a somber and pious artillery officer who had trained at the U.S. Army Field Artillery School at Fort Sill, Oklahoma, and risen like a rocket in the army purges and Kurdish wars, became land force commander.

The strategy Shirazi carried out was to cut the Khuzestan front off from the northern sectors and then, conscious that the Iraqi forces were all but immobile, break them up in detail. Men he had, but it was a matter of combining their strengths. The Guards, operating at night in small units, were effective in overrunning Iraqi positions but then lost them to tank and artillery counterattacks in daylight. In the "Mobilization of the Weak," a militia founded in 1979 for civil defense and neighborhood control, he had the makings of highly motivated shock troops. His tactic was to transform the Guards and volunteers from roaming bands into brigade-strength forces, which could break the Iraqi lines allowing the regular units to hold and reinforce the captured ground. Helicopters and aircraft would be deployed to reconnoiter the battlefield and to support the ground forces. Returning to the front after two years away, the correspondent of the *New York Times* saw full uniforms and even the occasional salute. In the fashion of military commanders everywhere, the joint command drew up a plan of campaign in fantastic detail for the southern theater, known as the Karbala Plan, with no fewer than twelve separate operations.

In a series of actions during the winter of 1981–82, the Iranians isolated the southern front, while preparing for a large-scale offensive of two armored divisions, two infantry divisions, and three Guard divisions. The code name "Manifest Victory" was chosen at random from the Koran, a practice known as *estekhareh* in Persian and in English as bibliomancy. The verse that came up was: "We gave you a manifest victory."[49] The first operations, using the lightly armed volunteers in so-called human waves, drove the Iraqis back from Shush (the ancient city of Susa) and Dezful. Despite a series of Iraqi spoiling attacks, on March 22, 1982, in the middle of the New Year's holiday, Manifest Victory was launched and maintained for a week. In one of the most dashing actions of the war, Iranian commandos silenced the batteries on the Ali Gereh Zad heights, which were pounding Dezful and Vahdati air base, and captured the guns intact.[50] Demoralized by eighteen months of inaction, the Iraqis retired to new positions at the pre-1980 border. Correspondents brought to the front on April 5 came on Iraqi entrenchments unmarked by tank or artillery fire, as if they had been taken without a shot. "Now we are going to write our own manuals, with absolutely new tactics that the Americans and British and French can study at their staff colleges," Colonel Behruz Suleiman, the deputy commander of the Iranian 21st Division, told the journalists.[51]

With the front now shortened, men and armor could be redeployed to relieve Khorramshahr. There, after twenty months, the Iraqis were entrenched in the ruins and had built a network of roads to link the port to strongpoints at Hamid Junction, on the railway, and the town of Jofeir. Just forty days after Manifest Victory, before Iraq could regroup let alone mount a counterattack, Iran had assembled seven divisions and five independent brigades for "Operation Holy House" (named for the city of Jerusalem). With some 70,000 fresh volunteers and about 200 battle-ready tanks, the operation began just after midnight on April 30 with advances down three axes: from the northeast at Susangard; across the plain southwest of Ahvaz; and down the west or right bank of the Karun.

In the first hours, the Iranians crossed the Karun River, negotiated the minefields and embankments protecting the Ahvaz-Khorramshahr highway, and broke the Iraqi force into two. Jawad Shitnah, the Kurdish commander of the Iraqi 3rd Armored Division, attempted to draw the Iranians on and break them up in open ground, but his men were overwhelmed when the Iranian infantry swarmed into their artillery positions. Hamid fell on May 6 and Jofeir was abandoned. On the 9th, the Guards and regulars of the 92nd Armored broke through to the border post at Shalamcheh, leaving Khorramshahr cut off except by the bridges over the Shatt now under constant Iranian air attack. On May 22, the Iranians captured the Iraqi supply road along the east bank of the Shatt, isolating the conscript army in Khorramshahr, which surrendered. After twenty-five days of fighting, Iran had 17,500 prisoners. The Iraqi army was broken, with 10,000 battle casualties, two armored divisions reduced to brigades, and no more than 100 usable combat aircraft.[52] Jawad Shitnah and the commander of the Third Corps, Salah al-Qadi, were executed. It was the greatest Iranian feat of arms since the eighteenth century. The "modern tradition of defeat" mentioned by that U.S. officer back in 1953 was ended.

Saddam sought new means to extricate himself. On June 3, on the pavement outside the Dorchester Hotel on Park Lane, London, Shlomo Argov, the Israeli ambassador who was well liked in London, was shot in the head. His assailant, who was critically wounded by Argov's British diplomatic-protection officer, was a member of a three-man group sent to London by Sabri al-Banna, known as Abu Nidal ("father of struggle"), a Palestinian assassin at that time operating out of Baghdad. The Metropolitan Police arrested all three men, including Nawaf Rosan, an officer in Iraqi intelligence. The cell had been established as a "sleeper" in London at the outset of the war, and activated at short notice.

Saddam believed, with justice, that the attempt on Argov's life would provoke an Israeli attack on the Palestinian ministate in Lebanon.[53] The Israeli cabinet, which had been planning to expel the Palestine Liberation Organization from Lebanon and had received endorsement from the Reagan administration, met the following morning and launched an air assault on Palestinian targets in Lebanon. On the 6th, Israeli armor and infantry crossed the border and besieged Beirut.[54] (Argov was paralyzed and died in Israel in 2003. At the time of writing his three assailants were still in custody in Britain.)

On June 10, the Iraqi Revolutionary Command Council (RCC) in Baghdad, with Tariq Aziz presiding, announced a unilateral cease-fire and the withdrawal of all its forces from Iranian ground in two weeks. "The RCC believes it is urgently necessary to concentrate all efforts to confronting the ferocious Zionist aggression against the Arab world," the statement said.[55] Iraq offered safe transit for Iranian forces to the Lebanese front. Iran's Arab allies, including Syria, Libya, and the PLO, urged Iran to accept the cease-fire and join the battle against Israel.

There was much in Saddam's offer that appealed to the Iranian revolutionaries. Shirazi, the architect of the successful offensives, was prepared to detach experienced men to Damascus and the Bekaa. Others, particularly in the Guards leadership and the hard-line clergy, saw in the Israeli invasion an American conspiracy to save Saddam from Iranian punishment. As the Political Office of the Guards noted later that summer: "To an extent we fell into the snare set by America, Israel and the Baathist regime. We turned our attention from continuing the war to the problem of Lebanon."

Those in favor of continuing the war against Iraq had two principal arguments. First, the Baath was not to be trusted and Iranian territory would not be secure until the Iraqi military was broken. Strategic areas of southern Iran were still under the Iraqi guns. Mohsen Rafiqdoust later summed up this argument: "The enemy was so powerful that accepting the ceasefire was not a logical decision. It was better to pursue the war onto Iraqi soil."[56] Second, the Baath was weakened and an Iranian success of the nature of Manifest Victory and Holy House might topple the Iraqi regime and project Islamic revolution toward the borders of Israel.[57] Montazeri, among others, was convinced that a *coup d'état* was in preparation in Iraq. Khomeini ended the debate on June 21, 1982, with a broadcast in which he called anew for the overthrow of Saddam. In a warning to the Arab regimes, he said that the people of Iraq would establish Islamic government, and "if Iran and Iraq unite, the other nations of the region will join with them."[58] The motto was: *The road to Jerusalem passes through Karbala.*[59] As the Political Office of the Guards wrote, "The Imam cried, Watch Out! and shattered the illusions we had made for ourselves. We realised that the only way to rescue the region from the clutches of America was to overthrow Saddam's regime and replace it with an Islamic and popular regime in Iraq."[60]

Iran did send approximately five hundred men to Baalbek, a lawless town famous for its Roman ruins and narcotics trade in the east of Lebanon, and opened an unconventional front on the streets of Beirut scarred by seven years of civil war. Among the Shia in Baalbek and in the southern districts of Beirut, the Corps of Guards provided cash and support to found a Lebanese *hezbollah* or Party of God, which came to dominate the south of the country and the capital and wage war with Israel. The Lebanese *hezbollah* announced its intentions early on the morning of October 23, 1983, when suicide bombers blew up the buildings housing U.S. Marines and French paratroopers who had come into Beirut as a peacekeeping force but been sucked into the conflict. *Hezbollah* also kidnapped foreigners, including Americans, many of them long settled in that once cosmopolitan city.

Meanwhile, the Iraqis had not been inactive. To protect Basra, the country's second city and only substantial port, army engineers began in 1981 to grade land on the Iraqi side of the border for flooding, lay roads, raise high earthworks, and sow minefields. The British reporters John Bulloch and Harvey Morris, traveling south in 1982, thought the defenses as formidable as anything devised since the setpiece battles of World War I.[61] Ten miles northeast of Basra, engineers threw up earth barriers around the perimeter of the marsh and then drew water along the Jasim channel to flood an area of about 120 square miles. At its heart, they dug a shallow trench running northwest to southeast, approximately half a mile wide and eighteen miles long, known as *qanat al-asmak* in Arabic, *kanal-e mahigiri* in Persian, and, in English, Fish Lake. Its forward shore was fortified with barbed wire, mines, and electrodes. North of Fish Lake, and stretching as far as the oil platforms of the Majnoon field in the marshes, were two parallel lines of triangular or pentagonal fortresses, capable of protecting a battalion and its supporting tanks and artillery, with interlocking fields of fire. (The traces of those fortifications, and of Fish Lake, are still visible in modern satellite photography.)

It was at this time that Saddam built laboratories and factory capacity, at Muthanna northwest of Baghdad, to manufacture chemical munitions, first tear gas and sulphur mustard gas, which had been deployed in the static warfare of World War I, and then the nerve agents tabun and sarin. The attack by Israeli Phantoms on the Tuwaitha complex on June 7, 1981, which destroyed the Osirak reactor and postponed to the remote future a nuclear deterrent, had brought an urgency to the chemical weapons project. Iraq later told inspectors from the United Nations that from 1982 until the end of the war in 1988, it manufactured some 3,000 tons of chemical agents and filled 100,000 aerial bombs, artillery shells, rockets, and missile warheads.[62] Such weapons, inefficient and hard to deploy, nonetheless had a discouraging effect on Iranian morale. Martyrdom is one thing. Martyrdom with extremities blistered by mustard gas or paralyzed by nerve agents is another.[63]

Against those colossal defenses, Iran now threw its children and young men. On the evening of July 13, 1982, after the men had broken their fast, Iran launched Karbala 4, or the Ramazan offensive, with the objective of capturing Basra and provoking a Shia uprising in Iraq. (The action is known in Iraq as the First Battle of Basra.) The assault, involving eight understrength divisions, consisted of thrusts through Shalamcheh and toward the northern shore of Fish Lake. Reconnaissance was poor, both before and during the battle, and the Iranian commanders underestimated the tenacity of the Iraqis on their home soil. Shirazi later blamed "overconfidence" as a result of the successes of the spring.[64]

In the south, the Iranians advanced to within sight of the city lights of Basra, but in the north the attack stalled in the fiercest large-scale fight since World War II. The Chieftains bogged down in mud on the shore of the lake.[65] Between them, volunteers were slaughtered in windrows. An Iraqi captain said: "They keep coming and we keep shooting, sweeping our [heavy machine guns] around like sickles. My men are eighteen, nineteen, just a few years older than these kids. I've seen them crying, and at times the officers have had to kick them back to their guns."[66] In the end, the Iranian assault was driven back under its guns to the border town of Zeid. One Iranian tank commander said that in the last action, of the volunteers attached to his unit of tanks, 70 percent perished before midday.[67] The Chieftains captured by the Iraqi Third Corps were paraded as prizes in Baghdad, and then sold to Jordan.

With the onset of autumn, once again there was stalemate. It was an appalling place for a static war, scalding in summer and swept by sandstorms from the northwest, which piled up drifts on the roads and filled the trenches by noon. Men cleaned their rifles twice a day, or wrapped them in cloth. Every vehicle threw up a telltale plume of dust and battles were fought in a fog of white. Soldiers suffered agonies of thirst. In winter, mist and rain rusted weapons, ruined ammunition, and shorted the telephone lines that the Guards used for their few communications.[68]

From the Iraqi side, Bulloch and Morris wrote:

The winter landscape of southern Iraq recalled pictures of the Somme in 1916: long lines of laden men moving in single file up to the front, the non-coms shouting at them to hurry past gaps in the ramparts where Iranian snipers 1,000 yards away might pick them off. Mud everywhere, clinging soft mud that worked its way into the operating rooms in the forward casualty posts and field hospitals, mud that got into the mess tins and made all food taste the gritty same. Where the groves of date palms had broken up the landscape there were now only the blackened stumps and burned trunks of the trees, the tops blown off by shell fire and cut down by heavy machine gun bursts. Where the mud ended the water began, great man-made lakes, only a few feet deep to make it difficult for assault boats to be used, a tremendous feat of engineering skill and sheer back-breaking labour as the pioneer battalions built the raised roads which allowed troops and vehicles to move about. There was constant danger, as the Iranians quickly found the co-ordinates and dropped shells and mortar bombs on the bottle-necks where traffic was held up, the narrow bridges over streams, the crossroads where the new tracks converged.[69]

As the war entered its third year, Iranian spirits were still high. An atmosphere of religious devotion, not seen in European armies since the seventeenth century, suffused the Guards and volunteers. The rituals of popular religion and the Karbala story, suppressed by the Pahlavis, burst into life. Miracles became commonplace. Red tulips sprouted from the graves of the dead. A trunkless head, blown off by a mine, was seen to mouth: *Salam alaik ya abu abdullah!* (Greetings to you, Hosein, father of Abdullah!) Soldiers dreamed their own deaths the next day or saw, amid the barrel flashes, the Prince of Martyrs on a white stallion galloping before them. A painting of that time shows a grieving mother, in the style of the Virgin in a Renaissance *Pietá* as seen by an Isfahan miniaturist, cradling the body of a dead volunteer.[70] Images of Martyr Fahmideh were plastered on house gables.

At the Tehran University grounds each Friday, the prayer leader preached holding a G3 or AK-47, while young boys in cut-down uniforms and the wounded on crutches or in wheelchairs muttered hosannas from the front rows. (Correspondents found irresistibly comic the sight of Montazeri with the bayonet of his G3 reaching his chin.) The college boys who commanded tank units were astonished by the cheerfulness of the volunteers, who ran laughing and without helmets between the Chieftains. The army itself took on a volunteer character. A young tank commander later said: "Army regulations were not in effect. I was not ordering so much as convincing."[71]

In vain the Iraqis put on show a lame twelve-year-old boy, named Hosein, captured in the battle for Khorramshahr. As they translated his story for the correspondent of the Hamburg *Der Spiegel*, unfamiliar clergymen had appeared in his village in the south and said that the Imam had called for volunteers to liberate Jerusalem. The village molla decreed that each family must send a boy. Hosein was chosen by his father by reason of his deformity from polio. On the outskirts of Khorramshahr, the boys were formed into platoons of twenty, given a weapon and twenty rounds, and sent against an artillery position. Hosein and two others survived. All the time, they believed they were fighting Israelis.[72]

In the course of 1983, Iran sought to put pressure on the enemy by occupying its territory and launched five minor offensives, code-named *Val Fajr* ("By the Dawn") from the Koran (chapter 89) in the northern and central sectors of the front. None was successful, and for the first time Iranian infantry came under chemical attack. That was a breach of the 1925 Geneva Protocol, but Iran had not thought to acquire friends abroad to support its protest at the United Nations. At the fronts, men became alert for a sweet scent in the air which reminded them of cucumber or watermelon. In February 1984, in response to Iranian shelling of Basra and to delay and disrupt the next Iranian offensive, Iraq launched missile attacks on Tehran and other towns. The Soviet rockets, at the limit of their range, appear to have had no targets except the city. At night, residents of Tehran drove out of town to take refuge in the hills and villages. It was the first episode in what became known as the "War of the Cities."

The main Iranian land offensive, when it came that February of 1984, was ambitious, well organized, and ingenious. Reconnaissance had identified a weakness in the Iraqi line in the Hoveizeh Marshes between the Third and Fourth Iraqi Army Corps. At that time of year, the marshes were underwater often above a man's head and scattered with clumps of impenetrable reeds and muddy hammocks. The marshes sit atop one of the largest oil fields in the world, discovered in 1975 by Brazilian engineers and named Majnoon ("Insane") by virtue of its colossal reservoir and explosive wellhead pressure. Two man-made islands, known as Majnoon North and Majnoon South, had been built to support some seventy wells and other oil-service installations. The Iraqi command thought the morass was protection enough and the sector between the two army corps was defended only by the conscript Popular Army.

Iran, in contrast, saw a way through to the Tigris and the main Baghdad-Basra road without fear of the armored counterattacks that had broken up Ramazan in 1982. Once the road was secured, forces could wheel south toward Basra. Assembling twelve divisions for the operation, six each from the army and the Guards, on February 22 Iran launched "Operation Khaibar" (named after a Jewish village captured by Ali in Year Seven of the Muslim era) across the entire extent of the marsh. In the main thrust, amphibious forces, using speedboats, Hovercraft, and Styrofoam rafts, captured the two oil islands and laid a ten-mile pontoon bridge from Majnoon South to bring up reinforcements.

Advance parties of Guards crossed the Tigris and reached the road, and even the outskirts of the town of Qurna, where the Euphrates joins with the Tigris to form the Shatt al-Arab. They were driven back into marshes by overwhelming airpower and artillery. Iraq then attempted to recapture the islands, with the first use of chemical nerve agents, but the Iranian forces crammed onto the platforms held. After eight days of the heaviest fighting of the war, Iran was left in possession of the islands, which it annexed and renamed Khaibar. In a more restricted operation in the flooded marshes in March 1985, known as "Operation Badr" (after another of the Prophet's battles), Guards again crossed the Tigris and captured the highway and again were driven back by Iraqi helicopters and armor. Saddam responded by launching a second "War of the Cities."

The tide was turning again. Iran was underequipped in all arms, while Iraq, financed by its rich allies on the Gulf, had rebuilt its air force with French Mirage fighters and Soviet MiG-25 high-altitude bombers and gained air supremacy. During Operation Badr, a Guards commander said: "The sky is full of Iraqi planes, and we have nothing in response, hardly even anything to shoot them down."[73] In contrast, Iran could keep airworthy only some fifty F-4 Phantoms and perhaps thirty F-14 Tomcats at any one time. Mohsen Rafiqdoust, the principal arms buyer for the Guards, persuaded Muammar Gaddafi to deliver Soviet Scud-B long-range surface-to-surface missiles and antiaircraft missiles. On the ground, Saddam's new T62 and T72 tanks were impermeable to the Guards' rocket-propelled grenades and were a match for the Iranian Chieftains, with their inadequate power-packs and tendency to overheat. In 1986, the old Iraqi palace guard known as the Republican Guard was expanded from a division to a corps of six divisions and recruited from the universities and technical colleges. Iraqi Military Intelligence managed to break the Iranian army codes.

CHAPTER 14

Convoys of Light

◇

*Happy are those who departed this world in martyr-
dom! Happy are those who ventured their lives in this
convoy of light! Happy are those who nurtured these
jewels in their laps!*

—Ruhollah Khomeini[1]

Above all, Saddam turned his attention to the waters of the Persian
Gulf, launching attack after attack on Iran's export terminal at Kharg
Island and tankers approaching it, sending out helicopters from a new
base at Umm Qasr and laying contact mines. His purpose in what
became known as "the Tanker War" was to provoke Iranian retaliation, draw in his maritime neighbors on the Arab shore of the Gulf,
and eventually force the great powers to intervene to secure the free
flow of oil. In that he was to succeed, but it was to take three more
years of bloodletting. Meanwhile, there occurred an episode which was
to shake Khomeini's government to its root and prove as decisive for
the future of the Islamic Republic as the battles at the front.[2] The episode, generally known as the Iran-Contra Affair, is documented in its
American aspect. The Iranian half of the story, with its roots lost in
the obscurity of Savak and its revolutionary successor, is not easy to
uncover.

At its simplest, the Guards needed weapons to deal with the T72s,
which were almost impossible to disable with an RPG rocket launcher
except from a range of 30 yards and a shot to the turret.[3] They had
in mind advanced American guided missiles such as the TOW (tube-
launched, optically-tracked, wire-guided) missile first deployed in

307

Vietnam. Iran also required surface-to-air missiles to protect Kharg Island and the air bases. In the end, there was talk of long-range artillery and importing U.S. or, at least, U.S.-trained technicians to bring the inoperable Phoenix missiles at Isfahan back into service.[4]

The opportunity arose in 1984 when Shia militants in Lebanon, operating under the front name of Islamic Jihad, kidnapped several foreigners, including four Americans. On March 16, 1984, William Buckley, CIA's head of station, was abducted from his apartment block in West Beirut and taken to the Bekaa Valley. Videotape of his interrogation, and the marks of torture on his face and upper body, were dispatched to Washington. President Reagan, a man who was often led by his heart, was desperate to secure the release of the U.S. citizens. Though it degenerated into a mere racket, the Iran-Contra Affair began in sympathy.

The trade started with an itinerant weapons merchant and former Savaki named Manucher Ghorbanifar. Despite his poor English, since 1980 he had been offering the CIA intelligence of doubtful veracity. After he failed two lie-detector tests, the CIA on July 25, 1984, issued a so-called Burn Notice, warning other U.S. agencies that Ghorbanifar "should be regarded as an intelligence fabricator and a nuisance."[5] He was also a double-crosser, but the Americans did not know that.

Undeterred and perhaps undeterrable, Ghorbanifar turned to General Manuchehr Hashemi, the former head of the Eighth Bureau (Counterespionage) of Savak, who had smashed a weak KGB operation in Tehran in 1977 and 1978 and had admirers in Washington.[6] In Hamburg that November, Hashemi introduced Ghorbanifar to a veteran of the CIA in Vietnam, Theodore Shackley. At the meeting, Ghorbanifar said that his contacts in Iran could arrange for the ransoming of the hostages. The State Department was not impressed. Ghorbanifar then approached the Israelis, who were anxious to recover their old relationship with Iran, to injure Saddam and the Arabs in general, to offload decayed munitions and replenish them from the United States, and make some money. David Kimche, a British-born intelligence officer who was now director general of the Israeli Foreign Ministry, later said: "We had very deep relations with Iran, cutting deep into the fabric of the two peoples. It was difficult for people to accept the fact that all of this intimacy was thrown out of the window."[7]

Congress would determine afterwards that it was the Israeli endorsement of Ghorbanifar that was fatal.[8]

In July, Kimche came to Washington and convinced Robert "Bud" McFarlane, Reagan's national security adviser, that certain circles in Iran were keen to reestablish relations with the United States and were willing to free the hostages as evidence of their bona fides.[9] William Sullivan's old fantasy, the Iranian "moderate," rose from the grave of revolution. In return, McFarlane was told a little later, the "moderates" wanted to buy 100 TOW missiles to improve their standing with the military. Reagan, then in hospital for cancer treatment, ignored objections from his secretaries of state and defense and approved the transaction.

From August 1985 to November 1986, Iran received seven shipments of military equipment invoiced at $48 million, first from Israeli stocks and then directly from the U.S. military inventory. Iran received a total of 2,004 TOW and 18 Hawk air-defense missiles plus spare parts for the Hawk system. Three American hostages were freed. (Buckley had been tortured to death.)

With no trust between the two sides, the deliveries required dubious middlemen and far-flung locations. As well as Ghorbanifar, the chief actors were Colonel Oliver North, like McFarlane a Marine Corps veteran at the National Security Council, and two businessmen, former Air Force general Richard Secord and the Iranian-American Albert Hakim; and, in Israel, associates and friends of Prime Minister Shimon Peres in business and government, including Jackob Nimrodi, an arms dealer who had been part of the first Mossad mission to Savak in the 1960s. Adnan Khashoggi, a free-spending Saudi arms dealer, provided bridging finance. The weapons were sold to the Iranians at mark-ups of 100 percent or more, and the profits used for commissions and bribes (including, Ghorbanifar said, in Iran),[10] and to sidestep a congressional ban on assistance to the anti-Communist rebels in Nicaragua, known as "Contras." The diversion of the profits or "residuals" to the Contras became the prime incentive for North. The Iranian side kidnapped three more Americans in Lebanon to replenish the security.[11]

The first shipment of ninety-six TOWs, packed on pallets of twelve apiece, was delivered to Mehrabad on August 30, 1985, in an unmarked Israeli DC-8 aircraft. No hostages were freed. Ghorbanifar claimed that the Guards had seized the missiles at the airport and that the "moderates" felt cheated. A second shipment on September 14 of 408 TOWs went to Tabriz, and this time the Reverend Benjamin Weir, a Presbyterian minister kidnapped in May 1984, was freed. There followed the first of several setbacks. For a delivery of eighty Hawk missiles in November, Portugal refused to grant transshipment rights through Lisbon. Because of the delay, the lease for the waiting Israeli aircraft expired. Oliver North finagled an aircraft from a CIA front company that turned out to have a cargo capacity of only eighteen missiles. After test-firing one missile, the Iranians found it lacked the 70,000-foot altitude they wanted. Nine of the missiles were marked with the Star of David, which the Iranians took as a calculated insult. They demanded a refund. No hostage was freed.

In December in London, McFarlane for the first time met Ghorbanifar. He was aghast, describing the Iranian as "the most despicable man" he had ever encountered and a "borderline moron."[12] Having now left office, he urged President Reagan to drop both the initiative and Ghorbanifar, who failed all but two questions of another polygraph test on January 11, 1986. ("This is a guy who lies with zest," a CIA officer commented.)[13] McFarlane's successor, Vice Admiral John Poindexter, persisted with both. On January 17, Reagan signed a new finding authorizing the trade with the goal of "establishing a more moderate government in Iran" and "furthering the release of the American hostages held in Beirut."[14] Rather than dispatch superannuated Israeli equipment, the CIA would purchase arms directly from the Pentagon. The United States thus became a direct supplier to Iran. Ghorbanifar was now telling Colonel North that Khomeini himself would stand down on the seventh anniversary of the victory of the Revolution: February 11, 1986.[15]

North and his associates arranged the sale of 1,000 TOWs in February, along with some intelligence on the Iraqi order of battle, but again the deliveries yielded no hostages. By now, Iran had captured the island of Fao and established forces on Iraqi territory. On May 25, 1986, at 9 a.m. a U.S. delegation including McFarlane and North, a Persian-speaking CIA veteran, George Cave, two communications specialists, and a Peres aide named Amiram Nir, left the United States without preparation for Tehran. They carried Irish passports issued under false names. With them were twelve pallets of Hawk spares, a couple of Colt handguns as presents, and also a chocolate cake that North had bought from a kosher bakery during the layover in Tel Aviv, iced with a skeleton key to symbolize the breakthrough in relations.[16] In Iran, it was Ramazan, the fasting month. They were not expected. After staring at one another for two hours in the VIP lounge at Mehrabad, they were whisked by the Foreign Ministry by way of the parkway to the former Hilton Hotel, now known as the Independence Hotel, in the northern suburbs of Tehran, and isolated on the fifteenth floor. Back at Mehrabad, the Hawk spares were carted off and the Guards wolfed the cake.[17]

Ghorbanifar and the Israelis had promised McFarlane meetings with Hashemi Rafsanjani, Prime Minister Mir Hosein Musavi, and President Khamenei. The Iranians, remembering what happened to Bazargan after meeting Brzezinski in Algiers in 1979, presented a strident junior Foreign Ministry official named Kangarlou ("little artichoke") and, some time later, the head of the Foreign Affairs Committee of Parliament. It was as if, McFarlane cabled Poindexter, "after nuclear attack, a surviving cobbler became Vice President; and a bookie became the interlocutor for all discourse with foreign countries."[18] After three and a half days, McFarlane took the delegation away. At Tel Aviv Airport, North tapped him on the shoulder and whispered: "Don't worry, Bud, it's not a total loss. At least we're using some of the Ayatollah's money in Central America."[19]

McFarlane reported on the Tehran fiasco to the president. A second hostage, Father Lawrence Martin Jenco, was released in late July and twelve further pallets of Hawk spare parts were flown to Bandar Abbas on August 3. Rather than end the trade, somebody took the catastrophic decision to cut Ghorbanifar out of the operation and explore a contact of Hakim's in Tehran. The Second Channel, as it was known, though it was identical to the first, entailed direct dealings with Ali Hashemi Bahramani, a nephew of Hashemi Rafsanjani's known as "The Relative," and a Guards intelligence officer or civilian known as "The Engine." Bahramani dazzled the Americans. He was invited to Washington and Colonel North gave him a clandestine tour of the Oval Office.

The Iranians, who were punctilious in payment, grumbled about the overcharging. At a meeting in Frankfurt in October 1986, North handed Bahramani a copy of the Bible inscribed by Reagan with a verse from St. Paul that stressed the common descent of Muslims and Christians from the Patriarch Abraham.[20] An officer of imagination, North said that the president had spent a weekend in prayer at Camp David before signing the book. One last shipment of 500 TOWs was made in late October, which resulted in the release of the hostage David Jacobsen, a hospital administrator, but by then three more U.S. hostages had been taken. The day after Jacobsen's release, November 3, a Lebanese newsmagazine broke the story of the McFarlane visit to Tehran.

In unraveling what occurred, it is necessary to reconcile two sets of Iranian sources. Hosein Ali Montazeri, who had been appointed successor presumptive to Khomeini in 1985, puts McFarlane at the heart of the scandal. Hashemi Rafsanjani, the Khomeini household, and the Intelligence Ministry make no mention of the American arms trade or the McFarlane visit whatsoever.

According to Montazeri, Ghorbanifar sent him photocopies of two letters he had written to Kangarlou in July that referred in detail to the McFarlane visit and the arms trade. Montazeri says that he was shocked at the Israeli connection and the implication that Iran was about to abandon "revolutionary activity overseas" (terrorism) to enter a new relationship with the United States.[21]

Montazeri was under the influence of a militant friend of his late son, Mohammed ("Ringo"), named Sayyid Mehdi Hashemi, a native of a village in the Isfahan oasis called Qahdarijan that had a tradition of religious violence going back to anti-Bahai riots of the later nineteenth century. Sayyid Mehdi's brother was married to Mohammed Montazeri's sister. Born in 1946, Sayyid Mehdi had attended the seminary, been conscripted, and then fallen under the spell of both *The Eternal Martyr* and Khomeini's Najaf lectures. In the early 1970s, his disciples went on a rampage of murder and mayhem in the Isfahan villages against landlords, those they considered immoral, and the quietist clergy. On April 7, 1976, his followers kidnapped and strangled with a handkerchief a respected congregational clergyman of Isfahan, Abol Hassan Shamsabadi. The murder caused a sensation in Pahlavi Iran, but Sayyid Mehdi escaped the gallows, whether because Mohammed Reza did not want to antagonize the clergy and Amnesty International or because, as Sayyid Mehdi later confessed (under duress), he had been turned by Savak.

Freed at the Revolution, Sayyid Mehdi became active both in the turbulent politics of Isfahan and the Qom Seminary and also, from a short-lived and chaotic bureau of the Guards called the Office for World Islamic Liberation Movements, in Afghanistan, Lebanon, and the Philippines. Khomeini thought him a hoodlum and detested him.[22] In late 1982, the Liberation Movements bureau was dissolved by Parliament, but Sayyid Mehdi hid the weapons and explosives he had assembled at a safe house in Tehran. In 1984, Khomeini appointed a supple clergyman named Mohammadi Reyshahri to head a new Ministry of Intelligence to bring the networks inherited from Savak and such loose cannons as Sayyid Mehdi under control of the Leader's Office.

According to Mohammadi Reyshahri, what provoked the crisis was the discovery of explosives in the safe house on Yusefabad Avenue on September 11. According to Montazeri, it was his protégé's hostility to the new relationship with the United States and the McFarlane mission. On October 4, Khomeini wrote to Montazeri demanding that he distance himself from an "accused murderer."[23] Montazeri wrote back in insubordinate language, saying that Sayyid Mehdi was a pious and committed Muslim and not a yes-man like the minister of intelligence and the commander of the Guards, Rezai.[24] On the 12th, Sayyid Mehdi and dozens of associates were arrested. Flyers protesting the arrest and describing "contacts with atheist countries," including the McFarlane mission, appeared in Tehran and Baalbek, Lebanon. At a meeting in Mainz, West Germany, on October 29, a panicked "Relative" reported to Colonel North that the story was out but was persuaded that they could ride the storm.[25] They could not. Either that day or the next, two Iranian emissaries called at the South Beirut offices of a little leftist magazine, *Al-Shiraa* (*The Sail*), and told the story of the McFarlane visit.[26] They had arrived by air. According to Montazeri, they had with them the Ghorbanifar letters. Though it was just four days to press, the owner-editor, a Lebanese Shia named Hassan Sabra, led the issue of November 3 with an account of the McFarlane mission and Montazeri's protest. The story inundated the news wires.

Hashemi Rafsanjani bluffed. The next day, he confirmed to Parliament that a four-man U.S. delegation had visited Iran, was "imprisoned in Iran for five days and afterward deported from the country."[27] There was no mention of Israelis. He used the cake (now key-shaped), the Bible from Reagan, and the two Colt handguns to fashion a comic burlesque of American oddity, submission, and "helplessness." Resolving that audacity was the only sanctuary, he told the merry deputies: "Why did he bring pistols? What we need is more sophisticated weapons." Reagan attempted to deny the story and then retreated into senescence, but the scandal shook his presidency and caused McFarlane to attempt suicide.

In Iran, Hashemi Rafsanjani and Ahmad Khomeini demanded to know Montazeri's source. "The jinns [fairies] told me," Montazeri said.[28] Such archness was to cost him. Sayyid Mehdi was broken by Reyshahri in a year of interrogation, and confessed on television to a catalogue of crimes, including the murder of Shamsabadi and cooperation with Savak. Montazeri protested that confessions under duress were unlawful. Ordinary Iranians wondered why a known Savaki who had murdered a devoted clergyman had been admitted into the Imam's house.[29] Khomeini appointed a sort of star chamber, called the Special Clerical Court. It met in Evin and found Sayyid Mehdi guilty of murder, terrorism, "sabotaging foreign relations," and another offense that was kept secret. On September 27, 1987, he became the first turbanned cleric to be executed in Iran since Fazlollah Nuri in 1908. It was the beginning of the end for Montazeri, for the scholastic basis of the Islamic Republic, and for the war.

In the pouring rain of February 9, 1986, in Operation "By the Dawn 8," Iran launched a three-pronged assault into Iraqi territory to regain the initiative in the war. While the northern thrusts by the army could not progress, an amphibious assault by a division of Guards crossed the tidal river near its mouth under heavy artillery support, established a beachhead on the marshy Fao peninsula, and captured the town of Fao on the 11th. Always quick to respond to battlefield developments, the Guards reinforced the Fao beachhead as a backdoor assault on Basra and Umm Qasr, the Iraqi naval base on the west side of the peninsula. The Iraqi high command, in contrast, continued to believe that the Fao attack was a diversion from an assault on the Sixth Corps at Majnoon, and was slow to respond.

Two Republican Guard brigades, advancing down a narrow road through the palm plantations, were enfiladed with missile and artillery fire from in front and from the east bank and disintegrated. Thick cloud hampered Iraqi air operations while the rain turned the ground to a quagmire, where infantry fought in mud to their knees in see-saw battles for a few yards. "Leaving there was like going from hell to heaven," an Iraqi general said later.[30] The ground was too marshy for tanks, and shells carrying chemical munitions (which are heavier than air) buried themselves twenty feet down in the mud before detonating. While the Guards were prevented from taking Umm Qasr by a battalion of Iraqi marines, they dug in around the saltworks known as Hawr al-Ahwar ("Marsh of marshes") at Fao behind reinforced concrete fortifications against air-burst shells. After the fiercest fighting of the war, Saddam Hussein recognized in late March that he would need time to dislodge the invader.

Khomeini announced that the year that began on March 21, 1986, would be "the year of destiny." The Corps of Guards planned a "final offensive" on Basra without precedent, involving no less than 1,500 battalions of volunteers or 450,000 men, the equivalent of the British Empire forces at the Somme in 1916. With the war in its sixth year, they had to settle for 300 battalions or 100,000 men, who were seen off at a rally at the Azadi (formerly Aryamehr) Stadium in Tehran and driven down in British-style double-decker buses to the front. The plan of attack was the Karbala 4 operational plan that had failed in the Ramazan offensive of July 1982, but with several differences that turned out to be insignificant. The battle was to take place in winter rather than summer, with better cloud cover against air attack and ground too sodden for the Iraqi armor. It was to be principally an operation of Guards and volunteers fighting at close quarters. Finally, the Guards had staged large-scale exercises in crossing water obstacles at Enzeli on the Caspian and had the experience of Fao behind them.

The first phase was a bloody fiasco. On December 24, 1986, there was an amphibious assault on the island of Umm al-Rassas ("Mother of Bullets") in the Shatt as a preliminary to cutting off the Fao peninsula and opening the way to Basra on the west bank of the river. The Iraqis were well prepared. The waterborne invasion ran into heavy fire, and the next morning the landing parties on Umm al-Rassas were overwhelmed and demolished from the air. The Iraqi Third Corps commander said his men had reaped "the largest crop of rotten heads" so far in the war.[31] The Reuters correspondent, brought to the scene on December 27, counted ninety-six fallen Iranians in a hundred-yard stretch.[32] The defeat, according to the Iranian army history, "plunged the Supreme Command into crisis"[33] Senior army officers opposed the continuation of the offensive. Rather than send the volunteers home, with small prospect of ever mustering such a force again, the Guards command resolved to have one last throw at Shalamcheh and Fish Lake, and the army agreed to provide artillery and helicopters and engineering support to surmount the water barriers.

This terrible battle, known as Karbala 5 in Iran and "The Great Day" in Iraq, began just before midnight on January 9, 1987. The Guards and volunteers reached the eastern side of Fish Lake, crossed the water in boats, and made a dash for the Shatt some ten miles distant. They were held by the Republican Guard and driven back to a salient about 500 yards deep on the western shore of the lake. A second assault through Shalamcheh penetrated the outer fortifications south of the lake. In hard fighting, the Iranians managed to reach the Jasim channel but could not gain more than a foothold on the further bank and never succeeded in linking up with the Fish Lake salient, which was collapsed at the end of the month. The Iranians had fought with valor and decency, but neither was adequate against the Iraqi fortifications and superior weaponry and an Iraqi army that had learned in seven years how to fight. I have heard that Iranian losses in the battle were 20,000 dead.

Iran was licked. The Guards' strategy had failed and they had no other. As the army historian wrote, "After these operations, the countdown began for the ending of the war."[34] On July 20, 1987, the UN Security Council unanimously adopted Resolution 598 calling for a cease-fire. The resolution, the sixth such by the Council since September 1980, made no mention of Iraqi reparations, nor did it condemn the Iraqi use of chemical weapons. As to who started the war, the secretary-general was to explore "the question of entrusting an impartial body with inquiring into the responsibility for the conflict."[35] It was a thin harvest for seven years of Iranian sacrifice and suffering. Unable to make peace or war, Iran neither accepted nor rejected the cease-fire but waited on events, which turned against it. Attempting to stage a demonstration at that year's pilgrimage to Mecca, the Iranian pilgrims were shot at by the Saudi security forces and over four hundred lost their lives.

With the Iranian armed forces spread out from Fao to Kurdestan, Iraq at last went on the offensive to recapture its territory. On March 16, 1988, Iraqi artillery and, according to eyewitnesses, aircraft dropped chemical agents on the town of Halabjeh in Iraqi Kurdestan, killing as many as 5,000 civilians. Ten days later, the Mojahedin "National Liberation Army," which had been established with Saddam's help at a camp north of Baghdad and provided with miscellaneous munitions, overran the Fakkeh sector in a twelve-hour attack called "Operation Sunshine," taking four hundred prisoners. The Iranian conscripts were astonished to see young women in combat and as battlefield medics. Morale, already sinking, plummeted the following month when the Iranians were driven from Fao. Laying gravel to support tanks, and preceded by a barrage of gas (which blew back), the Iraqi army pushed the Iranian garrison back over its pontoon bridges in under thirty-six hours. ("We did not even throw a shoe at them," an Iraqi intelligence agent later boasted to me in Basra.) Shalamcheh, the base for the attacks on Basra, was recaptured in May. In June, the Iranians were ejected from the Majnoon islands.

It was out over the sea that the war was finally decided. In response to Iraqi air attacks on tankers bound for Kharg Island, Iran retaliated against Iraq's Arab allies and financiers in the Gulf, principally Kuwait. By the middle of 1987, some 8 million tons of shipping had been destroyed (as much as the Allied tonnage sunk in 1942) and two hundred sailors killed.[36]

Kuwait appealed for assistance to both the Soviet Union and the United States. The day after Security Council Resolution 598, the U.S. Navy began operations to escort convoys of Kuwaiti vessels in the Gulf. On the morning of July 24, a Kuwaiti tanker renamed the *Bridgeton* and flying the U.S. flag struck a contact mine on its northward voyage. The U.S. Navy responded by boarding an Iranian troopship found laying mines, the *Iran Ajr*, and scuttling it. When a U.S. frigate, *Samuel B. Roberts*, struck a similar contact mine northeast of Qatar on April 13, 1988, the United States sank one of Iran's British-built frigates, the *Sahand*, disabled another, the *Sabalan*, and destroyed two oil platforms. By now, the United States was engaged in its largest naval action since

Korea. To add to the muddle and tension in the waterway, on May 17, 1988, an Iraqi Mirage F-1 fighter fired two 1,500-pound Exocet missiles at a Navy frigate, USS *Stark,* killing thirty-seven sailors. After the *Stark* incident, U.S. naval commanders in the Gulf were issued preemptive rules of engagement to protect their valuable commands.[37]

On July 3, 1988, a group of speedboats operated by the Guards tangled in the Straits of Hormuz with the new guided missile cruiser, the USS *Vincennes,* Captain Will C. Rogers commanding, and fired on one of its helicopters. At 10:13 a.m., *Vincennes* opened fire on the Guards' boats. Two minutes later, an Iran Air Airbus, carrying 290 passengers and crew, took off from Bandar Abbas Airport to the east, which had both military and civilian sectors, for the short flight down the commercial airway—known as Amber 59—to Dubai. In a flurry of misjudgments and mistaken assumptions, the *Vincennes* identified Iran Air 655 as an Iranian F-14 that had been transferred to the airfield on June 25, fired two surface-to-air missiles, and destroyed the airliner, killing all on board.

The destruction of Iran Air 655 left a profound impression in Iran. Iranians saw in the incident not an aggressive commander, untried technology, and a keyed-up crew, but a U.S. determination to bring an end to the war in Iraq's favor. "It was not a mistake," Rafiqdoust of the Guards said later. "Not at all. It was a warning by the Americans that they had come to the region."[38] Hashemi Rafsanjani, who had been appointed acting commander in chief in June, wrote in his diary: "It is an astonishing crime."[39] He was more than ever convinced that continuing the war could do the Revolution a lasting injury. The *Vincennes* incident also gave the Revolutionary Guards, without admitting defeat, a justification for armistice. It was their own *Dolchstosslegende,* as it was known in Germany after World War I, the stab in the back. They had been bested not by a tinhorn Arab, but by the most powerful nation on earth.

Before approaching Khomeini, and to protect his own position, Hashemi Rafsanjani commissioned from the Guards' command a list of their requirements to continue fighting.[40] In his response, Mohsen Rezai, the Guards' commander, wrote that the tide of war would not turn for five years: "If we deploy 350 infantry brigades and purchase 2,500 tanks, 3,000 artillery pieces, 300 warplanes and 300 helicopters, and master the manufacture of a substantial arsenal of laser and nuclear weapons which by then will be among the necessities of modern warfare, then, God willing, we can think of going on the offensive." Though Rezai appealed to continue the war, his words said the precise opposite, and Khomeini, seeing through it, called the letter "mere phrase-making." Prime Minister Musavi said the economy was on its knees.

At a meeting in the president's office on July 19, Ahmad Khomeini read out his father's decision: "Since commanders of both Army and Guards, who are specialists, openly admit that the Muslim army will not be victorious for some time and in the light of the recent setbacks and the enemy's wide use of chemical munitions and our lack of equipment to neutralise them, I give my consent to a ceasefire."[41] That day, President Khamenei wrote to UN Secretary-General Perez de Cuellar to say that Iran accepted Security Council Resolution 598. In a long statement, read out on Radio Tehran the next day, Khomeini expressed his bitterness and regret: "Had it not been for the interests of Islam and the Muslims, I would not have accepted this, and would have preferred death and martyrdom. Acceptance is more lethal to me than poison. Nonetheless, I drink this chalice of poison for the sake of the Almighty and for His satisfaction."[42] He then retired to his house and did not appear to the general public again.

In the eight years of war, Iran by its own computation had lost 123,220 men dead in action, with a further 60,711 missing in action (including deserters and prisoners of war), which was later increased to 72,753. Because, in the early years of the war, many of the volunteers were not registered, the death toll was certainly higher, though perhaps not by a great number. Ten years later, the Guards were still searching the battlefields for bodies. In addition, about 11,000 Iranian civilians died as a result of enemy action.[43] It was the greatest catastrophe to befall Iran since the Mongol invasions of the Middle Ages.

Disengagement was to have its own horrors. Fearful that S.C. Resolution 598 would spell the end of the Mojahedin, Masoud Rajavi, and his wife, Maryam, pleaded with Saddam to delay the implementation of the cease-fire. Keen to maintain pressure on Iran, Saddam gave the Mojahedin a week. At Camp Ashraf, the Mojahedin base near the town of Khalis in Diyala Province, a force was mustered and equipped with surplus Iraqi equipment, including Brazilian tanks. Masoud Banisadr, a cousin of the disgraced president, was shown how to fire a Kalashnikov. The bang "sent him reeling." At a meeting in the camp, Masoud Rajavi said they should not halt until they reached Khomeini's house in Jamaran. "We will not be fighting alone," he said. "We will have the people on our side."[44]

On July 25, the so-called National Liberation Army, numbering some 7,000 men and women, crossed the Iranian frontier at Qasr-e Shirin, climbed the Paitak Pass that General Slim had bypassed in 1941, and captured the town of Kerend. Advancing on the road without support and Iraqi air cover, they were halted before Kermanshah, and on July 29, they were bombed to pieces from the air. Many abandoned their tanks because they could not operate them and were terrified of being incinerated.[45] They left behind some 1,300 dead either in battle or to lynching. Banisadr woke up under anesthetic in a Baghdad dressing station. All around in the operating light were naked boys and girls, and the surgeons who were amputating their limbs.[46]

The horror was to be matched in Iran. According to the penal theory that had developed since the Revolution, the prisoners of the Islamic Republic were sick and the prisons their infirmaries. Evin was divided into two institutes. Prisoners were held first in solitary confinement, until they signed a confession and were sentenced. To encourage them, interrogators would apply to a judge for "discretionary punishment," which generally consisted of a beating on the soles of the feet with "His Excellency Lord Cable," such as a truck or tractor fan belt. Once they had confessed, they might be moved to the communal blocks, where they would be exposed to intensive religious education.[47] In a sort of no-man's-land of this system, there were in the summer of 1988 several thousand Mojahedin prisoners who had served out their sentences but, because they had not recanted, had not been released. Those men and women were known in prison slang as *mellikeshha* or "Lotto winners."

On July 28, while the battle for Kermanshah was yet in the balance, Ahmad Khomeini wrote down from his father's dictation the following opinion or *fatwa*:

In the Name of God the Compassionate, the Merciful,
Since the treacherous Hypocrites in no way believe in Islam and whatever they say arises in their deceit and hypocrisy;

And since the claims of their leaders have revealed they are renegades from Islam;

And since they wage war on God and pursue conventional warfare in the west, north and south of Iran in co-operation with the Baath Party of Iraq, and conduct espionage on behalf of Saddam against our Muslim nation;

And seeing that they are allied to the World Bullies [Britain and the United States] and have inflicted cowardly blows on the Islamic Republic's order since its foundation until now;

It is hereby decreed that those who are in prisons throughout the country who have remained and still remain steadfast in their Hypocrisy are Wagers of War on God and are condemned to death.

The task of executing this decree in Tehran is entrusted to the Proof of Islam, Mr. Nayyeri (May his bounty overflow!) as Holy Law Judge and his Excellency Mr. Eshraqi, the Public Prosecutor of Tehran, and a Representative of the Intelligence Ministry. Though unanimity is to be preferred, a simple majority will suffice.

Likewise, in the prisons of the country's provincial capitals, the majority opinion of the Holy Law Judge, the Revolutionary Prosecutor or Assistant Prosecutor, and the Representative of the Intelligence Ministry is binding.

To show clemency to those who make war on God is simple-minded. Islamic decisiveness in dealing with the enemies of God is one of the indubitable principles of the Islamic System. I hope that my revolutionary indignation and rancour towards the enemies of Islam will earn the satisfaction of God Almighty and that those gentlemen entrusted with carrying out this matter will not waver, doubt or hesitate but endeavour to be "The Hammers of Infidelity." Any hesitation in enforcing Islamic revolutionary justice is to avert the eyes from the pure and spotless blood of the martyrs. And so peace on you. Ruhollah Musavi Khomeini.[48]

Hossein Ali Nayyeri and Morteza Eshraqi arrived in Evin on the 29th. According to survivors' reports, the Mojahedin prisoners were called in batches to the tribunals, and asked if they renounced their affiliation. Those who answered in the negative were taken out to execution, the men mostly by hanging, the women by firing squad. One leftist secular prisoner recalled:

We had a loudspeaker in our ward and were able to listen to the radio news and heard that the government had accepted the UN Resolution. But after the ceasefire the guards came and took the televisions and newspapers and books and we didn't get any more papers and the family visits stopped. Then they came and took four MKO [Mojahedin-e Khalq Organization] girls from our ward. One of them came back to the ward later and talked to other MKO prisoners who told us "they are killing everyone." At night we could hear chants of "God is Great!" and "Death to the Hypocrites!" and then we would hear shooting. They would come each day and call a few more MKO so other prisoners would come and stand with them in the hallway to say goodbye and to cry. We just walked the MKO girls round the ward and told them stories to distract them. The MKO girls had all packed their bags to give to their families and we discussed how to keep the packages small in case big packages were not delivered.[49]

There was a lull in mid-August, to coincide with the first ten days of the mourning month of Moharram, by which time 750 prisoners had been killed in Evin and Gowhardasht prisons in Tehran. Then the executions resumed, this time of Communist prisoners on grounds of apostasy from Islam. Montazeri surmised that Khomeini had issued a second judgment or *fatwa*. If there was such an order, it has not been published. According to Montazeri, at least 2,800 prisoners were executed.[50]

In his lectures on *Islamic Government*, Khomeini had quoted the example of the Prophet, who in a single day beheaded all the men of a Jewish tribe for plotting against Islam. "They were damaging Islam and Islamic government so he annihilated them," Khomeini said.[51] That may be, but his ruling altered the course of the Islamic Republic. Hosein Ali Montazeri, since 1985 his designated successor, who had lost his son Mohammed at the bombing of the Islamic Republic Party headquarters in 1981 and was no lover of the Mojahedin, was aghast. He consulted the Koran. On July 31, he wrote to Khomeini, criticizing his order as an "act of vengeance and spite," inexpedient and unlawful. For good measure, he quoted at his old master a Tradition or saying of the Prophet that enjoined mercy.[52] He wrote again five days later. In a newspaper interview, and then again in a speech in Qom on the tenth anniversary of the Revolution the following February, he railed against the abridgment of liberties in Iran, the bloodthirsty sloganeering, the mismanagement of the war, and the sacrifice of principle to the exercise of power. Then he broke what, even today, is an Iranian taboo: "Did we prevail in the war?" he asked. "Or did the enemies who imposed it emerge as the victors?"[53]

Although his powers were ebbing, Khomeini had one more fight in him. On the morning of February 14, 1989, two days after Montazeri's speech, he sentenced to death the British-Indian writer Salman Rushdie. Brought up in a Muslim household in Bombay, Rushdie had lost his faith one day at the age of fifteen at Rugby School in England and celebrated by eating a ham sandwich.[54] Attracted to a new style of fictional literature, which liked to disrupt the ancient unities of style, narrative, and point of view, Rushdie in September 1988 published a long novel under the title *The Satanic Verses*. Diffused through a tale of Indian immigrants in England were dreams and fantasies in which there appeared, in fictional postures and lights, the Prophet of Islam, his wives, Mecca, the Koran, the Angel Gabriel, and Khomeini himself.[55] Rushdie took his title from the name in the West for an ancient and disputed Muslim Tradition that Mohammed had recited—at the dictation not of Gabriel but of the Devil—two verses favorable to polytheism, which he later repudiated.[56] The novelist Angela Carter described the book in her review in the *Guardian* as "a rollercoaster ride over a vast landscape of the imagination."[57] In contrast, the book brought protests from Muslims in Britain and in Pakistan and Indian-administered Kashmir.

Why Khomeini chose to condemn that author, that literary work, and at that time is not obvious to me. Some older Iranians thought their leader had become anxious that his successors might readmit the British, and the *fatwa* was designed to prevent that. Khomeini was thus like Hamilcar entrusting his son Hannibal with continuing the fight against Rome.[58] Others say that he wanted to show that the revolutionary fire of 1979 was not quenched or neutralized by the Chalice of Poison and that—very particularly—it was not to be taken over by the Sunni mainstream or (as Khomeini had put it in 1944) "the camel-grazers of Riyadh."

Early in March, Khomeini was infuriated to hear on the BBC the two letters Montazeri had written about the postwar executions. (According to Baqer Moin of the Persian Service, they had come to the broad-caster by way of Bani-Sadr's office in Paris.)[59] He ordered the Assembly of Experts to convene to reopen the question of the succession. On March 26, he wrote Montazeri a bitter and insulting letter, which was not published for ten years. In the letter, whose authenticity has been questioned, Khomeini stated:

> Since it has become apparent that after me you are going to hand over this country and the beloved Islamic Revolution of the Muslim people of Iran to the Liberals, and by way of them to the Hypocrites, you have no competence or legal right to succeed me. . . . Since you are a gull-ible person and easily agitated, do not interfere in political matters and perhaps then God will forgive your sins. Do not write to me ever again and do not allow the Hypocrites to pass state secrets to foreign radio stations. By God, I swear that from the beginning I never wanted you chosen as my successor.[60]

Time was running out. With Montazeri stripped of his titles and privileges, the succession was now up in the air. The problem was that those jurists considered to be "Sources of Imitation"—Golpayegani, Marashi-Najafi, and Shariatmadari—did not believe in clerical dic-tatorship. Khomeini's pupils did, but of them only Montazeri was an eminent scholar, and he was disgraced. So, as for Mossadeq and Mohammed Reza, for Khomeini the Constitution was at fault.

On April 24, Khomeini convened a body that called itself the Assembly for Revising the Constitution. Twenty of the members were appointed by Khomeini, five by Parliament. The Assembly duly amended the articles requiring that the Leader or *rahbar* be a divine of the first rank or "Source of Imitation" and, in default of such a scholar, a collegiate leadership (Articles 5, 107–12).[61] With one stroke, Kho-meini cut out from clerical government its scholastic basis. The "Stew-ardship of the Jurist" turned out to be just a mechanism for attaining power, and the Islamic Republic, after all, just another nationalist state, of which there was at the time no shortage in the Near East. At the same time, the Assembly abolished the post of prime minister.

Having made those arrangements to ensure the survival of his pol-ity, Khomeini prepared to face his Maker.

Ruhollah Musavi Khomeini died after repeated heart failure just before midnight on Saturday June 3, 1989, at the clinic near his house in Jamaran in the northern Tehran suburbs. His revolutionary companions, led by Hashemi Rafsanjani, the speaker of Parliament, and President Ali Khamenei, were at his bedside and resolved to delay the announcement to allow time to prepare the body; to impose a state of emergency; to put the borders on alert against Iraqi attack; and to lay plans for an orderly succession to Khomeini as *rahbar* or Leader.

Even so, rumors flew through the city and crowds began to make their way to Jamaran. It was not until seven o'clock on the Sunday morning that Radio Tehran announced his death. One newspaper ran the splash heading: "Imam Ascends to Highest Angelic Realm."[62] Dressed in black, people poured into the streets and mosques, or set out from the provincial cities, the women in their full-length black prayer chadors. At 9 a.m. in the Parliament building, Khamenei (known for his beautiful diction) read out Khomeini's last will and testament to the body of leading clerics known as the Assembly of Experts. With all the members in tears, the reading of the will, signed on February 15, 1983, took three hours. It opened with an attack on the Saudi royal family, a bugbear of Khomeini's since the 1920s. Convening again in the afternoon, the Assembly elected Ali Khamenei, though just fifty years old and not a prominent jurist, to be Leader. He tried to refuse, not just out of the Iranian courtesy known as *taarof*, but from the heart.[63] Hashemi Rafsanjani told the delegates that when he and some others had raised the question of succession after Montazeri's disgrace, and complained of a lack of suitable candidates, Khomeini said: "On the contrary, you have Mr. Khamenei."[64]

Early on Monday, June 5, Khomeini's body was transferred from Jamaran to the dusty vacant lot in northwest Tehran used for public prayers and sacrifices on the religious holidays, and known as the Musalla. On a high podium made out of steel shipping containers, Khomeini lay wrapped in a white shroud in an air-conditioned glass case, the indigo turban of a descendant of the Prophet on his chest. By midmorning, hundreds of thousands of mourners had come to bid farewell, beating their chests and drawing blood from their cheeks, crying, "We are orphaned!" (*yatim shodim*). In the crush to approach the body, eight people lost their lives and hundreds more were injured.

Amid clouds of dust and in blinding heat the Tehran fire brigade sprayed the mourners with jets of water, both to calm the excitement and also as an element of ritual. Iranian history is a sort of passion play, a constant recitation of the foundation tragedy of Shia Islam, which is the Prophet's family, ringed by murderous enemies and tormented by heat and thirst, at Karbala in Iraq in October 680. Many in the crowd were mourning not a revolutionary leader or a canon jurist, but the "Imam," a title applied in Iran up to then only to the perfect Shia saints of the Middle Ages.

It was decided that Khomeini should be buried not in Qom— where he had spent his years as a seminary professor until his exile by Mohammed Reza in 1964—but in the graveyard of the dead of the war and Revolution on the Qom road, Behesht-e Zahra or "the Paradise of Fatemeh the Radiant." This was ritual of a political type, for it reenacted in mourning Khomeini's triumphant visit by helicopter to the cemetery on the day of his return from exile, February 1, 1979.

Early on the morning of Tuesday, June 6, the body was brought down from its makeshift pyramid and the coffin opened for old Golpayegani to lead the prayers. Those twenty minutes were the only funerary solemnity a Westerner might have recognized. The plan was to set off south in orderly procession the twenty-five miles through town, but the crowds had swelled even from Monday. The numbers ran to several millions. Mohsen Rafiqdoust, who knew something about Tehran crowds, thought there were 8 million. "From the north of Tehran to Behesht-e Zahra," wrote Baqer Moin, "nothing could be seen but a black sea of mourners dotted only by the white turbans of some mollahs." [65]

The air-conditioned truck acting as hearse could make no progress through the crowds, and neither water cannon nor warning shots from the Revolutionary Guards could clear a path. In the end, in that mingling of metaphysics and aviation that has been such a feature of this story, the body was transferred to a helicopter and brought by air to a grave that had been hacked with mattocks out of the stony desert.

Yet even here, the crowd surged past the makeshift barriers. John Kifner of the *New York Times* wrote that "The body of the Ayatollah, wrapped in a white burial shroud, fell out of the flimsy wooden coffin, and in a mad scene people in the crowd reached to touch the shroud." [66] A frail white leg was uncovered. The shroud was torn to pieces for relics. Khomeini's son Ahmad was knocked from his feet. Men jumped into the grave. At one point, the Guards lost hold of the body. Firing in the air, the soldiers drove the crowd back, retrieved the body, and brought it to the helicopter, but mourners clung to the landing gear before they could be shaken off. The body was taken back to North Tehran to go through the ritual of preparation a second time.

To thin the crowd, it was announced by television and radio that the funeral had been postponed. Five hours later, the sound of rotors could be heard over Behesht-e Zahra and this time the Guards were better prepared. Three of Mohammed Reza's old Huey helicopters landed, and the body brought out sealed in what Kifner described as "a metal box resembling an airline shipping container." Once again, men broke through the cordon and reached the container, but by weight of numbers the Guards pushed through to the grave.

There, according to the reporters for *Time* magazine, "the metal lid of the casket was ripped off, and the body was rolled into the grave. The grave was quickly covered with concrete slabs and a large freight container."[67] In succeeding years, the Republic erected on the site a monumental mosque and shrine to Khomeini, fit to match the great monuments of the Shia at Karbala and Najaf, Mashhad, Qom and Lucknow.

For the outside world, for non-Shia Muslims, and for the Iranian *émigrés,* the funeral was "bizarre, frightening—and ultimately incomprehensible," as *Time* magazine said. Here was not tragedy but farce, idolatrous, makeshift, homicidal, frivolous, unmanly, and lacking in self-control. Tehran Radio said that 10,000 people were treated that day for self-inflicted wounds, heat exhaustion, and crush injuries.

For the Iranians, on the contrary, those events were evidence of what they prize above all things: unaffected sympathy, or what they call *del* or heart. The people wished to commemorate a revolution that seemed to stand outside the course of Iranian history, and the champion who had made it possible. Khomeini's funeral was also (or so it seems to me) an act of mourning for an Iranian way of life, antiquated perhaps, but not without amenity, that itself has been tipped into the earth and covered over with concrete.

Khomeini displayed traits of character that were to the Iranians appealing. Those were an indifference to phenomena, known in Persian as *tavakkol,* whether stepping into a helicopter or bathing in the sea; unbending determination; probity in matters of money; and if I may say so, a species of verbal wit of spotless propriety. Within Creation, he seemed to be but imperfectly detained, like a passenger in an airport lounge in thick weather. Yet for all his implacable will, he could have his mind changed, and in such matters as democracy, the powers of the state, and the rights and duties of women, he ended his life a long way from where he started.

In his home life he was said to be affectionate, but he could be surly, even rude, to strangers, and some Iranians regretted the exquisite courtesy of old Borujerdi. It is said that once in Isfahan, the great Safavid divine Majlisi gave an apple to a Jew. Once in Tyre in the 1970s, Moussa Sadr bought an ice cream from a Christian.[68] No such stories are told of Ruhollah Khomeini.

He has few admirers outside Iran. In the West, having done with Scholasticism centuries ago, we cannot understand a man who could know so much and, at the same time, so little. His mystical writings pass over our heads and his political statements, with their exaggerations and inaccuracies, beneath our notice. We wonder how, precisely, he explained to God the spots of blood on his robe and turban and the boys he left behind at Fish Lake.

Epilogue

◇

I cried: O Fate, you slept and now the sun is high!
She said: Do not despair, for all that has gone by.
—Hafez[1]

The state that Khomeini made has lasted. "God's Government," as he called it on April 1, 1979, is now in its fourth decade in Iran. The population since the Revolution has doubled (to about 75 million) and the country and its institutions have come unscathed through the decades of turmoil on its land borders. The Soviet Union disintegrated, the Baath was driven from power in Iraq, Western armies came into Afghanistan, but Iran continued on its solitary way.

Bin-Ladenism, which was the response of the extreme Sunni sectarians to the success of the Iranian Revolution, failed to provoke the Iranians into a fight and is now in decline. Despite the murder by the Taliban of ten Iranian diplomats and a journalist in Afghanistan and the dynamiting of the mosque in Samarra where the Tenth and Eleventh Imams lie buried, the Iranians refused to be drawn.[2]

At home, the bloodletting of the Revolution and its aftermath abated and the scum stirred up in 1979 sank back down into the sediment of an ancient society. In 1998, and again the following year, I was able to return to Iran and found a country that, though still attached to the language of war and revolution, was entirely becalmed. My friends had contrived to get on no better under Islamic government than under the monarchy. I was struck by the loss of amenity in Iranian life. Those who make great revolutions forget that prisons and torture chambers survive into the new era, but good manners, good food, the small pleasures of family life, and literary excellence all go to hell. What the Iranians most wished for they never gained, and what they most sought to preserve they lost.

The price of crude oil, in retreat since the early years of the war with Iraq, fell at the end of 1998 to a price in constant money not seen since World War II. Hashemi Rafsanjani, in his two terms as president (1989–97), attempted to repair the damage of war but was hampered by lack of revenue. Unwilling to raise oil production to the levels of Mohammed Reza's glory days, for lack of investment in the producing fields the Islamic Republic found it could not do so. The country slid into commercial mediocrity. The population outstripped the capacity to provide for it and it was thirty years before Iran achieved the per capita GDP of Mohammed Reza's time and, then, not for long.[3] A clientele of public employees, war veterans, and pensioners was maintained by printing money whose purchasing power decayed. Young men and women left the country and the cash and labor spent on their education was lost to the republic. Meanwhile, Iranian émigrés in North America helped found abroad businesses of which just one (Google Inc.) is more valuable than the entire Tehran Stock Exchange.[4]

In June 1997, a dapper clergyman of great charm and literary education, Mohammed Khatami, was elected president in a landslide. He sought to dispel the atmosphere of social gloom, encourage public expression, and open Iran to the world. He soon fell afoul of the Intelligence Ministry, the judiciary, and the Guardian Council. The checks and balances introduced with such care by the framers of the Constitution in 1979 ensured that the reformists could not reform.

The rise in the price of crude oil in the new century brought with it a new Iranian self-assertion. Mahmoud Ahmadinejad, elected president to succeed Khatami in 2005, attempted to revive the spirit of 1982 and pursue Iran's special destiny as the enemy of America and Israel and the favorite of the Lord of the Age. Research into nuclear physics, launched during the war but suspended or frozen when U.S. forces invaded Iraq in 2003 on the pretext of ending Saddam's nuclear ambitions, was revived. Ahmadinejad trumpeted Iran's success in mastering physics taught to high school students and manufacturing processes routine in the West and Russia for nearly seventy years. In 2007, a bank note of 50,000 rials was printed with a drawing of electrons circling an atomic nucleus and a sentence attributed to the Prophet: "If there were godliness in the Pleiades, one or other of them [Iranians] would still find it."[5] The president failed to draw the connection between his scientific pretensions and the all-but-worthless paper money.

Mohammed Reza had signed the United Nations' Nuclear Non-Proliferation Treaty in 1968. There is no evidence that he intended to use the nuclear reactors he ordered for Bushehr to produce explosive for a weapon. His strategy was to build up conventional forces to deter and dominate his neighbors while relying on the United States to restrain the Soviet Union.[6] He did seek to have access to those technologies and processes (uranium enrichment and the chemical treatment of spent reactor fuel) that can be used to produce bomb explosive, but did not press the matter.

The Islamic Republic is different. The present leaders share Khomeini's dislike and distrust of a Pahlavi-style standing army, while the war with Iraq revealed the limits of the Corps of Guards and the volunteer militia. A nuclear weapon suits the regime's strategic interests. On the evidence from India and Pakistan, which first tested nuclear devices in, respectively, 1974 and 1998, a bomb would be popular with the public. Even if Iran's intention is merely to master the processes within the limits of the treaty, the dispute with the nuclear powers (and above all the United States) keeps Iran in the public eye, a thing very necessary to a proud people. In a revolutionary state languishing in the doldrums, the dispute is productive of agitation and xenophobia.

The Iranian government says that its nuclear research is for peaceful purposes, and the fuel enriched is to supply a small (5-megawatt) "swimming-pool" reactor at Tehran University, installed in 1967 and long overdue for dismantling. Such claims would carry more weight had not the National Council of Resistance in Paris (in effect, the Mojahedin) revealed in 2002 that Iran was building underground enrichment and processing capacity that it had not declared to the International Atomic Energy Agency (IAEA), which polices the treaty on behalf of the United Nations. In 2006, the UN Security Council imposed sanctions on Iran. In 2009, Iran revealed it was building another underground nuclear site at a Corps of Guards base at Fordow, near Qom. When diplomacy produced no result, the United States and European Union placed an embargo on Iranian oil. By early 2013, Iranian oil revenues had fallen in money (adjusted for inflation) to the level of the early 1970s, and there were shortages of foreign luxuries and even necessities, such as certain pharmaceuticals.

The nuclear issue is now entangled with the future of revolutionary government. On June 12, 2009, Ahmadinejad stood for reelection and, within a couple of hours of the close of the polls, was pronounced victor. The reformist candidates, Mir Hosein Musavi, the wartime prime minister, and Mehdi Karroubi, disputed the result, and young men and women poured onto the streets, crying, "Where is my vote?" and then, "Death to the Dictator!" (Khamenei). They became known as the "Green Wave" after adopting that color to identify themselves. The Corps of Guards, which up to then had, at least in public, respected Khomeini's wish that it keep out of politics, warned that a democratic or "Velvet" revolution was in the making. Cheered on by the émigrés, and encouraged by Montazeri from seclusion in Qom, the Greens persisted with their protest. On June 20, a sniper shot a young woman named Neda Agha Soltan in the heart. The Islamic Republic reverted to its old practices of mass imprisonment, torture, show trials, and television confessions. On December 19, 2009, Montazeri died and the protest subsided. By then, not merely Ahmadinejad but the entire paraphernalia of state had lost affection and respect. The next presidential election, due in June 2013, promised another crisis for the revolutionary generation already gone in years.

Iran's fuel-enrichment centrifuges would be of smaller interest to the world but for Ahmadinejad's anti-Semitic speeches, and vice versa. Iran and Israel are separated by mountains and deserts and there is no tradition of enmity between the races, but rather the contrary. An antagonism that began in Khomeini's failed attempt in exile to garner Arab support for his cause has monopolized Iran's external policy and become an institution of state. In the early 1990s, Israel, having fought its Arab enemies to a standstill, found in Iran an adversary that was also loathed by the American public, its principal support and financier. Mojahedin agents operating on behalf of Israeli intelligence have assassinated Iranian nuclear scientists, while the United States and Israel have since 2008 introduced destructive code into the computer systems regulating the centrifuges.[7]

With its reservoirs of oil and gas, its vast extent and ingenious pop-

ulation, Iran is capable of fulfilling Mohammed Reza's dream and joining the ranks of the advanced nations. It may even overtake the United
Kingdom, which would have its charm. Yet Iran must first negotiate
the nuclear crisis.

This history has shown how on four occasions Iran persisted with a
weak hand long after it should have folded. Reza in 1941, Mossadeq in
1953, and Khomeini with the American hostages in 1979–81 and after
the recapture of Khorramshahr in 1982 stayed in the game and ended
with nothing. Each time, Iran's intransigence revealed not strength but
weakness and, each time, it underestimated the bloody-mindedness
of its adversaries. Contemptuous of diplomacy, the Islamic Republic
is now incapable of it. Yet even Khomeini, the most intransigent of all
Iranians, in 1988 drank the poison of compromise, and that action,
though it broke his heart, preserved the republic.

Khomeini's Letter of July 16, 1988, to Civil and Military Leaders, Accepting the United Nations Cease-fire

In the name of God the Merciful, the Compassionate

Saturday, 25 Tir '67
By the Grace of of God Almighty and Blessings and Peace
on the Mighty Prophets of God and the Infallible Imams
Praise be on Them One and All!

Now that our military commanders, both of Army and Corps of Guards, who are experts in war, openly confess that the army of Islam will not soon be victorious; and mindful that the competent authorities of the Islamic Republican regime, both military and civilian, no longer find in their hearts that war is in the country's interest, but insist that it is impossible at any price to procure one tenth of the weaponry the bullies of East and West have put at Saddam's disposal; and in light of the shocking letter of the Commander of the Corps of Guards [Mohsen Rezai], which is but one of dozens of such military and political reports sent me since our recent defeats; and informed by the Acting Commander in Chief [Hashemi Rafsanjani] that the Guards Commander is one of the very few officers who believes, in the event that the necessary equipment were available, that the war should be prosecuted; and in recognition of the wide deployment by the enemy of chemical munitions and our lack of means to neutralize them, I give my consent to the cease-fire.

To illuminate the reasons behind this bitter decision, I draw attention to certain points in the letter of the Guards Commander of 2/4/1367 [June 23, 1988]. The above-mentioned commander has written that we will have no victory for five years. In the event that we can assemble over that five years the necessary equipment, it is possible we will be in the position to embark on spoiling or retaliatory actions. After the close of 1371 [in March 1993], if we can deploy 350 infantry brigades and 2,500 tanks, 3,000 artillery pieces, 300 warplanes and 300 helicopters, and master the manufacture of a substantial quantity of laser and nuclear weapons which by then will be among the necessities of modern warfare, then, God willing, we can think of going on the offensive. He says that the strength of the Corps of Guards must be increased sevenfold and the regular Army by 150 percent. He has added that, of course, we must evict America from the Persian Gulf, else we shall not succeed. This commander has stated that the key to the success of his strategy is the prompt allocation of budget and resources and he doubts whether the Government or the General Staff will meet their commitments. For all that, he says that we should fight on which is mere phrasemaking.

The Prime Minister [Mir Hosein Musavi], on the strength of reports from the Ministers of Economy and [Planning and] Budget, has indicated that the government's financial capacity is less than zero. War commanders say that simply to replenish the weapons lost in the recent defeats will consume the entire budget allocated to the Corps of Guards and Army in the current year. Political officials say that the receding prospect of victory has diminished the public enthusiasm for service at the front.

You, my dear friends, know better than anybody that this decision is more lethal for me than poison, but I take it for the satisfaction of God Almighty, for the preservation of religion and for the protection of the Islamic Republic. Such honor as I possess in the eyes of men, I hereby cast aside.

O God, we rose up for the sake of Your religion, we went to war for Your religion and, to protect Your religion, we accept the cease-fire. O God, You Yourself are our witness that not for an instant did we compromise with America, the Soviet Union and all the Powers of the world; that we regard compromise with the Great Powers and other Powers as turning our backs on the principles of Islam. O God, we are strangers in a world of idolatry, heathenism and hypocrisy, a world of money, power, deceit and double-dealing. Aid us, O Lord. O God! In all of history, whenever prophets and saints and learned men resolved to reform society, to put their learning into practice and to organize societies free of corruption and decay, they ran into opposition from the Abu Jahls and Abu Sufyans of their age [opponents of the Prophet]. O God! For Your satisfaction, we sacrificed the sons of Islam and our revolution. But for You, we have nobody. Help us to fulfill Your commands and laws. O God, I beseech You, grant me a speedy martyrdom.

I said that an assembly should convene so that the religious-political leaders may prepare to defend our country against rumors and counterrevolutionary movements at home and abroad. Let them take steps to explain the cease-fire to the public. Be on your guard lest hotheads and zealots divert you with revolutionary slogans from what is best for Islam. Let me make this clear: All your efforts should be directed at justifying this course of action. The smallest deviation is a mortal sin and will provoke a reaction. You know that the high officials of the regime wept tears of blood in reaching this decision while their hearts brimmed over with love for Islam and our Muslim fatherland. Have God in your thoughts and whatever happens, take it in good part. *And so peace be upon you and upon the righteous servants of God.*

Ruhollah al-Musavi al-Khomeini

Two leaves of the manuscript letter, marked "1" and "2," are reproduced in Ali Akbar Hashemi Rafsanjani, *1367: Payan-e defa, aghaz-e bazsazi (From Defense to Reconstruction, 1988–89)*, pp. 215 and 580. The second leaf ends with the phrase "an assembly should convene." The remainder of the final paragraph I have translated from Hashemi Rafsanjani's printed text, p. 581.

Notes

1. The Origins of the Pahlavi State

1. *Gulistan* 1:19.
2. *Program-e tajgozariye alihazrat-e homayun-e shahinshahi* [Program of the Coronation of His Serene Majesty the King of Kings, Long May He Reign!] in Soleiman Behbudi, *Bist sal ba Reza Shah* [Twenty Years with Reza Shah], in Gholamhosein Mirza Saleh, ed., *Reza Shah: Khaterat-e Soleiman Behbudi, Shams Pahlavi, Ali Izadi* [Memoirs of Soleiman Behbudi, Shams Pahlavi, Ali Izadi], Tehran, 1371, p. 281; also FO 416/78, Loraine to Chamberlain, Tehran, May 1, 1926; Hosein Makki, *Tarikh-e bist saleye Iran* [Twenty-Year History of Iran], Tehran, 1363, Vol. 4, pp. 32ff; Melvin Hall, *Journey to the End of an Era: An Autobiography,* London, 1948, pp. 214–16; Vita Sackville-West, *Passenger to Teheran,* London, 1991, pp. 98–108.
3. V. B. Meen and A. D. Tushingham, *Crown Jewels of Iran,* Toronto, 1968, pp. 50–61. In a letter to Virginia Woolf on April 8, 1926, Vita Sackville-West described a visit to select jewels from the treasure chamber under the palace: "We came away shaking the pearls out of our shoes." V. Glendinning, *Vita: The Life of V. Sackville-West,* London, 2005, p. 158.
4. Violet Stuart Wortley, *Life Without Theory,* London, 1946, p. 94.
5. Meen and Tushingham, *Crown Jewels,* p. 78, say this jewel was made long after Nader.
6. FO 416/78, Loraine to Chamberlain, Tehran, May 1, 1926.
7. Text in Makki, *Tarikh-e bist saleye,* Vol. 4, p. 38.
8. Text ibid., p. 39.
9. FO 416/78, Loraine to Chamberlain, May 1, 1926.
10. According to Behbudi, Reza wanted, not "a likeness to any one particular kingdom, but a new style derived from different manners of dress." Behbudi, *Bist sal,* p. 292.
11. FO 416/78, Fraser, Intelligence Summary No. 9, May 1, 1926.
12. Sir Clarmont Skrine, *World War in Iran,* London, 1962, p. 120.
13. I noted this during a fortnight's walk in Rudbar in 1974.
14. Samples taken for the government of India's *Gazetteer of Persia* in 1900, and the national censuses of 1956 and 1966, all show that over 55 percent of villages housed fewer than 250 souls. Julian Bharier, *Economic Development in Iran 1900–1970,* London, 1971, p. 32.

NOTES

15. James Morier, *A Second Journey Through Persia*, London, 1818, pp. 197–98.
16. Joseph-Arthur de Gobineau, *Trois ans en Asie*, Ch. V, in *Oeuvres*, Paris, 1983, Vol. 2, pp. 328–29.
17. Charles Aitchison, *A Collection of Treaties, Agreements and Sanads Relating to India and Neighbouring Countries*, Calcutta, 1929–1933, Vol. 13.
18. Griboyedov was permitted to sit, but sat for too long and in a relaxed posture. The Shah was twice heard to use the word *morakhass* ("Dismissed!").
19. The Iranian secretary to the Russian mission, who survived the massacre, left an account, translated as "Narrative of the Proceedings of the Russian Mission, from Its Departure from Tabreez for Tehran of 14th Jummade 2d (December 20, 1828) Until its Destruction on Wednesday the 6th of Shaban (February 11, 1829)," *Blackwood's Edinburgh Magazine*, Vol. 28, No. 171, September 1830. He heard Griboyedov cry out: " 'Futh Alli Shah! Futh Alli Shah, jensoudre, jensoudre!' or some such expression" (p. 510). Most authors read *j'enfoutre* for "jensoudre." Laurence Kelly, *Diplomacy and Murder in Tehran: Alexander Griboyedov and Imperial Russia's Mission to the Shah of Persia*, London, 2006, p. 192.
20. FO 60/204, "Translation of a Memorandum Given by the Persian Government," Murray to Clarendon, camp near Tehran, October 29, 1855, No. 77, enclosure.
21. Nassereddin's first prime minister, Mirza Taqi Khan, said there were "eighteen crores" (nine million) in the 1850s, but other estimates are lower. Abbas Amanat, *Pivot of the Universe*, London, 1997, p. 128.
22. Charles Issawi, ed., *The Economic History of Iran 1800–1914*, Chicago, Ill., 1971, pp. 339–42.
23. Edward Stack, *Six Months in Persia*, London, 1882, Vol. 2, p. 36.
24. J. Rabino, "Banking in Persia," *Journal of the Institute of Bankers*, Vol. 13, January 1892, pp. 1–56.
25. Haj Zeinolabedin Maraghei, *Siahatnameye Ebrahim Beg* [The Travel Diary of Ebrahim Beg], Tehran, 1364, p. 30.
26. "During the harvest, peddlers and small storekeepers who have advanced goods on credit to the peasants during the year, go to the villages and secure the payment in opium sap. Occasionally, at this time, gifts of sap are made to the village mullahs; and the village barbers and carpenters are paid for their services in the same medium. As soon as the gathering of the sap begins, thousands of vendors of small articles and sweetmeats go out from the large towns and barter their wares for sap, in the poppy fields. Dervishes, story-tellers, beggars, musicians, and owners of performing animals go from one field to another, and are rewarded or given alms by having the flat side of the opium knife scraped on their palms or on the small bowls carried by the dervishes. These itinerants sell their accumulations to travelling opium-buyers, who also purchase from the peasants. When it is realised there may be easily from three [thousand] to five thousand strangers in a single area during the harvest season, each with opium sap in his or her possession, the difficulty of centralizing the entire crop becomes apparent." A. C. Millspaugh, *The American Task in Persia*, New York, 1925, pp. 190–91. A. T. Wilson, "The Opium Trade Through Persian Spectacles," *Asiatic Review*, Vol. 21, 1925, pp. 181–93.
27. Rabino, "Banking in Persia."

28. Maraghei, *Siahatnameye Ebrahim Beg*, p. 82.
29. Denis Wright, *The English Amongst the Persians*, London, 1977, p. 103.
30. G. N. Curzon, *Persia and the Persian Question*, London, 1892, Vol. 1, p. 480.
31. Ebrahim Teimuri, *Asr-e bi khabari* [The Age of Innocence], Tehran, 1332, p. 105.
32. Rabino, "Banking in Persia."
33. FO 539/40, Wolff to Salisbury, Tehran, November 3, 1888.
34. W. Litten, *Persien: Von der "pénétration pacifique" zum "Protektorat": Urkunden und Tatsachen zur Geschichte der europäischen "pénétration pacifique" in Persien 1860–1919*, Berlin and Leipzig, 1920, p. 226.
35. Behbudi, *Bist sal*, p. 373.
36. Hamideh Amani, "Farar az charqeye nabudi" [Rescued from Oblivion], *Hamshahri*, 25 Bahman 1383.
37. MS Add. 200 f. 40, Cambridge University Library, quoted in Persian in E. G. Browne, *A Literary History of Persia*, Cambridge, 1902, Vol. 4, pp. 22 and 53.
38. There are other traditions relating to the Twelfth Imam, but I have selected just one.
39. Joseph-Arthur de Gobineau, *Les religions et les philosophies dans l'Asie centrale*, in *Oeuvres*, Paris, 1983, Vol. 2, p. 618.
40. *Voyages du chevalier Chardin en Perse*, Paris, 1811, Vol. 5, pp. 208ff; Vol. 6, p. 295. Sir John Chardin was a Huguenot jeweler who made three journeys to Iran in the seventeenth century.
41. Gobineau, *Les religions*, in *Oeuvres*, Vol. 12, p. 598.
42. It was thought as many as half of Hoveyda's ministers were Bahai. Asadollah Alam, *Yaddashtha*, Tehran, 1380, 22 Shahrivar 1352; *The Shah and I*, ed. Alinaghi Alikhani, London, 1991, p. 317. E. A. Bayne, *Persian Kingship in Transition: Conversations with a Monarch*, New York, 1968, p. 51, said that seven members of the cabinet in 1966 had Bahai family connections.
43. Moojan Momen, *An Introduction to Shi'i Islam*, New Haven, Conn., 1985, p. 141.
44. British diplomats report Russian demands for an opium *régie*. FO 539/48, Salisbury to Wolff, London, April 13, 1890.
45. M. R. Rahmati, *Naqsh-e mojtahed-e Fars dar nezhat-e tonbaku: Zendeginameye siasi-ejtemaiyeh Sayyid Ali Akbar Fal Asiri* [The Role of the Fars Mujtahed in the Tobacco Movement: Sayyid Ali Akbar Fal Asiri], Qom, 1371–1372, p. 78.
46. Jean-Baptiste Feuvrier, a French military doctor who had access to the harem, wrote in his diary on December 3, 1891: "Personne ne fume plus, ni en ville, ni dans l'entourage du chah, ni même dans son anderoun. Quelle discipline! [Nobody smokes anymore in town or at the court, or even in the Shah's private quarters. What discipline!]." Feuvrier, *Trois ans à la cour de Perse*, Paris, 1906, p. 284.
47. Meeting of the Royal Central Asian Society, with Taqizadeh (deputy from Tabriz) and Muazid as-Saltaneh (Tehran) in February 1909. E. G. Browne, *The Persian Constitutionalists: An Address*, London 1909, p. 12.
48. Wilfred Sparroy, *Persian Children of the Royal Family*, London, 1902, p. 242.
49. FO 60/542, Lascelles to Rosebery, January 16, 1892.
50. R. W. Ferrier, *The History of the British Petroleum Company*, Vol. 1: *The Developing Years, 1901–1932*, Cambridge, 1982, App. 1.1.
51. Ahmad Kasravi, *Tarikh-e mashruteye Iran* [The History of the Iranian Constitution], Tehran, 1384, p. 172.

52. E. G. Browne, *The Persian Revolution of 1905–1909,* Cambridge, 1910, pp. 372–73.

53. Homa Rezvani, ed., *Lavaih-e Aqa Sheikh Fazlallah Nuri* [Sheikh Fazlollah Nuri's Broadsides], Tehran, 1362, pp. 29–30.

54. "Dar hajve Sheikh Fazlollah Nuri," in *Divan-e Iraj Mirza,* Bethesda, Md., 1992, p. 25. The word *fokoli* (from French *faux col,* or stiff collar) was a term of contempt for the Europeanized Iranians of the democratic party. In the Revolution of 1979, the insulting word was *kravati* (from French *cravate,* or necktie). No enthusiast of the Islamic Republic in Iran is seen with either tie or collar.

55. Lambert Molitor to his brother Philippe, Tehran, December 12, 1907. Papiers Molitor in Annette Destrée, *Les fonctionnaires belges au service de la Perse, 1898–1915,* Tehran/Liège, 1976, p. 180.

56. Sir Arnold Wilson, *SW Persia: A Political Officer's Diary, 1907–1914,* Oxford, 1941, p. 42.

57. Ferrier, *British Petroleum,* Vol. 1, p. 190.

58. *Times,* June 30, 1914.

59. Curzon to Inter-Allied Petroleum Conference, London, November 18, 1918.

60. Ferrier, *British Petroleum,* Vol. 1, p. 361.

61. Litten, *Persien,* p. 261.

62. Reza's date of birth was later given as 24 Esfand 1256 (March 15, 1878). Donald N. Wilber, *Riza Shah Pahlavi,* Hicksville, New York, 1975, gives March 16, 1878.

63. Abbas Ali's gravestone in the shrine of Shah Abdolazim, south of Tehran, has the date of his death as 1 Dhulhijja 1295, or November 26, 1878.

64. Shams Pahlavi, *Khaterat,* in Behbudi et al., *Reza Shah,* p. 431.

65. The translator at the German Legation told Major Hall in 1927 that he used to give leftovers from the legation kitchen to a tall soldier named Reza who stood guard in a box at the gates. Hall, *Journey,* p. 220.

66. In contrast, four Swedish officers of the government gendarmerie lost their lives. Litten, *Persien,* p. 234.

67. Behbudi, *Bist sal,* p. 332.

68. There are references to Reza's use of opium in the diplomatic correspondence from at least 1927. FO 371/12296, "Persia Annual Report," January 26, 1927. Mohammed Reza said: "My father . . . smoked a little opium and never once caught cold." Alam, *Yaddashtha,* 4 Dey 1349; English edition, ed. Alikhani, p. 179.

69. Lord Ironside, ed., *High Road to Command: The Diaries of Major-General Sir Edmund Ironside, 1920–1922,* London, 1972, p. 149.

70. Unpublished Ironside diaries quoted by Richard Ullman, *Anglo-Soviet Relations, 1917–1921,* Vol. 3: *The Anglo-Soviet Accord,* Princeton, N.J., 1972, p. 384.

71. Ironside, *High Road,* pp. 159 and 178.

72. Ibid., p. 152. The Shah wanted to borrow British military trucks to transport a consignment of silver *krans,* worth about £500,000, to Bombay, where the exchange into sterling was more favorable. Ironside, who needed the *krans* to pay his men, was disgusted.

73. Unpublished Ironside diaries quoted by Philip Mallet, "Sixty-Eight Snipe and a Revolution," *Journal of the Royal Society for Asian Affairs,* Vol. 25, No. 2, June 1994, p. 175.

74. Unpublished Ironside diaries quoted by Wright, *The English Amongst the Persians,* p. 184.

75. "If Reza wants to play false he will." Unpublished Ironside diary entry for February 12 in Mallet, "Snipe," p. 175.
76. Ironside, *High Road*, p. 118.
77. The estimated number of men involved ranges from 600 (Yazdanpanah) to "2,500 to 3,000" (British Legation). The different accounts are collated in Cyrus Ghani, *Iran and the Rise of Reza Shah*, London, 1998, pp. 166ff.
78. See the declaration of 23 Jumadi 2, 1340 (February 21, 1922) signed by Reza, though probably written by Sayyid Zia. It is printed in Bagher Agheli, *Ruzshomar-e tarikh-e Iran* [Historical Calendar of Iran], Tehran, 1384, Vol. 1, pp. 506ff.
79. FO 416/78, Loraine to Chamberlain, December 31, 1925.
80. Text in Agheli, *Ruzshomar-e*, entry for 12 Farvardin 1303.
81. Geoffrey Jones, *Banking and Empire in Iran: The History of the British Bank of the Middle East*, Cambridge, 1986, Vol. 1, p. 196.

2. Cossack Government

1. Mehdi Qoli Hedayat, *Khaterat va khaterat* [Memories and Hazards], Tehran, 1330, p. 386.
2. This is the *Nutuk* [Speech], running to six hundred pages of print, which Kemal Pasha delivered in six sessions of the convention of the Republican People's Party in Ankara, October 15–20, 1927. In public statuary in Turkey, Kemal is often shown carrying a bound volume of the speech.
3. *Safarnameye Mazanderan, 1305/2485*, Tehran, 1355, p. 53.
4. Hedayat, *Khaterat va khaterat*, p. 385.
5. Soleiman Behbudi, *Bist sal ba Reza Shah* [Twenty Years with Reza Shah] in Gholamhosein Mirza Saleh, ed., *Reza Shah: Khaterat-e Soleiman Behbudi, Shams Pahlavi, Ali Izadi* [Memoirs of Soleiman Behbudi, Shams Pahlavi, Ali Izadi], Tehran, 1371, p. 359.
6. Hedayat, *Khaterat va khaterat*, p. 386.
7. Hosein Makki, *Doktor Mossadeq va nutuqhaye tarikhiye u* [Dr. Mossadeq and His Historic Speeches], Tehran, 1356, p. 148.
8. "The most important fact is that while two years ago the Shah was merely disliked by the people here, to-day he is hated by all." FO 371/18997, Gault in Kermanshah to Knatchbull-Hugessen in Tehran, August 2, 1935, "Memorandum on the Political and Economic Situation in Kermanshah, July 1935."
9. FO 371/12296, "Persia Annual Report," January 26, 1927.
10. Behbudi, *Bist sal*, p. 391.
11. *Izvestiya*, December 16, 1925. "Cinq ans de rapports du gouvernmente soviétique avec la Perse," *Novy Vostok*, Vol. 4, p. 218.
12. FO 371/11483, Nicolson to Chamberlain, Gulhek, July 3, 1926.
13. A. C. Millspaugh, *Americans in Persia*, Washington, D.C., 1946, p. 25n.
14. FO 416/82, Intelligence Summary No. 7 for the period ending March 31, 1928; also, Clive to Chamberlain, March 30, 1928. The British correspondence, based on reports from the Indo-European Telegraph Department station at Qom, is nearest in time to events. Hosein Makki, *Tarikh-e bist saleye Iran*, Tehran, 1361,

multiplies the number of armored cars but places the event a year too early, as does Bagher Agheli, *Ruzshomar-e tarikh-e Iran*, Tehran, 1384, ad loc. Behbudi, *Bist sal*, p. 322, says it was only Princess Shams who showed her face and she was ten years old and therefore not required to veil. E. A. Bayne has a squadron of cavalry riding through the mosque. Bayne, *Persian Kingship in Transition: Conversations with a Monarch*, New York, 1968, p. 47.

15. "Imam Khomeini in his lessons on ethics while teaching at Madrasseh Faiziyeh would often remark: 'These days anyone wishing to visit a staunch believer who has suppressed his appetitive soul and reformed it, should travel to the city of Ray and after performing the pilgrimage to the shrine of Lord Abdolazim should meet Mr Bafqi.' And he used to recite the following couplet: 'What a wonder that a single miracle should accomplish two tasks, / The pilgrimage of Shah Abdolazim and a meeting with the beloved.'" "The Teachers of Imam Khomeini," at imam-khomeini.com.

16. FO 416/82, Clive to Chamberlain, March 30, 1928.

17. Hedayat, *Khaterat va khaterat*, p. 382.

18. Ibid., p. 383.

19. Donald Wilber, *Riza Shah Pahlavi*, Hicksville, N.Y., 1975, p. 233.

20. *Ettelaat*, 15 Tir 1324.

21. FO 371/18992, Daly in Mashhad to Knatchbull-Hugessen, July 15, 1935.

22. In his defense before the revolutionary court, Matbui said he had instructed the 250 soldiers to use only maneuver cartridges (training blanks) to clear the 800 people from the shrine. See iranrights.org under Matbui.

23. FO 371/ 18992, Knatchbull-Hugessen to FO, August 23, 1935.

24. The British consul in Kermanshah reported tentative approaches from traders and clergy for a *bast* in the consulate grounds. FO 371/18997, Gault in Kermanshah to Knatchbull-Hugessen, August 2, 1935.

25. Hosein Ali Montazeri, *Khaterat*, Vol. 1, p. 78, at amontazeri.com.

26. M. Jafari et al., eds., *Vaqayeye kashf-e hejab* [Incidents of the Unveiling Act], Tehran, 1373, Introduction.

27. Photograph in Farah Pahlavi, *An Enduring Love*, New York, 2004, after p. 150.

28. FO 371/120048, Urquhart to Legation, February 20, 1936.

29. Montazeri, *Khaterat*, Vol. 1, p. 79.

30. For example, Ch. LIV, "Hajji Baba Becomes a Promoter of Matrimony," in James Morier, *The Adventures of Hajji Baba of Ispahan*, London, 1824.

31. Jafari et al., *Vaqayeye kashf-e hejab*, Doc. 90.

32. Kan, now engulfed in the western suburbs of Tehran. M. R. Mahdavi-Kani, *Khaterat*, Tehran, 1385, p. 29.

33. Sir Clarmont Skrine, *World War in Iran*, London, 1962, p. 75.

34. R. W. Ferrier, *The History of the British Petroleum Company*, Vol. 1: *The Developing Years, 1901–1932*, Cambridge, 1982, pp. 370 and 601.

35. The fields manager at Masjed-e Suleiman, R. R. Thompson, said the company's concession was entirely different from those in other territories where "the sole idea of the various interested Companies has been anxiety to tap the oil horizon before their rivals, regardless of the damage done to the oil-bearing strata by faulty drilling to the detriment of the prolonged productive capacity of the field." Ibid., p. 403.

36. BP H13/132. Cadman's Address to the American Petroleum Institute, December 6, 1928. Ibid., p. 514.

37. *Safarnameye Khuzestan, 1303/2483*, London, 1983, pp. 170ff. Figures for the labor force are in Ferrier, *British Petroleum*, Vol. 1, p. 40.

38. *Shafaq-e sorkh* [Red Horizon], December 5, 1928.

39. Ferrier, *British Petroleum*, Vol. 1, p. 601.

40. Jacks to Cadman, June 1, 1928, ibid., p. 599.

41. The "personal request" for £50,000 to found a museum in Tehran was made in correspondence with Cadman. BP H16/50, quoted ibid., p. 623.

42. American Legation Dispatch 710, November 26, 1928. Quoted in Wilber, *Riza Shah Pahlavi*, p. 130.

43. Hedayat, *Khaterat va khaterat*, p. 395.

44. Hassan Arfa, *Under Five Shahs*, London, 1964, p. 236.

45. Ghassem Ghani, *Yaddashtha*, London, 1985, Vol. 1, p. 215.

46. Arfa, *Under Five Shahs*, p. 235.

47. FO 371/16935, Hoare to Oliphant, January 14, 1933. Hoare proposed to show the letter to Davar and warn that if there were no progress "we would have no alternative but to produce the letter."

48. *Times*, January 9, 1933.

49. "C'est la politique anglaise qui m'a fichu par terre [It is British policy that has brought me low]." Letter of February 1933, quoted in Miron Rezun, "Reza Shah's Court Minister: Teymourtash," *International Journal of Middle East Studies*, Vol. 12, 1980, pp. 119–37.

50. Mir Jafar Pishehvari, *Khaterat*, in *Zendan-e Reza Shah* [Reza Shah's Prison], Tehran, 1384, p. 118.

51. FO 416/92, Hoare to Simon, March 11, 1933.

52. FO 416/92, Mallet to Simon, July 1, 1933.

53. Hedayat, *Khaterat va khaterat*, p. 397.

54. FO 371/16941, Mallet to Simon, October 6, 1933.

55. Cadman to Simon, April 19, 1933, in J. H. Bamberg, *The History of British Petroleum*, Vol. 2: *The Anglo-Iranian Years*, Cambridge, 1994, p. 45.

56. American Legation Dispatch, May 4, 1933, quoted in Wilber, *Riza Shah*, p. 150.

57. Speech of January 27, 1949, quoted in L. P. Elwell-Sutton, *Persian Oil: A Study in Power Politics*, London, 1955, p. 73.

58. Bamberg, *British Petroleum*, Vol. 2, p. 325.

59. "Iran's New Darius," *Time*, April 25, 1938.

60. Angelo Polacco, *L'Iran di Rezà Schià*, Venice XV/1937. For the construction, Steen Anderson, "Building for the Shah: Market Entry, Political Reality and Risks on the Iranian Market, 1933–1939," *Enterprise and Society*, Vol. 9, No. 4, December 2008, pp. 637–69. J. H. Shotton, "Building a Railroad Through Iran," *Compressed Air Magazine*, Vol. 41, No. 12, December 1936.

61. Wilber, *Riza Shah*, p. 185.

62. FO 371/18992, Knatchbull-Hugessen to FO, August 23, 1935.

63. "Iran's New Darius."

64. An export tonnage of 6,115 in 1928–1929 was not matched until 1957–1958. A. C. Edwards, *The Persian Carpet*, London, 1975, p. 373.

65. Anthony Smith describes how in 1950 in Mahun, near Kerman, the representa-

tive of the Iranian Carpet Company, Nahidi, took his knife to a man's loom and slashed down through all the *jufti* wefts. Both men were in tears. Smith, *Blind White Fish in Persia,* London, 1953, p. 151.

66. FO 416/92, Hoare to Simon, November 3, 1934.

67. Polacco, *L'Iran,* p. 107. According to Polacco, p. 8, "He [Reza] has refashioned [Iran] in his image and to his will as an artist transforms brute matter into a work of art."

68. Travel diaries quoted in James Knox, *Robert Byron,* London, 2003, p. 304.

69. "'Vieux Téhéran,' Conférence à l'Institut Franco-Iranien," 1951. Reprinted in *Téhéran de Jadis,* Geneva, 1971, p. 9. Also in Vincent Monteil, *Iran,* Paris, 1962, p. 53.

70. For Sultanabad, renamed Arak, Edwards, *Persian Carpet,* p. 135.

71. Behbudi, *Bist sal,* p. 321.

72. Mohammed Reza Pahlavi, *Mission for My Country,* London, 1961, p. 46.

73. Behbudi, *Bist sal,* p. 295.

74. Fardoust says Reza retired each night with a glass each of red and white wine beside his bedroll. Hosein Fardoust, *Zuhur va suqut-e saltanat-e Pahlavi: Khaterat-e arteshbod-e sabeq Hosein Fardoust* [The Rise and Fall of the Pahlavi Monarchy], Tehran, 1374, Vol. 1, p. 71. I am informed that wine will counteract the insomniac effects of opium.

75. Behbudi, *Bist sal,* p. 359.

76. Ibid., p. 297.

77. Fardoust, *Zuhur va suqut,* Vol. 1, p. 72.

78. Behbudi, *Bist sal,* p. 11.

79. Clive to Henderson, March 19, 1930, quoted in Ferrier, *British Petroleum,* Vol. 1, p. 610.

80. The British Legation reported in 1935 that Reza had bought the village of Siahdehan, where the road from Qazvin forks to Hamadan and Tabriz, which had revenues of 15,000 tomans for 100,000 tomans (£12,500) and had begun to erect a hotel. According to the seller, Reza did not pay. FO 371/18992, Mallet to FO, November 28, 1935.

81. More probably, half the size of Belgium.

82. Behbudi, *Bist sal,* pp. 377–79.

83. V. Kosogovskii, commander of the Cossack Brigade in the late 1880s, said Nassereddin's private quarters housed four wives and 106 concubines or temporary wives, and with servants and visitors comprised never fewer than 1,500 persons. Elena Adreeva, *Russia and Iran in the Great Game,* London, 2007, p. 158.

84. Colonel C. E. Stewart, an Indian Army officer stationed at Khaf in Khorasan, saw Nassereddin pass through Quchan, with a retinue of 18,000, in August 1883. The following spring, there was no grain or fodder for horses for eighty miles around. Antony Wynn, "Colonel C. E. Stewart—A Spy in Khaf," *Journal of the Iran Society,* Vol. 2, No. 7, September 2008.

85. Jean-Baptiste Feuvrier, *Trois ans à la cour de Perse,* Paris, 1906, p. 2. A photogravure of the night palace, or *khabgah,* is on p. 143 in this edition.

86. A modest house, set back from the street by a small courtyard and entrance porch, or *ivan,* was pointed out to me in 1974. I do not know its fate.

87. Ashraf Pahlavi, *Faces in a Mirror,* Englewood Cliffs, N.J., 1980, p. 1.

88. Fardoust, *Zuhur va suqut,* Vol. 1, p. 75.

89. "Interview with Esmat ol-Moluk Dowlatshahi," *Tarikh-e moaser-e Iran,* Vol. 6, No. 23, 1381, p. 325.

90. "Shah, particularly since the fall of Temourtache, is weighed down . . . by the flood of trivial details on which he alone can decide." FO 371/18992, Knatchbull-Hugessen to FO, May 1, 1935.

91. Behbudi, *Bist sal,* p. 353.

92. Mohammed Reza Pahlavi, *Mission,* p. 53.

93. Arfa, *Under Five Shahs,* p. 226.

94. At the request of the British Legation in Tehran, Mrs. Armstrong, wife of the vice-consul in Geneva, lunched with the headmaster, M. Carnal, and his American wife at the Château du Rosey. Carnal told her the Crown Prince was an "excellent all round athlete, being especially prominent in the football field." He had won the school's Prix d'Excellence. Among the sixty-five pupils were English and American boys and the sons of such well-known continental families as Radziwill and Thurn und Taxis, who spoke to Mohammed Reza in the familiar form (*tu*) and slapped him on the back. His only privileges were having his own bedroom and not being required to file in line into meals. A tutor gave him lessons in Persian every day. FO 371/18992, Shone in Berne to FO, November 11, 1935.

95. Farah Pahlavi, *An Enduring Love,* p. 134.

96. Behbudi, *Bist sal,* p. 395.

97. "A curious decadent fellow, about twenty-five, dressed like a musical comedy Bohemian, who also reads characters from hand-writing and the palms of your hands and makes the most surprising statements on the strength of it about your 'vie sexuelle'! . . . It is rather alarming that such an odd specimen should have such a hold over the young Prince. The Belgian Chargé here, a most sensible fellow, has said that he would not entrust any young man to Monsieur Perron, let alone a future monarch." FO 371/20048, Butler in Tehran to Shone in Berne, August 31, 1936.

98. Fardoust, *Zuhur va suqut,* Vol. 1, p. 58.

99. Fathollah Minbashian. Interview recorded by Habib Ladjevardi, December 1, 1981, Cagnes-sur-Mer, France. Iranian Oral History Collection, Harvard University, Transcript 1.

100. Mohammed Reza Pahlavi, *Mission,* p. 64.

101. "He wanted to find a princess of good descent to marry his son; and . . . through a marriage link with another royal family, to cement relations with a nearby state." Ibid., p. 218.

102. *Life,* September 21, 1942, p. 28. Cecil Beaton, who photographed her at Saadabad, described Fauzia as an "Asian Venus" with "a perfect heart-shaped face and strangely pale but piercing blue eyes."

103. Antony Wynn, "Ziegler's Man in Persia: Condensed from the Private Memoirs of W. L. Flinn," *Journal of the Iran Society,* Vol. 2, No. 8, September 2009, p. 44.

104. Ghani, *Yaddashtha,* Vol. 7.

105. Winston Churchill, *The Grand Alliance,* London, 1950, Ch. 26.

106. Bullard to FO, August 25, 1941, in Reader Bullard, *Letters from Tehran: A British Ambassador in World War II Persia,* ed. E. C. Hodgkin, London, 1991, p. 69.

107. Ashraf Pahlavi, *Faces,* p. 40.

108. Arfa, *Under Five Shahs,* p. 298.

109. Lambton and Bullard say it was with the flat of his sword. Bullard, *Letters*, pp. 73 and 80.
110. FO 416/99, Intelligence Summaries, August 24 to September 24, 1941.
111. BBC Written Archives Centre, BBC Persian News Bulletins, September 6–17, 1941; also "Some of the Acts of Reza Shah" in Bullard, *Letters*, p. 80.
112. Behbudi, *Bist sal*, p. 397. "All that is for show" is, literally, "These occurrences are all for Molla's blanket." The folk hero Molla Nasreddin, hearing a thief one night, ran out dressed in a blanket, which the thief then stole. He came back and told his wife, "It was just about some blanket."
113. Skrine, *World War*, p. 83.
114. "Esmat Interview," *Tarikh-e moaser-e Iran*, Vol. 6, No. 23, 1381, p. 325.
115. Printed in Behbudi, *Bist sal*, p. 564.

3. The Boy

1. E. A. Bayne, *Persian Kingship in Transition: Conversations with a Monarch*, New York, 1968, p. 66.
2. FO 416/99, Intelligence Summary for November 11–18, 1941.
3. FO 416/99, Intelligence Summaries for August 24, 1941, to September 24, 1941.
4. In a circular letter of November 5, 1943, Bullard wrote: "Most Persians will surely be blow-flies in their next incarnation." Reader Bullard, *Letters from Tehran: A British Ambassador in World War II Persia*, ed. E. C. Hodgkin, London, 1991, p. 216. Churchill wrote: "Sir Reader Bullard has a contempt for all Persians which however natural is detrimental to his efficiency and our interest." Prime Minister to Foreign Secretary, April 28, 1943, in Bullard, *Letters*, p. 187. Hosein Fardoust says the Shah told him that he asked London to have Bullard recalled, but was refused. Fardoust, *Zuhur va suqut-e saltanat-e Pahlavi: Khaterat-e arteshbod-e sabeq Hosein Fardoust* [The Rise and Fall of the Pahlavi Monarchy], Tehran, 1374, Vol. 1, p. 127.
5. FO to Bullard, September 19, 1941, in Bullard, *Letters*, p. 82.
6. *Life*, September 21, 1942, p. 96.
7. The figure £5 million is taken from the "70m tomans" mentioned by Asadollah Alam in a conversation with Mohammed Reza on November 30, 1970, and converted at the 1941 exchange rate of fourteen tomans to one pound sterling. Asadollah Alam, *Yaddashtha*, Tehran, 1380, 9 Azar 1349; *The Shah and I*, ed. Alinaghi Alikhani, London, 1991, pp. 176–77. Forughi told Parliament there was a credit of 68 million tomans in Reza's account at the National Bank. G. M. Majd, *Great Britain and Reza Shah*, Gainesville, Fla., 2011, pp. 323–25. Ann Lambton provided a figure of £6 million to the BBC Persian Service. Bullard, *Letters*, p. 80. In a deed done before Public Notary No. 17 at Isfahan, and witnessed by Mahmood Jam, Minister of Court, on 28 Shahrivar 1320 (September 19, 1941), Reza passed "all our properties, chattels, factories etc. . . . whatsoever to His Imperial Majesty for and in consideration of 10 grammes of sugar." An English translation of the deed is included in FO 371/52371. "Ten grammes of sugar" is *yek habeh qand* [one lump of sugar], which plays roughly the same role in Iranian transactions as, in the past in England and the United States, a peppercorn.

8. Mohammed Reza Pahlavi, *Mission for My Country,* London, 1961, p. 75.

9. CIA (Donald Wilber et al.), "Clandestine Service History: Overthrow of Premier Mossadeq of Iran, November 1952–August 1953," App. E, p. 2.

10. Eve Curie, *Journey Among Warriors,* London, 1943, p. 111.

11. FO 248/1406, Bullard to FO, October 4, 1941.

12. Bullard reported to London that he had received a secret message from the Shah saying "he would like to see me fairly often, alone and without the knowledge of the politicians." Bullard replied he could not do so without informing the cabinet and his Soviet colleague. FO 248/1406, Bullard to FO, October 16, 1941.

13. Bullard to FO, December 9, 1942. Bullard, *Letters,* p. 160.

14. "My brother and I were like faces in a mirror." Ashraf Pahlavi, *Faces in a Mirror,* Englewood Cliffs, N.J., 1980, p. 20.

15. Bullard, *Letters,* p. 228.

16. Ghassem Ghani, *Yaddashtha,* London, 1985, Vol. 3, pp. 356–73. Ali Dehbashi, ed., *Yadnameye Allameh Mohammed Qazvini* [Memoir of Qazvini], Tehran, 1378, p. 233.

17. "I was most tempted." Mohammed Reza Pahlavi, *Mission,* p. 80.

18. Mohammed Reza Pahlavi, *Answer to History,* New York, 1980, p. 137.

19. Greely to Somervell, May 30, 1942, in T. H. Vail Motter, *United States Army in World War II: The Persian Corridor and Aid to Russia,* Washington, D.C., 1952, p. 167.

20. Stimson to Welles, September 1, 1942, ibid., p. 171.

21. Ibid., p. 468.

22. "The sound course would have been to abolish the Army altogether and build up and equip the gendarmerie to the requirements of country-wide policing." A. C. Millspaugh, *Americans in Persia,* Washington, D.C., 1946, pp. 104–5.

23. Ibid., p. 105n.

24. Motter, *Persian Corridor,* p. 243.

25. Ibid., p. 436.

26. Secretary of State to Secretary of War, December 21, 1944, ibid., p. 472.

27. Ghani, *Yaddashtha,* Vol. 7.

28. Mohammed Reza Pahlavi, *Answer to History,* p. 77. Those exploits are not mentioned in the earlier *Mission.*

29. Farah Pahlavi, *An Enduring Love,* New York, 2004, p. 25.

30. *Entretien avec le Shah, 8 mars 1947 de 17 h 30 à 19 h 30,* at amiscorbin.com/textes/francais/shah.

31. Marshall Wainwright, "The Flying Fortress Airliner," *Aeroplane Monthly,* Vol. 38, No. 6, June 2010, pp. 56–59.

32. Mohammed Reza Pahlavi, *Mission,* p. 56.

33. Pari Ghaffari had some success as a film actress in the 1960s, playing opposite Fardin, the "king of hearts" of Iranian commercial cinema, in melodramas such as *Faryad-e nim-e shab* [Cry at Midnight], 1961. In 1997, Ghaffari published a kiss-and-tell memoir, *Ta siahi . . . Dar dam-e Shah* [Into the Dark . . . In the Clutches of the Shah], Tehran, 1376. In this work, as with other memoirs published since the Revolution, it is necessary to separate the obviously false from the possibly true.

34. Mohammed Reza Pahlavi, *Mission,* p. 57. Ashraf Pahlavi, in *Faces,* p. 112, says her brother recognized the weapon as a "Belgian Herstell" and therefore knew it car-

ried only six rounds. He may have said that it was the six-round FN Model 1910, manufactured at Herstal in Belgium. She may have misheard him.

35. Mohammed Reza Pahlavi, *Mission*, p. 57. "When you think I've been wounded by a good five bullets . . . you have to believe in miracles. I've had so many air disasters, and yet I've always come out unscathed—thanks to a miracle willed by God and the prophets." Oriana Fallaci, *Interview with History*, trans. John Sheppey, New York, 1976, p. 269.

36. Dean Acheson, *Present at the Creation: My Years at the State Department*, London, 1970, p. 502.

37. Ghani, *Yaddashtha*, Vol. 8, entry for November 24, 1949.

38. "I refrained from pointing out that this wasn't the first time I had been told." Alam, *Yaddashtha*, 6 Dey 1348 and 5 Dey 1349; English edition, ed. Alikhani, pp. 115, 180.

39. Soraya Esfandiary Bakhtiary, *Le palais des solitudes*, Paris, 1991, p. 93. "The Shah's Wedding," *British Pathé*, February 22, 1951. "The Shah Takes a Bride," *Life*, February 26, 1951. The dress, made by Dior of silver lamé with a train of while tulle, was sold for 1.3 million euros in 2002 at Maison Drouot in Paris.

40. Soraya, *Le palais*, p. 76.

41. Ibid., p. 101.

42. Ibid., pp. 124–25.

43. Hosein Fardoust says that after the first year of her marriage, Soraya did not receive Shams or the Queen Mother. Fardoust, *Zuhur va suqut*, Vol. 1, p. 208.

44. FO 375/133065, Stevens to FO, March 17, 1958.

45. According to Ann K. S. Lambton, *The Persian Land Reform, 1962–1966*, Oxford, 1969, p. 54, their gross annual revenue was 88 million rials.

46. J. H. Bamberg, *The History of British Petroleum*, Vol. 2: *The Anglo-Iranian Years*, Cambridge, 1994, p. 325.

47. Secretary of State Acheson wrote from Paris after a meeting with British officials on November 10, 1951: "The cardinal purpose of Brit policy is not to prevent Iran going commie; the cardinal point is to preserve what they believe to be the last remaining bastion of Brit solvency." *FRUS, 1952–1954*, Vol. X: *Iran (1952–1954)*, Secretary of State to Department of State, Paris, November 10, 1951.

48. L. P. Elwell-Sutton, *Persian Oil: A Study in Power Politics*, London, 1955, p. 65.

49. Soraya, *Le palais*, pp. 145, 157.

50. Alam, *Yaddashtha*, 25 Shahrivar 1352; English edition, ed. Alikhani, p. 318.

51. In the summer of 1950, a group of Oxford University undergraduates studying the fish, flora, and geography of the underground irrigation canals at Kerman in the southeast, found even in remote villages "the constant refrain: 'Give us our oil and then there is nothing which we will not be able to do.'" Anthony Smith, *Blind White Fish in Persia*, London, 1953, p. 95.

52. Acheson, *Present at the Creation*, p. 504.

53. M. Navvab Safavi, *Fedayan-e Islam: Tarikh, amalkard, andisheh*, ed. Hadi Khusrowshahi, Tehran, 1375. "Resume of Program of Fedayan Islam as Made by Weekly *Tehran Mosavvar*," enclosure in Tehran Embassy to Department of State, Dispatch No. 21, July 1951.

54. Sohrab Behdad, "Islamic Utopia in Pre-Revolutionary Iran: Navvab Safavi and the Fada'ian-e Eslam," *Middle Eastern Studies*, Vol. 33, No. 1, 1997, pp. 40–65.

55. CIA (Wilber et al.), "Clandestine Service History," p. 3. This account was written in March 1954 and published by the *New York Times* on June 16, 2000.

56. Ibid., pp. 8–9.

57. FO 371/104562, Eden to FO, February 27, 1953.

58. *FRUS, 1952–1954*, Vol. X: *Iran (1952–1954)*, Henderson to Department of State, February 25, 1953; FO 371/104562, British Embassy, Washington, D.C., to FO, February 27, 1953.

59. *FRUS, 1952–1954*, Vol. X: *Iran (1952–1954)*, Henderson to Department of State, March 10, 1953.

60. According to CIA, "Clandestine History," p. 24, she met her brother on June 29, but Ashraf Pahlavi, in *Faces*, p. 140, denies this.

61. CIA, "Clandestine History," App. B, " 'London' Draft of the TPAJAX Operational Plan."

62. Ibid., p. 38. The name of the officer is redacted and is my conjecture.

63. *Ettelaat*, 20 Mordad 1352.

64. Text of broadcast in *Ettelaat*, 25 Mordad 1352.

65. Soraya, *Le palais*, p. 158.

66. Interview with Abolfath Atabai by Ahmad Ghoreishi, New York, June 6, 1982, FISOHA, p. 34, quoted in G. R. Afkhami, *The Life and Times of the Shah*, Berkeley, Calif., 2009, p. 179.

67. FO 371/10457, Bromley in Baghdad to FO, August 19, 1953; *FRUS, 1952–1954*, Vol. X: *Iran (1952–1954)*, Berry in Baghdad to Department of State, August 17, 1953.

68. Soraya, *Le palais*, pp. 165ff.

69. British Secret Intelligence Service (SIS), Nicosia, also wanted to continue. A proposal by SIS to fly Darbyshire and Leavitt to Baghdad by RAF jet fighter on August 17 to persuade the Shah to stay was refused by Churchill. CIA, "Clandestine History," p. 51.

70. Kennett Love, "Shah Flees Iran After Move to Dismiss Mossadegh Fails," *New York Times*, August 17, 1953; Ardeshir Zahedi, *Khaterat*, Vol. 1, Bethesda, Md., 2006, p. 175.

71. *Ettelaat*, 26 Mordad 1352.

72. CIA, "Clandestine History," p. 64.

73. Ibid., p. 62.

74. *Kayhan*, 29 Mordad 1332.

75. Evidence of Captain Madani to his captors in General Teymour Bakhtiar et al., *Evolution of Communism in Iran: From Shahrivar 1320 (September 1941) to Farvardin 1336 (April 1957)*, Tehran, 1959, p. 293.

76. *FRUS, 1964–1968*, Vol. XXII: *Iran*, Country Team to Department of State, Tehran, November 28, 1965.

77. E. A. Bayne, *Persian Kingship in Transition: Conversations with a Monarch*, New York, 1968, p. 66.

78. Soraya, *Le palais*, p. 170.

79. Ibid.

80. CIA, "Clandestine History," p. 38.

81. *Middle East Journal*, Vol. 8, No. 2, Spring 1954, pp. 184–204.

82. Bakhtiar et al., *Evolution of Communism*, p. 392; Mohammed Reza Pahlavi, *Mission*, p. 105.

83. Mohammed Reza and Soraya were in the United States from December 13, 1954, to February 11, 1955.

84. Denis Wright. Interview recorded by Habib Ladjevardi, October 10 and 11, 1984, Aylesbury, England. Iranian Oral History Collection, Harvard University, Transcript 2.

85. FO 248/1560, Fearnley to Ambassador, May 22, 1955.

86. FO 248/1560, Stevens to FO, May 12, 1955.

87. FO 248/1560, Wright to FO, September 18, 1955.

88. Wright, Iranian Oral History Project (IOHP) interview, Transcript 2.

89. "Ghasl-e shahadat," at navabsafavi.com.

90. Wright, IOHP interview, Transcript 1.

91. Klaus Koerner, "Erst in Goebbels,' dann in Adenauers Diensten" [Goebbels's Man in Adenauer's Service], Die Zeit, August 24, 1990.

92. Robert Graham, Iran: The Illusion of Power, London, 1978, p. 159.

93. FO 371/133065, Stevens to FO, March 17, 1958.

94. Ibid.

95. Oriana Fallaci, Interview with History, trans. John Sheppey, New York, 1976, p. 269.

96. "Yo no tenía ningunas ganas de casarme, ni vocación para ser Reina. También el Sha de Irán me pidió en matrimonio y tampoco acepté. Afortunadamente." Diario de Mallorca, July 20, 2010.

97. "Pope Bans Marriage of Princess to Shah," New York Times, February 24, 1959.

98. Alam, Yaddashtha, 5–12 Esfand 1348; English edition, ed. Alikhani, p. 135. According to Fardoust, Zuhur va suqut, Vol. 1, p. 207, the Princess's brother, Prince Vittorio Emmanuele, reported Pari Sima's indiscretions to Mohammed Reza and said they were the cause of his sister's refusal. The Prince later went into business in Tehran. Pari Sima was invited to the Persepolis celebrations in 1971, and a new tiara and earrings were made for her to wear.

99. Information from a fellow student.

100. Farah Pahlavi, Enduring Love, p. 80.

101. Described in V. B. Meen and A. D. Tushingham, Crown Jewels of Iran, Toronto, 1968, p. 138. Soraya, in Le palais, p. 185, said the tiara was actually made for her.

102. Mohammed Reza Pahlavi, Mission, pp. 54–55.

4. Ruhollah

1. Ruhollah Khomeini, Mobarezeh ba nafs ya jihad-e akhbar [The Battle with the Self, or the Greater Jihad], Tehran, 1357, p. 28.

2. Mehdi Haeri-Yazdi. Interview recorded by Zia Sedghi, January 28 and February 4, 1989, and April 29, 1992, Bethesda, Md. Iranian Oral History Collection, Harvard University, Transcript 1.

3. Ebrahim Yazdi, who accompanied Khomeini in his failed attempt to enter Kuwait in 1978, says the passport was in the name of Mostafavi. Yazdi, Akharin talashha dar akharin ruzha [The Final Push], Tehran, 1388, p. 74.

4. Baqer Moin, Khomeini: Life of the Ayatollah, London, 1999, p. 37, quoting the newspaper Resalat of July 11, 1989.

5. Hosein Ali Montazeri, Khaterat, Vol. 1, p. 202, at amontazeri.com.

6. In his Turkish exile once, Khomeini preferred to work in the dark rather than ask one of his guards to draw back the curtains or undertake that operation himself. Sadeq Khalkhali, *Khaterat*, Tehran, 1379, p. 136.

7. "The Imam [Khomeini] generally refrained from overt political activity until 1962 not only because of an unwillingness to dispute the quietist attitude of the senior 'ulama [clergyman] of the day, but also because an essential process of inner preparation was underway." Hamid Algar, "The Fusion of the Gnostic and the Political in the Personality and Life of Imam Khomeini (R. A.)," *Al-Tawhid*, June 2003.

8. Montazeri, in *Khaterat*, Vol. 1, p. 197, reported one of the gentlemen saying: "Lucky his mother is not a philosopher and let's hope the lad takes after her."

9. Muhsin al-Amin, *Rihlat al-Sayyid Muhsin al-Amin* [Travels], Beirut, 1985, p. 170.

10. Montazeri, *Khaterat*, Vol. 1, p. 54. The sweet, called *suhan*, is made from roasted almonds, sugar, honey, and saffron. François Villon in *Le testament*, p. 30, said of his fellow-students in Paris in the fifteenth century: "Et pain ne voient qu'aux fenestres [All the bread they see is in shopwindows]."

11. Montazeri, *Khaterat*, Vol. 1, p. 90. Shahrough Akhavi, *Religion and Politics in Contemporary Iran*, Albany, N.Y., 1980, App. Table 1 derives from Ministry of Education annuals a figure for all Iran of 784 for 1940–1941, and 1,010 for 1941–1942. Those figures exclude students in Iraq.

12. Moin, *Khomeini*, p. 42, believes this work was written in 1942. An essay or sermon, attacking Reza as an "ignorant Mazanderani" and Kasravi as a "worthless person from Tabriz," dated the equivalent of May 4, 1944, has survived and gives the starting point for his political writing: Ruhollah Khomeini, *Sahifeye nur* [The Page of Light], Tehran, 1361, Vol. 1, pp. 3–4.

13. Ruhollah Khomeini, *Resalah fi at-talab wal-iradah* [Epistle on Will and Requirement], Tehran, 1363, p. 153 (in Arabic).

14. Ruhollah Khomeini, *Kashf ol-asrar*, n.p., n.d., pp. 223–24.

15. Ibid., p. 184.

16. Ibid., p. 185.

17. "I remember we were present at Ayatollah Khomeini's house, about five or six of us, including Mr. Motahhari, and we fell to talking about the Fedayan-e Islam, and Mr. Khomeini said: 'What sort of program is this? What are they doing? They collect up three or four students, then start slandering everybody, the police will get involved, they'll start interfering, what is all this extremism for?'" Montazeri, *Khaterat*, Vol. 1, p. 140.

18. Ibid., Vol. 1, p. 143; Khalkhali, *Khaterat*, p. 48.

19. Mohammed Reza Pahlavi, *Mission for My Country*, London, 1961, p. 200.

20. Mohammed Reza was heard to use the phrase to parliamentary deputies during the bread riots of December 1942. "Yesterday he said to some deputies whom he had summoned that unless something drastic was done there would be a revolution from below and suggested that a revolution from above would be better." Bullard to FO, December 9, 1942. Reader Bullard, *Letters from Tehran: A British Ambassador in World War II Persia*, ed. E. C. Hodgkin, London, 1991, p. 160.

21. Chapour Bakhtiar, *Ma fidélité*, Paris, 1982, p. 112.

22. *International Affairs* (Moscow), No. 3, March 1963.

23. Montazeri, *Khaterat*, Vol. 1, p. 188.

24. "Not a single person came." Ibid.
25. Khalkhali, *Khaterat,* p. 56.
26. Hamid Rouhani, *Nehzat-e imam Khomeini* [Imam Khomeini's Movement], Tehran, 1381, Vol. 1, pp. 142ff.
27. Bahauddin Nuri in Savak weekly report dated 1 Khordad 1342, printed in holograph in Javad Mansuri, ed., *Tarikh-e qiyam-e 15 Khordad be ravayat-e asnad* [The Uprising of June 5, 1963, According to Official Documents], Tehran, 1377, No. 4/101.
28. *Towzih al-masael* [Clarification of Problems], Mashhad, 1367. Portions of an English translation of this work were printed in *Harper's Magazine,* June 1985.
29. Montazeri, *Khaterat,* Vol. 1, p. 211.
30. Ibid., p. 212.
31. Khalkhali, *Khaterat,* p. 64.
32. Bagher Agheli, *Ruzshomar-e tarikh-e Iran,* Tehran, 1384, ad loc.
33. Mohammed Reza used that phrase in a conversation with Denis Wright on April 16, 1963, FO 248/1590.
34. Khomeini, *Sahifeye nur,* Vol. 1, p. 16.
35. Montazeri, *Khaterat,* Vol. 1, p. 207.
36. *Gahnameyeh panjah sal shahanshahiye Pahlavi* [Chronology of Fifty Years of the Pahlavi Empire], Paris, 1364, ad loc.
37. I have written this account from the recollections of Montazeri, Khomeini, and Khalkhali; Rouhani's *Nehzat;* and Khomeini's speech at the Faizieh of June 3, 1963.
38. Montazeri, *Khaterat,* Vol. 1, p. 218.
39. Khalkhali, *Khaterat,* p. 74.
40. Ruhollah Khomeini, *Majmuei az maktubat, sokhanraniha va . . . Imam Khomeini* [Collected Letters, Speeches, etc.], Tehran, 1365, p. 36.
41. Montazeri, *Khaterat,* Vol. 1, p. 223.
42. Khomeini, *Majmuei,* p. 49.
43. Farah Pahlavi, *An Enduring Love,* New York, 2004, p. 130.
44. Khomeini, *Majmuei,* p. 59.
45. Khalkhali, *Khaterat,* p. 105.
46. Literally, "The cannon and musket are in my hand." Asadollah Alam, *Yaddashtha,* Tehran, 1380, 25 Farvardin 1354.
47. Mansuri, *Tarikh-e qiyam,* No. 4/61.
48. Ibid., Nos. 4/62 and 4/63.
49. Telegram from Savak station, Semnan, 17 Khordad 1342, ibid., No. 4/65.
50. "On 15 Khordad 42, the proud nation of Iran . . . sacrificed nearly fifteen thousand martyrs at the throne of God Almighty." 'Message on the anniversary of 15 Khordad 1342,' June 5, 1981. Khomeini, *Sahifeye nur,* Vol. 13, p. 260.
51. Denis Wright. Interview recorded by Habib Ladjevardi, October 10 and 11, 1984, Aylesbury, England. Iranian Oral History Collection, Harvard University, Transcript 2. Queen Farah gives a figure of fifty "in Tehran and the provinces," *Enduring Love,* p. 131. Emadeddin Baghi, who analyzed the returns at the Martyrs Foundation after the Revolution, gave a figure of thirty-two dead in Tehran, all males, emadbaghi.com/en/archives/000592.php. Moin, *Khomeini,* p. 110, quotes General Mobasher, who took over command in Qom at mid-afternoon on June

5, as saying twenty-eight were killed in that town. I could find no figures for the dead at Baqerabad.

52. Conversation with author.

53. Montazeri, *Khaterat,* Vol. 1, p. 234.

54. "It was . . . General Hassan Pakravan, a man of great culture, intelligence, and humanity, who pleaded clemency to the king." Farah Pahlavi, *Enduring Love,* p. 131.

55. Khalkhali, *Khaterat,* p. 125.

56. Montazeri, *Khaterat,* Vol. 1, p. 243.

57. Fatemeh Pakravan, interview recorded by Habib Ladjevardi, March 3, 1983, Paris, France. Iranian Oral History Collection, Harvard University, Transcript 1.

58. *FRUS, 1964–1968,* Vol. XXII: *Iran,* Embassy in Iran to Department of State, April 6, 1964.

59. *FRUS, 1961–1963,* Vol. XVII: *Near East,* pp. 519–20.

60. *FRUS, 1964–1968,* Vol. XXII: *Iran,* Embassy in Iran (Rockwell) to Department of State, October 14, 1964.

61. Khomeini was mistaken here. Under Article 37 of the Vienna Convention, local staff members such as cooks and servants are under the host country's jurisdiction. See http://untreaty.un.org/ilc/texts/instruments/english/conventions/9_1_1961.pdf.

62. Khomeini, *Majmuei,* pp. 129ff.

63. *FRUS, 1964–1968,* Vol. XXII: *Iran,* Embassy in Iran (Rockwell) to Department of State, November 5, 1964.

64. Ahmet Kahraman, "Türkiye'deki Hümeyni: İranli dini liderin sürgün günleri" [Khomeini in Turkey: The Iranian Religious Leader's Days of Exile], *Milliyet,* August 16–22, 1987.

65. *Milliyet,* August 18, 1987.

66. *Tahrir al-wasila* [Edition of the "Way"], Beirut, 1403/1982, 2 vols. (in Arabic).

67. Rouhani, *Nehzat,* p. 141.

68. Ibid., p. 159.

69. Ibid., pp. 221ff.

70. Ibid., p. 396.

71. Robert Graham, *Iran: The Illusion of Power,* London, 1978, p. 116.

5. Ruritania

1. Eskandar Beg Munshi, *Tarikh-e alamaraye Abbasi* [History of Shah Abbas the Great], Tehran, 1334, Vol. 1, p. 475.

2. Author's visits; Farah Pahlavi, *An Enduring Love,* New York, 2004, pp. 161–62; Pascal Hinous and Philippe Jullian, "Architectural Digest Visits the Empress of Iran," *Architectural Digest,* December 1977, pp. 68–76; *Jansen Decoration,* Paris, n.d.

3. Asadollah Alam, *Yaddashtha,* Tehran, 1380, 9 Azar 1349; *The Shah and I,* ed. Alinaghi Alikhani, London, 1991, p. 177.

4. Ashraf says she inherited the equivalent of $300,000, a hundred hectares on the Caspian, and properties in Gorgan and Kermanshah. *Faces in a Mirror,* Englewood Cliffs, N.J., 1980, p. 78.

5. Alam, *Yaddashtha*, 2 Farvardin 1351, "Prince Pimp" in English, English edition, ed. Alikhani, p. 207.

6. Alam, *Yaddashtha*, 12 Ordibehesht 1351; English edition, ed. Alikhani, p. 214.

7. *Tarikh-e moaser-e Iran*, Vol. 1, No. 4, Zemestan 1367.

8. Minou Reeves, *Behind the Peacock Throne*, London, 1986, p. 89.

9. "I asked HIM what expenses she should be allowed. 'As much as she wants,' he said. 'Maybe then she'll keep her gob shut.'" Alam, *Yaddashtha*; English edition, ed. Alikhani, p. 342.

10. Speech of September 20, 1951, in *Gahnameyeh panjah sal shahanshahiye Pahlavi* [Chronology of the Pahlavi Empire], Paris, 1364, Vol. 1, ad loc; also Farah Pahlavi, *Enduring Love*, p. 151. Hoveyda quoted the Shah as saying on 15 Esfand 1344: "The day I put on the crown is when the country's difficulties have been alleviated and my kingdom is on the path of progress and development. That time has come." Mokhtar Hadidi, "Asnad-e mehramaneye jashnehaye 2,500 saleh shahinshahi" [Confidential Documents on the 2,500th Anniversary Celebrations], *Tarikh-e moaser-e Iran*, Vol. 2, No. 5, Bahar 1377, p. 108.

11. Text in *Gahnameh*, ad loc; Farah Pahlavi, *Enduring Love*, p. 157.

12. Ruhollah Khomeini, *Velayat-e faqih: Hokumat-e Islami* [The Stewardship of the Jurist: Islamic Government], Tehran, 1357, p. 106; Hamid Algar, trans., *Islam and Revolution: Writings and Declarations of Imam Khomeini (1941–1980)*, Berkeley, Calif., 1981, p. 86.

13. Farah Pahlavi, *Enduring Love*, p. 153.

14. Described in V. B. Meen and A. D. Tushingham, *Crown Jewels of Iran*, Toronto, 1968, p. 57. Two of the loose, unset emeralds are illustrated on p. 64.

15. Hadidi, "Asnad-e mehramaneh," p. 109.

16. Mohammed Reza Pahlavi, *Mission for My Country*, London, 1961, p. 321.

17. FO 371/62017, Ead to Sargent, October 13, 1947.

18. Abbas Milani, *The Persian Sphinx*, Washington, D.C., pp. 197ff.

19. Alam, *Yaddashtha*, 20 Tir 1351: English edition, ed. Alikhani, p. 229.

20. FO 371/170526, Chevallier, July 17, 1963.

21. For example, Alam, *Yaddashtha*, 30 Ordibehesht 1348; English edition, ed. Alikhani, p. 65.

22. Alam, *Yaddashtha*, 6 Aban 1352; English edition, ed. Alikhani, p. 330.

23. Theodore Sorensen, *Kennedy*, New York, 1965, p. 628.

24. "Recent Trends in Iranian Arms Procurement," U.S. Central Intelligence Agency, Directorate of Intelligence/Office of Economic Research, May 1972.

25. Denis Wright. Interview recorded by Habib Ladjevardi, October 10 and 11, 1984, Aylesbury, England. Iranian Oral History Collection, Harvard University, Transcript 2.

26. FO 248/1694, Wright to Suffield, MOD, November 25, 1970. DEFE 24/1317, Street to Secretary of State, July 11, 1977.

27. U.S. Congress, Committee on Foreign Relations of the U.S. Senate, *U.S. Military sales to Iran: A Staff Report of the Subcommittee on Foreign Assistance*, Washington, July 1976, p. 7.

28. Sir Peter Ramsbotham. Interview recorded by Habib Ladjevardi, October 18, 1985, London, England. Iranian Oral History Collection, Harvard University, Transcript 1.

29. Robert E. Huyser, *Mission to Tehran,* London, 1986, p. 27.
30. According to William Safire, *Before the Fall,* New York, 2005, p. 458, "the Shah was about the President's favorite statesman." An entry in Alam's diaries suggests Mohammed Reza may have been asked by Nixon for contributions to his reelection campaign in 1972. Alam, *Yaddashtha,* 31 Tir–8 Mordad 1351.
31. Alam, *Yaddashtha,* 2 Bahman 1348; English edition, ed. Alikhani, p. 126.
32. Julian Bharier, *Economic Development in Iran, 1900–1970,* London, 1971, p. 120.
33. Alam, *Yaddashtha,* 17 Esfand 1347; English edition, ed. Alikhani, p. 39.
34. Alam, *Yaddashtha,* 2 Farvardin 1349; English edition, ed. Alikhani, p. 137.
35. Alam, *Yaddashtha,* 28 Mehr–30 Aban 1349; English edition, ed. Alikhani, p. 174.
36. David Holden and Richard Johns, *The House of Saud,* New York, 1982, p. 310.
37. Robert Graham, *Iran: The Illusion of Power,* London, 1978, p. 36.
38. Alam, *Yaddashtha,* 27 Bahman 1349; English edition, ed. Alikhani, p. 202.
39. Conversation with author, Haddenham, 1973; N. W. Browne, *British Policy on Iran, 1974–1979,* FCO, London, 1980, NBP 020/28, pp. 10 and 23, available at fco.gov.uk/en/about-us/our-history/historical-publications/documents-british-policy/british-policy-on-iran-1974–1978.
40. A letter from King Juan Carlos of Spain, written in French from Zarzuela on June 22, 1973, and asking for $10 million to support a centrist political party "pour la consolidation de la monarchie espagnole [to strengthen the Spanish monarchy]," is reproduced in Alam, *Yaddashtha,* Vol. 6, pp. 531ff.
41. *Bazm-e Ahriman* [Satan's Feast], Tehran, 1377, p. 9.
42. Interview with French television, 23 Bahman 1337, quoted in Hadidi, "Asnad-e mehramaneh," p. 104.
43. Mohammed Reza Pahlavi, *Mission for My Country,* London, 1961, p. 23.
44. That was my impression from two visits to Persepolis in 1974 and 1975.
45. Ruhollah Khomeini, *Message to the Proud People of Azerbaijan,* 19 Rabi 1, 1398, in *Majmuei az maktubat, sokhanraniha va . . . Imam Khomeini* [Collected Letters, Speeches, etc.], Tehran, 1360, p. 307.
46. Denis Wright. Interview recorded by Habib Ladjevardi, October 10 and 11, 1984, Aylesbury, England. Iranian Oral History Collection, Harvard University, Transcript 4.
47. Nassereddin's son and successor, Muzaffareddin, was admitted to the Garter in 1902.
48. Hadidi, "Asnad-e mehramaneh," p. 109.
49. Alam, *Yaddashtha,* 7 Shahrivar 1349. The Queen wrote later: "All I could do was accept the choices that had already been made." Farah Pahlavi, *Enduring Love,* p. 217.
50. Charlotte Curtis, "Tent City Awaits Celebration," *New York Times,* October 12, 1971.
51. Alam to Dr. Fazlollah Mushavar of NIOC, 21 Esfand 1350, in Hadidi, "Asnad-e mehramaneh," p. 182.
52. Interview with Abdolreza Ansari by Cyrus Kadivar, December 25, 2001, in "We Are Awake: 2,500-Year Celebrations Revisited," at Iranian.com.
53. Alam, *Yaddashtha,* 28 Mehr–30 Aban 1349; English edition, ed. Alikhani, p. 173. Abdolreza Ansari, an official in Princess Ashraf's office, said Alam threatened to resign if his plans were altered. Interview with Abdolreza Ansari by Gholamreza

Afkhami, 1991, Bethesda, Md., FISOHA, quoted in Afkhami, *The Life and Times of the Shah,* Berkeley, Calif., 2009, p. 408.

54. Alam, *Yaddashtha,* 17 Farvardin 1349; English edition, ed. Alikhani, p. 143. Farah Pahlavi, *Enduring Love,* p. 223.
55. *New York Times,* October 12, 1971.
56. Queen Elizabeth's handwritten letter of February 2, 1971, is reproduced in Alam, *Yaddashtha,* Vol. 2, pp. 196–97.
57. Alam, *Yaddashtha,* 28 Mehr–30 Aban 1349; English edition, ed. Alikhani, pp. 173–74.
58. Khomeini, *Majmuei,* pp. 170ff.
59. Marc Kravetz, *Irano Nox,* Paris, 1982, p. 23.
60. Anthony Parsons, *The Pride and Fall: Iran 1974–1979,* London, 1984, p. 24.
61. Bagher Agheli, *Ruzshomar-e tarikh-e Iran* [Historical Calendar of Iran], Tehran, 1384, 2 Aban 1350. AP, October 25, 1971. In his interview with Kadivar, Ansari gave a figure for the government expense of 1.6 billion rials, or about $22 million in the money of the day. William Shawcross, *The Shah's Last Ride: The Fate of an Ally,* New York, 1988, p. 47, says that the "whole affair cost anything up to $300m." That amount, $300 million, was a third of Iran's oil revenue in 1970. Had the festival cost that much, Iran's civil servants, armed forces, and trade and public creditors could not have been paid and the country would have been bankrupt.
62. Alam, *Yaddashtha,* 12 Azar 1351; English edition, ed. Alikhani, p. 263.
63. James Archer Abbott, *Jansen,* New York, 2006, p. 306.
64. Alam, *Yaddashtha,* 20 Mehr 1352.
65. Sir Peter Ramsbotham, interview recorded by Habib Ladjevardi, October 18, 1985, London, England. Iranian Oral History Collection, Harvard University, Transcript 1.

6. The Storm Gathers

1. Literally, "Behold the moon! And there are the Pleiades!" *Gulistan,* 1:31.
2. FO 1110/1770, General Pakravan in London, December 1964.
3. Parviz Radji, *In the Service of the Peacock Throne,* London, 1983, p. 123.
4. Pakravan himself was more philosophical. "One must move with the times," he told his wife Fatemeh. Madame Pakravan, interview recorded by Habib Ladjevardi, March 3 and 7, 1983, Paris, France. Iranian Oral History Collection, Harvard University (in English).
5. Sabeti to Abbas Milani, 2003, in Milani, *Eminent Persians,* Syracuse, N.Y., 2008, Vol. 1, p. 479.
6. Hosein Fardoust, *Zuhur va suqut-e saltanat-e Pahlavi: Khaterat-e arteshbod-e sabeq Hosein Fardoust* [The Rise and Fall of the Pahlavi Monarchy], Tehran, 1374, Vol. 1, pp. 413–4.
7. Richard Savin, *Vakil Abad,* Edinburgh, 1979, p. 122.
8. On June 1, 1976, a group of Iranian students overran the Savak station at the consulate general in Geneva and found a fifty-eight-page list of Iranian students who were to be questioned. "Schah-Spitzel: 'Bohnen' und 'Sauberfinger,'" *Der Spiegel,* September 6, 1976, pp. 124–25.

9. When Mohammed Reza attended the commencement ceremonies at the University of Los Angeles in 1964, a hired aircraft twice flew over, towing a streamer that read, "Need a fix? See the Shah," *FRUS, 1964–1968*, Vol. XXII: *Iran*, Department of State, Washington, D.C., to the Embassy in Iran, June 16, 1964.

10. Farah Pahlavi, *An Enduring Love*, New York, 2004, p. 236.

11. Alam, *Yaddashtha*, Tehran, 1380, 17 Shahrivar 1352; *The Shah and I*, ed. Alinaghi Alikhani, London, 1991, p. 315.

12. *Gharbzadegi* [Sick from the West], Tehran, 1341, p. 78.

13. *Islamshenasi* [Islamology], Mashhad, 1347, pp. 30ff.

14. "The history of Shi'ism mustn't be written from the perspective of Imam Hussain's movement alone; his movement was an exception in the history of Shi'ism, not the rule." "An Interview with Abdulkarim Soroush by Reza Khojasteh-Rahimi," June 2008, at drsoroush.com.

15. Ali Rahnema, *An Islamic Utopian: A Political Biography of Ali Shariati*, London, 1998, p. 315.

16. "Nameye montasher nashodeye Doktor Shariati," *Iran-e Farda*, No. 16, Esfand 1383.

17. Rahnema, *Utopian*, p. 278.

18. Ibid., p. 334.

19. The plot may have had little substance, but the Queen believed in it. Farah Pahlavi, *Enduring Love*, p. 191.

20. Translated from the court newsreel, video available at youtube.com/watch?v=buTIBLGdUfo (in Persian).

21. Ruhollah Khomeini, *Sahifeye nur* [The Page of Light], Tehran, 1361, Vol. 1, p. 227. Rahnema, *Utopian*, p. 275. According to Hamid Rouhani, *Nehzat-e Imam Khomeini* [Imam Khomeini's Movement], Tehran, 1361, Vol. 2, pp. 701–2, Khomeini showed his disapproval by remaining silent regarding Shariati and, after Shariati's death, refusing to accord him the conventional honorific *marhum*, "blessed."

22. Hosein Ali Montazeri says that in their discussions in Qom before 1964, "there was no hint of the Stewardship of the Jurist." Montazeri, *Khaterat*, Vol. 1, p. 199, at amontazeri.com.

23. Ruhollah Khomeini, *Velayat-e faqih: Hokumat-e Islami* [The Stewardship of the Jurist: Islamic Government], Tehran, 1357, p. 63; Hamid Algar, trans., *Islam and Revolution, I: Writings and Declarations of Imam Khomeini (1941–1980)*, Berkeley, Calif., 1981, p. 62.

24. Ibid., pp. 173–74; Algar, trans., pp. 126–27.

25. For example, Mohsen Kadivar, *Nazarihaye dowlat dar fiqh-e Shia* [The State in Shia Jurisprudence], Tehran, 1376; and its successor volume, *Hokumat-e velayi* [Delegated Government], Tehran, 1377.

26. Khomeini, *Velayat*, p. 58; Algar, trans., p. 58. Both pen and inkpot are visible in the photograph of Khomeini's room on the cover of the first Tehran edition of *Velayat*.

27. It is not true that the Israelis staged the Persepolis celebrations.

28. Ruhollah Khomeini, *Majmuei az maktubat, sokhanraniha va . . . Imam Khomeini* [Collected Letters, Speeches, etc.], Tehran, 1360, p. 168.

29. Adam Smith, *The Theory of Moral Sentiments*, London, 1759, VII.iii.3.15.

30. Reza Hajatpour, *Der brennende Geschmack der Freiheit: Mein Leben als junger*

Mullah im Iran [The Burning Taste of Freedom: My Life as a Young Mullah in Iran], Frankfurt am Main, 2005, p. 187.

31. Rouhani, *Nehzat,* Vol. 2, p. 323.

32. Khomeini, *Sahifeye nur,* Vol. 2, p. 250.

33. Reuters, March 20, 1973.

34. *New York Times,* December 24, 1973; Robert Graham, *Iran: The Illusion of Power,* London, 1978, p. 15; and *Kayhan International,* December 23, 1973, have slightly different wording.

35. Alam, *Yaddashtha,* 5 Mehr, 1352; English edition, ed. Alikhani, p. 321. Graham, *Illusion,* p. 77.

36. Graham, *Illusion,* p. 112.

37. *Gahnameye panjah sal shahinshahiye Pahlavi* [Chronology of Fifty Years of the Pahlavi Empire], Paris, 1364, entry for August 3, 1974; *Kayhan International,* August 4, 1974; Graham, *Illusion,* p. 80.

38. Graham, *Illusion,* p. 83.

39. Ibid., p. 87.

40. In Qajar times, the New Town stood just outside the city walls beyond the Qaz-vin Gate. It was used by the city authorities as a sort of quarantine or dumping ground to remove streetwalkers and other prostitutes from the city proper. A police report of June 27, 1907, records an incident when an old notable named Qavam Daftar turned up at the gate "in night-cap and pyjamas" and was not admitted, because the women had been frightened by the local *lutis,* or rough-necks. The report is reproduced in *Yaghma,* Ordibehesht 1339 (May 1960).

41. Asef Bayat, *Street Politics,* New York, 1997, p. 27. Zurabad was in Karaj.

42. Speech in Najaf of February 18, 1978. Khomeini, *Sahifeye nur,* Vol. 1, p. 30.

43. Abdolreza Ansari, deputy head of the Central Council of the Festival, to Mayor Nikpay, 2 Shahrivar 1350. Mokhtar Hadidi, "Asnad-e mehramaneye jashnehaye 2,500 saleh shahinshahi," *Tarikh-e moaser-e Iran,* Vol. 2, No. 5, Bahar 1377, p. 179, Doc. 44.

44. *Kayhan International,* October 26, 1976; *Der Spiegel,* November 22, 1976.

45. U.S. Senate, Committee on Foreign Relations, *U.S. Military Sales to Iran: A Staff Report of the Subcommittee on Foreign Assistance,* Washington, D.C., July 1976, p. vii.

46. "A General View of the Region," n.p., n.d. [1973], in "A Life in Intelligence: The Richard Helms Collection," at foia.cia.gov/helms.asp.

47. U.S. Congress, *U.S. Military Sales to Iran,* p. vi.

48. Dennis Romano, a Grumman test engineer who was in the backseat of the air-craft, recalled: "We took the airplane up into the vertical, cleaned up the gear and flaps, pulled it upside down, and rolled out at about eight hundred to a thou-sand feet headed south. Then came a 90-degree turn to the right, followed by a 270-degree turn to the left to come back to runway heading. Next came a knife-edge pass, the airplane rolled 90 degrees, to the vertical, to give reviewing stands a plain view of the variable sweep wing. This meant sweeping the wings manually from 68 degrees full aft to full forward, 22 degrees—a very uncomfortable maneu-ver. . . . We did a quarter-roll right over the top of where the Shah was standing. Then we landed with a maximum-performance braking maneuver, stopping the airplane probably in about twelve hundred feet. The F-14 was never outside the

field boundaries for the entire air show, it was always visible." G. M. Skurla and W. H. Gregory, *Inside the Iron Works: How Grumman's Glory Days Faded,* Annapolis, Md., 2004, pp. 116–17.

49. Ibid., p. 119.
50. "The critical variable . . . is the degree to which the IIAF can recruit and train the technical personnel required to perform operation, maintenance and logistical functions associated with its sophisticated inventory." U.S. Congress, *U.S. Military Sales to Iran,* p. 25.
51. I was witness of the last.
52. Abbas Gharabaghi, *Vérités sur la crise iranienne,* Paris, 1985, p. 77; Iraj Yahyapur, "Naqsh-e artesh dar enqelab-e islami, motaleye muredi: Homafaran" [The Role of the Armed Forces in the Islamic Revolution: The Case of the Air Force Technicians], *Motalaat tarikhi-nezami* [Historical and Military Studies], Vol. 1, Nos. 5 and 6, p. 165.
53. Alam, *Yaddashtha,* 15–16 Mehr 1353; English edition, ed. Alikhani, pp. 390–91.
54. U.S. Congress, *U.S. Military Sales to Iran,* p. xiii.
55. George Ball, *The Past Has Another Pattern,* New York, 1982, pp. 453–58.
56. Geoffrey Moorhouse, *The Diplomats: The Foreign Office Today,* London, 1977, p. 294.
57. Alam, *Yaddashtha,* 1353; English edition, ed. Alikhani, p. 234.
58. N. W. Browne, *British Policy on Iran, 1974–1979,* FCO, London, 1980, p. 47.
59. "Comment by Sir A. D. Parsons, Her Majesty's Ambassador, Tehran: 1974–1979." Ibid., Annex B.
60. Ibid., p. 47.
61. Alam, *Yaddashtha,* 16 Esfand 1353; English edition, ed. Alikhani, pp. 417–18.
62. "Treaty Concerning the State Frontier and Neighbourly Relations (with Protocol Concerning the Delimitation of the River Frontier), Dated 13 June 1975," *United Nations Treaty Series,* No. 14903.
63. Anthony Parsons, *The Pride and the Fall: Iran, 1974–1979,* London, 1984, p. 24.
64. Ken Perkins, "The Death of an Army: A Short Analysis of the Imperial Iranian Armed Forces," *Royal United Services Institute,* Vol. 125, June 1980, pp. 21–23; Graham, *Illusion,* p. 180.
65. Alam, *Yaddashtha,* 15 Azar 1352; English edition, ed. Alikhani, pp. 340–41.
66. Alam, *Yaddashtha,* 21 Azar 1351; English edition, ed. Alikhani, p. 264.
67. Alam, *Yaddashtha,* 30 and 31 Tir 1352; English edition, ed. Alikhani, pp. 306–7.
68. Alam, *Yaddashtha,* 10 Shahrivar 1352; English edition, ed. Alikhani, p. 313.
69. Alam, *Yaddashtha,* 25 Shahrivar 1352.
70. *New York Times,* February 23, 1976.
71. *Kayhan,* 27 Shahrivar 1354.
72. "In the event of a transition in the regime, following the natural death or removal of the Shah by other means, the military is likely to be the dominant force in controlling political developments. If forced to choose the key military figure in a transition, we would pick General Mohammed Khatami, as the husband of the Shah's sister well-connected in the establishment, and as head of the Air Force, leader of the most effective of the three Services." *FRUS, 1969–1976,* Vol. XXVII: *Iran; Iraq (1973–1976),* Embassy in Iran to Department of State, January 9, 1973. Robert Graham, the *Financial Times* correspondent in Tehran in the mid-1970s,

wrote that Khatami "was generally regarded as the man who would hold the armed forces loyal if anything were to happen to the Shah." Graham, *Illusion*, p. 74.

73. Alam, *Yaddashtha*, 21 Dey 1354; English edition, ed. Alikhani, p. 460. Alam thought that a "wild overstatement."

74. Alam, *Yaddashtha*, 3 Mehr, 1354; English edition, ed. Alikhani, p. 444.

75. Mohammed Reza Pahlavi, *Answer to History*, New York, 1980, App. III.

76. Alam, *Yaddashtha*, 20 Farvardin 1353; English edition, ed. Alikhani, p. 363.

77. "Obituary: Jean Bernard," *British Medical Journal*, Vol. 332, No. 7554, June 8, 2006.

78. Alam, *Yaddashtha*, 20 Farvardin 1353; English edition, ed. Alikhani, p. 363.

79. Flandrin assumes this was "at the end of 1973." Flandrin to Professor Bernard, in Farah Pahlavi, *Enduring Love*, p. 245.

80. Interview with Dr. Georges Flandrin and others by William Shawcross, in Shawcross, *The Shah's Last Ride: The Fate of an Ally*, New York, 1988, pp. 232–33.

81. Alam, *Yaddashtha*, 26–31 Khordad 1353; English edition, ed. Alikhani, p. 377. Alam had the courtier's habit of putting his opinions into the mouths of others, so it is possible that Bernard did not say this.

82. Alam, *Yaddashtha*, 18 Shahrivar 1353; English edition, ed. Alikhani, pp. 386–87.

83. Transcript of interview with Amir Aslan Afshar for BBC documentary film, *Iran and the West*, 2009, Liddell Hart Centre for Military Archives, King's College, London.

84. Lawrence K. Altman, M.D., "The Shah's Health: A Political Gamble," *New York Times Magazine*, May 17, 1981.

85. Lord Owen, "Diseased, Demented, Depressed: Serious Illness in Heads of State," *QJM*, Vol. 96, No. 5, 2003, pp. 325ff.

86. Farah Pahlavi, *Enduring Love*, pp. 266–67. Valéry Giscard d'Estaing, *Le pouvoir et la vie*, Paris, 2004, p. 98.

87. "That he, the Shah, knowing that his elder son, who was going to be the Shah, hadn't got what it takes, really, to do what he was doing to hold the country together, was putting off his own retirement. I think he said to me—or Asadollah, I can't remember which—that he would carry on till he was sixty-five, or thereabouts, and would gradually retire. But he wouldn't wholly . . . he wouldn't leave all the reins of office for that reason. And that's why he was in such a hurry—much too much of a hurry—to industrialize and change. It brought about his downfall." Peter Ramsbotham. Interview recorded by Habib Ladjevardi, October 18, 1985, London, England. Iranian Oral History Collection, Harvard University, Transcript 1.

88. Graham, *Illusion*, p. 132.

89. Flandrin to Bernard, quoted in Farah Pahlavi, *Enduring Love*, p. 187.

90. Alam, *Yaddashtha*, 7 Mordad 1354; English edition, ed. Alikhani, pp. 431–32.

91. Mohammed Reza Pahlavi, *Mission for My Country*, London, 1961, pp. 162 and 173.

92. Alam, *Yaddashtha*, 18 Azar 1352; English edition, ed. Alikhani, p. 341.

93. Nahavandi interview, *France 24*, February 10, 2010.

94. Farah Pahlavi, *Enduring Love*, pp. 260–61.

95. Alam, *Yaddashtha*, 4 and 5 Esfand 1353; English edition, ed. Alikhani, pp. 413–14.

96. *Kayhan,* 12 Esfand 1353.
97. Gholam Reza Afkhami, *The Life and Times of the Shah,* Berkeley, Calif., 2009, pp. 433ff, says that the idea for "a political movement . . . called the Resurrection Movement of the Iranian Nation" arose from a group of intellectuals (including himself) working for the Queen over the winter of 1971–1972.
98. Rahnema, *Utopian,* p. 349, concludes that the articles were extracted from Shariati by Savak.
99. *New York Times,* June 18, 1979.
100. Alam, *Yaddashtha,* 12 Ordibehesht 1354. The young men, seven from the Fedayan and two from the Mojahedin, had been in prison since the late 1960s. They were killed in the hills above Evin by Savak officers in revenge for the assassination of a successful Savak double-agent who had infiltrated the armed Left, Abbas Shahriari. Jazani is buried in Behesht-e Zahra cemetery, Section 33, Row 119, No. 4.
101. Ebrahim Yazdi, *Akharin talashha dar akharin ruzha* [The Final Push], Tehran, 1388, p. 51.
102. Abbas Milani, *Tales of Two Cities: A Persian Memoir,* Washington, 1996, p. 164. In Shia jurisprudence, what constitutes the unclean or *najes* varies according to the jurist. Khomeini himself was considered by some in Qom to be unclean by reason of his teaching philosophy.
103. Ruhollah Khomeini, *Majmuei az maktubat, sokhanraniha va . . . Imam Khomeini* [Collected Letters, Speeches, etc], Tehran, 1360, p. 223.
104. Khomeini, *Sahifeye nur,* Vol. 4, p. 26.
105. Savin, *Vakil Abad,* p. 156.
106. Farah Pahlavi, *Enduring Love,* p. 190.
107. Audio recording at presidency.ucsb.edu/mediaplay.php?id=25953&admin=39.
108. Radji, *Peacock,* p. 42.
109. "The total number of political prisoners has been reported at times throughout the year to be anything from 25,000 to 100,000 but AI is not able to make any reliable estimate." *Amnesty International Annual Report,* London, 1975, p. 129.
110. *Amnesty International Annual Report,* London, 1977, p. 298.
111. Savin, *Vakil Abad,* p. 187.
112. Ali Akbar Hashemi Rafsanjani, *Douran-e mobarezeh* [The Years of Struggle], Tehran, 1386, pp. 303ff.
113. Alam, *Yaddashtha,* 5 Tir 1356; English edition, ed. Alikhani, p. 549.
114. Ali Asghar Hajj Sayyid Javadi, *Namehha* [Letters], Tehran, 1357.
115. Radji, *Peacock,* p. 89.
116. Ibid., p. 91.
117. Interview with Nasser Minachi, 1996, in Rahnema, *Utopian,* p. 368.
118. The coroner's report of June 21 gave "cardiac failure" as the cause of death. The philosopher Soroush, who hurried down from London at the news of Shariati's death, said: "Mr. Minachi and I entered the cold chamber [of the hospital mortuary] and I saw Dr. Shariati's body lying in one of the many drawers that they had there. He looked very serene and there weren't any signs of injury on his face or body." See drsoroush.com/English/Interviews/E-INT-Shariati_June2008.html.
119. Alam, *Yaddashtha,* 7 Mehr 1356; English edition, ed. Alikhani, p. 557.
120. Gharabaghi, *Vérités,* pp. 23–24.
121. Nasser Moazzen, *Dah shab: Shabhaye shaeran va nevisandegan dar Anjuman-e*

Farhangiye Iran va Alman [Ten Nights: Poets and Writers at the Irano-German Cultural Institute], Tehran, 1978.

122. Koran 2:156.
123. Khomeini, *Majmuei,* pp. 264–66.
124. Farah Pahlavi, *Enduring Love,* p. 270.
125. Jimmy Carter, *Keeping Faith: Memoirs of a President,* New York, 1982, p. 434.
126. Ibid., p. 437.
127. Graham, *Illusion,* p. 213.
128. "I have never heard a foreign statesman speak of me in quite such flattering terms." Mohammed Reza Pahlavi, *Answer,* p. 152.
129. "Toasts of the President and the Shah at a State Dinner, Tehran, Iran, December 31, 1977," at presidency.ucsb.edu.

7. The Indian

1. PREM (Prime Minister's Office) 16/1719, Parsons to FCO, September 25, 1978.
2. *Ettelaat,* 17 Dey 2036 by the Imperial calendar.
3. Ziauddin Tabaraian, "Enfejar-e yek maqaleh va paslarzehhaye an" [A Newspaper Article and Its Aftershocks], *Tarikh-e moaser-e Iran,* Vol. 6, No. 24, Zemestan 1381, pp. 5ff.
4. *Politica,* 1303b.
5. "A common soldier, a child, a girl at the door of an inn, have changed the face of fortune, and almost of Nature." Edmund Burke, *First Letter on a Regicide Peace,* London, 1795.
6. *Ettelaat,* 17 Dey 2036.
7. *Ettelaat* first appeared on July 11, 1926.
8. Daryoush Homayoun, *Zendegi pas az mordan, pish az marg* [Returned to Life], at d-homayoun.net.
9. "High-ranking security official" (that is, Sabeti) in Abbas Milani, *The Persian Sphinx,* Washington, D.C., 2004, p. 286.
10. Tabaraian, "Enfejar."
11. Anthony Parsons, *The Pride and the Fall: Iran, 1974–1979,* London, 1984, p. 61.
12. Tabaraian, "Enfejar," and Homayoun, *Zendegi,* go into detail.
13. There was no edition of *Ettelaat* on January 6, a Friday, which is the weekly holiday.
14. The government figure was nine dead. The Queen gives a figure of eight, including two policemen: Farah Pahlavi, *An Enduring Love,* New York, 2004, p. 274. The Islamic Republic has not so far attempted to enumerate or name the dead of the Revolution year.
15. Bagher Agheli, *Ruzshomar-e tarikh-e Iran* [Historical Calendar of Iran], 22 Dey 1356.
16. Richard Savin, *Vakil Abad,* Edinburgh, 1979, p. 218.
17. Parsons, *Pride and Fall,* p. 62.
18. Hamid Rouhani, *Nehzat-e Imam Khomeini* [Imam Khomeini's Movement], Tehran, 1381, Vol. 2, p. 570, makes this point.
19. Ruhollah Khomeini, *Sahifeye nur* [The Page of Light], Tehran, 1361, Vol. 2, pp.

22–34; Hamid Algar, trans., *Islam and Revolution, 1: Writings and Declarations of Imam Khomeini, 1941–1980,* Berkeley, Calif., 1981, pp. 213 and 217. The reference is to Koran 7:107.

20. Hosein Alai in *Hamshahri,* 28 Bahman 1389.
21. Farah Pahlavi, *Enduring Love,* p. 275.
22. Agheli, *Ruzshomar,* 29 Bahman 1356.
23. Gary Sick, *All Fall Down,* New York, 1985, p. 35.
24. Farah Pahlavi, *Enduring Love,* p. 274.
25. Ruhollah Khomeini, *Majmuei az maktubat, sokhanraniha va . . . Imam Khomeini* [Collected Letters, Speeches, etc.], Tehran, 1360, pp. 305–7; Algar, trans., *Islam,* pp. 228–30.
26. Quoted from the Congress papers by G. R. Afkhami, *The Life and Times of the Shah,* Berkeley, Calif., 2009, p. 261. Afkhami's wife, Mahnaz, was secretary general of the Women's Organization of Iran. Agheli, *Ruzshomar,* 8 Esfand 1356, omits the dog, which is from Sadi among others: "Mah feshanad noor o sag oo-oo konad / har kasi bar tinate khod mikonad." ["The moon shines and the dog howls/ Each acts according to its own nature."]
27. Parsons, *Pride and Fall,* pp. 63–64.
28. Farah Pahlavi, *Enduring Love,* p. 275.
29. Sick, *All Fall Down,* p. 35.
30. *Dar bareye qiyam-e Qom va Tabriz* [Concerning the Uprisings in Qom and Tabriz], Belleville, Ill., 1978, Vol. 3, pp. 22–26.
31. Parsons, *Pride and Fall,* p. 66.
32. Ibid., pp. 63–64.
33. *Focus,* October 31, 1994.
34. Mehdi Bazargan, *Khaterat,* Tehran, 1377, Vol. 2, p. 236.
35. Ibid., p. 246.
36. Parviz Radji, *In the Service of the Peacock Throne,* London, 1983, pp. 169–70, diary entry for April 21, 1978.
37. Ibid., p. 179, entry for May 13, 1978.
38. Mohammed Reza Pahlavi, *Answer to History,* New York, 1980, p. 155.
39. Agheli, *Ruzshomar,* 23 Ordibehesht 1357.
40. Sick, *All Fall Down,* p. 36.
41. Agheli, *Ruzshomar,* 26 Ordibehesht 1357.
42. PREM 16/1719, Parsons to FCO, May 10, 1978; Parsons, *Pride and Fall,* p. 66.
43. William H. Sullivan, *Mission to Iran,* New York, 1981, p. 148.
44. Radji, *Peacock,* p. 187, entry for June 6, 1978.
45. Agheli, *Ruzshomar,* 14 Mordad 1357.
46. Radji, *Peacock,* p. 210, entry for August 5, 1978.
47. Ibid., p. 215, entry for August 9, 1978.
48. UPI, August 13, 1978.
49. Jimmy Carter, *Keeping Faith,* New York, 1982, p. 438.
50. Shaida Nabavi, "Abadan, 28 Mordad 1357: Sinema Reks," *Cheshmandaz,* No. 20, Bahar 1378.
51. For example, *Time,* September 4, 1978.
52. "For me the revolution started with the fire at the Rex Cinema in Abadan." ". . . The revolution—everything—started for me with the fire at the Rex Cinema."

Haleh Esfandiari, ed., *Reconstructed Lives: Women and Iran's Islamic Revolution,* Washington, D.C., 1997, p. 62.

53. "The nucleus of the oil-workers' strike must be sought in this event." Reza Baraheni, "Che shodeh ast va che khahad shod" [What Happened and What Will Happen], 21 Azar 1357, in Baraheni, *Dar enqelab-e Iran che shodeh ast va che khahad shod,* Tehran, 1358, p. 105.

54. *Kayhan,* 28 Mordad 1359.

55. The hearing was conducted by a single judge and two assistants over twelve half-day sessions. For comparison, the inquest into the London bombings of July 7, 2005, heard evidence from 310 witnesses over sixty-three days and cost £5 million.

56. Genesis 4:15, Authorized Version: "And the Lord set a mark upon Cain, lest any finding him should kill him." Koran 5:23–31 omits the mark.

57. *Ettelaat,* 5 Shahrivar 1359.

58. *Kayhan,* 15 Shahrivar 1359.

8. The Burnt Cinema

1. Koran 5:32. Author's translation.

2. *Ettelaat,* 6 Shahrivar 1359.

3. "Armed assault" is *chaqukeshi,* or "knife-pulling." *Kayhan,* 3 Shahrivar 1359.

4. Monika Faber, Azar Nafisi, and John P. Jacob, *Inge Morath: Iran,* Göttingen, 2009, pp. 213ff.

5. Kamin Mohammadi, *Financial Times,* July 15, 2005.

6. *Kayhan,* 4 Shahrivar 1359.

7. "After a while I said to Yadollah, Faraj, and Fallah that sitting in the mosque and reading the Koran was pointless, and I quit." *Ettelaat,* 6 Shahrivar 1359.

8. Ibid.

9. For example, Ruhollah Khomeini, *Sahifeye nur* [The Page of Light], Tehran, 1361, Vol. 2, pp. 218 and 259.

10. *Kayhan,* 4 Shahrivar 1359. A high school teacher and reader at the Hoseinieh of the Isfahanians in Abadan, Rashidian, was named in the arraignment, but by then he was a member of parliament for Abadan and he was not called or questioned by the court. Shaida Nabavi, "Abadan, 28 Mordad 1357: Sinema Reks," *Cheshmandaz,* No. 20, Bahar 1378.

11. "Because the thinner was volatile (*furi*), it evaporated and had no effect." *Ettelaat,* 6 Shahrivar 1359.

12. *Roghan,* which can also mean clarified butter or ghee. So the newspaper reports.

13. *Ettelaat,* 6 Shahrivar 1359.

14. Minou Reeves, *Behind the Peacock Throne,* London, 1986, pp. 176–77.

15. The syllogism is: (A) The Rex Cinema fire was a great crime. (B) Muslims do not commit great crimes. Therefore, (C) a Muslim could not have caused the Rex Cinema fire.

16. There is wordplay in *Shahkar,* which means both "action by the King" and the "masterpiece" of an artist, poet, athlete, or craftsman. Khomeini, *Sahifeye nur,* Vol. 2, p. 91; Hamid Algar, trans., *Islam and Revolution, 1: Writings and Declarations of Imam Khomeini, 1941–1980,* Berkeley, Calif., 1981, p. 232.

17. Nabavi, "Abadan," p. 3.
18. Ibid., p. 2.
19. PREM 16/1719, Parsons to Secretary of State, October 9, 1978.
20. "This incident broke the spirit of the Shah, setting him on the path of concession and then surrender to the revolutionary forces." Daryoush Homayoun, *Zendegi pas az mordan, pish az marg* [Returned to Life], at d-homayoun.net.
21. William Sullivan, *Mission to Iran*, New York, 1981, p. 157.
22. Farah Pahlavi, *An Enduring Love*, New York, 2004, pp. 280–81.
23. Ibid., p. 278.
24. PREM 16/1719, Chalmers to FCO, August 29, 1978.
25. *Kayhan*, 4 Shahrivar 1359; *Ettelaat* of the same day.
26. *Kayhan*, 1 Shahrivar 1357.
27. Mohammed Reza Pahlavi, *Answer to History*, New York, 1980, p. 160. Houchang Nahavandi, who was meeting Shariatmadari at the time, has Shariatmadari calling for "a radical decision" and "a capital decision." Nahavandi, *The Last Shah of Iran*, Slough, 2005, pp. 141–42.
28. "I should never have allowed this wise and unbiased counselor to withdraw." Mohammed Reza Pahlavi, *Answer*, p. 160.
29. Alam reports Mohammed Reza speculating whether Freemasons were behind the events of June 1963.
30. Nahavandi, *Last Shah*, pp. 157–58.
31. Ibid., p. 164.
32. Sullivan, *Mission*, p. 165.
33. Nahavandi, *Last Shah*, p. 178.
34. A translation of *Baradar-e arteshi, chera baradarkoshi?*
35. *Kayhan*, 16 Shahrivar 1359.
36. Nahavandi, *Last Shah*, p. 200. Compare Anthony Parsons, *The Pride and the Fall: Iran, 1974–1979*, London, 1984, p. 71, on his audience of September 16: "The Shah then asked plaintively why it was that the masses had turned against him after all that he had done for them."
37. N. W. Browne, *British Policy on Iran, 1974–1979*, FCO, London, 1980, NBP 020/28, p. 20.
38. Ashraf Pahlavi, *Faces in a Mirror*, Englewood Cliffs, N.J., 1980, pp. 205–6. Also, Parviz Radji, *In the Service of the Peacock Throne*, London, 1983, p. 226.
39. Ruhollah Khomeini, *Majmuei az maktubat, sokhanraniha va . . . Imam Khomeini* [Collected Letters, Speeches, etc.], Tehran, 1360, p. 25; Algar, trans., *Islam*, p. 234.
40. Mohammed Reza Mahdavi-Kani, *Khaterat*, Tehran, 1385, p. 182.
41. I visited this district in 1974 and again, with greater attention, in 1999. Also, "Plan Prepared by the Geographical Section, General Staff, Persian Army," April 1945; and the 1:2000 Tehran mosaic of the National Cartographical Center of the Plan Organization, March 1964, Sheet B53.
42. Nahavandi, *Last Shah*, p. 189.
43. Qom, Tabriz, Mashhad, Isfahan, Shiraz, Abadan, Ahvaz, Qazvin, Kazerun, Jahrom, and Karaj.
44. Audio interview for BBC Persian Service, *Dastan-e enqelab* [The Story of the Revolution], printed in Omid Parsanejad, *Jomeh Siah* [Black Friday], September 6, 2008, at bbc.co.uk/persian/iran/story/2008/09/080906_op-black-friday.shtml.

45. PREM 16/1719, Chalmers to FCO, September 8, 1978.
46. *Kayhan,* 16 Shahrivar 1359.
47. Printed in full in *Kayhan,* 18 Shahrivar 1357: that is, the next day, Saturday, as there was no edition on Friday afternoon.
48. Information from racecourse employee.
49. Bagher Agheli, *Ruzshomar-e tarikh-e Iran* [Historical Calendar of Iran], Tehran, 1384, Vol. 2, 20 Shahrivar 1357; Trevor Mostyn, *Coming of Age in the Middle East,* London, 1987, p. 160.
50. For example, Vladimir Kuzichkin, *Inside the KGB,* London, 1990, p. 241.
51. Emaduddin Baghi, "Amar-e qorbaniun-e enqelab" [Figures for the Victims of the Revolution], *Iran-e Emruz,* 8 Mordad 1382, at emadbaghi.com.
52. Mohammed Reza Pahlavi, *Answer,* p. 160.
53. Général Abbas Gharabaghi, *Vérités sur la crise iranienne,* Paris, 1985, p. 225.
54. Nahavandi, *Last Shah,* p. 195.
55. Parviz Radji, review of Abbas Milani, *The Persian Sphinx,* Iran Press Service, December 18, 2000.
56. PREM 16/1719, Chalmers to FCO, September 11, 1978.
57. Mohammed Reza Pahlavi, *Answer,* p. 161.
58. PREM 16/1719, Prime Minister to Parsons, September 14, 1978.
59. PREM 16/1719, Parsons to FCO, September 16, 1978.
60. With the annexation in 1856 of the kingdom of Lucknow, the government of India became trustee of a valuable fund for the endowment of the Shia holy places in Iraq known as the Oudh Bequest. In 1902, the British minister in Tehran, Arthur Hardinge, had proposed making careful payments to subsidize the clergy in Iran and Iraq as a counter to Russian influence: FO 60/664, Hardinge to Lansdowne, August 27, 1902. His successor, Spring-Rice, allowed the Constitutionalists, led by the "Two Proofs of Islam," Behbehani and Tabatabai, to take asylum in the British Embassy garden in 1906. From then on, British contacts with the clergy diminished and then ceased.
61. Parsons, *Pride and Fall,* p. 72.
62. Farah Pahlavi, *Enduring Love,* p. 283.
63. Ibid.
64. PREM 16/1719, Parsons to FCO, October 3, 1978. Also Parsons, *Pride and Fall,* p. 78.
65. Sharif-Emami related that to Parsons. PREM 16/1719, Parsons to FCO, October 3, 1978.
66. Ebrahim Yazdi, *Akharin talashha dar akharin ruzha* [The Final Push], Tehran, 1388, p. 96.
67. Fouad Ajami, *The Vanished Imam: Musa al Sadr and the Shia of Lebanon,* Ithaca, N.Y., 1986, pp. 182–83.
68. PREM 16/1719, Parsons to FCO, October 6, 1978. Also Parsons, *Pride and Fall,* p. 83.
69. PREM 16/1719, Parsons to Secretary of State, October 9, 1978.
70. Browne, *British Policy,* p. 21.
71. Richard Savin, *Vakil Abad,* Edinburgh, 1979, p. 225. This was possibly on October 16.
72. Farah Pahlavi, *Enduring Love,* p. 285.

9. The Junction

1. Mohammed Reza Pahlavi, *Answer to History*, New York, 1980, p. 167.
2. Gary Sick, a White House official, received a frantic telephone call from Professor Richard Cottam of Pittsburgh University, who was Yazdi's friend. Sick, *All Fall Down*, New York, 1985, p. 57.
3. Ebrahim Yazdi, *Akharin talashha dar akharin ruzha* [The Final Push], Tehran, 1388, p. 79.
4. Ibid., p. 81.
5. Text of Carter letter in PREM 16/1720, President Carter to Prime Minister Callaghan, November 24, 1978.
6. Mohsen Sazegara, *Financial Times Magazine*, February 9, 2009.
7. Valéry Giscard d'Estaing, *Le pouvoir et la vie*, Paris, 2004, pp. 107ff.
8. Mohammed Reza Pahlavi, *Answer*, p. 163; Christine Ockrent and Alexandre de Marenches, *Dans le secret des princes*, Paris, 1986, p. 254.
9. PREM 16/1719, Parsons to FCO, October 11, 1978.
10. PREM 16/1719, Parsons to FCO, October 12, 1978. Sharif-Emami said this in a meeting with Parsons on October 11.
11. PREM 16/1719, Cartledge to Prime Minister, October 13, 1978.
12. Yazdi, *Akharin*, p. 78.
13. Ibid., p. 98.
14. The Air France charter to Tehran alone cost Khomeini's bazaar supporters $50,000.
15. Baqer Moin, *Khomeini: Life of the Ayatollah*, London, 1999, p. 193.
16. Yazdi, *Akharin*, p. 104.
17. Moin, *Khomeini*, pp. 192–93.
18. Bani-Sadr says the answers were prepared by himself, Yazdi, Qotbzadeh, Ahmad Khomeini, and, later, Mousavi-Khoeiniha. Abol Hassan Bani-Sadr, *L'espérance trahie*, Paris, 1982, p. 275.
19. "Whether directly, or in the process of translation, the answers given were those that had been discussed and agreed." Yazdi, *Akharin*, p. 84.
20. Said Amir Arjomand, *The Turban for the Crown*, Oxford, 1988, pp. 148–49.
21. Yazdi, *Akharin*, p. 87.
22. Bani-Sadr, *L'espérance*, p. 286.
23. N. W. Browne, *British Policy on Iran, 1974–1978*, London, 1980, p. 7.
24. Mehdi Bazargan, *Khaterat*, Tehran, 1377, Vol. 2, p. 256; Mehdi Bazargan, *Shuraye enqelab va doulat-e movaqqat* [The Revolutionary Council and the Provisional Government], Tehran, 1361, pp. 19–20.
25. William H. Sullivan, *Mission to Iran*, New York, 1981, p. 221.
26. PREM 16/1719, Parsons to FCO, November 1, 1978.
27. Colin Powell with Joseph E. Persico, *My American Journey*, New York, 1995, pp. 240–42.
28. PREM 16/1719, Parsons to FCO, October 25, 1978.
29. PREM 16/1719, Parsons to FCO, October 31, 1978.
30. PREM 16/1720, Parsons to FCO, November 8, 1978. Parsons says he drafted this message before November 5.

31. PREM 16/1719, Parsons to FCO, October 11, 1978.
32. PREM 16/1719, Parsons to FCO, October 19, 1978.
33. Ehsan Naraghi, *Des palais du chah aux prisons de la révolution,* Paris, 1991, p. 137; Sullivan, *Mission,* p. 178.
34. Hosein Ali Montazeri, *Khaterat,* pp. 397ff, at amontazeri.com.
35. *Time,* November 13, 1978.
36. Chapour Bakhtiar, *Ma fidélité,* Paris, 1982, pp. 138–39.
37. Dated 14 Aban 1357 [November 5, 1978] and printed in Yazdi, *Akharin,* p. 124.
38. PREM 16/1720, Parsons to FCO, November 12, 1978.
39. PREM 16/1719, Parsons to FCO, October 31, 1978.
40. Mohammed Reza Pahlavi, *Answer,* p. 165.
41. Anthony Parsons, *The Pride and the Fall: Iran, 1974–1979,* London, 1984, p. 92.
42. Vladimir Kuzichkin, *Inside the KGB,* London, 1990, p. 251.
43. Trevor Mostyn, *Coming of Age in the Middle East,* London, 1987, pp. 167–68 and conversation with author.
44. PREM 16/1720, Parsons to Department of Trade, November 16, 1978.
45. Parsons, *Pride and Fall,* p. 99.
46. Ibid., p. 95. "It is now clear . . . that the army made no attempt to prevent the wholesale destruction which took place in Tehran on November 5." PREM 16/1720, Parsons to FCO, November 9, 1978.
47. Parsons, *Pride and Fall,* p. 96.
48. Sullivan, *Mission,* p. 180.
49. PREM 16/1720, Parsons to FCO, November 9, 1978. General Gharabaghi, the Interior Minister, claims the Chief of Police told him that he was under instruction from Oveissi not to intervene. Gharabaghi, *Vérités sur la crise iranienne,* Paris, 1985, p. 53.
50. Parsons, *Pride and Fall,* p. 99.
51. PREM 16/1720, Parsons to FCO via U.S. Embassy, Tehran, November 5, 1978.
52. PREM 16/1720, Parsons to FCO, November 23, 1978.
53. Sullivan, *Mission,* p. 75.
54. Asadollah Alam, *Yaddashtha,* Tehran, 1380, 15 Azar 1352; *The Shah and I,* ed. Alinaghi Alikhani, London, 1991, pp. 340–41.
55. Text in Mehdi Bazargan, *Enqelab-e Iran dar do harakat* [The Iranian Revolution in Two Phases], Tehran, 1363, pp. 207ff.
56. PREM 16/1720, Parsons to FCO, November 6, 1978.
57. A fragment of newsreel of the speech was broadcast in 2009 in the BBC documentary film *Iran and the West.*
58. Yazdi, *Akharin,* p. 140. The poem, *Mush o gorbeh* [Mice and Cats], is by Obaid Zakani of Qazvin. English translations include M. Farzaad, *Rats Against Cats,* London, 1945; and Basil Bunting, *The Pious Cat,* Verona, 2005.
59. Daryoush Homayoun, *Zendegi pas az mordan, pish az marg* [Returned to Life], at d-homayoun.net.
60. PREM 16/1720, Parsons to FCO, November 7, 1978; Parsons, *Pride and Fall,* pp. 100–1.
61. Parsons, *Pride and Fall,* pp. 101–2.
62. Farah Pahlavi, *An Enduring Love,* New York, 2004, p. 288.
63. Abbas Milani, *The Persian Sphinx: Amir Abbas Hoveyda,* Washington, D.C., 2004, p. 300.

64. Desmond Harney, *The Priest and the King*, London, 1998, pp. 92–93.
65. PREM 16/1720, Parsons to FCO, November 29, 1978. The list included people who were no longer living. As Parsons reminded London, commissions on foreign contracts, the chief source of corrupt payments under Mohammed Reza, were paid into foreign, not Iranian, bank accounts. Also, UPI, November 27, 1979.
66. PREM 16/1720, Parsons to FCO, November 12, 1978.
67. *New York Times*, November 14, 1978.
68. That figure, which is approximate, is based on obituaries printed in the Iranian newspapers after they restarted publication in early January 1979. The British Embassy estimated the number at two hundred. Parsons, *Pride and Fall*, p. 104.
69. *Khaterat-e amir shahid sepahbod Sayyad Shirazi* [Memoirs of Sayyad Shirazi], Tehran, 1378, p. 81.
70. Mohammed Reza Pahlavi, *Answer*, p. 168.
71. Ibid., p. 167.

10. A Box of Earth

1. Anthony Parsons, *The Pride and the Fall: Iran, 1974–1979*, London, 1984, p. 126.
2. Farah Pahlavi, *An Enduring Love*, New York, 2004, p. 293.
3. Gary Sick, *All Fall Down*, New York, 1985, p. 63.
4. Parsons, *Pride and Fall*, p. 102.
5. PREM 16/1720, Parsons to FCO, November 19, 1978.
6. Ibid.
7. PREM 16/1719, Cartledge to FCO, October 27, 1978.
8. *Hansard*, House of Commons, November 6, 1978, Vol. 957, Cols. 504–12.
9. PREM 16/1720, Mulley to Prime Minister, November 13, 1978.
10. William H. Sullivan, *Mission to Iran*, London, 1981, p. 202; Sick, *All Fall Down*, pp. 83–85, criticizes these arguments.
11. Jimmy Carter, *Keeping Faith*, New York, 1982, p. 440, diary entry for November 10, 1978.
12. "Conversation with Engineer Amir Entezam, 22 Dey 1375," in Mehdi Bazargan, *Khaterat*, Tehran, 1377, Vol. 2, pp. 330ff.
13. George Ball, "Iran Memorandum," December 1978, George Ball Papers, Mudd Manuscript Library, Princeton University, Box 30, Folder 8.
14. Carter, *Keeping Faith*, p. 441, diary entry for November 21, 1978.
15. PREM 16/1719, Parsons to FCO, October 19, 1978.
16. PREM 16/1720, Parsons to FCO, November 23, 1978.
17. *Pravda*, November 19, 1978.
18. PREM 16/1720, Carter to Callaghan, November 20, 1978.
19. PREM 16/1720, Callaghan to Carter, December 2, 1978.
20. Ruhollah Khomeini, *Sahifeye nur* [The Page of Light], Tehran, 1361, Vol. 3, p. 227; Hamid Algar, trans., *Islam and Revolution, 1: Writings and Declarations of Imam Khomeini, 1941–1980*, Berkeley, Calif., 1981, p. 244.
21. Farah Pahlavi, *Enduring Love*, p. 288.
22. Desmond Harney, *The Priest and the King*, London, 1998, p. 98.

23. PREM 16/1720, Parsons to FCO, December 3, 1979.
24. Harney, *Priest*, p. 102.
25. Vladimir Kuzichkin, *Inside the KGB*, London, 1990, p. 252.
26. Sullivan, *Mission*, p. 208.
27. PREM 16/1720, Callaghan minute on Prendergast, FCO, to Cartledge, December 11, 1978.
28. PREM 16/1720, Parsons to FCO, December 7, 1978.
29. Harney, *Priest*, p. 112.
30. Parsons, *Pride and Fall*, p. 111.
31. "The Shah Averts a Showdown as a Parade of Protest Ends Peacefully," *Time*, December 18, 1978.
32. "Report of the Commission Dispatched to Isfahan and Najafabad," dated 7 Dey 1357 [December 28, 1978]. Printed in "Asnadi az akharin talashhaye kargo-zaran-e hakimiat-e Pahlavi" [Documents from the Last Efforts of the Agents of the Pahlavi Regime], *Tarikh-e moaser-e Iran*, Vol. 2, No. 8, 1999, p. 190.
33. FBIS, USSR, December 12, 1978.
34. PREM 16/1720, Parsons to FCO, December 12, 1978. The Queen, who visited the wounded, said there were thirteen dead.
35. "Report of the Commission," pp. 190ff; *Khaterat-e sepahbod Sayyad Shirazi*, [Memoirs of Sayyad Shirazi], Tehran, 1378, p. 83.
36. "If he were to abdicate or [withdraw temporarily,] the armed forces . . . would be very likely to react with a military coup." PREM 16/1720, Parsons to FCO, December 19, 1978.
37. General Robert E. Huyser, *Mission to Tehran*, London, 1986, p. 91.
38. Harney, *Priest*, p. 122.
39. PREM 16/1720, Parsons to FCO, December 19, 1978.
40. PREM 16/1720, Parsons to FCO, December 21, 1978; Sullivan, *Mission*, p. 212.
41. PREM 16/1720, Parsons to FCO, December 22, 1978.
42. UPI, December 25, 1978.
43. PREM 16/1720, Given in Bahrain to Tehran, December 31, 1978.
44. *New York Times*, December 27, 1978.
45. Hosein Ali Montazeri, *Khaterat*, Vol. 1, pp. 416–17, at amontazeri.com.
46. Bazargan, *Khaterat*, Vol. 2, pp. 282–85.
47. Parsons, *Pride and Fall*, p. 118.
48. Information from courtier.
49. Letter to Professor Bernard in Farah Pahlavi, *Enduring Love*, p. 295.
50. Ibid.
51. PREM 16/1720, Parsons to FCO, December 29, 1978.
52. Ibid.
53. Chapour Bakhtiar, *Ma fidélité*, Paris, 1982, p. 47.
54. Sullivan, *Mission*, p. 235.
55. Bakhtiar, *Ma fidélité*, p. 56.
56. PREM 16/1720, Parsons to FCO, December 30, 1978.
57. Mohammed Reza Pahlavi, *Answer to History*, New York, 1980, p. 173.
58. PREM 16/1720, Owen to Prime Minister, Guadeloupe, enclosing Parsons to FCO, January 4, 1979.
59. Sullivan, *Mission*, p. 231.

60. PREM 16/2131, Jay in Washington, D.C., to FCO, January 3, 1979.
61. N. W. Browne, *British Policy on Iran, 1974–1978,* London, 1980, pp. 31, 62.
62. PREM 16/2131, Jay in Washington, D.C., to FCO, January 3, 1979; Owen to Washington, D.C., January 4, 1979.
63. Carter, *Keeping Faith,* p. 446.
64. Huyser, *Mission,* p. 24.
65. Sullivan, *Mission,* p. 222.
66. Sick, *All Fall Down,* p. 137.
67. Sullivan, *Mission,* p. 223.
68. Ibid., p. 224.
69. Carter, *Keeping Faith,* p. 446.
70. Huyser, *Mission,* pp. 22–23.
71. *Izvestiya,* January 6, 1979.
72. "Stenographic Protocol" Zhivkov-Brezhnev, January 13, 1979, Central State Archive, Sofia, Fond 1-B, Record 60, File 248, in Bulgarian. Cold War International History Project (CWIHP), at www.CWIHP.org, by permission of Woodrow Wilson International Center for Scholars.
73. Partial text of the President's message in Huyser, *Mission,* p. 18.
74. Sick, *All Fall Down,* p. 139.
75. Huyser, *Mission,* p. 80.
76. Ibid., p. 77.
77. Mohammed Reza Pahlavi, *Answer,* p. 172.
78. "Note confidentielle de Michel Poniatowski au Président," in Valéry Giscard d'Estaing, *Le pouvoir et la vie,* Paris, 2004, pp. 761ff. Transcript of interview with Amir Aslan Afshar for BBC documentary film *Iran and the West,* 2009, Liddell Hart Centre for Military Archives, King's College, London. *New York Times,* January 3, 1979.
79. Ebrahim Yazdi, *Akharin talashha dar akharin ruzha* [The Final Push], Tehran, 1388, pp. 188–92. Khomeini refers to Carter in the polite third person plural. He also thanked the French government for Giscard's stand at Guadeloupe, and promised that once the economy was restored "Iran will export oil to the West and indeed to any place where there are customers." One of the French officials, Claude Chayet, describes the meeting in similar terms in *Iran and the West,* BBC documentary film, February 7, 2009.
80. Sick, *All Fall Down,* pp. 141–47.
81. Bakhtiar, *Ma fidélité,* p. 136.
82. Ibid., p. 137.
83. Parsons, *Pride and Fall,* pp. 125–26.
84. Abbas Gharabaghi, *Vérités sur la crise iranienne,* Paris, 1985, p. 129.
85. Conversation with Mehdi Jami, Purmerend, 2009.
86. Kambiz Atabai, interview with Gholam Reza Afkhami, FISOHA, February 3, 2003, Tape 1, quoted in Gholam Reza Afkhami, *The Life and Times of the Shah,* Berkeley, Calif., 2009, p. 527.
87. *Kayhan,* 27 Dey 1357.
88. Ibid.
89. Gharabaghi, *Vérités,* p. 131.
90. *New York Times,* January 17, 1979. *Ettelaat,* 27 Dey, 1357, has 1:08 p.m. Gharabaghi, *Vérités,* p. 142, has 13:10 hours.

91. Amir Aslan Afshar, interview with Mahnaz Afkhami, September 10 and 12, 1988, FISOHA, quoted in Afkhami, *Life and Times,* p. 528.
92. Harney, *Priest,* pp. 157–58.
93. *Kayhan,* 27 Dey 1357.

11. God Is Great

1. There are different versions of this statement. This is from Ebrahim Yazdi, *Akharin talashha dar akharin ruzha* [The Final Push], Tehran, 1388, p. 90.
2. General Robert E. Huyser, *Mission to Tehran,* London, 1986, p. 130.
3. Ibid., p. 131.
4. Ibid., pp. 83, 105.
5. Gary Sick, *All Fall Down,* New York, 1985, p. 151.
6. *New York Times,* January 7, 1979.
7. Huyser, *Mission,* pp. 64, 285.
8. Mohammed Reza Pahlavi, *Answer to History,* New York, 1980, pp. 64, 172.
9. *Kayhan,* 25 Dey 1357.
10. *New York Times,* January 16, 1979.
11. Huyser, *Mission,* p. 157.
12. Abbas Gharabaghi, *Vérités sur la crise iranienne,* Paris, 1985, p. 153.
13. Yazdi, *Akharin,* pp. 352–53.
14. Chapour Bakhtiar, interview with Zia Sedghi, 1984, Paris, France. Iranian Oral History Collection, Harvard University, Transcript 4 (in Persian).
15. Resignation letter dated 1 Bahman 1357 is printed in Bagher Agheli, *Ruzshomar-e tarikh-e Iran* [Historical Calendar of Iran], Tehran, 1384, Vol. 2, ad loc.
16. The *formul* of 3 Bahman 1357 (in Bazargan's hand) and the draft letter of resignation (in Amir Entezam's hand) are reproduced in holograph in Mehdi Bazargan, *Khaterat,* Tehran, 1377, Vol. 2, pp. 461 and 462. Another hand, presumably Bakhtiar's, has crossed out in the resignation letter the two references to "the great leader Khomeini."
17. Desmond Harney, *The Priest and the King,* London, 1998, p. 171.
18. Farah Pahlavi, *An Enduring Love,* New York, 2004, p. 302.
19. Ibid., p. 306.
20. The receipt is reproduced in Farah Sepahbody, "The Last Flight of the Persian Eagle," at users.sedona.net.
21. *New York Times,* January 27, 1979.
22. Sadeq Khalkhali, *Khaterat,* Tehran, 1379, p. 273. Montazeri later admitted that his son had "mental problems."
23. According to a discharged technician speaking to the *New York Times* in Qom. *New York Times,* February 10, 1979.
24. Huyser, *Mission,* p. 219.
25. Gharabaghi, *Vérités,* p. 164.
26. "Je suis au courant et attentif, ne soyez pas inquiet." [I am carefully watching developments. Do not worry.] Ibid., p. 188.
27. *Ettelaat,* 10 Bahman 1357.
28. Huyser, *Mission,* p. 242.

29. Sick, *All Fall Down*, p. 140.

30. Huyser, *Mission*, p. 241.

31. *New York Times*, February 1, 1979.

32. Peter Scholl-Latour, *Allah ist mit den Standhaften*, Frankfurt am Main, 1983, p. 94.

33. Sadeq Tabatabai, transcript of interview for BBC documentary *Iran and the West*, 2009, Liddell Hart Centre for Military Archives, King's College, London.

34. *Daily Telegraph*, February 7, 2009.

35. Yazdi, *Akharin*, pp. 374–75, reports having heard such an explanation from Haeri-Yazdi. In his long interview with the Harvard Oral History Program, Haeri-Yazdi makes no such claim. The British Persianist Michael Axworthy writes: "The mojtahed on the path to becoming the Perfect Man had no place for feelings or the manifestation of feelings." Axworthy, *Empire of the Mind: A History of Iran*, London, 2007, p. 266.

36. Yazdi, *Akharin*, pp. 106–7.

37. "Je restais un moment en haut de la passerelle. On avait le sentiment que les intellectuels avaient accompagné M. Khomeyni jusqu'à l'aéroport et qu'une fois là, les clercs l'avaient l'enlevé. [I paused for a moment at the top of the airstairs. I sensed that the intellectuals had brought Mr. Khomeini to the airport and now the clergy had kidnapped him.] Abol Hassan Bani-Sadr, *L'espérance trahie*, Paris, 1982, p. 309.

38. *New York Times*, February 2, 1979.

39. "Div chu birun ravad, fereshteh dar ayad." Hafez, *Divan*, No. 232.

40. Bakhtiar, Iranian Oral History Project (IOHP), Transcript 4.

41. "Khial nakonid . . . ma miayim shomara be dar mizanim" Ruhollah Khomeini, *Sahifeye nur* [The Page of Light], Tehran, 1361, Vol. 5, pp. 3–9; Hamid Algar, trans., *Islam and Revolution, 1: Writings and Declarations of Imam Khomeini, 1941–1980*, Berkeley, Calif., 1981, p. 260.

42. This account is based on three sources: the eyewitness report in *Kayhan*, 12 Bahman 1357; the transcript of Rafiqdoust's interview for the 2009 BBC documentary film *Iran and the West* at the Liddell Hart Centre for Military Archives, King's College, London; and conversations with older residents when I retraced the route in 1999.

43. Gharabaghi, *Vérités*, p. 191.

44. Khalkhali, *Khaterat*, p. 277.

45. Mohammed Reza Mahdavi-Kani, *Khaterat*, Tehran, 1385, p. 196.

46. Ali ibn Abi Talib, *Nahj al-balaghah* [The Way of Eloquence], Sermon No. 229. This is a collection of sermons and writings attributed to the patriarch of the Shia and assembled in the eleventh century AD.

47. *Pravda*, January 30, 1979.

48. Huyser, *Mission*, p. 236.

49. Ibid., p. 265.

50. Ibid., pp. 270–1.

51. Sick, *All Fall Down*, p. 149.

52. Mehdi Bazargan, *Masael va moshkelat-e nakhostin sal-e enqelab* [Difficulties and Problems of the First Year of the Revolution], Tehran, 1362, p. 5.

53. Khomeini, *Sahifeye nur*, Vol. 5, p. 31.

54. Baqer Moin, *Khomeini,* London, 1999, p. 204.
55. *Kayhan,* 17 Bahman 1357.
56. Transcript of Rafiqdoust interview, BBC documentary film *Iran and the West.*
57. Amir Entezam interview, Bazargan, *Khaterat,* Vol. 2, pp. 333–34.
58. In their *mémoires justificatifs* from Paris, neither Gharabaghi nor Bakhtiar mentions this meeting.
59. *Kayhan,* 21 Bahman 1357.
60. Ibid.
61. Alireza Mahfoozi. Interview recorded by Zia Sedghi, April 7, 1984, Paris, France. Iranian Oral History Collection, Harvard University.
62. Gharabaghi claims that Bakhtiar himself ordered the broadcast in the hope that Khomeini's "Nothing" in answer to Jennings of ABC might cause a bad impression.
63. *Daily Telegraph,* February 12, 1979. The report, by James Allan, is the clearest by a newspaper correspondent of the events of February 9 and 10.
64. Gharabaghi, *Vérités,* p. 208.
65. *Daily Telegraph,* February 12, 1979. The *New York Times,* February 11, 1979, reports this event as occurring during the night.
66. "Dès 8 h 30 le matin," according to Gharabaghi, *Vérités,* pp. 209, 236. During the night, according to the *New York Times,* February 11, 1979.
67. *Daily Telegraph,* February 12, 1979.
68. Documentary film, *Baraye azadi* [For Liberty!], dir. Hossein Torabi, in Persian with English subtitles, at iranian.com.
69. *Kayhan,* 22 Bahman 1357.
70. Khomeini, *Sahifeye nur,* Vol. 5, p. 49.
71. Hosein Fardoust, *Zuhur va suqut-e saltanat-e Pahlavi: Khaterat-e arteshbod-e sabeq Hosein Fardoust* [The Rise and Fall of the Pahlavi Monarchy], Tehran, 1374. Vol. 1, p. 623.
72. Khalkhali, *Khaterat,* p. 279.
73. Gharabaghi, *Vérités,* p. 228. Also interview with Gharabaghi in *Dastan-e Enqelab* [The Story of the Revolution], BBC Persian Service, at bbc.co.uk/persian/revolution.
74. Chapour Bakhtiar, *Ma fidélité,* Paris, 1982, p. 180, says he ordered the bombardment at the National Security Council meeting on the Saturday evening.
75. *Kayhan,* 22 Bahman 1357, 2nd edition.
76. Gharabaghi, *Vérités,* p. 230.
77. *Kayhan,* 23 Bahman 1357. The Organization of Physicians reported 166 dead and 634 wounded.
78. Fardoust, *Zuhur va suqut,* Vol. 1, p. 625.
79. Gharabaghi, *Vérités,* p. 238.
80. Ibid., p. 241.
81. Ibid., p. 243.
82. Translated from the Persian holograph printed in ibid., p. 245.
83. Bakhtiar, *Ma fidélité,* p. 182.
84. Reza Baraheni, *Dar enqelab-e Iran che shodeh ast va che khahad shod* [What Happened and What Will Happen], Tehran, 1358, p. 123.
85. Bakhtiar, *Ma fidélité,* p. 183.
86. William H. Sullivan, *Mission to Iran,* New York, 1981, p. 253.

87. Huyser, *Mission*, p. 284.
88. Michel Poniatowski to AP, March 31, 1979.
89. Bakhtiar, *Ma fidélité*, pp. 192ff. He does not say what passport he used, or where it came from.
90. *Kayhan*, 7 Esfand 1357.
91. *Kayhan*, 23 Bahman 1357.
92. Ibid.
93. Daryoush Homayoun, *Zendegi pas az mordan, pish az marg* [Returned to Life], at d-homayoun.net.
94. Fereshteh Ensha in Abbas Milani, *The Persian Sphinx*, Washington, D.C., 2001, p. 307.
95. *Kayhan*, 30 Bahman 1357.
96. Rasool Nafisi, "Firmly Planted," at iranian.com.

12. Dog Wedding

1. "Mokhtaseri az zendegi-am" [A Brief Life] in Sadeq Khalkhali, *Ayyam-e enzeva* [The Wilderness Years], Tehran, 1380, p. 27.
2. Pakravan's daughter, Saideh, to *Omid*, at iranrights.org, ad loc. The trial report, *Ettelaat*, 22 Farvardin 1358, does not record this sally.
3. Sadeq Khalkhali, *Khaterat*, Tehran, 1379, p. 380.
4. Ibid., p. 291, which also reproduces the letter of commission.
5. The *Arveh* is a collection of legal rulings (*Al-urwat ul-wuthqa* in Arabic) issued in 1919 by Mohammed Kazem Tabatabai Yazdi. Khomeini may be referring to the new edition with commentary that was published at Qom in 1961.
6. Khalkhali, *Khaterat*, p. 292.
7. "*C'était véritablement comme si l'ère de Djamchid s'ouvrait à nouveau!* [It was truly as if the Age of Jamshid had returned]" Abol Hassan Bani-Sadr, *L'espérance trahie*, Paris, 1982, p. 68.
8. *New York Times*, February 13, 1979.
9. This mode of execution, with a paralyzing shot to the nape and a second to the skull, became widespread in the twentieth century, notably in Russia, under the Third Reich, and in East Germany. It is known in German as the *Genickschuss* or the *unerwartete Nahschuss* ("sudden point-blank shot").
10. *Tehran Journal*, February 17, 1979. *Kayhan International* of the same date prints photographs of all twenty-four men. Khalkhali, *Khaterat*, p. 362, says the executions were delayed by Yazdi's interference until 2 a.m.
11. Amnesty International, *Law and Human Rights in the Islamic Republic of Iran*, London, February 1, 1980, lists (mostly by name) 438 men and women executed up to August 12, 1979, and approximately 120 in the following month.
12. *Kayhan*, 24 Bahman 1357.
13. Khalkhali, *Ayyam-e enzeva*, p. 12.
14. Charles-Louis de Secondat, Baron de Montesquieu, *De l'esprit des lois*, Book VI, Ch. XXI.
15. Reza Baraheni, *Dar enqelab-e Iran che shodeh ast va che khahad shod* [What Happened and What Will Happen], Tehran, 1358, p. 5.

16. *Kayhan,* 28 Bahman 1357.
17. *Tehran Journal,* February 17, 1979.
18. "True Justice must prevail at all times." Ibid.
19. For example, the charge of heroin smuggling against Hoveyda.
20. Marc Kravetz, *Irano Nox,* Paris, 1982, p. 32.
21. Khalkhali, *Khaterat,* p. 378.
22. Bani-Sadr, *L'espérance,* p. 54.
23. Ibid., p. 55. Abbas Milani, *The Persian Sphinx,* Washington, D.C., 2001, pp. 330–31, differs in some details.
24. Reuters in Amnesty International, *Law and Human Rights.*
25. Khalkhali, *Khaterat,* p. 379.
26. Ibid., p. 381. Milani, *Persian Sphinx,* p. 324, has "refrigerator"; Baqer Moin, *Khomeini: Life of the Ayatollah,* London, 1999, p. 208, has "fridge."
27. Named by Milani, among others.
28. *Kayhan,* 19 Farvardin 1358.
29. Milani, *Persian Sphinx,* p. 339. His account of Hoveyda's death came from Ehsan Naraghi, who while in Evin Prison had it from a member of the firing squad, a young man named Karimi. Khalkhali has claimed both that he himself killed Hoveyda, in V. S. Naipaul, *Among the Believers,* London, 1981, p. 56; and that he killed nobody with his own hand, in Khalkhali, *Ayyam-e enzeva,* p. 12.
30. Khalkhali, *Khaterat,* p. 393.
31. Ibid., p. 394.
32. Television interview of November 6, 1979, printed in Mehdi Bazargan, *Masael va moshkelat-e nakhostin sal-e enqelab* [Problems and Difficulties of the First Year of the Revolution], Tehran, 1362, p. 281.
33. AP, March 7, 1979.
34. *New York Times,* October 14, 1979.
35. "Die Tudeh-Partei erkennt die objectiv fortschrittlichen Elemente in seiner Bewegung an." "Tudeh und die iranische Revolution," *horizont,* No. 16, 1979, pp. 14–15.
36. Its indebtedness was 60 billion tomans in March 1981. Ali Akbar Hashemi Rafsanjani, *Obur az bohran* [Weathering the Storm], Tehran, 1378, entry for 4 Farvardin 1360.
37. *New York Times,* February 14, 1979.
38. *Kayhan,* 12 Esfand 1357.
39. *New York Times,* April 1, 1979.
40. BBC documentary film *Iran and the West,* 2009; Sadeq Tabatabai, transcript of interview for the film, Liddell Hart Centre for Military Archives, King's College, London; Peter Scholl-Latour, *Allah ist mit den Standhaften,* Frankfurt am Main., 1983, p. 94.
41. *New York Times,* June 16, 1979.
42. Plato, *Republic,* pp. 373ff.
43. Bani-Sadr, *L'espérance,* p. 316.
44. Ibid., p. 70.
45. *Surat-e mashruh modarekat-e majles-e barresi nemai qanun-e eslami* [Comprehensive Record of the Deliberations of the Assembly Investigating the Basic Law], Tehran, 1362, Vol. 1.

46. Interview with Marc Kravetz in January 1979. Kravetz, *Irano Nox*, p. 113.

47. Those numbers imply that as many died or were injured on each day of 1978 as in the fighting of February 10, 1979. There is no evidence for this and much to the contrary. The ratio of wounded to dead (1.7:1) belongs to the pitched battles of antiquity, not to a rich country equipped with emergency services and modern hospital surgery.

48. *Qanun-e asasiye jomhuriye eslamiye Iran* [The Fundamental Law of the Islamic Republic of Iran], Tehran, 1376. This edition includes both the Constitution of 1979 and the revisions of 1989.

49. Jimmy Carter, *Keeping Faith*, New York, 1982, p. 457.

50. Ray Takeyh, *Guardians of the Revolution*, Oxford, 2009, pp. 39ff, sets out this view.

51. Preface to Massoumeh Ebtekar (as told to Fred A. Reed), *Takeover in Tehran*, Vancouver, 2000.

52. Michael P. Zirinsky, "Blood, Power and Hypocrisy: The Murder of Robert Imbrie and American Relations with Pahlavi Iran, 1924," *International Journal of Middle East Studies*, Vol. 18, No. 3, 1986, pp. 275–92.

53. William H. Sullivan, *Mission to Iran*, New York, 1981, pp. 270–71.

54. PREM 19/76, FCO to Graham, September 13 and November 13, 1979. Both the Moroccan and the Egyptian embassies were also attacked.

55. Farah Pahlavi, *An Enduring Love*, New York, 2004, p. 310.

56. Sullivan, *Mission*, p. 277.

57. Gary Sick, *All Fall Down*, New York, 1985, p. 178.

58. PREM 16/2132, British Embassy, Rabat, to FCO, February 28, 1979. The Shah had also put out a feeler by way of a freelance journalist, Alan Hart. FCO to British Embassy, Rabat, February 22, 1979.

59. Mohammed Reza Pahlavi, *Answer to History*, New York, 1980, pp. 25–26; Margaret Thatcher to author, Bonn, 1982.

60. Farah Pahlavi, *Enduring Love*, p. 312.

61. *New York Times Magazine*, May 17, 1981.

62. Flandrin to Professor Bernard, in Farah Pahlavi, *Enduring Love*, p. 318.

63. Sir Denis Wright, interview recorded by Habib Ladjevardi, October 10 and 11, 1984, Aylesbury, England. Iranian Oral History Collection, Transcript 6. Wright, a director of Shell Transport and Trading, says he did not wish to embarrass his new employer.

64. Ibid.

65. Mohammed Reza Pahlavi, *Answer*, p. 15. William Shawcross was told that Mohammed Reza spent $1.2 million in the Bahamas. Shawcross, *The Shah's Last Ride: The Fate of an Ally*, New York, 1988, p. 147.

66. *El País*, February 4, 1981.

67. Carter, *Keeping Faith*, p. 454.

68. *New York Times Magazine*, May 17, 1981.

69. Flandrin to Professor Bernard, in Farah Pahlavi, *Enduring Love*, p. 328.

70. Hamilton Jordan, *Crisis: The Last Year of the Carter Presidency*, New York, 1982, p. 32; indirect speech in Carter, *Keeping Faith*, p. 455; and Sick, *All Fall Down*, p. 184.

71. Carter, *Keeping Faith*, p. 456.

72. Ebrahim Asgharzadeh, transcript of interview for BBC documentary film *Iran*

and the West, 2009, Liddell Hart Centre for Military Archives, King's College, London.

73. Interview with Mohsen Milani, in Milani et al., "Hostage Crisis," *Encyclopaedia Iranica*, at iranicaonline.org.
74. *Hamshahri* (Monthly), Vol. 1, No. 9, December, 2001.
75. Sadegh Tabatabai, transcript of interview for BBC documentary film *Iran and the West*.
76. Reuters, November 4, 1979.
77. Sick, *All Fall Down*, p. 186.
78. John Kifner, *New York Times Magazine*, May 17, 1981.
79. Bani-Sadr, *L'espérance*, p. 144.
80. Mohammed Reza Mahdavi-Kani, *Khaterat*, Tehran, 1385, pp. 218–19.
81. PREM 19/76, Wyatt to FCO, November 5, 1979.
82. Text dated 14 Aban 1358, in Bazargan, *Masael*, p. 67.
83. Scholl-Latour, *Allah*, p. 195.
84. PREM 19/76, Wyatt to FCO, November 6, 1979.
85. Conversation with U.S. sound engineer, Beirut, 1982. This story may have become true in the telling.
86. Transcript of Asgharzadeh interview in BBC documentary film *Iran and the West*.
87. Mahdavi-Kani, *Khaterat*, p. 220.
88. Ebtekar, *Takeover*, p. 101.
89. "Ce qu'il y a d'étonnant dans cette Révolution, c'est qu'on a fait une république avec des vices; faites-en avec des vertus; la chose n'est pas impossible." Saint-Just, 1793, quoted by C.-A. de Sainte-Beuve, *Causeries du lundi*, 26 janvier 1852.
90. *New York Times*, December 4, 1979.
91. *Kayhan*, 20 Dey 1359.
92. Bani-Sadr, *L'espérance*, p. 38.
93. Ibid., p. 41.
94. *Federal Register*, Executive Order 12170, November 14, 1979.
95. PREM 19/76, "Telephone Conversation Between the Prime Minister and the President of the United States of America on Monday, 19 November, 1979."
96. Author's conversation with PLO official, Beirut, 1982.
97. Farah Pahlavi, *Enduring Love*, p. 362; Jehan Sadat, *A Woman of Egypt*, New York, 1987, pp. 422ff.
98. Khalkhali, *Khaterat*, pp. 341ff.
99. Carter, *Keeping Faith*, p. 504.
100. *Koran* 105.
101. Jimmy Carter, *White House Diary*, New York, 2010, entry for April 24, 1980.
102. Admiral James Holloway, *Rescue Mission Report*, Special Operations Review Group, U.S. Joint Chiefs of Staff, August 23, 1980.
103. *Kayhan*, 24 Bahman 1357.
104. "The Nuzhih Plot and Iranian Politics," *International Journal of Middle East Studies*, Vol. 34, No. 4, 2002, pp. 645–66.
105. At a press conference on July 13, Reyshahri, the head of the army revolutionary court, said that the authorities had advance intelligence of the plan but allowed it to proceed. *Kayhan*, 23 Tir 1359.
106. Listed by name at sarafrazan.net.

107. "Soir 3," *France 3*, July 18, 1980.
108. *Amnesty International Report 1981*, London, 1981, p. 355.
109. Kravetz, *Irano Nox*, p. 71.
110. *Kayhan*, 2 Ordibehesht 1359.
111. *Kayhan*, 16 Tir 1359.
112. Shirin Hakimzadeh, "Iran: A Vast Diaspora," *Migration Information Source*, September 2006.
113. Mohammed Reza Pahlavi, *Answer*, p. 155.
114. Stiftung Archiv der Parteien und Massenorganisationen der DDR im Bundesarchiv (Berlin-Lictherfelde), DY30 JIV 2/201/1342. In English at Cold War International History Project (CWIHP), CWIHP.org, by permission of the Woodrow Wilson International Center for Scholars.
115. "Saddam and High-Ranking Officials Discussing Khomeini, etc." Conflict Records Research Center, National Defense University, SH-SHTP-A-000-851.
116. *Financial Times*, December 30, 2010.
117. SH-GMID-D-000-842, "General Military Intelligence Directorate Report Assessing Political, Military, and Economic Conditions in Iran," January 1–June 30, 1980. Conflict Records Research Center, National Defense University, Washington, D.C. (author's translation from Arabic).
118. Lieutenant General Raad al-Hamdani, in Kevin M. Woods et al., *Saddam's Generals: Perspectives of the Iran-Iraq War*, Alexandria, Va., 2010, p. 55.
119. Ibid., p. 115.
120. *Kayhan*, 20 Shahrivar 1359.
121. Tom Cooper, "Persian Cats," *Air and Space*, September 2006.
122. Author's interview, Baghdad, May 16, 1999. The cities are, from north to south, Suleimaniyah, Kirkuk, Baqubah, Kut, Amarah, and Basra.
123. SH-SHTP-A-000-835, "Saddam and His Advisers Discussing Iraq's Decision to Go to War with Iran," September 16, 1980, Conflict Records Research Center, National Defense University.

13. The Scent of Watermelon

1. Political Office of the Islamic Revolutionary Guards, *Gozari bar do sal-e jang* [A Glance at Two Years of War], Tehran, n.d.
2. Ibid., pp. 23–27.
3. Ibid.
4. Major General Alaeddin Al-Makki, in Kevin M. Woods et al., *Saddam's Generals: Perspectives of the Iran-Iraq War*, Alexandria, Va., 2010, p. 28.
5. General Alwan Al-Abousi, ibid., p. 197.
6. SH-SHTP-D-000-847, "Transcript of a Meeting Between Saddam and His Commanders Regarding the Iran-Iraq War," after September 30, 1980, Conflict Records Research Center, National Defense University (author's translation from Arabic).
7. I visited Khuzestan in 1974 and 1999.
8. Reuters, October 5, 1980.
9. *New York Times*, October 12, 1980.

10. "Zendeginameh," at fahmideh. javanblog.com (in Persian).

11. Ahmad Salamatian and Simine Chamlou, "Les dix années de la Révolution islamique en Iran," *Tiers Monde*, Vol. 31, No. 123, 1990, p. 529.

12. Ebrahim Asgharzadeh, transcript of interview for BBC documentary film *Iran and the West*, 2009. Liddell Hart Centre for Military Archives, King's College, London.

13. *New York Times*, November 2, 1980.

14. Massoumeh Ebtekar (as told to Fred A. Reed), *Takeover in Tehran*, Vancouver, 2000, p. 232.

15. Seventy according to Ground Forces of the Army of the Islamic Republic, Colonel Mojtaba Jafari, ed., *Atlas-e nabardhaye mandegar* [Atlas of Unforgettable Battles], Tehran, 1386, ad loc.

16. Robert Armao, *Financial Times*, February 8, 2011.

17. Interview with Gholam Reza Afkhami, in Afkhami, *The Life and Times of the Shah*, Berkeley, Calif., 2009, p. 547.

18. Abol Hassan Bani-Sadr, *L'espérance trahie*, Paris, 1982, p. 263.

19. Ali Akbar Hashemi Rafsanjani, *Karnameh va khaterat 1360: Obur az bohran* [Weathering the Storm], Tehran, 1378, entry for 29 Farvardin 1360.

20. Ibid., entry for 14 Farvardin 1360.

21. Jafari, ed., *Atlas-e*, ad loc. does not varnish the failure of these operations but points to the pressure of public opinion for action.

22. Bani-Sadr, *L'espérance*, p. 261.

23. Hashemi Rafsanjani, *Obur*, 8 Farvardin 1360.

24. Ibid., 17 Farvardin 1360.

25. The text of the revolutionary prosecutor's order is in ibid., 17 Khordad 1360, fn.

26. Ibid., 18 Khordad 1360.

27. Ibid., 21 Khordad 1360.

28. Reuters, June 15, 1981.

29. Hashemi Rafsanjani, *Obur*, 25 Khordad 1360.

30. Ibid., 31 Khordad 1360.

31. Reuters, June 22, 1981.

32. Reuters, June 29, 1981.

33. Mohammed Reza Mahdavi-Kani, *Khaterat*, Tehran, 1385, p. 310.

34. Mir Hosein Musavi to Hashemi Rafsanjani, in Hashemi Rafsanjani, *Obur*, 8 Tir 1360.

35. AP, July 9, 1981.

36. Mahdavi-Kani, *Khaterat*, p. 313.

37. Ehrsan Naraghi, *Des palais du chah aux prisons de la révolution*, Paris, 1991, p. 268.

38. "Letter of Mr. Amir Entezam," in United Nations Commission on Human Rights, *Final Report on the Situation of Human Rights in the Islamic Republic of Iran*, New York, 1993, Annex II.

39. *Amnesty International*, MDE 13/12/81, December 13, 1981. Shahrnush Parsipour reports that one night in September 1981 a cellmate counted 250 coups de grâce.

40. Shahrnush Parsipour, *Khaterat-e zendan*, Stockholm, 1996, pp. 83–84.

41. Montazeri, *Khaterat*, Vol. 1, p. 622, at amontazeri.com.

42. *Le Monde*, 25 June 2003.

43. Shaul Bakhash, *The Reign of the Ayatollahs,* London, 1985, p. 221.

44. Amnesty International, in its 1983 *Annual Report,* said it had recorded 5,447 executions since the Revolution, of which 399 took place in 1983.

45. Reynaldo Galindo Pohl, *Report on the Situation of Human Rights in the Islamic Republic of Iran,* United Nations Economic and Social Council, New York, 1990. Kianuri, his wife, and his daughter were arrested by Guards early in the morning of January 7, 1983, and taken to the Komiteh, now known as Detention Center 3000.

46. *New York Times,* October 9, 1980.

47. Manoucher Avaznia, *Path to Nowhere,* Concord, Mass., 2007, Ch. Six.

48. *Gozari bar do sal,* p. 113.

49. *Koran* 48:1.

50. *Gozari bar do sal,* p. 134.

51. *New York Times,* April 7, 1982.

52. *New York Times,* May 29, 1982.

53. Conversation with PLO official, Beirut, June 1982.

54. I reported for the *Financial Times* on the attempt on Argov's life and the war in Lebanon.

55. AP, June 10, 1982.

56. Transcript of Rafiqdoust interview, BBC documentary film *Iran and the West,* 2009, Liddell Hart Centre for Military Archives, King's College, London.

57. Sayyad Shirazi quoted in Ray Takeyh, *Guardians of the Revolution,* Oxford, 2009, p. 93.

58. *Kayhan,* 1 Tir 1361.

59. A translation of *Rah-e quds az karbala migozarad.*

60. *Gozari bar do sal,* p. 162. Ahmad Khomeini, *Majmueye asar-e yadegar-e Emam,* Tehran, 1375, Vol. 1, p. 718, claims his father was opposed in 1982 to continuing the war onto Iraqi territory but was persuaded by his commanders. That is hard to credit. Khomeini was reluctant to make peace in the incomparably less favorable circumstances of 1988.

61. John Bulloch and Harvey Morris, *The Gulf War,* London, 1989, p. 148.

62. UN Special Commission on Disarmament, "Status of the Verification of Iraq's Chemical Weapons Program," January 1999.

63. Conversation with Guards veteran, Tehran, 1999.

64. Jafari, ed., *Atlas-e,* ad loc.

65. General Makki, in Woods et al., *Saddam's Generals,* p. 125.

66. Bulloch and Morris, *Gulf War,* p. 150.

67. Adar Forouzan to Ed McCaul, *Military History* (Herndon, Va.), Vol. 21, No. 1, April 2004, pp. 44ff.

68. Conversation with Guards veteran, Tehran, 1999.

69. Bulloch and Morris, *Gulf War,* pp. 148–49.

70. M. A. Rajabi, *Miraj-e shahid* [The Ascent of the Martyr], Muze Shuhada [Martyrs Museum], Tehran.

71. Forouzan, in *Military History,* pp. 44ff.

72. Erich Wiedemann, "Mit dem Paradies-Schlüssel in die Schlacht," *Der Spiegel,* August 2, 1982.

73. Quoted in Tom Cooper and Farzad Bishop, *Iran-Iraq War in the Air,* Atglen, Pa., 2000, p. 194.

14. Convoys of Light

1. Radio Tehran, July 20, 1988. Printed in Ali Akbar Hashemi Rafsanjani, *Karnameh va Khaterat 1367: Payam-e defa, aghaz-e bazsazi* [1988-1989: From Defense to Reconstruction], Tehran, 1390, p. 628.

2. For example, Mohammadi Reyshahri, *Khaterat-e siasi* [Political Memoirs], Tehran, 1369, pp. 51 and 54.

3. Saed Abu Taleb, transcript of interview, BBC documentary film *Iran and the West*, Liddell Hart Centre for Military Archives, King's College, London.

4. *Report of the Congressional Committees Investigating the Iran-Contra Affair*, Washington, D.C., 1987, p. 260.

5. Ibid., p. 164.

6. For General Hashemi, see Vladimir Kuzichkin, *Inside the KGB*, London, 1990, pp. 195ff; and Abbas Milani's interview with Hashemi, in Milani, *Eminent Persians*, Syracuse, N.Y., 2008, pp. 462–67c.

7. Interview by Trita Parsi, Tel Aviv, 2004, in *Encyclopaedia Iranica*, "Israeli Relations with Iran."

8. "There is no doubt, however, that it was Israel that pressed Mr. Ghorbanifar on the United States." *Report of the President's Special Review Board* (hereafter cited as *Tower Report*), February 26, 1987, iv-12.

9. Robert McFarlane and Zofia Smardz, *Special Trust*, New York, 1994, p. 20.

10. *Tower Report*, B-53.

11. "Relative" to North, *Report of the Congressional Committees*, p. 252.

12. Ibid., pp. 193 and 199.

13. *Tower Report*, B-53.

14. Ibid., B-60; *Report of the Congressional Committees*, pp. 206–9.

15. *Tower Report*, B-73.

16. McFarlane and Smardz, *Special Trust*, p. 56.

17. Hashemi Rafsanjani later told Parliament: "The lads were hungry and ate the cake." *New York Times*, November 5, 2012 (correcting mistranslation). Once, driving north from Bushehr with two cases of dates for my host in Isfahan, I was stopped on the road by Guards, who sampled the dates, then returned one case to me and kept the other.

18. McFarlane and Smardz, *Special Trust*, p. 58; *Tower Report*, B-101.

19. McFarlane and Smardz, *Special Trust*, p. 66.

20. "And the scripture, foreseeing that God would justify the heathen through faith, preached before the gospel unto Abraham, saying, In thee shall all nations be blessed." Galatians 3:8, in *Report of the Congressional Committees*, p. 265, n152.

21. Montazeri, *Khaterat*, Add. 130 and 131, prints Ghorbanifar's holograph letters to Kangarlou of 18 and 19 Tir 1365 at amontazeri.com. This is contrary to *Report of the Congressional Committees*, p. 261, which says, "The source was neither Ghorbanifar nor his financiers, who had made earlier threats to do so."

22. Reyshahri, *Khaterat*, p. 26.

23. Ibid., pp. 65–66; Ahmad Khomeini, *Ranjnameh* [The Book of Pain], Tehran, 1384, p. 14.

24. Printed in Reyshahri, *Khaterat*, p. 49.

25. *Report of the Congressional Committees,* p. 259; George Cave, *Washington Report on Middle East Affairs,* September–October, 1994, p. 89.
26. Hassan Sabra, editor of *Al Shiraa,* to AP, December 6, 1986.
27. *New York Times,* November 5, 2012.
28. Montazeri, *Khaterat,* Vol. 1, p. 607.
29. Conversations in Isfahan, 1999.
30. Woods et al., *Saddam's Generals: Perspectives of the Iran-Iraq War,* p. 70.
31. AP, December 25, 1986.
32. Reuters, December 27, 1986.
33. Jafari, ed., *Atlas-e nabardhaye mandegar,* ad loc.
34. Ibid.
35. At un.org/Docs/scres/1987/scres87.htm.
36. AP, July 12, 1987.
37. Rear Admiral William M. Fogarty, *Formal Investigation into the Circumstances Surrounding the Downing of Iran Air Flight 655, July 3, 1988,* Department of Defense, Washington, D.C., 1988, "Rules of Engagement."
38. Transcript of Rafiqdoust interview, BBC documentary film *Iran and the West.*
39. Ali Akbar Hashemi Rafsanjani, *Karnameh va khaterat 1367: Payan-e defa, aghaz-e bazsazi* [From War to Reconstruction], Tehran, 1390, entry for 12 Tir 1367.
40. Transcript of Rafiqdoust interview, BBC documentary film *Iran and the West.*
41. The two letters were released by Hashemi Rafsanjani in September 2006 in response to a statement by Rezai accusing him of defeatism in 1988 (English translation at cfr.org).
42. *Ettelaat,* 29 Tir 1367.
43. H. W. Beuttel, "Iranian Casualties in the Iran-Iraq War: A Reappraisal," *International TNDM Newsletter,* Vol. 2, No. 3, December 1997.
44. Masoud Banisadr, *Masoud: Memoirs of an Iranian Rebel,* London, 2004, pp. 282–83.
45. Ibid., p. 291; National Liberation Army of Iran, "Operation Eternal Light," at iran-e-azad.org; *Kayhan,* 12 Mordad 1367.
46. Banisadr, *Masoud,* p. 290.
47. Roger Cooper, *Death Plus Ten Years,* London, 1993, pp. 77 and 98. Cooper was in Evin from 1986 to 1991.
48. Translated from the holograph letter reproduced in Geoffrey Robertson, QC, *The Massacre of Political Prisoners in Iran, 1988,* London, 2009, p. 42; and Montazeri, *Khaterat,* Add. 152, p. 624. The letter is undated, but Montazeri believes it was dictated on Thursday, that is, July 28. The edition of Montazeri's memoirs printed in Iran, Asadollah Badamchian, ed., *Khaterat-e Montazeri va naqd-e an* [Montazeri's Memoirs and a Critique of Them], Tehran, 1386, omits the Khomeini letter and much else besides.
49. Fariba Sabet in Robertson, *Massacre,* p. 55.
50. Montazeri, *Khaterat,* Vol. 1, p. 628. The Mojahedin say they lost 3,208 of their own number in the prison massacres.
51. Ruhollah Khomeini, *Velayat-e faqih: Hokumat-e Islami* [The Stewardship of the Jurist: Islamic Government], Tehran, 1357, p. 111; Hamid Algar, trans., *Islam and Revolution, I: Writings and Declarations of Imam Khomeini, 1941–1980,* Berkeley, Calif., 1981, p. 89.

52. Holograph letter in Montazeri, *Khaterat,* App. 153, pp. 629ff.

53. AP, February 12, 1989.

54. Salman Rushdie, "In God We Trust," in *Imaginary Homelands,* London, 1991, p. 377.

55. Salman Rushdie, *The Satanic Verses,* London, 1988.

56. The two verses were said to have come after Koran 53:20. The term "Satanic Verses" was coined by Sir William Muir in *The Life of Mahomet,* London, 1861.

57. Angela Carter, "Angels in Dirty Places," *Guardian,* September 23, 1988.

58. Titus Livius, *Ab urbe condita* [History of Rome], Lib. XXI.

59. Baqer Moin, *Khomeini: Life of the Ayatollah,* London, 1999, p. 287.

60. Montazeri, *Khaterat,* App. 172, pp. 673ff. Montazeri thought the letter a forgery.

61. *Qanun-e asasi* [The Basic Law], Tehran, 1390, prints both original and revised articles.

62. A translation of *Emam be malkut-e ala peivast.*

63. Video from the meeting was shown in the BBC documentary film *Iran and the West.*

64. At youtube.com/watch?v=Lre995bov_k.

65. Moin, *Khomeini,* p. 312.

66. *New York Times,* June 7, 1989.

67. *Time,* June 19, 1989.

68. Mohammed Suleiman Tunakbuni, *Qissas al-ulama* [Anecdotes of the Learned], Tehran, n.d., ad loc. Fouad Ajami, *The Vanished Imam,* Ithaca, N.Y., 1986, p. 133.

Epilogue

1. Hafez, *Divan,* 407.

2. Correspondence captured by the U.S. Special Forces that assassinated bin Laden in Pakistan in 2011 reveals that the Iranians were holding hostages in Iran for his good behavior. Atiya to "our noble Sheikh," June 11, 2009, No. 12 in Don Rassler et al., *Letters from Abbottabad,* Combating Terrorism Center, West Point, N.Y., 2012.

3. International Monetary Fund, World Economic Outlook Database, September 2000, September 2002, and April 2012.

4. As of close of business, 10 Tir 1391 (June 30, 2012). Nasdaq.com and irbourse.com.

5. Bukhari, *Al-jami as-Sahih,* Book 6, Ch. 60, No. 420.

6. According to Akbar Etemad, head of the prerevolutionary Atomic Energy Organization of Iran, Mohammed Reza said, "Against [neighboring] countries we are the superior power and therefore we do not need atomic weapons for our defense. Against the Soviet Union, we cannot defend ourselves with one, two, or even ten bombs. Today . . . we do not need atomic bombs." Etemad interview with Gholam Reza Afkhami in Afkhami, *The Life and Times of the Shah,* Berkeley, Calif., 2009, p. 360.

7. "Obama Order Sped Up Wave of Cyberattacks Against Iran," *New York Times,* June 1, 2012.

Acknowledgments

I would like to thank Dr. Fereydoun Ala, Caroline Dawnay, Christopher de Bellaigue, Bijan Golshaian, Andrew Goodson, Dr. John Gurney, Peter James, Mehdi Jami, Jamshid Kashkooli, Emily Loose, Dr. Philip Mansel, Shabnam Mirafzali, Trevor Mostyn, Dr. James Mumford, Ardeshir Naghshineh, Roland Philipps, Dr. Gary Sick, Lord Tweedsmuir, Caroline Westmore, Professor Dr. Stefan Wild and Gerlind Wülker-Wild, and Antony Wynn. My principal debt is to the late Ali Boroumand of Isfahan.

ILLUSTRATION CREDITS

© Abbas/Magnum Photos: 7, 8, 9 below, 10 below, 11, 12, 13, 14 above, 15 above. © Amanat Architect: 5 below. © Bruno Barbey/Magnum Photos: 6 below. © Raymond Depardon/Magnum Photos: 6 above. © Jean Gaumy/Magnum Photos: 16 below. © Getty Images: 1 below left and right; above right/De Agostini; 2 below, 3 below left/ Gamma-Keystone; below right/Time & Life Pictures; 9 above/Michel Setboun/Gamma-Rapho; 14 centre/Alain Mingam/Gamma-Rapho; 16 centre/Jean-Claude Delmas/AFP. © Thomas Hoepker/Magnum Photos: 4 below right. © Inge Morath © The Inge Morath Foundation/Magnum Photos: 4 above and below left. © Press Association Images: 2 above, 3 above, 5 above right, 10 above, 14 below, 15 below, 16 above. © Marilyn Silverstone/Magnum Photos: 5 above left. Smithsonian Institution, Washington, DC: 1 above left/Myron Bement Smith Collection, Antoin Sevruguin Photographs, Freer Gallery of Art and Arthur M. Sackler Gallery Archives, Gift of Katherine Dennis Smith.

Index

INDEX

INDEX